HOPE ABUNDANT

HOPE ABUNDANT

Third World and Indigenous Women's Theology

Edited by Kwok Pui-lan

ORBIS BOOKS

Maryknoll, New York 10545

Founded in 1970, Orbis Books endeavors to publish works that enlighten the mind, nourish the spirit, and challenge the conscience. The publishing arm of the Maryknoll Fathers and Brothers, Orbis seeks to explore the global dimensions of the Christian faith and mission, to invite dialogue with diverse cultures and religious traditions, and to serve the cause of reconciliation and peace. The books published reflect the views of their authors and do not represent the official position of the Maryknoll Society. To learn more about Maryknoll and Orbis Books, please visit our website at www.maryknollsociety.org.

Copyright © 2010 by Kwok Pui-lan.

Published by Orbis Books, Maryknoll, New York 10545-0302.
Manufactured in the United States of America.

Library of Congress Cataloging-in-Publication Data

Hope abundant / third world and indigenous women's theology / edited by Kwok Pui-lan.
    p. cm.
  Includes bibliographical references.
  ISBN 978-1-57075-880-5 (pbk.)
  1. Women in Christianity—Developing countries. 2. Theology, Doctrinal—Developing countries. I. Kwok, Pui-lan.
  BV639.W7H59 2010
  230.082'091724—dc22
                                        2010003009

To
Virginia Fabella, M.M.
and
Mercy Amba Oduyoye

Contents

PART 3: CHRISTOLOGY

PART 4: BODY, SEXUALITY, AND SPIRITUALITY

Acknowledgments

In 1988, Virginia Fabella from the Philippines and Mercy Amba Oduyoye from Ghana co-edited *With Passion and Compassion: Third World Women Doing Theology*, based on the work of the Women's Commission of the Ecumenical Association of Third World Theologians. The book has been widely used as an important resource for understanding women's liberation theologies in Africa, Asia, and Latin America emerging out of women's struggles for justice in church and society. More than twenty years have passed and it is time to bring out a new collection of essays to signal newer developments and to include emerging voices. I would like to thank Susan Perry, senior editor at Orbis Books, for her support and encouragement for the project from the beginning. The editorial and production teams at Orbis Books provided guidance and assistance during the many stages of the process.

Colleagues and friends from various parts of the world supported the project with enthusiasm and graciously granted permission to reprint their essays. I am very grateful for their friendship, solidarity, and critical contribution to enlarging the theological discourse. I am much indebted to María Pilar Aquino, Nancy Elizabeth Bedford, J. Shannon Clarkson, Mary E. Hunt, Nami Kim, Boyung Lee, Mercy Amba Oduyoye, and Mary Judith Ress for their suggestions on the selections for this volume, although, because of space and other considerations, I may not always have been able to follow their advice. My research assistant Susan Spilecki offered timely help in preparing the manuscript for publication during the Christmas holidays. Without her meticulous work, publication of the book would have taken much longer. I also want to acknowledge the prompt feedback and valuable input I received from members of the Postcolonial Theology Network on Facebook when I solicited their opinions on the use of the term "Third World." It was amazing that we could have global conversations on this topic through the Internet. Finally, I am particularly grateful to the Episcopal Divinity School for supporting this book project through the Theological Writing Fund and to my colleagues there for their encouragement.

This book is lovingly dedicated to Virginia Fabella and Mercy Amba Oduyoye, two pioneers who have been midwives for the development of Third World women's theology. Proceeds from the book will be used to support the Institute of Women in Religion and Culture at Trinity

Theological College in Accra, Ghana, founded by Mercy for the training of future African women leaders.

I am very grateful to Loi Che Rakhorst-Chan for allowing me to use the image of her sculpture "Woman" for the cover art. Loi Che and I have been good friends since college. She developed as a multi-media artist integrating Eastern and Western sensibilities in the past several years after a career in broadcasting.

Source information for each article is provided at the bottom of the article's first page. I am grateful to the following publishers for permission to reprint materials: Cluster Publications (Petermaritzburg) for the article by Musimbi R. A. Kanyoro; the Christian Conference of Asia for the article by Wong Wai Ching Angela; the *Journal of Feminist Studies in Religion* for the article by Andrea Smith; Musa W. Dube for her article; Continuum for the article by Monica Melanchthon; Sheffield Academic Press for the article by Laura E. Donaldson; Cambridge University Press for the article by Mercy Amba Oduyoye; *Concilium* for the articles by Sharon A. Bong and Maria José Rosado-Nunes; ISPCK (Delhi) for the articles by Lee Miena Skye and Carmelita Usog; the *Chinese Theological Review* for the article by Meng Yanling; and *In God's Image* (Yogyakarta) for the poem of Sun Ai Park.

Introduction

Kwok Pui-lan (Hong Kong/USA)

In December 1986, twenty-six women from Africa, Asia, and Latin America gathered in the city of Oaxtepec, Mexico, for the Intercontinental Conference of Women Theologians of the Third World, a conference sponsored by the Women's Commission of the Ecumenical Association of Third World Theologians (EATWOT). The outcome of this groundbreaking meeting was the book *With Passion and Compassion: Third World Women Doing Theology*, co-edited by Virginia Fabella and Mercy Amba Oduyoye and published in 1988.[1] Since then, Third World women theologians have met in other ecumenical gatherings, and they have made significant contributions to broadening the theological discourse. Many newer voices have joined this multicultural and multilingual theological chorus, bringing theology into dialogue with contemporary issues.

The past twenty-five years have seen dramatic changes in the world: the disintegration of the former Soviet Union, the transformation in Eastern Europe, the war on terrorism, the rise of China and India as economic powers, the impact of the HIV/AIDS epidemic, and the current global financial crisis. With the end of the Cold War era, many have questioned whether the term "Third World" still makes sense, since it was originally used to designate the non-aligned countries, in contrast to the capitalist First World and the socialist Second World. In place of the term "Third World," other names have been suggested, such as the "developing world," "global South," "Two-Thirds World," and "majority world," but these terms are not without problems.

This book still uses the term "Third World" because it connotes not simply a geographical area but the tremendous power imbalance between the powerful and the disenfranchised. As Virginia Fabella and R. S. Sugirtharajah note:

It describes a relationship marked, in the past, by power and mediated through old colonial ties and, currently, through the cultural and economic presence of neocolonialism. Such iniquitous relationships exist both globally and locally. In this sense, there is already a Third World in the First World, just as there is a First World in the Third World—the world of economic and political

1

elite who are in collusion with the world powers. Ultimately, what is important is not the nomenclature but the idea it conveys and the analysis it provides.[2]

In the theological context, "Third World" theologies develop out of the struggles against social and political oppression, cultural alienation, and injustice as a result of sexism, racism, classism, colonialism, and other forms of oppression. Theologians of EATWOT have advocated for the liberation of the poor, the integrity of creation, gender justice, racial and ethnic equality, and interfaith dialogue. The term "Third World" can also be used metaphorically to convey a "Third Space," a space that is not bound by a binary mindset or dualistic and hierarchal constructions. Homi Bhabha calls the "Third Space" the in-between space, which questions established categorizations of culture and identity and opens up the possibilities of renegotiating power and creating new cultural meanings.[3] Since the term "Third World" has such a rich trajectory of meanings in the field of theology, I continue to use it in this volume instead of following other newer nomenclature.

This book is concerned not only with women in the Third World, the majority of whom have experienced external colonization, but also with the plight of indigenous women whose lands have been taken by the settlers in a form of internal colonialism. The indigenous peoples argue that their issues are quite different from those of the Third World, and some of them call themselves the "Fourth World." The "Fourth World" denotes "nations without a sovereign state, emphasizing the non-recognition and exclusion of ethnically- and religiously-defined peoples from the politico-economic world system."[4] The voices of indigenous women have been least heard in the theological discourse. The inclusion of their critical contributions to the global voices of Christian women struggling for justice, liberation, and peace is long overdue.

Globalization and Its Impacts

The end of the Cold War has ushered in not a period of peace but the escalation of militarism and warfare, ethnic and religious strife, and violence in many parts of the world. Globalization and the neoliberal economy, because they have changed the distribution of resources and roles of nation states, have created greater disparity between the rich and poor. Global warming, deforestation, and the breakdown of ecological systems have especially threatened the survival and subsistence of poor families, indigenous communities, and endangered species. While these affect both women and men, women and children bear the brunt of the problem. Theologians in the Third World are keenly aware of the need to develop social and theological analyses that address the socio-political issues caused by globalization.[5]

The current phase of globalization characterized by a free-market economy is gendered and biased against women. Mexican scholar María Arcelia Gonzáles Butron, who specializes in economics and Latin American studies, points to the sexual division of labor and its implications for women's lives:

> Given the permanence of division of labour as a result of the sexual differentiation of work, women are still found mainly in certain types of employment, usually less qualified and so less well paid. Globalization processes have not changed this tendency. With industrialization aimed at overseas markets, there has been a growth in the presence of transnational "brand" manufacturing companies and an increase in agribusiness units, in both of which women workers predominate.[6]

Although women have been absorbed in the global labor market, for many of them, working conditions continue to be precarious. Citing countries in the Latin American region as examples, the author notes that working conditions include provisional contracts, regimentation of work, lack of social security or benefits, and, in many places, prohibitions against forming labor unions. Women who work part-time or provide paid domestic services find that job security is even less protected as well as being contingent upon changes in the economy.

Writing from the South African context, Puleng LenkaBula argues that the consequences of globalization in Africa have been detrimental to the poor and vulnerable, women, and the working class, since millions are excluded from any meaningful participation in the economy. In addition, the "market logic" of globalization requires the opening up of national boundaries, structural adjustments of societies, and non-intervention from the state. Privatization of state-owned enterprises leads to outsourcing of services to private companies, and in South Africa, for example, provision of basic goods and services such as water, pensions, and healthcare is contracted to the business sector. Deregulation has reduced the role of the state in bringing businesses under the authority of the law and in setting price controls. While trade and financial liberalization both attract foreign investors that poorer countries desperately need, they also allow profits to easily move out of the country across borders.[7]

In Asia, economic growth in the Pacific Rim region has improved the livelihood of women, especially in the newly industrialized countries. Cheap female labor has supported the growth of labor-intensive industries, such as the manufacture of garments, toys, and electronics. But outside the export processing zones and industrialized regions, many women still live in abject poverty, with no share in the "Asian economic miracle." The financial crisis of 1997 further showed how the Asian economies were subject to the vicissitudes of the rapid movement of foreign capital and the control of international financial agencies. South Korea, Indonesia, and Thailand were the countries most affected. Kyungmi Park of South Korea wrote in the aftermath of the financial crisis:

> The globalization of capitalism would be more concerned inevitably with the interest of advanced capital, in that its process is controlled by the economics of western Europe and the U.S. capital. Who would rule the world market now? They would be none other than those transnational entrepreneurs who hold control over the world market, transcending their nationality and acting outside of the control of their national governments.[8]

The outsourcing of industries in the "race to the bottom" affects the volume, scale, and nature of migration of labor. Gemma Tulud Cruz notes that "today, migration in the Asian region is marked not only by its velocity and multidirectionality but also by its increasing feminisation and significant shift in destination, that is, from the Atlantic to the Pacific."[9] The Philippines is the global labor exporter *par excellence*, with almost 10 percent of its population of 84 million working outside the country. Millions of Filipinas toil as domestic helpers and in service-oriented jobs in East Asian and Southeast Asian countries, and as far away as Africa, Australia, Russia, and the Middle East. Cruz has written on the exploitation of female migrant workers and horizontal violence between women of "developed" countries and of "developing" countries.

Women's sexual labor has also been exploited to bolster the economy. The sex industries in Southeast Asia were developed during the Vietnam War for the "rest and recreation" of the American service personnel. Today, sex tourism is highly institutionalized and globalized, with the tacit cooperation of local law enforcement agencies, national governments, travel agencies, and the international business community. Many women and girls are illegally trafficked to Europe, North America, Southeast Asia, Japan, and Australia. Young African girls, for example, are exported to Europe through an international ring of criminals to serve as prostitutes in the lucrative sex industry. Sex trafficking of women and children is on the rise, causing unspeakable suffering to the victims and their families.[10] In the United States alone, the government estimates that there are as many as fifty thousand women and children trafficked into the country each year, primarily from Latin America, Eastern Europe, and Southeast Asia for commercial sexual exploitation.[11] Because of the fear of HIV/AIDS, some customers prefer to have sex with very young girls.

The grossly unjust world order, which benefits the elites but leaves 2.7 billion people of the world to survive on two American dollars per day or less, contributes to social unrest, rebellions, and, in some cases, prolonged civil wars. To maintain its global hegemony, the United States has resorted to the threat and use of military force, which enables it to reign supreme in the world. The preemptive strike against Iraq was a prime example. In the Third World, there is also the craze to build up military arsenals, draining valuable resources from education, health-care, and other social services. Between 1960 and 1988, military expen-ditures of the "least developed countries" quintupled in real terms.[12] Following the end of the Cold War, world military expenditures de-creased during the 1990s, but rose again in the late 1990s. In 2008, they reached $1.46 trillion, representing a 45 percent increase over the ten-year period since 1999. While the military expenditures of the United States account for 41.4 percent of the total, the expenditures of poorer countries, such as Algeria, Azerbaijan, Chile, and Peru have also in-creased.[13] But military expenditures have not been an effective deterrent to rebellions in developing countries, and have had an adverse effect on economic growth.[14]

War and civil conflicts result in violence, bloodshed, instabilities, mass migration, and refugees across country borders. Women trapped in war situations "become easy prey to rape, sexual slavery, torture, geno-cide, and other forms of gender-specific violence," says Marlene Perera of Sri Lanka, whose country suffers because of a prolonged civil war.[15] For example, during the 1994 Rwandan genocide, women were the victims of immense sexual violence and trauma, while the powerful nations stood by and did nothing to stop the genocide. Another example that, once it be-came known, caused public outcry was the systematic raping of Kosovar Albanian women by Serbian forces in Kosovo in the late 1990s.

Globalization has prompted much debate on the future of liberation theology, especially the adequacy of its social and economic analyses.[16] For example, some have questioned whether Latin American liberation theology with its Marxist analyses is outdated, since the world economy has changed so drastically. Others have pointed out that such criticism often originates in the North and is voiced by people who have not fol-lowed the latest developments. Latin American scholars, in particular the economist-theologian Franz J. Hinkelammert, have provided perceptive insights for analyzing the world economic order and suggested alterna-tives to the tyranny of capital.[17] Argentinean theologian Enrique Dussel has used a world-system approach in his analysis of the development of Latin American theology. He insists that liberation theology, with a com-mitment to the poor of the South, who are excluded from the globaliza-tion modernization process, is still highly relevant because it aims "to-ward an alternative of greater justice for the people at the periphery."[18]

Feminist liberation theologians have also charged that Marxist analysis has not paid sufficient attention to gender, sexuality, and women's reproductive issues, and the Latin American male theologians are often blinded by their *machismo*. One of the sharpest critics is the late Argentinean theologian Marcella Althaus-Reid, who charges that liberation theology must be demythologized and demystified. In particular, she argues that we need to "denounce the attempts to harmonize in a hegemonic and authoritarian way the positive and revolutionary elements of difference and dissent in our communities, in order to be able to continue the *caminata* [the walk] of theology."[19] By focusing primarily on class, male liberation theologians have failed to integrate the issues of gender and sexuality in their liberation project. Althaus-Reid concludes: "To keep unveiling the political and sexual masks and to keep rediscovering the true face of God in Latin America is a daring and risky project which still has not finished."[20] The same can be said for other contexts, and feminist liberation theologians must continue to articulate their vision that a more inclusive and alternative world is possible.

Cultural Criticism

Globalization not only restructures economics and alters the roles of the state but also affects people's worldviews, behavior, and cultural and religious identities. The mass media, the information highway, and social websites have created a kind of global mass culture, and it both absorbs and threatens local cultures. As a response to the pervasiveness of the forces of globalization, religious fundamentalisms of various kinds have emerged, often in the name of protecting "traditional" values and identities. The tensions between tradition and modernization are not new, since modernization usually means Westernization, though there are different ways of conceiving modernity. But the scope, scale, and pace of globalization have exacerbated some of these tensions. Women have often been caught in the "culture wars," whether in the West or in so-called traditional societies, because women are often seen as the symbols and guardians of tradition. Religious fundamentalisms in general treat women as subordinate to men and prescribe strict codes of female conduct and acceptable behavior.

In the past, there has been a perception that Latin American theologians are preoccupied with the socio-economic dimensions of liberation, while the Asian and African theologians focus on the religio-cultural aspects. In the age of globalization, these two aspects are so closely connected that one cannot be separated from the other. CNN and Hollywood movies are both cultural productions and transnational businesses. The same macro-level economic and cultural forces are shaping the world, though their impact and the responses they trigger may vary in local contexts. When I reviewed recent theological writings by Third World and indigenous women, I found that they are concerned both with the economic and the cultural aspects of oppression and liberation, though the emphases may be different because of the particular issues within the writers' contexts.

In the past two decades, Third World and indigenous women theologians have deepened their cultural criticism, especially with regard to the impact of colonialism on their culture, multiplicity and hybridity, and the role of popular religion in shaping women's lives. Some have turned to cultural studies, postcolonial criticism, poststructuralist theory, as well as studies on women, gender, and sexuality for theoretical insights for their work. In 1994, Kenyan theologian Musimbi Kanyoro saw the importance of the inclusion of cultural analysis in doing theology. She used the term "cultural hermeneutics" to describe the analysis of cultural ideologies regarding gender roles and power, cultural violence against women, and women as victims and perpetrators.[21] She now prefers to call this method "engendering cultural hermeneutics" to signal clearly that African women bring a gender and feminist perspective to a theology of inculturation (see chapter 1).

African women theologians are concerned about the impact of colonization and globalization on the rich diversity of local cultures and their in-built structures of human relationships. Teresa Okure, a Nigerian Catholic religious sister and biblical scholar, reminds us that Africa contains more than fifty-five countries, each with many languages and cultures. She says, "The globalization and Westernization of Africa started with the slave trade by Europeans and Arabs. It intensified through colonialism and continues through neo-colonialism and modern globalization."[22] The aggressive slave trades resulted in the destabilization and destruction of the social and political fabrics of the people. Cultural imperialism in the colonial era engendered a loss of faith of people in themselves and in the cultural heritage passed down over generations. The current culture of consumerism, individualism, and exploitative capitalism has wreaked havoc on African communal life.

Some Third World theologians have used postcolonial theory in analyzing colonial discourse and the impact of colonialism on biblical interpretation and theology. Postcolonial studies began in the late 1970s and have exerted considerable impact on the disciplines in the humanities and the social sciences. In biblical studies, Musa W. Dube of Botswana has authored the pioneering text *Postcolonial Feminist Interpretation of the Bible*.[23] It has received critical acclaim in the scholarly world. In theology and cultural studies, Wong Wai Ching Angela from Hong Kong has used postcolonial theology to scrutinize Asian theology, including Asian feminist theology.[24] Sharon A. Bong from Malaysia has discussed the Bible and ethics through the lense provided by postcolonialism, while several Asian diasporic scholars, including myself, have also used postcolonial theory in our works.[25]

Native and indigenous scholars have chastised genocide and cultural theft by the settlers, particularly the misappropriation of cultural and spiritual traditions. Andrea Smith, a Cherokee scholar, has studied the abuses of missionary schools and whitewashing of Native American children's minds. She also points out that sexual violence against Native women was a critical strategy of conquest.[26] Laura E. Donaldson, also of Cherokee heritage, has applied postcolonial theory to scrutinize the collusion with colonialism in white feminists' works. In *Decolonizing Feminisms*, Donaldson challenges the woman=colonized, man=colonizer homology because it fails to note that gender is a contested field and that white, middle-class women occupy the contradictory social positioning as "both colonized patriarchal objects and colonizing race-privileged subjects."[27] Using the theoretical tools provided by Mary Louise Pratt, Gayatri Chakravorty Spivak, and other postcolonial theorists, Donaldson has presented influential readings of the Bible from Native American perspective (chapter 8).

In Latin America, feminist theologians have paid more attention to cultural analysis and theories of gender since the 1990s. Elsa Tamez, a well-known Mexican biblical scholar, was among the first to write on cultural abuse against women with reference to the multiple layers of culture in Latin America: aborigine, black, *mestizo*, and white. While the patriarchal occidental society was imposed by colonialism, Tamez also notes the intercultural violence perpetrated by people of the *mestizo*-white culture against aborigines and black people. She proposes an intercultural dialogue based on mutual respect and recognition.[28] In recent years, Latina feminist theologians and social scientists from Latin America and the United States have met to develop a feminist intercultural theology.[29] An intercultural theology moves beyond mere recognition of differences toward creating common spaces and new forms of living together (*convivencia*). María Pilar Aquino, who plays a key role in developing this intercultural theology, argues that an intercultural approach recognizes the values of all cultures, relativizes our own ways of thinking, and debunks hegemonic monocultural and Eurocentric claims. As such, an intercultural framework provides theoretical tools for feminist theologians to develop "an alternative ethical-political project for advancing toward a new world of justice."[30]

Latin American feminist theologians have paid increasing attention to popular culture and religion, such as the devotion to Mary of Guadalupe and other religious practices of women. An important development is the analysis of hybridity between Christianity and African traditions and indigenous traditions. Several theologians have discussed Christian symbols, such as Jesus and Mary, as they interact with the rich traditions of African religions.[31] In addition, María Pilar Aquino has paid homage to indigenous traditions, which have seldom been brought into a feminist theological framework. She discusses the possibilities and conditions of bringing this *Teología India* into dialogue with the Catholic Church and the wider theological community.[32]

Asia is the birthplace of the historical religions of humankind. With approximately four billion people, Asia hosts roughly 60 percent of the world's population. Christians make up less than 3 percent of the population of this densely populated continent. Except in the Philippines, where Christians are the majority, and in South Korea, where Christians constitute about 30 percent of the population, Christians make up a tiny minority in most Asian societies. Living in a culturally, religiously, and racially diverse continent, Asian feminist theologians caution against the homogenization of Asian culture. Some question the colonial construct of "Asia"[33] and the essentialized description of "Asian-woman-ness." In urban Asian cities, global culture collides with local culture to such a degree that it is difficult to separate the two. Wong Wai Ching Angela questions whether the binary construction of East and West still holds, and whether this is not a replication of the colonial mindset.[34] Namsoon Kang of South Korea goes further in her critique, noting that Asian feminist theology in the past has been "geographically deterministic" and "culturally essentialist." She proposes reconceptualizing Asian feminist theology as "a *glocal* feminist theology, in which the global context and the local context are proactively combined to resist Empire(s) of all forms and to strengthen solidarity with the women and the marginalized who are dislocated and displaced."[35]

Since globalization and the current form of Empire are de-centered and de-territorialized, transnational and intercultural alliances among marginalized women doing theology are necessary. I have already mentioned the recent development of Latina feminist intercultural theology of the Americas. Another example is the network of Pacific, Asia, and North American Asian Women in Theology and Ministry. Since its small beginning in 1985, the group has met annually to facilitate exchanges between Asian and Asian North American women theologians.[36] Asia is poised to play an important role in shaping the world in the twenty-first century. The East Asian Economic Community is being developed as a regional bloc to challenge the hegemony of the European Union and America. Asian feminist theologians must keep a close eye on how this new geopolitical alliance is shaping the world economically, politically, and culturally.

Many new feminist theological voices are emerging from the Asian and Pacific region. Dalit women in India have articulated their biblical hermeneutics and theology. The Dalits occupy the lowest rung in the Indian caste system and they are discriminated against as a socio-cultural group.[37] Tribal women and indigenous women in India and the Philippines have described the threat of economic development to their ecological system and ways of life, and their vision for a holistic theology and spirituality.[38] In the Pacific region, women in Tonga, Fiji, Papua New Guinea, Australia, and Aotearoa/New Zealand gathered at Brisbane to form Women Scholars of Religion and Theology in 1998. They have met in other regional conferences and publish an electronic journal entitled *SeaChanges*.[39]

About This Volume

This volume aims to give readers an overview of recent developments in Third World and indigenous women's theology. These authors have to struggle against patriarchal church structures and create alternative spaces in which to nurture their theological thinking. In Africa, the Circle of Concerned African Women Theologians (the Circle) was founded in 1989 in Accra, Ghana, to undertake research and publication of African women's theological scholarship.[40] Since its founding in 1988 in Hong Kong, the Asian Women's Resource Centre for Culture and Theology has played a pivotal role in promoting Asian women's theology, and publishes the quarterly journal *In God's Image*.[41] The Con-spirando Collective in Santiago, Chile, formed in 1991, provides a forum for Latin American women to exchange their ideas and publishes the journal *Con-spirando: Revista latinoamericana de ecofeminismo, espiritualidad y teología*.[42] In addition, the Women's Commission of EATWOT continues to provide support for women to meet and discuss regional and intercontinental concerns.

Third World and indigenous women have published a substantial number of books and articles in the past two decades. The majority of the essays included in this volume were published after 2000, with a few dating from the late 1990s. In selecting these essays, I have tried to present both Catholic and Protestant perspectives, established and emergent voices, and contributions from scholars and activists. I have included authors from several countries on a given continent to give diverse viewpoints. Each section of the book begins with a poem or a prayer, because Third World and indigenous women use poetry and creative writing in their theology and liturgy.[43] As the reader will see, several contributors also include poetry in their respective chapters.

This book is limited to essays written in English, or articles that have been translated into English. It does not claim to be representative, because articles published in other languages without English translation have not been included. But it does include some of the most important essays coming out of these various contexts. The book does not include contributions from women of African American, Asian American, and Latina heritages, though some of them are members of EATWOT. This is because there are substantial theological anthologies from womanist

(African American), Latina, and Asian and Asian North American women showcasing their recent works.[44]

In contrast to the 1988 book, *With Passion and Compassion: Third World Women Doing Theology*, this book has been organized thematically, rather than according to continents—Africa, Asia, and Latin America. In an increasingly interconnected world, it would be quite arbitrary to narrowly define theological works according to continents, because many authors address the global context. *With Passion and Compassion* addresses the following themes: methodology, spirituality, women and the church, Christology, and the Bible in women's theology. *Hope Abundant* retains some of these themes, and adds the crucial topic of body and sexuality, which has become a very important area of theological discussion.

The book is divided into four parts. Part 1, "Context and Theology," reviews the development of women's theology in Africa, Asia, and Latin America and discusses the possibility of developing Native feminist liberation theologies in America. Musimbi Kanyoro, who has coordinated the Circle for many years, explains why inculturation is not sufficient and African women need to engage in engendered communal theology. Wong Wai Ching Angela, who served as a member of the presidium of the Christian Conference of Asia, provides the context for the development of Asian theology and discusses the struggles to build an inclusive community. Latin America's best-known ecofeminist theologian Ivone Gebara observes that women have made few inroads in changing Latin America's patriarchal church hierarchy. She proposes that an epistemological rupture is necessary to overcome essentialist metaphysical presuppositions of patriarchal discourse. The issues facing Native feminist scholars are quite different, and some hesitate to call their project "theology." The term is often linked to Christian theology, which has been complicit in the missionization and genocide of Native peoples. Andrea Smith, the U.S. coordinator of EATWOT, discusses these complex issues and explains why Native American theology must include a critical analysis of nation building.

Part 2, "Scripture," presents critical essays in biblical interpretation that have broadened the scope and strategies of feminist hermeneutics. In the first essay, Musa W. Dube explains that since the Bible has been used as a tool for colonialism, a reading that focuses on gender is insufficient in the Third World. She proposes a post-colonial feminist reading strategy that attends to the imperial settings of ancient texts and gender construction in imperialist narratives. Monica Jyotsna Melanchthon's essay offers reading methods from the perspective of Dalit women in India. She points out that Dalit women form the majority of church members in most cases, and yet their voices have been excluded. She highlights storytelling and role-play as useful methods in the oral culture of Dalits. The next two essays are closely related and can be read in tandem. Jean Zaru, a Palestinian and a Quaker, explains why the indigenous people of

Palestine look at the Bible differently from Third World theologians. For many liberation theologians, the exodus story is a story of liberation from oppression; for Palestinians, it can be read as a story that justifies occupation and genocide.[45] Though living in an occupied land, Zaru does not lose her sense of hope and offers a vision for peace and non-violence. In the following chapter, Laura E. Donaldson interprets the story of Ruth through the relationship between Native Americans and the European colonizers. Instead of siding with Ruth who is assimilated into Jewish culture, Donaldson lifts up Orpah, the marginalized figure in the text, as the one who connotes hope for Native women. The last chapter is an excerpt from Elsa Tamez's book. It offers an insightful reading of 1 Timothy 2:8–14, a passage that tells women to keep silent and forbids them to teach or have authority over men. Like other authors in Part 2, Tamez complicates feminist reading by asking who the targeted women in the passage are. The answer can be found through analyzing class and gender within the Greco-Roman imperial patriarchal society.

Part 3, "Christology," attempts to answer Jesus' question "Who do you say that I am?" While the four essays chosen are in dialogue with traditional doctrine of Christ, they have also asked new questions and expanded our Christological inquiry. Mercy Amba Oduyoye, a pioneer in African women's theology, elucidates how the images of Christ as king, liberator, friend, prophet, and suffering servant have been appropriated by African women theologians to address the oppression and suffering in Africa. Since African traditions have both male and female saviors, African women have no problem with the fact that Jesus was male and they have not insisted on seeing Christ as the wisdom (*Sophia*) of God. Sharon A. Bong's chapter looks at the suffering Christ through Asian women's bodies. She reminds us that Asian women's bodies suffer, but also resist and seek healing. The embodied Christ in Asian women's theology both suffers and is resurrected. The next chapter is by Lee Miena Skye, a *Palawa* (Tasmanian Aboriginal) who describes herself as a *womanist* theologian, adapting a term used by some African American women. The essay is the last chapter of her book in which she interviews Aboriginal women to understand their Christology. Since Aboriginal women have a holistic worldview, Skye suggests a Creation/Identity methodology to understand how Christ becomes "one" with creation. This chapter is one example of ecofeminism, which has increasingly become a concern for Third World and indigenous women.[46] The last chapter by Clara Luz Ajo Lázaro takes us to the Afro-Cuban context and asks what happens to the symbols of Christ and Mary when Cubans go to Mass and also attend rituals of Santería and other Afro-Cuban forms of religious worship. The result is an interesting discussion of interfaith dialogue and hybridization between cultures.

Part 4—the book's final section—on "Body, Sexuality, and Spirituality," articulates the need to include women's body and sexuality in the discussion of feminist theology and spirituality. The HIV/AIDS epidemic has wreaked havoc in the countries of Africa, and women are susceptible to the virus if they have little control over their body and sexuality. Isabel Apawo Phiri's article details why we need a gender-response to the crisis and a new theology that is life-giving and not condemning. Meng Yanling's essay outlines the challenges Chinese Christian women face when they make decisions about marriage and sexuality. The chapter offers examples of feminist interpretations of biblical teachings on marriage and discusses the relevance of feminist theology in China. In the next chapter, Maria José Rosado-Nunes, an academic and activist on women's reproductive choice in Brazil, discusses why women's rights are human rights. She details how the Catholic Church has intervened in women's freedom to control their bodies and live their sexuality in responsible ways. The book closes with Carmelita Usog's uplifting article on women's spirituality for justice. Using the Philippines as an example, she describes how Catholic women have rediscovered the women's mystical tradition and experiment with new liturgies and symbols to sustain their work for justice.

When we look at the complexity of global issues and the dense matrices of structural oppression, we might sometimes wonder whether an alternative world is indeed possible. This collection of essays, written by Third World and indigenous scholars and theologians, testifies to the strength of their Christian faith and the resilience of the human spirit. Their words and action offer us a rare gift—hope abundant.

Notes

1. Virginia Fabella and Mercy Amba Oduyoye, eds., *With Passion and Compassion: Third World Women Doing Theology* (Maryknoll, NY: Orbis Books, 1988).

2. Virginia Fabella and R. S. Sugirtharajah, "Introduction," in *Dictionary of Third World Theologies*, ed. Virginia Fabella and R. S. Sugirtharajah (Maryknoll, NY: Orbis Books, 2000), xxii.

3. Homi K. Bhabha, *The Location of Culture* (London: Routledge, 1994), 36–39; see also Jonathan Rutherford, "The Third Space: Interview with Homi Bhabha," in *Identity: Community, Culture, Difference*, ed. Jonathan Rutherford (London: Lawrence and Wishart, 1990), 207–21.

4. "Fourth World," in *Wikipedia*, <http://en.wikipedia.org/wiki/Fourth_World>.

5. See the issue on "Globalization and Its Challenges to Doing Theology in Asia," *The Journal of Theologies and Cultures in Asia* 2 (2003); the issue on "Theology in the Context of Globalization," *Voices from the Third World* 20, no. 2 (1997); and the articles by Third World scholars in *Globalization and Its Victims*, ed. Jon Sobrino and Felix Wilfred, *Concilium* 2001, no. 5 (London: SCM Press, 2001).

6. María Arcelia Gonzáles Butron, "The Effects of Free-Market Globalization on Women's Lives," in Sobrino and Wilfred, *Globalization and Its Victims*, 46.

7. Puleng LenkaBula, "Justice and Fullness of Life in the Context of Economic Globalization: An African Woman's Perspective," *Reformed World* 52, no. 4 (2002): 163–74.

8. Kyungmi Park, "A Preview of Challenges for Asian Feminist Theology in the 21st Century," *PTCA Bulletin* 13, no. 1–2 (June and December, 2000): 8.

9. Gemma Tulud Cruz, "Faith on the Edge: Religion and Women in the Context of Migration," *Feminist Theology* 15, no. 1 (2006): 10.

10. Nantawan Boobprasat Lewis, "When Justice Collapses: A Religious Response to Sexual Violence and Trafficking in Women in Asia," in *Off the Menu: Asian and Asian North American Women's Religion and Theology*, ed. Rita Nakashima Brock, Jung Ha Kim, Kwok Pui-lan, and Seung Ai Yang (Louisville, KY: Westminster John Knox Press, 2007), 217–30.

11. Janice G. Raymond and Donna M. Hughes, "Sex Trafficking of Women in the United States: International and Domestic Trends," <http://www.uri.edu/artsci/wms/hughes/sex_traff_us.pdf>.

12. Ariya Abeysinghe, "Military Expenditure in LDC's: A Case Study of Sri Lanka," *People's Bank Economic Review* (January 1992), 33–47, quoted in Marlene Perera, "Militarism: A Thrust towards Globalization," in *Women Resisting Violence: Spirituality for Life*, ed. Mary John Mananzon et al. (Maryknoll, NY: Orbis Books, 1996), 109.

13. Anup Shah, "World Military Expenditure," <http://www.globalissues.org/article/75/world-military-spending>.

14. Paul Collier, "War and Military Expenditure in Developing Countries and Their Consequences for Development," *The Economics of Peace and Security Journal* 1, no. 1 (2006): 9–13.

15. Perera, "Militarism," 111.

16. See G. de Schrijver, ed., *Liberation Theologies on Shifting Grounds: A Clash of Socio-Economic and Cultural Paradigms* (Leuven: Leuven University Press, 1998); and Joerg Rieger, ed., *Opting for the Margins: Postmodernity and Liberation in Christian Theology* (New York: Oxford University Press, 2003).

17. See, for example, Ulrich Duchrow and Franz J. Hinkelammert, *Property for People, Not for Profit: Alternatives to the Global Tyranny of Capital* (London: Zed Books, 2004).

18. Enrique Dussel, "The Sociohistorical Meaning of Liberation Theology (Reflections about Its Origin and World Context)," in *Religions/Globalizations: Theories and Cases*, ed. Dwight N. Hopkins, Lois Ann Lorentzen, Eduardo Mendieta, and David Batstone (Durham, NC: Duke University Press, 2001), 33–45.

19. Marcella Althaus-Reid, "Class, Sex, and the Theologian: Reflections on the Liberationist Movement in Latin America," in *Another Possible World*, ed. Marcella Althaus-Reid, Ivan Petrella, and Luiz Carlos Susin (London: SCM Press, 2007), 27.

20. Ibid., 38.

21. Musimbi Kanyoro, "Cultural Hermeneutics: An African Contribution," in *Women's Visions: Theological Reflection, Celebration, Action*, ed. Ofelia Ortega (Geneva: World Council of Churches, 1995), 18–28. See also Kanyoro's *In-*

troducing Feminist Cultural Hermeneutics: An African Perspective (Cleveland, OH: Pilgrim Press, 2002).

22. Teresa Okure, SHCJ, "Africa: Globalization and the Loss of Cultural Identity," in Sobrino and Wilfred, *Globalization and Its Victims*, 68.

23. Musa W. Dube, *Postcolonial Feminist Interpretation of the Bible* (St. Louis, MO: Chalice Press, 2000).

24. See *The Poor Woman: A Critical Analysis of Asian Theology and Contemporary Chinese Fiction by Women* (New York: Peter Lang, 2002).

25. Sharon A. Bong, "An Asian Postcolonial and Feminist Methodology: Ethics as a Recognition of Limits," in *Gender and Religion: Cross-Cultural Approaches*, ed. Ursula King and Tina Beattie (London: Continuum, 2004) 238–49; Bong, "Postcolonialism," in *Blackwell Companion to the Bible and Culture*, ed. John Sawyer (Oxford: Blackwell Publication, 2006), 497–514; and Kwok Pui-lan, *Postcolonial Imagination and Feminist Theology* (Louisville, KY: Westminster John Knox Press, 2005).

26. Andrea Smith, *Conquest: Sexual Violence and American Indian Genocide* (Cambridge, MA: South End Press, 2005).

27. Laura E. Donaldson, *Decolonizing Feminisms: Race, Gender, and Empire-Building* (Chapel Hill, NC: University of North Carolina Press, 1992), 6.

28. Elsa Tamez, "Cultural Violence against Women in Latin America," *Voices from the Third World* 28, no. 1 (June 1995): 177–91.

29. Two symposia have been organized, one on intercultural feminist theology, and the other on violence against women. The papers from the first symposium have been published as *Feminist Intercultural Theology: Latina Explorations for a Just World*, ed. María Pilar Aquino and Maria José Rosado-Nunes (Maryknoll, NY: Orbis Books, 2007).

30. María Pilar Aquino, "Feminist Intercultural Theology: Toward a Shared Future of Justice," in Aquino and Rosado-Nunez, *Feminist Intercultural Theology*, 9.

31. See chapter 13 in this volume, and Silvia Regina de Lima Silva, "Dialogue of Memories: Ways toward a Black Feminist Christology from Latin America," in Aquino and Rosado-Nunez, *Feminist Intercultural Theology*, 166–78.

32. María Pilar Aquino, "Theology and Indigenous Cultures of the Americas: Conditions of Dialogue," *Catholic Theological Society of America Proceedings* 61 (2006): 19–50. I am grateful to Aquino for drawing my attention to this important work.

33. Nami Kim, "The 'Indigestible' Asian: The Unifying Term 'Asian' in Theological Discourse," in Brock, Kim, Kwok, and Yang, *Off the Menu*, 23–43.

34. Wong, *"The Poor Woman."*

35. Namsoon Kang, "Re-constructing *Asian* Feminist Theology: Toward a *Glocal* Feminist Theology in an Era of Neo-Empire(s)," in *Christian Theology in Asia*, ed. Sebastian C. H. Kim (Cambridge: Cambridge University Press, 2008), 222.

36. Kwok Pui-lan and Rachel A. R. Bundang, "PANAAWTM Lives," *Journal of Feminist Studies in Religion* 22, no. 2 (2005): 147–58.

37. See the issue on "Haunts of Pain: Theologizing Dalits," *In God's Image* 26, no. 3 (September 2007).

38. See. for example, Lalrinawmi Ralte, "Tribal Eco-Feminist Spirituality," in *Breaking Silence: Theology from Asian Women*, ed. Meehyun Chung (Delhi:

ISPCK, 2006), 3–22; and Victoria Tauli-Corpuz, "Reclaiming Earth-Based Spirituality: Indigenous Women in the Cordillera," in *Women Healing Earth: Third World Women in Ecology, Feminism, and Religion*, ed. Rosemary Radford Ruether (Maryknoll, NY: Orbis Books, 1996), 99–106.

39. Kathleen McPhillips, "Feminism and Religion in the Pacific Region," *Journal of Feminist Studies in Religion* 18, no. 2 (2002): 83-90. See also <www.wsrt.net.au>.

40. See the Circle's website, <http://www.thecirclecawt.org>.

41. See the Center's website, <http://www.awrc4ct.org>.

42. Josefina Hurtado and Ute Seibert, "Con-spirando: Women 'Breathing Together'—Female Congregation Dealing with Spirituality and Sociopolitical Issues," *Ecumenical Review* 53, no. 1 (January 2001), <http://findarticles.com/p/articles/mi_m2065/is_1_53/ai_71190356>, and Mary Judith Ress, "The Conspirando Women's Collective: An Historical Perspective," in *Circling In, Circling Out: A Con-spirando Reader*, ed. Mary Judith Ress (Santiago, Chile: The Con-spirando Collective, 2005), 11–17. The website of the Collective is <http://www.conspirando.cl>.

43. Poetry by Asian women can be found in the Asian women's theological journal *In God's Image*. For samples of African women's poetry, see *Transforming Power: Women in the Household of God*, ed. Mercy Amba Oduyoye (Accra: Sam-Woode, 1997), 148–60; for the use of poetry in liturgy, see "'This is My Body Broken for You'—Liturgical Resources for Dealing with HIV/AIDS," by Devarakshanam Betty Govinden, in *African Women, HIV/AIDS and Faith Communities*, ed. Isabel Apawo Phiri, Beverley Haddad, and Madipoane Masenya (Pietermaritzburg: Cluster Publications, 2003), 259–90.

44. Stacey M. Floyd-Thomas, ed., *Deeper Shades of Purple: Womanism in Religion and Society* (New York: New York University Press, 2006); María Pilar Aquino, Daisy L. Machado, and Jeanette Rodríguez, eds., *A Reader in Latina Feminist Theology: Religion and Justice*, (Austin, TX: University of Texas Press, 2002); and Brock, Kim, Kwok, and Yang, *Off the Menu*.

45. See the section on interpretation of the Exodus stories in R. S. Sugirtharajah, ed., *Voices from the Margin: Interpreting the Bible from the Third World*, 3rd ed. (Maryknoll, NY: Orbis Books, 2006), 207–78.

46. See Ruether, *Women Healing Earth*.

PART 1
Context and Theology

A Circle expands forever
It covers all who wish to hold hands
And its size depends on each other
It is a vision of solidarity
It turns outwards to interact with the outside
And inward for self-critique
A circle expands forever
It is a vision of accountability
It grows as the other is moved to grow
A circle must have a center
But a single dot does not make a Circle
One tree does not make a forest
A circle, a vision of cooperation, mutuality and care

—Mercy Amba Oduyoye (Ghana)

1

ENGENDERED COMMUNAL THEOLOGY

African Women's Contribution to Theology in the Twenty-first Century

Musimbi R. A. Kanyoro (Kenya)

The African Dilemma

Africa is a land wealthy in proverbs. One of my favorites relates the dilemma of the hyena. The hyena was following the general direction of the aroma of barbecuing meat. He wanted a share of this enticing and mouth-watering meat. Suddenly his path forked. He was not sure which fork would lead him to the meat. In his uncertainty, he put his legs astride the two paths and tried to walk along both but the poor hyena split in the middle.

The African Christian often walks with one foot in African religion and culture and another in the church and Western culture. While the former is seen as tradition that must disappear with time, the latter is presented as progress and encouraged. The dilemma of the African Christian cannot simply be wished away, especially today when it seems as if the center does not hold and things are falling apart.[1] Christian women of Africa inhabit these two worlds. Oftentimes they feel the strain of splitting apart when trying to correlate the pull of the culture on the one hand with that of the church on the other. It is wishful thinking to believe that it is possible and desirable to live in the tension between the varying demands of the gospel and culture.

The reality is that, in the African indigenous thought system, culture and religion are not distinct from each other. Therefore, culture and

Musimbi R. A. Kanyoro, "Engendered Communal Theology: African Women's Contribution to Theology in the 21st Century," in *Talitha Cum! Theologies of African Women*, ed. Nyambura J. Njoroge and Musa W. Dube (Pietermaritzburg: Cluster Publications, 2001), 158–78. *Talitha Cum!* is available from Cluster Publications at <www.clusterpublications.co.za>.

religion in Africa embrace all areas of one's total life. There is no sphere of existence that is excluded from the double grip of culture and religion. The presence or absence of rain, the well-being of the community, sexuality, marriage, birthing, naming children, success or failure, the place and form of one's burial, all these and other aspects of life come within the scope of religion and culture. It is, therefore, a great threat to communal security to be critical of culture, for there are elements in the culture that are the very roots through which the solidarity of the community is nurtured.

However no culture or religion can ever be static. Hence, culture and religion in Africa today, while bearing a direct link to the past, have had contact with other cultures through colonial occupation, trade, religious encounters, and other diverse links. Change today is made even faster and easier by communication networks and their technological artifacts, travel, and the globalization of Western education.

In addition, African religions and cultures have had to contend with new political realities, the formation of new identities, and interactions with surrounding and new contact cultures and religions. Despite such encounters, it amazes both Africans and foreigners alike to see how cultural practices in Africa are alive and well, and how they remain intact despite their exposure to new encounters.

The African Woman's Dilemma

Women in Africa are the custodians of cultural practices. For generations, African women have guarded traditional practices that are strictly observed for fear of breaking taboos. In many cases, women themselves are the objects of these practices and are diminished by them. Harmful traditional practices are passed on as "cultural values" and therefore are not to be discussed, challenged, or changed. In the guise of culture, harmful practices and traditions are perpetuated. Practices such as female genital mutilation,[2] early betrothals[3] and marriages, and the stigmatization of single women, barren women, and widows hinder the liberation of women. Yet, in fact, it is women who sustain these practices. Such a state of affairs illustrates the reality of women's powerlessness and their vulnerability in the face of cultural prescriptions.

When trained women theologians begin to make connections between what happens at home and in church with a view to suggesting change in the name of justice, they have to be cautious about disturbing the set order. It takes time and extended discussions with other women in order to establish the trust necessary to begin advocating change. It would be easier simply to pursue the study of academic theology, that is, reading, reflecting, and writing. But for us in Africa, it does not matter how much we write about our theology in books; the big test before us is whether we can bring change to our societies. This is a tall order and we agonize over it.

A majority of African Christian women have been raised in evangelical and conservative churches. We therefore often find ourselves struggling with our history and the personal changes we have experienced as a result of our theological studies, ecumenical exposure, and encounters with the analysis of women's global issues. Sometimes being at this crossroad leaves us in great pain, as Nyambura Njoroge suggested in "Groaning and Languishing in Labour Pains: But for How Long Lord?" the paper she presented at the meeting of the Circle of African Women Theologians in Nairobi in 1994.[4] Njoroge, a woman pastor raised in a Presbyterian home and church, laments that her training as a pastor never equipped her to deal with social or gender issues. Instead, she was trained to see people as souls without bodies, a perspective that made her ministerial work narrow and limited, if not impossible.

Whether in the pews or among theologically trained women, only a handful are comfortable with challenging the text of the Bible by subjecting the hermeneutics of critical analysis to the biblical text, as theologian Elisabeth Schüssler Fiorenza has suggested in her framework of feminist hermeneutical theory.[5] At this point, one of the immediate tasks before us is to gain the confidence to face the dilemmas and contradictions that are part of our history and our present. When we advocate that women be included in the ordained ministries of the churches in Africa, we are hoping that these women pastors will be strong pillars for establishing relationships of trust and mutuality with women in the congregations. We are hoping that women pastors will be willing to talk about the reality of women's experiences in their sermons, and therefore be able to make connections between church, home, and society. This would open up the possibility for women to be included in the telling of the story of faith to the community of faith. We also trust that the actuality of women and men working together in ministry will demonstrate not only the possibility but also the effectiveness of having men and women share leadership and responsibility. This could have a far-reaching impact in other areas, including the home. However, we have come to find out that it is not enough to have trained and ordained women: the nature of the training is even more important if change is to come to our societies.

The African continent's history of colonialism and Western imperialism causes a dilemma for African women theologians and activists at large. There is always a struggle regarding how to relate to Western culture, indigenous culture, and religious culture, coupled with the daily need to support life against all odds. The quest for justice for women is trivialized in favor of "larger" issues such as national liberation, famine, disease, war, and poverty. Acts of individual resistance to injustice and inequality in the church are seen as immoral rather than as prophetic and

scripturally based. Women who subject recent and current church practice to analysis are accused of being in pursuit of the Western ideals of
feminist liberation rather than African and Christian ones. This often
makes women vulnerable.

There are also many issues on which women do not agree. We are
especially at odds on issues concerning culture. For instance, there are
huge differences about how to regard cultural practices such as female
circumcision (genital mutilation), *lobola* (bride price), polygamy, the
male prerogative to inherit land, and numerous other practices. Some
perceive these practices as the essence of our culture, and therefore central to our identity. In other words, some believe that these practices help
to underpin who we are and therefore they give us a stable base and a
uniform community. Yet for some among us, many of these practices are
acts of injustice to women and they need to change. Such practices are
harmful and oppressive, and they reduce women to mere instruments of
men and culture in general. These dilemmas continue to divide us, but
the stage has been reached at which diversity of opinion will ensure that
the women of Africa will not remain silent.

Gender as a Concept of Theological Analysis

Theological engagement with gender issues seeks to expose harm
and injustices that are in society and are extended to scripture and the
teachings and practices of the church through culture. Today, most
women's scholarship globally recognizes the web of oppression that can
even lead women to oppress other women. Gender analysis seeks to
identify cases of injustice and to suggest societal correction that may be
warranted. African women have benefited from the theological work
being done by women globally. African women are part of the trend
whereby women now study theology. African women's theology places
emphasis on women's humanity, on the fact that women too are created
in the image of God. The roots and responses of this theology relate to
the dilemmas and celebrations of God's people on the African continent.
While African women's theology requires that the African worldview be
taken into account in analysis, it does not embrace the assumption that
the African or feminist worldview is universal, or that there is only one
mode of interpretation.

If African women today are able to name some of the oppressive aspects of African cultures, such a stance has not come easily. Telling the
stories of dehumanizing cultural practices is still rare and involves struggle. There are still many women who will not speak of their own experiences as victims, as perpetrators, or even as sympathizers. African
women theologians who have encountered feminist analysis do not
quickly jump to condemn women for being custodians of dehumanizing

cultural practices. It is appreciated that even women's actions may be deeply rooted in patriarchal socialization, and, therefore, the analysis of women's oppression has to be undertaken in the context of gender analysis.[6] Using gender analysis for our theological explorations, we seek to learn about and understand how our societies are organized and how power is used by different groups of people, by men and women, by young and old, and by people of varying economic means. Who benefits from a particular interpretation of culture and how is the system kept in place? We strive to clarify for ourselves ways in which roles, attitudes, values, and relationships regarding women and men are constructed in our societies and, indeed, by societies all over the world. The concepts and practices of equality and discrimination as determined by social, economic, religious, and cultural factors lie at the heart of the theology of women in Africa in this new millennium.

The task confronting women theologians in Africa is how to incorporate discussions on culture in our African communities so that women may find it safe to speak about issues that harm their well-being. The biblical conviction that men and women are created in God's image in itself demands that women too must live in dignity. Any pattern of discrimination, domination, or oppression is contrary to God's justice.

Cultural Hermeneutics as a Key to the Liberation of Women in Africa

In 1994 I first clearly saw the need for analyzing culture as a process for seeking out liberation for African women. I made the following preliminary remarks:

> The complexities inherent in cultural debate require space and a safe environment of mutual trust and mutual vulnerability in order for dialogue to take place... A new aspect of feminist analyses has been brought to theology mainly by studies of women from Africa. This new thing deserves its rightful place in the theological paradigms. It could be called "Cultural Hermeneutics."[7]

I suggested that cultural hermeneutics is an important first step toward an African women's liberation theology. All questions regarding the welfare and status of women in Africa can be explained within the framework of culture. Women are not permitted to inherit land or own property because it is not culturally "right." Women may not participate in leadership because it is culturally the domain of men. Whether the subject is politics, economics, religion, or social issues, in Africa, none of these can be extricated from the all-pervading culture.

However, it is not enough simply to analyze culture without reference to the people who maintain the culture and those whom the culture impacts. Here is where the need arises for a gender-sensitive cultural hermeneutics that addresses issues of culture while being critical of that culture from a gender perspective.

The church is part and parcel of the subject of analysis. It is in the church that the dilemma of how Africans should live as Christians and people of a particular culture persists. The status of women within their church is a microcosm of their status within the society of which the church is a part. Even when the rights of women are enshrined in law, popular attitudes and values lag far behind and continue to oppress women. Since the Bible forms the base of Christianity and informs African Christians on what they can or cannot validate in their culture, I have since 1982 been working in the framework of reading the Bible with African women's cultural eyes. It was through reading the Bible with women in my village for a very long time that I came to realize the importance of culture in people's lives and the consequent influence of that culture on their interpretation of the Bible. I stay with the Bible as the source of my own research, while acknowledging that cultural hermeneutics could also be done from a different standpoint.[8] It is important to recognize how the Bible is understood in order to locate the accountability of the church with regard to gender issues in church and in society. Cultural hermeneutics seeks to find ways to raise questions regarding the accountability of society and church to women, and the accountability of women in taking responsibility for their own lives.

I have presented my work in seminars in Africa and abroad and tested various hypotheses with other African women who have expertise in different disciplines. Three years ago I began to develop a theory based on previous hypotheses and my continuing encounter with the text of the Bible in Africa as well as the various ways in which the Bible has been interpreted by preachers, translators, and Bible study groups. My theory is that the culture of the reader in Africa has more influence on the way the biblical text is understood and used in communities than does the historical culture of the text. In stating this I suggest that not knowing the nuances of the culture within which the Bible is read or preached has much wider-reaching repercussions on the exegesis of the texts than is often acknowledged by biblical scholars and preachers. I further argue that cultural hermeneutics is a necessary tool for those who prepare others for pastoral work or teach homiletics in seminaries and other institutions for training clergy. More important, though, I claim that cultural hermeneutics is a prerequisite for understanding African women's liberation theology.

I base much of my theory on the experiences gained by reading the Bible with communities of African rural women between 1982 and 1996. The lessons gained from such readings underscored for me the urgency of affirming the concepts of social and cultural hermeneutics that have been dealt with so well by many authors.[9] I contend that we have to analyze both personal and communal experiences in religion and culture. The stories of African women unmask sins of oppression and injustice and call for collective repentance and change from society as a whole.

A Context of Much Suffering

Theological study in Africa today takes place among people who have suffered greatly. There is so much death on our continent that reality makes a mockery of the suffering of Job, the biblical figure associated with tribulations. As if illnesses and diseases were not enough, in Africa there are successive and simmering wars. There are repressive government regimes all over the continent, regimes that receive world attention only when their actions are the subject of global media coverage. Such actions include recent atrocious events in Liberia, Somalia, Rwanda, Burundi, the Congo, and Sierra Leone. Economic conflict has been aggravated by globalization, the aftermath of structural adjustment programs, corrupt leadership, and bad management of national economies. All these things affect women's lives, prompting prayers, liturgies, songs, and poems as ways of theologizing issues on the continent. Much of the time our loud lamentations are heard only as tiny whimpers. At other times, we are simply unable to cry. We preserve our tears for mourning our dead. In such a difficult context, culture can be seen as the only constant element for communities. Challenging culture amidst such upheavals is no small task, yet there is a need to address cultural questions and, when required, to dare challenge culture and much of what it stands for.

Cultural Nationalism

In pre-independence years, African nationalists sought the re-establishment of coherence and integrity in African life through programs of cultural retrieval. Literary efforts resulted in works characterized as expressions of "cultural nationalism" that debunked European culture and extolled African traditions. Novelists such as Camara Laye[10] and Chinua Achebe,[11] in addition to anthropologists such as Jomo Kenyatta,[12] paid attention to the wholesome dignity of African traditions and institutions.

In the wake of liberation movements seeking independence from European colonialists, African politicians such as Kwameh Nkrumah of Ghana, Jomo Kenyatta of Kenya, and others claimed cultural identity as a badge of African solidarity as well as uniqueness. The white government in South Africa interpreted the cultural uniqueness of Africans as one reason for asserting that cultures must develop separately. They introduced the evil system of apartheid, the demolition of which has been stained by the blood of many people. Scholars of African religions stated categorically that there are no boundaries between the sacred and the secular in African cultural and religious life. It was stated repeatedly that in the African religions, the "sacred" and the "profane" are on the same level of experience and not cut off from one another.[13]

African theologians of the last three decades, in reaction to the colonial mentality of the church in its interpretation of Christianity to Africans, have posited a theology of inculturation, various aspects of which have been presented by Simon S. Maimela, Jesse Mugambi, John Parratt, and John Pobee.[14] Inculturation theology attempts to "Africanize" in the sense of affirming African culture and positing it as the basis for developing African liberation theology.[15] The dominant participants in the theory of inculturation—whether novelists, politicians, or theologians—have been men, and have indeed been perceived to be speaking for all African people.

Inculturation Is Not Sufficient

In coming late to the scene, African women theologians are caught in the dilemma of disagreeing with the presentation of inculturation as the basis for African liberation theology. While affirming the need for reclaiming culture through the theology of inculturation, we African women theologians make the claim that inculturation is not sufficient unless the cultures we reclaim are analyzed and are deemed worthy in terms of promoting justice and support for life and the dignity of women.

Undertaking a theology of inculturation from a women's perspective requires that one draw wisdom from the methods used by both African and feminist theologies of liberation. While utilizing these theologies and means of analysis and systemization, we also employ an African method of storytelling familiar to our African communities. In using this method, we seek to examine the cultural conditioning of African women's thinking in order to discover the roots of the belief system of which they are also a part. We choose feminist methodology because it challenges cultural socialization by rejecting the assumption that the roles of men and women have been fixed, either by the Creator or by culture. In addition, feminist theologians begin by recognizing that existing stories, structures, and beliefs do not tell the stories of women or that they have distorted the truth about women.

Both feminist and inculturation theologies are contextual. They have to do with the present state of the world and thus adapt a hermeneutic approach to the text. They base their power of analysis on people's own named experiences. These factors are important for us as women of Africa as we begin to add our experiences to those of Western feminists, African American "womanists," and Latin American *mujeristas*, as well as Asian and Latin American women's perspectives in theology. The choice of feminist methodology as a frame of analysis for pursuing African women's theology is useful because feminist theology has been tested and subjected to critiques by other women[16] and we can learn from its identified weakness.[17]

In recent years, African women have strongly suggested that liberation theology in Africa can be credible only if it also subjects culture to stringent exegesis. Using their lives as examples, African women question the premises that celebrate all cultural practices regardless of their negative impact on women. "How can a theology of liberation be based on non-liberating cultural practices?" they ask.[18] As Christian women in Africa, we see the need to take responsibility for ourselves to illustrate the consequences of reading the Bible through a cultural lens by bringing our own experiences to bear on the texts of the Bible. In so doing, we address the place of women in the story of faith.

Engendered Communal Theology

The issues on which we focus in our theological work are African: they are both religious and cultural at the same time, but they affect women differently from the way they affect men. Labeling this method of undertaking theology, a method that analyzes culture as "cultural hermeneutics," seemed sufficient in 1994.[19] At the present time, I do not see that as an appropriately distinctive name for labeling the struggles of African women. Hence, I have moved on and would now elect to refer to this method as "engendering cultural hermeneutics." The term reflects and captures the challenges with which African women approach the theology of inculturation by examining culture with women's eyes. Thus, pursuing a theology of inculturation from a gender and feminist perspective is a new step forward. The process of breaking a long-held silence is very difficult. It requires a safe place to discover and build solidarity with the others in the community. In Africa, commitment to the changing of oppressive systems has to be done within the community; otherwise its validity will be questioned. It is for this reason that I would prefer to refer to theology currently being done by women in Africa as "engendered communal theology."

A method of theology that gives us African women our own voice and space is timely. The result of personal experience is the creation of new literature in which truths about women of Africa can be told. The new literature from women sheds light on new ways of reading the Bible.

African Women Undertaking Engendered Communal Theology

The Circle of Concerned African Women Theologians:
A Safe Place to Speak for Ourselves

In 1989 we founded our African women's theological community, the Circle of Concerned African Women Theologians (hereafter, "the Circle"). In 1992 our first continental volume, *The Will to Arise: Women, Tradition and Church in Africa*, was published by Orbis Books.[20] Since that time our efforts have continued unabated. We are writing, speaking, preaching, and studying the Bible and meeting to reject the dehumanization of African women. Today, the Circle has a membership scattered all over the continent. Women write papers and then meet to present these papers to each other for joint critiques. Some of the papers end up in books, while others appear in journals and still others in the media. More than nine books have been produced since 1989.

The Circle has become for many of us a circle of solidarity. Talking about various research projects in the company of the Circle is important so that African women can make their voices heard and increase the amount of literature that presents women's perspectives from the continent. The professional "death" of trained scholars in Africa is the norm and this particularly affects African women.[21] The Circle's approximately four hundred women members from all over Africa, extending from Cairo to Cape Town, are pursuing theology in the context of their own settings. Currently, we are divided into four study commissions, namely:

1. Cultural and Biblical Hermeneutics
2. Women in Culture and Religion
3. History of Women
4. Ministry and Theological Education and Formation

Each commission has a team of two people, trained in the appropriate discipline, to coordinate the study. The coordination involves designing the nature of the studies and inviting members from different parts of Africa to carry out relevant field research on the topics identified and then write about them. The Circle's efforts are important in that they contribute something new to theology by including the voices of women in Africa. Actions, such as returning to our villages to do theological work with our communities, make our task exciting. We do not stop at simply identifying issues in our communities as subjects for research, as has been done in the past. We stay with the issues, slowly discovering with the communities what the Word of God or our culture is sending us to do. We conduct our analyses with feminist hermeneutical tools and then we engage ourselves practically in some form of change.

It is for this reason that women who belong to the Circle believe that the study of theology from women's perspective is a gift to the church and a gift to women. It is a gift to the church because it calls the church to repentance for its role in the subordination of women. It is a gift to women because it has opened our eyes to the fact that the future of society and the future of women depend on our placing our trust in the message of God rather than the message of men. We can read and interpret the Bible by ourselves and we can count on God's word that says God created men and women in God's own image (Gen 1:27). The study of theology by women is the proverbial equivalent of the lion learning to write.

The Circle's vision is to encourage African women to write and publish their works. The goal of the Circle is to promote the well-being of African women and all women through theological analysis and the study of the Bible. This, in turn, commits us to social action. The discovery of women's theology has provided for us a renewal and a reformation not yet realized or acknowledged by the church. It is a renewal that we wish for all women in Africa and for the whole church in Africa. Since the birth of the Circle in Ghana in 1989, African women have found, through membership in the group, a safe place in which they can dare speak and write about many subjects considered "taboo" in African culture. The most courageous move has been to talk openly about sexuality. Circle women talk of sexuality as much as they talk about anything else. Bernadette Mbuy Beya, a Roman Catholic religious sister from Congo (formerly Zaire), pinpoints this cultural taboo in categorical terms:

> The implications of sexuality in our culture make it anything but comfortable for us to address this topic. In our culture, the subject is a taboo. Despite the difficulties, however, some of us African women determined to study this matter in depth. After all, sexuality is a prime factor in the determination of behavioral reality, both of human beings in general and of women in particular.[22]

It is remarkable that in almost all of the writings of the Circle, women have something to say on sexuality even if it is only by implication. Sexuality is defined in very broad terms as an expression of our identity and a means by which we express our relationships with each other in our communities. Thus, for us in Africa, relationships are at the heart of sexuality. Bernadette Mbuy Beya provides an African definition of sexuality as: "...the ensemble of activities by which human beings seek and attain satisfaction of their sexual inclination. Our traditional behavior and customs include a whole series of sexual initiatory practices."[23]

Beya goes on to explore sexuality in categories such as marriage, fidelity, prostitution, and single life. Other African women address sexuality through discussions of polygamy, clitoridectomy, secret societies, barrenness, and child marriages. Behind all of these practices there are certain implications for sexuality in society.

I have singled out sexuality because it is the foundation for engendering cultural hermeneutics. Many cultural behaviors that are detrimental to women's health are closely linked to sexuality. Sexuality and fertility are one issue. Attached to fertility is a whole string of factors that include the value of children, the impact of AIDS, female circumcision, and polygamy. Many women in Africa testify to the church's fears and suspicions of "women's sexuality." Sexuality is given as an excuse for denying ordination to women. Not only are women's bodies seen as symbols of sexuality but also, because of that, women are considered to be unacceptable as church leaders. It is interesting to me that African society, which is very hospitable to new life, has not provided a theology that affirms the woman through whom new life finds the possibility for growth.

Polygamy is another issue closely connected to sexuality. Here the church, too, has found itself in a dilemma. Until recently, the subject of polygamy has appeared in Christian debates mainly as a moral issue relating to marriage. Convinced that the scriptures advocate monogamy through texts such as the creation of Adam and Eve (Gen 2:23–25), the Christian church has taken pains to condemn those cultures in which polygamy is an accepted form of matrimony. As far as the church is concerned, polygamy is deemed immoral, those who engage in it are sinners, and thus men, women, and children in polygamous families cannot be accepted as church members. Often men have been asked to choose one wife and to leave the others in order to be accepted in the church. The Christian church is also in contention with Islam, which legally stipulates that a man may have up to four wives. Recent studies by Judith Mbula Bahemuka, Anne Nasimiyu-Wasike, Lloyda Fanusie, Bernadette Mbuy Beya, as well as studies that I have conducted, indicate that polygamy is an institution that oppresses women.[24] Polygamy thrives in patriarchal cultures that uphold the superiority of male persons. In such societies men may own not only property, they may also own women and their productive powers as well. Polygamy has been the basis of the exploitation of women and children's labor because polygamy is justified as a means of enhancing the productivity of property for men. Polygamy also depicts women as weak and in need of the constant protection of men. It reduces women's capacity to cope with physical circumstances such as barrenness. Both in the Bible and in African cultures, women who do not give birth or who give birth only to girl children are degraded to a degree, and this helps to perpetuate polygamy.

The church is often in a dilemma about polygamy because on the one hand it finds support for its position in the scriptures, which seem to advocate monogamy, and yet there is no direct condemnation of polygamy. African feminists argue that the case for monogamy should be based on the dignity of women, rather than on moral judgments or the "advantages" of one form of marriage over another. Failure to teach true equality of the sexes is failure to instill in society an understanding that the superiority of man over woman is contrary to God's intention for human beings. Today, however, books and articles by African women theologians, published locally and internationally, are serving as a resource that casts fresh new gender perspectives on these lasting issues.

Learning to Accommodate Diversity in Communitarian Contexts

Often detractors choose to perceive the efforts of African women to promote the perspectives of women as foreign and Western and not in accord with our African values and religious beliefs, especially when we struggle to come to terms with our differences. These people want African women theologians to be silent and submissive in the face of injustice and oppression. They condemn us when we do not sing in unison on all issues affecting women. This denigration takes its toll on women and threatens many women who genuinely seek the way of justice. To choose to move forward, despite these criticisms, is the privilege of only the few women who can rely on other support systems, such as families who understand, or who have the advantage of being economically and socially self-reliant. This defines the social location of those women who choose to actively protest against the current status of women through theology, the legal system, political activism, or any other possible means.

Such issues weigh heavily on women who have received a theological education. Many simply do not have time to sit and write long papers with footnotes and quotations from numerous other scholars. Many do not have the opportunity for academic study and pursuits. Many do not have access to books and libraries, and money is short and theological books are expensive. Those who judge African women as people who lack theological expression and reflection need to hear, read, and respect our choked silence. In some instances the seeming silence may well be the expression of a strategy of protest. But it may also be an expression of despair, anger, overloaded daily lives, and other circumstances that continually weigh us down. The reality is that African women live daily in vulnerable situations, and whether speaking or remaining silent, they are engaged in a daily struggle to transcend their reality.

Illiteracy as a Marginalizing Factor

The practice of theology in Africa today has to take into account rural non-literate women. This is a question of method, not content. Many women on our continent cannot read and write but they sing, they dance, and they speak. However, when it comes to the written scriptures as the basis for belief, they will always depend on other people interpreting the scriptures for them. Thus, the image of who they are in the story of faith largely depends on the teaching they receive.

For a long time, print media have marginalized the voices of African women. African rural women are singing songs; they are also creating poetry, proverbs, and dirges. Their reflections should challenge us to undertake theology in a different way. We who can write must explore new areas and new avenues for the words of our sisters to be heard beyond the confines of our borders. We must not repeat the theft by other researchers who have often taken these words without giving credit to their original owners. Sitting in comfortable offices producing complete manuscripts in dominant languages will leave out many of our own sisters from participating in theological reflection. When we African women cry for inclusion and participation, we cannot at the same time opt for struggle by and for individuals. Our success depends entirely on our ability to make our theology a communal theology. While maintaining global sisterhood with other women, we must seek to establish our own methodology. Illiteracy on our continent will not determine our access to the grace of God, but it is a real factor with critical consequences for those pursuing theology in Africa. My own experience of taking part in Bible studies with rural women in Africa, and more specifically with those in my village, shows that it is possible to work with illiterate communities and that inclusion should be a matter of justice, not simply one of choice.

Prophetic Engagement

Finally, we must ask about what the consequences for the church in Africa will be if women's perspectives and methods in theology are incorporated. I see first and foremost the possibilities in awakening the church to the fact that biblical history did not stop at the end of the first century of the Common Era. It is important for the Christian church in Africa to realize that the power of God, which enabled the Hebrew people to preserve their history by telling stories about their encounters with each other and with God, is the same power that led early Christians to tell their stories and by so doing relating the powerful story of Jesus. That same power of God still lives with us for whom the promise of the Holy Spirit was given and fulfilled at Pentecost.

I see our work as only one of the beginning parts of a long journey for African women and the African church as a whole. It is a journey that could lead toward envisioning a new beginning for women in Africa and for the church in Africa. A faith that holds itself aloof from people seeking to escape marginalization poses serious risk to the future of the church and the church of the future in Africa. In order to safeguard the prophetic witness of the church, action is needed now, for justice delayed is justice denied.

Speaking up on issues that diminish life has been the most difficult part of our self-understanding as individuals and churches. Speaking out is a prophetic task and therefore we, the African women engaged in theology, are participating in a prophetic mission. It involves some very serious risks. In our situation, where democracy is thought to be a luxury, speaking up involves risking the wrath of the powerful. Those who have dared to speak out despite all the risks involved are the prophets that our continent badly needs today. During the World Council of Churches Ecumenical Decade, 1988–1998, many women in the churches of Africa spoke up.[25] Some were reprimanded, others were excommunicated by the churches, and still others lost their positions in the church.[26] I yearn for a time when the men in the churches of Africa will be prophetic about the things that adversely affect the lives of African women!

Women of Africa are asking the church to be credible as we link our theological analysis to cultural hermeneutics. We give credibility to the church when we make it aware of its own shortcomings and the need for repentance. Perhaps, with the knowledge that other women have gone courageously before us, we as African women will be able to refuse to be victims of history and claim our share of the right to be God's dignified persons.

We must also listen to each other. To seek justice is to break the boundaries of injustice. The European theologian Dorothee Sölle says: "The question posed by feminist liberation theology is not 'Is there God?' but, 'Does God happen among us, too?'"[27] Engendered communal theology is about God happening among us as African women who are daughters of God and daughters of Anowa.[28]

Notes

1. Chinua Achebe, *Things Fall Apart* (London: Heinemann, 1958).

2. D. Efua, *The Cutting of a Rose: Female Genital Mutilation, the Practice and its Prevention* (London: Minority Rights, 1994). Female circumcision is the cultural term used for cutting parts of the female genital organ to mark the coming of age of a woman or to reduce her sexual pleasure with a view to curbing her need for sex. In the recent past, human rights groups have renamed this practice "female genital mutilation" (FGM). It is argued that removing a healthy organ or irremediably deforming it cannot be anything other than mutilation.

3. Early betrothals are a common practice in parts of Africa. Basically an early betrothal involves parents promising their girl child in marriage to another family. A girl child can be betrothed soon after birth. A dowry may be paid for her at the time of the betrothal. This means that in reality she is bonded and will be forced, when she grows up, to marry into the family chosen by her parents.

She may marry a younger man in the family or even a man old enough to be her great grandfather.

4. Nyambura J. Njoroge presented her paper at a meeting of the Circle of African Women Theologians in Nairobi, Kenya, in January 1994, and it was later published in *Groaning in Faith: African Women in the Household of God*, ed. Musimbi R. A. Kanyoro and Nyambura J. Njoroge (Nairobi: Acton Publishers, 1996), 3–15.

5. Elisabeth Schüssler Fiorenza, *Bread Not Stone: The Challenge of Feminist Biblical Interpretation* (Boston: Beacon Press, 1985).

6. For feminists, patriarchy does not just mean the rule of the father, or the rule of males for that matter, but it carries with it connotations of an unjust hierarchical and dualistic ordering of life that discriminates against women. Patriarchy should not be seen as the opposite of matriarchy. For further reading, see Rosemary Radford Ruether, "Patriarchy," in *The Dictionary of Feminist Theologies*, ed. Letty M. Russell and J. Shannon Clarkson (Louisville, KY: Westminster John Knox Press, 1996), 205–6.

7. See the report of the United Nations on the Fourth World Conference on Women: Beijing Declaration and the Platform for Action, 1995, United Nations Information Center, New York.

8. In her book, *Daughters of Anowa: African Women and Patriarchy* (Maryknoll, NY: Orbis Books, 1995), Mercy Amba Oduyoye presents the best example of engendered cultural hermeneutics available today. She does not use the terminology because her book is about content and begins with an analysis of oral literature. This work starts by analyzing the reading of the Bible in a cultural context and seeks to name the theologies of African feminists. The Akan people understand themselves as "children of Anowa" (a legendary Akan woman who represents Africa in contemporary Ghanaian creative literature), and women are her "daughters."

9. Norman K. Gottwald and Richard A. Horsley, eds., *The Bible and Liberation: Political and Social Hermeneutics* (Marynoll, NY: Orbis Books, 1993); Fernando F. Segovia and Mary Ann Tolbert, eds., *Reading from This Place*, vol. 2, *Social Location and Biblical Interpretation in Global Perspectives* (Minneapolis, MN: Fortress Press, 1995); and Frederick C. Tiffany and Sharon H. Ringe, eds., *Biblical Interpretation: A Roadmap* (Nashville, TN: Abingdon Press, 1996).

10. Camara Laye, *The African Child* (London: Fontana, 1959).

11. Achebe, *Things Fall Apart*; and Achebe, *Arrow of God* (London: Keinemann, 1964).

12. Jomo Kenyatta, *Facing Mount Kenya: The Traditional Life of the Gikuyu* (London: Secker and Warburg, 1938).

13. Edward E. Evans-Pritchard, *Theories of Primitive Culture* (London: Oxford University Press, 1965).

14. Simon S. Maimela, ed., *Culture, Religion and Liberation* (Pretoria, South Africa: Penrose Books, 1994); Jessie N. K. Mugami, *African Heritage and Contemporary Christianity* (Nairobi: Longman, 1990); John Parratt, *Reinventing Christianity: African Theology Today* (Grand Rapids, MI: Eerdmans, 1995); and John S. Pobee, *Towards an African Theology* (Nashville, TN: Abingdon Press, 1979).

15. Refer to the bibliography in *Talitha Cum! Theologies of African Women*, ed. Nyambura J. Njoroge and Musa W. Dube (Pietermaritzburg: Cluster Publications, 2001), 260–64.

16. Ada María Isasi-Díaz, *En la Lucha, In the Struggle: A Hispanic Women's Liberation Theology* (Minneapolis, MN: Fortress Press, 1993); Katie G. Cannon, *Black Womanist Ethics* (Atlanta: Scholars Press, 1988); Delores S. Williams, *Sisters in the Wilderness: The Challenge of Womanist God-talk* (Maryknoll, NY: Orbis Books, 1993).

17. Womanist and *mujerista* theologians have provided the most significant critique to feminist theology.

18. Mercy Amba Oduyoye, *Hearing and Knowing: Theological Reflections on Christianity in Africa* (Maryknoll, NY: Orbis Books, 1986); Oduyoye, *Daughters of Anowa*; and Mercy Amba Oduyoye and Musimbi R. A. Kanyoro, eds., *The Will to Arise: Women. Tradition, and the Church in Africa* (Maryknoll, NY: Orbis Books, 1992).

19. Musimbi Kanyoro, "Cultural Hermeneutics: An African Contribution," in *Women's Visions: Theological Reflection, Celebration, Action*, ed. Ofelia Ortega (Geneva: World Council of Churches, 1995), 18–28.

20. Oduyoye and Kanyoro, *The Will to Arise*.

21. Musa Dube points out that professional death comes to Third World people because they are trained in methods that stifle their own questions; see Dube, "An Introduction: How We Come to Read with," *Semeia* 73 (1996): 10–15.

22. Bernadette Mbuy Beya, "Human Sexuality, Marriage and Prostitution," in Oduyoye and Kanyoro, *The Will to Arise*, 155.

23. Ibid., 156.

24. See chapters by these authors in Oduyoye and Kanyoro, *The Will to Arise*.

25. Isabel Apawo Phiri, "Women, Church and Theological Identity," *Ministerial Formation* 71 (1995): 39-43.

26. The Presbyterian Church, Blantyre Synod in Malawi, for example, fired women church-workers and penalized Dr. Isabel Phiri when the women in the church talked about injustice toward women in the church and society.

27. Dorothee Sölle, "Liberating Our God-Talk," in *Liberating Woman Conference Reader*, ed. Ursula King (Bristol: University of Bristol, 1991), 42–52.

28. Oduyoye, *Daughters of Anowa*.

2

WOMEN DOING THEOLOGY
WITH THE ASIAN ECUMENICAL MOVEMENT

Wong Wai Ching Angela (Hong Kong, China)

Despite the increased number of feminist theological writings in Asia, it is not an easy task to write about the development of Asian feminist theology in a systematic way. One of the factors has been the vast geographical context—Asia—where Asian feminist theology is supposed to be primarily based. Another factor has been the "multitude" of women involved—none has the sole authority or capacity to define the path of Asian feminist theology, and thus it is very difficult to delineate a genealogy of representative theologies or their speakers.

There is yet another difficulty in the present task of outlining the development of Asian feminist theology by institutions since institutional identities seem to be the last thing women have in mind during their conferencing among one another. For of all these reasons, this chapter is not going be about the historical development of Asian feminist theology as such but rather will be an attempt to chart the development of women's consciousness and women's theologizing work in relation to the Asian ecumenical networks, including three main institutions, namely the Christian Conference of Asia (CCA), the Asia and Pacific Alliance of YMCAs, and the World Student Christian Federation (WSCF) Asia-Pacific Region, as well as the others such as the Asian Women's Resource Centre for Theology and Culture (AWRC) and the Women's Commission of the Ecumenical Association of Third World Theologians (EATWOT).

Why Asian Feminist Theology?

In one of her speeches to the young women of Student Christian Movement (SCM), Sun Ai Lee Park of Korea reiterates a liberationist

---

Wong Wai Ching Angela, "Women Doing Theology with the Asian Ecumenical Movement," in *A History of the Ecumenical Movement in Asia*, ed. Ninan Koshy (Hong Kong: Christian Conference of Asia, 2004), 2: 85–86; 96–114.

stance of framing the question of woman: "Third world women must prioritize national liberation together with their men. The women's issue is a secondary issue."[1] The same was said by some Third World women who were actively involved in national liberation movements of the seventies. Nevertheless, women who were active in human rights or labor struggles over the years came to realize that sexism among progressive male partners was not uncommon—women activists gradually found themselves being discriminated against by male colleagues who had devoted their services to all the other human right issues. There was definitely a need to pursue a different theological vision for a new community that would genuinely include women as equal partners.

The theological reflection on "The Search for Full Humanity" introduced by the Report of the Life and Action Committee to the Penang Assembly of the CCA in 1977 identified the mission of Asian Christians as a work of liberation:

> The offer of a full humanity means that Christians are obligated to work for an environment in which people can discover their freedom and human dignity. At the simplest level this means working at structures to ensure that every person has the basic requirements of food, shelter and clothing; it means the guarantee of work for every person as a right; it means giving all people the right to self-determination to participate in the shaping of their own destinies.[2]

Theologically, the search for full humanity provided a very important framework for the reflection of women in Asia who found them trapped in traditions of religions, cultures, and customs that "dehumanized" women.

The calling of Jesus for people to receive life in abundance was taken by women as the call to resist dehumanizing forces and to rise as subjects shaping their own destinies. The need for a systematic articulation of theology from the perspective of Asian women was strongly felt and resulted in the organization of subsequent theological consultations in the early eighties.

In the introduction to *Reading the Bible as Asian Women* (1987), two women committee members, Lee Oo-Chung and Sylvia Jenkin, joined the then Women's Secretary of CCA Mizuho Matsuda, to denounce the marginalization of women by men in the church. They contended that for centuries the Christian documents, including the biblical stories and texts, had been filled with only men's voices. With few exceptions, women were excluded from any opportunity to speak to the church; their voices were silenced.[3]

In this respect, doing theological and biblical reflection from a women's perspective is a way to liberate women from the Christian traditions as patriarchally constituted:

Once oppressed and marginalized in spirit, mind and body, women are moving with arms outstretched towards the church and towards the world, so that the truth which has been silenced and therefore has been absent, may be lifted up and offered to make up that which is lacking in the whole.[4]

Similarly, in the introduction to the first anthology in Asian feminist theology *We Dare to Dream* (1989), the editors, Virginia Fabella and Sun Ai Lee Park, explained the need for a distinction between the voices of Asian women and those of male Asian theologians. Like the male Asian theologians, Fabella and Park found that Asian women theologians in the early stage had largely depended on the thinking of Third World male liberation theologians. In many cases, women were used as manifestations of the oppression of people in the Third World or the most seriously affected victims of the imperialist structure of injustice and poverty. By conscious efforts to articulate a distinctive women's theology in Asia, women refused to let their experience be taken as a "token appendage" to either Third World theology or Asian theology. Rather, they insisted that Asian women's theology must be an integral part of the whole.[5] In Fabella and Park's words, without the inclusion of the distinctive voices of Asian women, theologies in Asia cannot be liberating or relevant for men, for women, or for the church and society at large.[6]

At the same time, Asian women sensed that it was necessary to distinguish their voices from those of First World feminists as well. Despite the admission of many Asian feminist theologians of their debt to Western feminists for their inspiration and the theological affinities between Western feminists and Asian feminist theologians,[7] Asian women felt the need to identify their own voices as distinctively Asian and women's.

The discussion of whether women theologians or women's theologies should be called "feminist theologians" or "feminist theologies" was one example of such a debate. In her introductory work to Asian feminist theology, Kwok Pui-lan notes that not all women theologians in Asia would like to be identified as feminist theologians. Rather, some of them prefer to call themselves Asian women theologians and their works Asian women's theology in order to avoid the negative, militant, separatist connotation of the term "feminist"—which is a term often also referred to as Western.[8] In this light, the setting forth of an Asian women's process of doing theology through a series of theological consultations in the early eighties was an attempt to elicit the unique voices of women in the context of Asia.

Following the definitive characterization of Asia in its prevalent poverty and its religio-cultural plurality provided by Aloysius Pieris, the liberation theologian from Sri Lanka,[9] Asian feminist theology has identified strongly with women in poverty, women who have been politically and economically victimized, culturally oppressed, colonially exploited, and theologically undermined in the Christian traditions.[10] In one of her early articles, Kwok Pui-lan defines Asian feminist theology as nothing but a story of suffering.

> Feminist theology in Asia will be a cry, a plea and invocation. It emerges from the wounds that hurt, the scars that hardly disappear, the stories that have no ending. Feminist theology in Asia is . . . scribed on the hearts of many that feel the pain, and yet dare to hope.[11]

Moreover, the suffering of women in Asia has been aggravated by Western colonialism and neocolonialism. Therefore, grounding Christianity in Asian soil involves a theology that can take account of the victimization and liberation of women from among the poor farmers, factory workers, slum dwellers, dowry victims, and prostitutes.[12]

Providing an overview or a particular description of the sufferings of Asian women in the background characterizes nearly all Asian feminist theological writings. One of the most representative descriptions of the suffering context of Asian women was produced by women theologians in an ecumenical forum in Manila in 1985 under the title "Asian Church Women Speak."[13] So far it has provided the most comprehensive statement on the understanding of the situation of Asian women, and thereby the vision and mission for the first generation of Asian women theologians:

> In all spheres of Asian society, women are dominated, dehumanized and dewomanized; they are discriminated against, exploited, harassed, sexually used, abused, and viewed as inferior beings who must always subordinate themselves to the so-called male supremacy. In the home, Church, law, education, and media, women have been treated with bias and condescension. In Asia and all over the world, the myth of subservient, servile Asian women is blatantly peddled to reinforce the dominant male stereotype image.[14]

Concern for the poor and marginalized women remains central in almost all Asian feminist theological writings to this day. Women in Asia are often seen as the poorest of the poor, the most exploited among the exploited, the most marginalized of the marginalized. Because women know best the pain of suffering people, they are the ones who can best discern the corruption and injustice of a society and they are the ones who know the *han* of the people and the time when *han* is to bring peace.[15] Because of their experience of the worst oppression, Asian women must be inclusive in their theology. It must take women's humanity and experience seriously. It must discern both the life-enhancing and the death-threatening aspects of our faith tradition for the marginalized, among whom women are the most affected.[16]

Women Doing Theology in Asia

Fabella and Park's introduction to *We Dare to Dream* (the first and still most representative volume on Asian feminist theology) states very clearly that Asian feminist theology needs to take seriously the context of oppression of women in Asia. This means that Asian feminist theologians must take "a critical look at their own and other women's experience, trace the roots of their secondary and subservient position in Church and society, and venture towards a new world of just and reciprocal relationships."[17] In this respect, Asian feminist theology must be practical and down to earth, speaking the language and the experience of women in their daily lives. The emphasis on "doing theology" reflects this very imperative to do theologizing work on the ground.

It was in the seventies that "doing theology" first emerged as an important term of reference for the theological work of Asian women.[18] The aim was to explore ways and methodologies through which women's experience could be included in Asian theological writings. "Doing" has at least two basic meanings: first, it is something coming out of life in practice; second, it is something always in process. In short, theologizing work for Asian women always takes place and should be ongoing. It is neither a finished product nor something separate from women's lives, experiences, and continuous reflection. In reaction to the kind of philosophical theology that tries to explain the logic between ideas and concepts independent of socio-political reality, the theological reflection of women in Asia must be not only a kind of speculative activity but also an active engagement in response to women's daily living experience and a commitment to strive toward full humanity. It must liberate and empower women in their living contexts.

Using a term coined by Paulo Freire, Christine Tse of Hong Kong sees the doing of women's theology as a process of *conscientization*. It signifies a movement that actively engages women in actions that can break the "culture of silence"—a culture in which Asian women are induced almost automatically and spontaneously to assume a role inferior to that of men.[19] In this regard, the agent doing theology is not confined to trained theologians but includes all women who care enough about their own experience, their faith, and the future of the church to do some serious reflection together. Adopting the EATWOT methodology of narrating the experience of the poor and oppressed peoples and attending critically to their socio-economic, political, and religio-cultural reality, the action-reflection-action process has become the most effective way of doing theology among Asian women from the eighties through to now.

Because of the identification of Asian feminist theologians with the poverty and oppression of women in Asia, the definition of Asian feminist theology includes not only the subject of theological reflection— Asian women, their experience, their stories, and the issues concerned— it includes also an explicit ethical-political goal. This ethical-political commitment to the people who are "disprivileged" and marginalized runs through the various themes and topics of discussion in the regional workshops and conferences held by the CCA, the WSCF, the YMCA, and the others. It was translated into three clear criteria for doing women's theology in Asia:

> First, the work must be contextualized, that is, it starts with an aspect of our Asian experience and is rooted in our Asian reality. It necessarily includes a critical examination of the context, not a mere description. Second, it must be theological, with references to our faith tradition, and not simply be a historical, sociological or analytical study of the Asian context and peoples. And third, it must be from the perspective of women that shows an awareness of the subordinate and oftentimes degrading situation of women and reveals a commitment to work towards its transformation.[20]

On a heavier note, Kwok Pui-lan argues that Asian feminist theology must not be an intellectual discipline or a rational reflection of Christian faith only. She says Asian feminist theologians cannot afford to engage in the academic exercise of mental gymnastics, when so many people are daily dehumanized or die of malnutrition and unsafe drinking water. Theology must be embodied; and reflection and action must be integrally linked together.[21]

Kwok Pui-lan goes on to explain that Asian feminist theology must proceed beyond "the confines of the Church"—its audience must not be limited to the church congregations. Rather, Asian feminist theologians must work closely with feminists and workers of the civil society to bring about the needed changes in their respective societies.[22]

Besides doing theology with the experience of the poor and the oppressed women, Asian women must "do" their theology with Asian indigenous resources, in order to address the issue of women locally in their religio-cultural contexts. Locating themselves in the larger context of Asian nation building at the time, Asian women joined male theologians in the construction of a unique "Asian" cultural identity in distinction from the West. Quoting C. S. Song, Kwok Pui-lan highlights "a new paradigm" in Asian theology as the basis for Asian feminist theology:

> Doing theology in Asia today is exciting because it is no longer dictated by rules and norms established elsewhere outside our

living space called Asia. Its contents are not determined any
more by schools and systems of theology formed under the influence of cultural elements alien to cultural experiences of Asia.
Its styles...[do] not have to be shaped by thought-forms and
life-experiences remote from Asian humanity.[23]

In her appeal to do theology with Asian indigenous resources,
Kwok drew the attention of Asian women to the pool of folk literature,
people's history, and religious texts in Asian cultures, including poems,
songs, stories, dances, rituals, and even lullabies that are most familiar
to women.[24] Other indigenous resources include Indian references to
their heroines, including a defiant Hindu mystic who survived the oppression of her husband and family, or Panditha Ramabai, a scholar and
an activist who brought about social reforms for child widows and victims of other misogynist Hindu practices.[25] The most outstanding example of the use of indigenous traditions and resources in Asian feminist
theology can be found in the work of Chung Hyun Kyung. Her theologizing of the *han* and its liberation for women living through the discrimination and oppression of Korean society is one of the most powerful works in Asian feminist theological literature. Her re-conception
of the role of the shaman priestess has opened up a new possibility for
women's search into alternative spiritualities within and/or without the
Christian tradition.[26]

Calling for a Partnership of Women and Men

During the period of increased awareness of women, there was at the
same time increased resistance from men. Recalling the experience of relationships between men and women over the period, Yong Ting Jin
could still feel the pain of intensive confrontation between members of
the same community at each given occasion:

The women were told that women's issues and movement were
western and liberal; that their liberation would come [when] the
national struggle for liberation was achieved; that they were perceived as emotional, inferior, less capable than men in almost
every field of work...For their part, the men were told that they
were male chauvinists, ego-centric, sexist, oppressive, more
mind than heart, without much feeling; that they were perceived
to have thought of themselves as superior [to] women...[27]

Views like these have caused both women and men much hurt and
pain and given rise to threats and reactions. It took some time before
there were any signs of a new and growing awareness in the more en-

lightened men. This development made it possible to take the next step, to begin rethinking the whole concept of partnerships between women and men in concrete terms. After serious discussion and reflection, women and men of the SCMs and the WSCF came to understand the idea of partnership as an "open-ended" discovery of life together.

This type of understanding means recognition of women's problems as men's problems, and of women's struggle for liberation as also men's struggle for liberation. It calls for "a covenant between women and men to search and find out the true and meaningful partnership in their personal/individual lives and their collective life . . . [it implies] life with new dimensions and dynamics."[28]

One of the greatest achievements in the SCM/WSCF Women's Programme has been the discovery of men's needs for liberation. From having seen women as the victims of gender oppression and violence, SCM/WSCF women began to discover that the more progressive and enlightened men did not play the role of supporters only; they too needed to be liberated from patriarchy in order that a new humanity in God's image could emerge. Ruth Harris, a longtime supporter of the Asian women's ecumenical movement, reflected on the development of the WSCF Women's Programme and was greatly impressed with the initiative taken by federation women to relate to men as partners in women's struggle for liberation. Rather than setting women over and against men in the federation, women looked for ways to bring men together with women into a deepening consciousness of the patriarchy that makes captives of men as well as of women. In a WSCF Asia-Pacific Regional three-week student and staff formation program in 1994, the twenty-four participants from eleven countries came to a consensus that "unless both sexes come to a similar level of understanding about the need to do away with patriarchy, the two cannot work together in true, mutually supportive, partnership."[29]

Similarly, in 1995 Esther Byu, the then executive secretary for Women's Concerns of CCA, edited a volume titled *Affirming Difference Celebrating Wholeness: A Partnership of Equals*. In its preface, Byu introduces the notion that improved participation of women in decision-making processes and in all aspects of church life is not so much a matter of acquiring positions or fostering token representation; rather, the purpose of women's participation is "to strengthen and accelerate the process for the partnership of women and men as equal participants in the total life of the church." She then lays out four goals of equal participation, including the following:

> To share ecumenical vision, theological reflection and explore avenues . . . beyond . . . boundaries; to question dominant power structures and systems . . . ; to take responsibility for, and share resources in building a just society; [and] to stand in solidarity

as women and men working towards the establishment of a new community based on the values of the Kingdom of God.[30]

On the surface, the emphasis seems to be a return to the early agenda of men and women working in harmonious relation for the larger good of the society, but underlying it is a call to equal partnership after twenty years of women's struggle against discrimination. Rather than a harmonious relationship between the sexes, the goal this time is the inclusion, recognition, and valuing of women's leadership and their wisdom, conviction, and commitment to building and transforming community. The exclusive right to leadership for men is no longer acceptable for the vision of a new society of equals. In the introduction to the same text, Ranjini Rebera adds that only when the social and political differences between men and women and among women themselves are recognized can common concerns be identified and a common plan of action be formulated by men and women as equals.[31]

In 2000, a sub-regional consultation on the theme "Partnership of Women and Men in Inclusive Community" was held in Colombo, Sri Lanka. This consultation noted that it has been the deep conviction of women that they are called not to give up or to be apathetic toward the church but to "restore inclusiveness, equality, and harmony" in it. Women have recognized that women and men are created equal, that each is made in the image and likeness of God, and that the church affirmed that Jesus of Nazareth during his ministry demonstrated a liberating relationship with women, although this model of partnership has not been consistently followed.

What women wanted to see was the churches' relinquishing of power and control over their people and an unceasing commitment to building genuine human relationships among men and women, and clergy and lay, on an equal basis. In the words of Yong Ting Jin,

> Women were active participants in all areas of life and mission of the early Christian communities. They were apostles, teachers, prophetesses, providers, workers, [and] preachers, each according to her potential and God-given talents. Indeed, they were full-time partners alongside men in the Gospel of Christ.[32]

Jesus the Risen Christ called on all to live an abundant life. Beginning first with women, the invitation has been extended and opened to all men, brothers, and friends to journey in equal partnership toward a new humanity and creation. As R. L. Hnuni points out, feminist theology has always been a search for partnership, equality, mutuality, and reciprocity. It aims for a new anthropology, a new dimension of what it means to be a human person with all persons made in the divine image.[33]

The Dream Shall Continue: Building an Inclusive Community

In her address to the young women of the SCM/WSCF in a workshop in Singapore in 1986, Sun Ai Lee Park identified the objectives of the ecumenical movement to be the seeking of human unity in a divided world and "the fostering of a renewal movement in the stifled traditional church and in the world."[34] The Asian ecumenical feminist movement since the nineties has launched an agenda of its own while maintaining a strong commitment to the Christian faith and the Asian churches in general. The community of Asian ecumenical women, though small and diverse, has provided one of the major resources for women from churches in various parts of Asia to explore the limits prescribed by the institutional authorities and to break boundaries by reaching out to women of other faiths, ethnicities, and classes in their respective countries, hoping that one day a new community of equals will emerge within and beyond the church.

In support of call of the World Council of Churches for an "Ecumenical Decade of the Churches in Solidarity with Women" from 1988 to 1998, the Colombo Assembly of the CCA mandated the Women's Concerns Programme to "work for full participation of women, men and children in creating an inclusive community, in educating and empowerment, liberation and faith," to "create a society free of violence against all people, especially women and children," to create "a participatory peace process which leads to a just society," and to strengthen "the leadership of women as co-partners with men in church and society." If the Ecumenical Decade for Women has served as something more than the staging of an international banner, it has provided the platform for many women to relate to each other, cultivate mutual exchange and support, and build networks and alliances on common issues. In the Asian ecumenical scene, advocacy for women's rights during the decade has been translated into numerous regional and national conferences and workshops on a wide range of issues related to women in their different contexts.

Under one of the decade's subthemes on fighting violence inflicted on women, the CCA organized a workshop in collaboration with the AWRC and the WSCF Asia-Pacific to address the needs of women suffering from violence. The workshop was designed to be an avenue for the breaking of silence; women who have been victims of violence were encouraged to tell the forbidden stories of their lives. These stories of violence from churchwomen, indigenous women, women factory workers, and single pregnant women had rarely been told in the church or in families. Once the voices of these women were heard, steps could be taken to identify the root causes of the violence and discover ways to heal the victimized.[35] The other important development over the Ecumenical

Decade was a growing concern for indigenous tribal women and Dalit women. The problem being faced by indigenous women was like the one all indigenous communities were facing. They had lost their distinctive cultural and communal roles and identities to the fast-growing industrialized economies of many Asian countries. Instead of being the chief providers of their tribal communities, many women fell into the traps of tourist and sex industries for the trading of their cultural artifacts or their bodies.[36]

Since the mid-eighties, the YMCA has sponsored programs that specifically focus on women, such as that on "Women in Society" (1985). Tan Chi Kiong, the former general secretary of the Asia Alliance of YMCAs, called for more serious reflection on women's issues and posed this question to the delegates of the Asia YMCA Forum on Leadership Development in 1992: "Can we become more inclusive to include women in the YMCAs and take up the issue in a dynamic way?"[37] In response to this question, the Asia Alliance of YMCAs decided to prioritize its work with migrant workers and domestic workers, who have mostly been women.[38] In relation to this concern for marginalized women and the communities of migrant workers, the Asia Alliance has extended its programs to cover issues relating to globalization, where once again women are the most seriously affected. In the globalized scheme of industrial employment, women workers' adversities are aggravated. They are subjected to lower wages, less bargaining power, constant displacement, worse health conditions, and further alienation from technology.

"Interfaith dialogue" has been another important development in women's ecumenical programs through the nineties. There is a clear need for women of different religious confessions to come together and work across their religious boundaries to understand their situation and build a common platform for women's liberation.

Efforts to engage in dialogue with women of other faiths were initiated together by the AWRC, the CCA Women's Concerns Unit, and the the WSCF Asia-Pacific Women's desk. Two pioneer volumes were produced on the subject, including *Faith Renewed: A Report on the First Asian Women's Consultation on Interfaith Dialogue, Kuala Lumpur, 1989* and *Faith Renewed II: A Report on the Second Asian Women's Consultation on Interfaith Dialogue, Colombo, 1990.*[39] Interfaith cooperation in building peace among women of various religious backgrounds has become even more important since September 11, 2001.

In a Leadership Formation Program of the WSCF Asia-Pacific in 2003, participants expressed their reservations about judging other religions, and confessed their belief in God's salvation in multidimensional forms and possibly through different religions. There should be no discrimination from Christians against other religions but rather Christians should learn and understand more about them in order to enrich the

Christian faith. Nevertheless, they added, there is for women one more task: they have to assess critically the patriarchal practices of the different religions, including fundamentalism, in Christianity as well as in other religions.[40]

For young women, issues of body and sexuality have become more and more important and personal. In 2004, the WSCF Asia-Pacific produced a *Reflective Liturgy for SCM Women*, which collected several stories of young women in search of God through their experience with their own bodies. Together they raised the question of the devaluation of women's bodies in the media and traditional cultures, they shared the pain of seeing and experiencing the violation of women's bodies in the Bible and the Christian tradition, they traced the source of the sacredness of women's bodies and sexualities to God's creation, and they found new affirmations of their bodily experience through reinterpretations of the Bible and their faith in the eyes of the Mother God who knows and cares for the bodies of women. The book announced powerfully the faith of young Christian women in their struggle to recognize the unique beauty of their bodies, despite all kinds of social ostracism imposed on them.[41]

The future of the women's movement and genuine partnership between women and men depends very much on the training and ecumenical education done today. Since 1996, the CCA Women's Concerns Unit, the Asian Christian Women's Conference, and the AWRC have coordinated their efforts in a common program of Gender Awareness and Sensitivity Training (GAST), which will form a team of trainers over a period of three to five years for the training of young women leaders in various Asian countries. Concern for young women led the GAST organizers to also invite the WSCF Women's Programme to participate. Representatives of the four organizations came together in Manila in 1997 to develop a GAST curriculum. In a concluding statement, the four organizations affirmed their vision to nurture "a whole new woman-consciousness that informs our life style, and as a consequence [eliminates] oppressive powers and principalities."[42] The work of gender sensitivity training and gender consciousness raising among men and women in Asian churches will be an ongoing task that will not end until the fulfillment of God's kingdom on earth.

As occasions for meeting and conferencing with women grow, it becomes increasingly apparent that Asian women are diverse and sometimes even divided because of their different backgrounds and experiences. In her introduction to *Affirming Difference Celebrating Wholeness* (1995) Ranjini Rebera reflects on the many layers of differences she has experienced as an Asian woman. There are differences in languages and cultures, religions and ethnicities, classes and castes, and political and theological affiliations, but there are also individual differences that every woman carries and that should not be lost in the mass of all women. The question to be answered by women of this vast continent is this: In what ways can women celebrate a sense of wholeness when the differences seem insurmountable?[43]

In Fabella and Park's 1990 volume on Asian feminist theologies, they state: "Our vision is to see men and women in communities of genuine partnership, with true reciprocity and mutual respect, in communities that care not only for people but for our whole planet earth. We envision a new world; a transformed world; a world that truly mirrors God's design; a just, caring, and peace-filled world—indeed, a new creation. We dare to dream..."[44] Women will continue to dream that women's right to freedom and full development will be given priority; that issues affecting women will become integral concerns of all; that one day women and men of different faiths, ethnicities, classes, and castes will be true partners in building an inclusive community in the churches as well as in society.

Notes

1. Sun Ai Park, "The Women's Movement and the Ecumenical Agenda," in *Weaving New Patterns: Women's Struggle for Change in Asia and the Pacific*, ed. Jennie Clarke (Hong Kong: WSCF Asian-Pacific Region, 1986), 65.

2. Christian Conference of Asia, *Christian Conference of Asia Sixth Assembly, Penang* (Singapore: Christian Conference of Asia, 1977), 102.

3. Lee Oo-Chung, Sylvia Jenkin, and Mizuho Matsuda, *Reading the Bible as Asian Women: Twelve Bible Studies on Mobilizing Women in Struggles for Food, Justice and Freedom* (Singapore: Christian Conference of Asia Women's Concerns Unit, 1987), 1.

4. Ibid.

5. Virginia Fabella and Sun Ai Lee Park, "Introduction," in *We Dare to Dream: Doing Theology as Asian Women*, ed. Virginia Fabella and Sun Ai Lee Park (Hong Kong: AWRC, 1989), x.

6. Ibid., vii.

7. A recent chapter written by Hisako Kinukawa, a Japanese feminist biblical scholar, traces a very important moment in the development of Asian feminist theology to a study seminar jointly held by the Association of Women Doing Theology in Japan and the Korean Association of Women's Theology in Seoul, Korea, January 15–17, 1987, at which Letty M. Russell delivered the keynote address. Several other Asian feminist theologians recall the seminar as an initiation event. See Kwang-Rye Chun et al., *Women Moving Mountains: Feminist Theology in Japan* (Kuala Lumpur: AWRC, 2000), 62–64.

8. Kwok Pui-lan, *Introducing Asian Feminist Theology* (Sheffield: Sheffield Academic Press, 2000), 32.

9. Aloysius Pieris, *An Asian Theology of Liberation* (Maryknoll, NY: Orbis Books, 1988), xi.

10. See my argument in the chapter, "'The Poor Woman': Representation of Women in Asian Theology," in Angela Wai Ching Wong, *"The Poor Woman": A Critical Analysis of Asian Theology and Chinese Contemporary Stories by Women* (New York: Peter Lang, 2002), 33–62.

11. First included in her article: "God Weeps with Our Pain," *East Asian Journal of Theology* 2, no. 2 (1984): 228, then recalled again in Kwok, *Introducing Asian Feminist Theology*, 32.

12. Chung Hyun Kyung, *Struggle to Be the Sun Again: Introducing Asian Feminist Theology* (Maryknoll, NY: Orbis Books, 1990), 113.

13. First issued as the "Final Statement" of the Manila conference, later collected in Fabella and Park, *We Dare to Dream*, 147–50.

14. "Final Statement: Asian Church Women Speak (Manila, Philippines, November 21–30, 1985)," in Fabella and Park, *We Dare to Dream*, 148.

15. Lee Oo-Chung, "Peace, Unification and Women: A Bible Study," in Fabella and Park, *We Dare to Dream*, 70.

16. Fabella and Park, "Introduction," in *We Dare to Dream*, viii.

17. Ibid., vii.

18. Ibid.

19. Christine Tse, "New Ways of Being Church: A Catholic Perspective," in Fabella and Park, *We Dare to Dream*, 38.

20. Fabella and Park, "Introduction," in *We Dare to Dream*, ix.

21. Kwok Pui-lan, *Introducing Asian Feminist Theology* (Sheffield: Sheffield Academic Press, 2000), 32.

22. Ibid.

23. Quoted by Kwok Pui-lan in her "The Emergence of Asian Feminist Consciousness of Culture and Theology," in Fabella and Park, *We Dare to Dream*, 98.

24. Kwok, "The Emergence of Asian Feminist Consciousness," 98.

25. Crescy John, "Woman and the Holy Spirit: From an Indian Perspective," in Fabella and Park, *We Dare to Dream*, 54.

26. Chung Hyun Kyung, "'Han-pu-ri': Doing Theology from Korean Women's Perspective," in Fabella and Park, *We Dare to Dream*, 136–39.

27. Yong Ting Jin, "Women's Journey With and Within the SCMs and WSCF: A Perspective from the Asia-Pacific Region," in *Towards a Women's History in the World Student Christian Federation*, ed. Clarissa Balan-Sycip (Geneva: World Student Christian Federation, 1994), 62.

28. Ibid., 62–63.

29. Originally taken from *Praxis*, combined issue, 4 (1994) and 1 (1995). Quoted here from Ruth Harris, "Gender Equality in the WSCF—Inter-Regional Encounters," in Balan-Sycip, *Towards a Women's History in the World Student Christian Federation*, 43.

30. Esther Byu, preface to *Affirming Difference Celebrating Wholeness: A Partnership of Equals*, ed. Ranjini Rebera (Hong Kong: CCA Women's Concerns, 1995), 7.

31. Ranjini Rebera, "Introduction: Difference and Identity," in *Affirming Difference Celebrating Wholeness*, 11.

32. Yong Ting Jin, "New Ways of Being Church: A Protestant Perspective," in Fabella and Park, *We Dare to Dream*, 47.

33. R. L. Hnuni, "Feminist Theology: History, Meaning and Concern," in *Transforming Theology For Empowering Women: A Theological and Hermeneutical Reflection in the Context of North East India*, ed. R. L. Hnuni (Jorhat: Eastern Theological College Women's Studies, 1999), 8.

34. Park, "The Women's Movement and the Ecumenical Agenda," 64.

35. Christian Conference of Asia, *Colombo to Tomohon: Christian Conference of Asia 1995–2000* (Hong Kong: Christian Conference of Asia, 2000), 60.

36. Christian Conference of Asia, *Narrative Report 2003–2004* (Hong Kong: Christian Conference of Asia, 2004).

37. M. D. David, *A Symbol of Asian Solidarity: A History of the Asia Alliance of YMCAs* (Hong Kong: Asia Alliance of YMCAs, 1998), 181.

38. Ibid., 223.

39. See Dulcie Abraham, Sun Ai Park, and Yvonne Dahlin, eds., *Faith Renewed: A Report on the First Asian Women's Consultation on Interfaith Dialogue, November 1–8, 1989, Kuala Lumpur, Malaysia* (Hong Kong: Asian Women's Resource Centre for Theology and Culture, 1989); and Asian Women's Resource Centre for Theology and Culture, ed., *Faith Renewed II: A Report on the Second Asian Women's Consultation on Interfaith Dialogue, November 1–7, 1991, Colombo, Sri Lanka* (Seoul: Asian Women's Resource Centre for Theology and Culture, 1991).

40. Shin Seung Min, ed., *Leadership Formation for Students and Youth*, Resource Book Series 1 (Hong Kong: World Student Christian Federation Asia-Pacific, 2003), 29-36.

41. See Wong Yock Leng, ed., *Reflective Liturgy for SCM Women*, Resource Book Series 2 (Hong Kong: World Student Christian Federation Asia-Pacific, 2004).

42. Christian Conference of Asia, *From Colombo to Tomohon*, 65.

43. See Rebera, "Introduction: Difference and Identity," in *Affirming Difference Celebrating Wholeness*, 9–12.

44. Fabella and Park, "Introduction," in *We Dare to Dream*, x.

3

A FEMINIST THEOLOGY OF LIBERATION

A Latin American Perspective with a View toward the Future

Ivone Gebara (Brazil)

The present study seeks, in a certain sense, to continue in my own way the commitment of feminist theologians like Elisabeth Schüssler Fiorenza to the construction of more just relationships between individuals and peoples. It seeks to mix, within the context in which I live, my own experience as a feminist theologian of liberation in Latin America with what I have learned from her. I dialogue with her, and with other women and men theologians, in an attempt to understand certain aspects of the complex religious reality of Latin American women. I like to see my work as a bridge that brings together realities that are sometimes similar and sometimes different. Since 1990 I have not been associated with any university or center of studies in theology or philosophy, but I journey through them, both in Brazil and throughout the world, as guest professor. With my neighborhood and the women's movement to which I belong as points of departure, I open the dialogue and make connections with the world of the university. It is from this "mixed" reality that I wish to share in this study questions of concern to me regarding the present and future of Latin American, Christian, feminist women. I will proceed in three stages: the hermeneutics of suspicion; Latin American feminism and kyriarchy; and metaphysical and essentialist presuppositions of patriarchal theological discourses.

Ivone Gebara, "A Feminist Theology of Liberation: A Latin American Perspective with a View toward the Future," trans. by Fernando F. Segovia from the Portuguese original, "Teologia Feminista da Libertação—uma perspectiva latino americana em vista do futuro," in *Toward a New Heaven and a New Earth: Essays in Honor of Elisabeth Schüssler Fiorenza*, ed. Fernando F. Segovia (Maryknoll, NY: Orbis Books, 2003), 249–68.

The Hermeneutics of Suspicion

To be suspicious is common in human existence. It shows lack of trust in certain interpretations of life advanced by either ourselves or others; it means distrust regarding the given facts; it means, in short, a sense of unease or discomfort with respect to the beliefs, interpretations, and individuals in which one trusted or still trusts. Suspicion can also signify progress in our daily quests, although now accompanied by a lack of credibility on the part of our former references, to which we had become accustomed. In this meaning, suspicion comes close to the critical sense, to an awareness of the need to look for new references to help us live.

When feminism speaks of suspicion, the latter takes on a concrete gendered meaning. It is not a question of human suspicion regarding things in general but rather of the specific suspicion of women with respect to a cultural system that was constructed and continues to be constructed by rejecting them as full "historical subjects." Suspicion arises regarding authoritarian cultural and social constructions that would constitute us as "satellites" of the masculine, defined "by and for men," obedient to that value system which they have established with our complicity. Our suspicion has a history and a plural history, which can be discovered in different human cultures and in different situations. Our suspicion relates to the past and to the present and develops by way of the new challenges that come to face us.

Feminism introduced the hermeneutics of suspicion in relation to the organization of the patriarchal world, with all of its cultural dimensions, including the sciences and religions. Therefore, as Schüssler Fiorenza notes, a feminist hermeneutics begins with a "hermeneutics of suspicion."[1] In this sense, we begin again to interpret the world, to read "with suspicion" the ancient texts and ancient philosophies. We perceive more and more that inequality ruled human relations and interpreted history with only partial respect for the facts, insofar as it concealed the actions of women and the poor. For a long time, such doings were looked upon as normal, the fruit of the social division of labor and of male and female roles that was essential to social order. At the same time, such normality or normativity began to be questioned and understood as an expression of the production of injustice in human relations. The systematic critique of masculine normativity brought about the eruption of different organizations or different fronts of struggle that came to constitute the feminist movement in all of its historical diversity. These struggles are making progress throughout the different countries of the world in such a way that one can say that, as a result of feminism, local cultures are no longer the same. Traditions are beginning to change, and the continuation of the unjust treatment of women can no longer be justified on the simple grounds that such practices form part of a cultural tradition. The cultural process marked by suspicion has brought about a process of "empowerment" on the part of women in different areas of human activity.

The hermeneutics of suspicion also opened enormous gaps within the Christian tradition, above all since the second half of the past century. Many women from this tradition began to recover an "other history" in which we were present and active, although it had been concealed by a patriarchal conception of history that reduced the feminine to the private sphere.[2] Such was the work of the 1970s and the 1980s. There were many publications in the fields of biblical, theological, and ethical studies. The debates were intense: the patriarchal theological perspective against the new feminist perspective. Women were beginning to recover spaces and, above all, to look upon their bodies and their feminine identity as realities with value in themselves and not by virtue of service to other bodies.

These debates took place also in Latin America, but with less intensity than in certain European countries and in the United States and Canada. The spaces available in the Latin colonialist culture and the culture of the Americas itself did not favor a major confrontation with the world of patriarchal religion. There were few manifestations of women in solidarity within the churches, women united by a common realization that certain things had to change within religious institutions with the collective help of women. The patriarchal system was able to prevent such manifestations and to punish instances of insubordination. Such punishments always had the effect of instilling fear in women. At the same time, a more or less concealed, more or less public solidarity always made itself felt, especially among women. However, this public expression was not sufficient to provoke an institutional crisis capable of bringing about a change in relations at the very heart of the institution. The "good upbringing" of many Christian women, the fear of criticism, and above all their dependence in relation to the institution did not allow them to move forward with a public confrontation of the religious authorities.

Toward the end of the 1980s and during the 1990s, the hermeneutics of suspicion began to make its way among women working in different church organizations. These suspicions with respect to what had been learned and assumed as "truth" spread through different groups of women, from the popular groups to the universities. This consciousness, tied to a political feminist consciousness, spread in irregular fashion through the different countries of Latin America and was able to bring about significant gains.

Today we live through a different moment. The great majority of feminists working in theology and Bible in Latin America, above all at the institutional level, have integrated the hermeneutics of suspicion into their discourses, yet the grounding of their framework remains philosophical-metaphysical and, to a certain extent, masculine in nature. Unless this framework changes, we pose, in my opinion, no great danger to Christian institutions. Unless this framework changes, we cannot, in fact, constitute ourselves as an alternative "public power." Unless this framework changes, there is no possibility of a new understanding of human relations based on justice and equity. In effect, we continue to live under masculine power, softened by a few feminist victories. Consequently, I believe that the hermeneutics of suspicion beckons us at present to take different steps, designed to lead us to new strategies in the exercise of power.

Without doubt, we must take into account an issue of the highest importance. Changes require not only objective conditions for change but also subjective conditions. This means that, from the point of view of Christian and Latin American feminine subjectivities, we are marked by a culture of dependence in relation to the schemes of patriarchal authority. We see the existing contradictions; we witness to them; we speak of them; we criticize the oppression that they produce at the domestic level; but we do not succeed in leaving them behind in order to "create" something new. This is especially true of religious institutions, since feminist advances in the institutions of civil society have been more significant in terms of a vindication of rights.

Too often we have recourse to a rather innocent type of discourse to speak of the need for "something new." At the same time, we experience real difficulty in undertaking the collective use of certain public "transgressions" as possible ways of access to the creation of different social relations. This cultural situation is heightened by the reality of economic poverty present in different countries of Latin America. Poverty often works as a block against any type of thinking in search of new alternatives. We keep fighting at the level of everyday survival, and as a result we often fail to advance proposals that would serve to bring about, in effect, structural change. We end up favoring a politics of survival, even at the level of religious institutions, instead of a politics of confrontation and ethical demand for structural change. The aggression suffered by many women as a result of an unjust social and economic system is so widespread and so heavy that we often deem it better to let them find in patriarchal religion a temporary consolation for their afflictions. Even if many of us are aware of the ambiguity of this attitude and even if we are rationally aware of the interdependence of all aspects of life, the pain of suffering and the immediate need for relief prevent us from making progress in a more collective and combative fashion. The dilemma of misery, marginality, and privation constitutes an obstacle on the way toward a relationship of gendered social justice. This dilemma manifests itself as well in a type of "cultural poverty" that limits the horizons and possibilities for effective change. Education for survival is highly immediate in character, while education for structural change is slow and demanding.

Religion, in all of its different forms, plays an important role in this regard, especially when it manages to buy off conscience through an appeal to sentimentality and the different expressions of religious catharsis that seem to multiply at present through the different countries of Latin America. Women continue to be the greatest "consumers" of this "religion of consolation" (*religião consolo*), since those spaces characterized as religious are the ones that are most open to women. Religious space, although public in nature, is assimilated to domestic space and becomes more or less bearable. Many women end up, by reason of their need for consolation and protection, strengthening the traditional roles of priests or pastors and of patriarchal religious institutions as a whole.

Today, it should be noted, institutional authority seems to assert itself in a different way, namely, through the use of the "media" and the tricks of communications technology. Priests and pastors continue to act as mediators between the faithful and the divine powers, above all in radio and television programs. Priests and pastors become God's "superstars," masters in mass communication, while their work ends up buying off both pain and conscience as well as creating new forms of dependence.

In this "wasting away" at work in Latin America, a good number of women from the Christian tradition also live "at the margins" of the institution. They find themselves more or less without a place. At times, they are "guests" in the worship ceremonies or celebrations of their churches, but they do not feel "in communion" with the system of relations that the churches continue to reproduce. To them, the hermeneutics of suspicion now finds itself in another phase. The suspicion of the exclusion and the concealment of women has transformed itself into certitude. Women now know the history of their mothers and grandmothers, and they see the path of their own history. They are critical of religious institutions and capable of taking clear political positions regarding both the national and international scenes. They assume their feminine identity and the consequences of a feminist public identity. Often they are like a voice crying in the wilderness or in the midst of the deafening noises of the big city, "Build relations of justice and equity!" Their voices, however, seem to lose themselves amid noises and sounds of all sorts. Once in a while, some groups join these voices or they join other groups, but it is impossible, taking them as a point of departure, to foresee a future of different human relations at the structural level. I situate myself among these minorities of women who are fearful and marginalized by the official religious system.

Within this context, a new suspicion is born among isolated feminist women theologians here and there in the world and particularly in Latin

America. After the critique and rescue of our biblical history, after the deconstruction of patriarchal theology, after the denunciation of the authoritarianism present in patriarchal religious institutions, after the struggle for the right to our own bodies, what is for us the path seemingly indicated by contemporary history? This question does not mean that we find ourselves already in possession of what these banners of struggle represent; it points rather to the concern and the need for direction in the feminist movement at the heart of the Christian tradition, insofar as we find ourselves continuing to affirm the banners of struggle previously mentioned. Many of us ask ourselves whether a change in patriarchal institutions is still possible or whether, taking advantage of what we have learned from our own history, we should try the gradual creation of alternative institutions. The tension between established structure and critical thought is a well-known social force, and the feminist movement seems to point more toward the creation of different alternatives than to coexistence with the old patriarchal structures, where even the right to survival can hardly be claimed.

There is no single response to this question. Indeed, it is precisely this diversity of living experiences, of interrogations, and of doubts that constitutes the originality of our historical moment. In the course of such reflection, both explicitly and implicitly, a number of intuitions and possible resolutions regarding this problematic are touched upon. However, the question itself continues with all of its intensity and actuality.

Latin American Feminism and Kyriarchy

Elisabeth Schüssler Fiorenza has coined one of the most interesting and significant feminist concepts for understanding the interrelationships at work among the different structures of domination in our world. This is the concept of "kyriarchy"—a term that makes explicit the hierarchical relations centered on the figure of a master, a mistress, a superior, or an aristocracy ruling and controlling social relations. In light of this concept, a number of things seem clearer. We leave behind the oversimplification, mechanistic at times, of oppressors and oppressed and enter into the complexity of human relations and the reproduction of structures of domination at different levels of human life. In light of this concept, one can understand the interdependence and transversality of powers as well as the appeal to nature and its natural law for the legitimation of hierarchical social, political, and religious patterns of behavior.[3]

In the same way, one can understand how the structures of domination penetrate our understanding, often in imperceptible fashion. One can speak, therefore, of kyriarchal knowledge as a knowledge intersected by unjust positions on gender, race, and class domination—Eurocentric as well as "North-American-centric" domination.[4] In our culture such positions are introduced in the midst of discourses on the equality of all human beings and the common right to citizenship. Yet we know that such discourses mask our real rights, turning them into rights merely actualized on paper and in demagogic speeches, with no real effect whatsoever.

The concept of kyriarchy has been used relatively little in Latin America, given the difficulty of introducing an erudite concept based on Greek terminology. However, if the concept has been but seldom used, the reality that points to the concept or that lies behind the concept has indeed been reflected upon by different groups of women. The observations that I offer on the basis of this concept are limited above all to the ecclesial context; that is, I seek to grasp the consequences of action within the religious institutional spaces of Latin America on the part of women with a feminist critical consciousness.

In these official spaces, I believe, the critical analyses undertaken of patriarchal power in all of its different expressions will not, in fact, bring about change in the official structures of the churches. One finds some personal efforts on the part of men more or less isolated, but officially we continue as second-rank citizens. One also finds clearer positions on the part of some women in the face of institutional pressures, but structural changes seem quite slow. What feminist analyses within the institutions have produced for many of us women has been a sort of ennui and disenchantment regarding the struggles within these same religious institutions. It is as if some women who had for a long time managed to preserve a hope for change in religious institutions began to perceive the ineffectiveness of their methods of criticism and their proposals for dialogue. One gets the impression that the institutions seem to absorb such criticisms and look upon them as exceptions or as the fruit of personal "rebellions." At most, they receive them as interesting expressions of the women's movement, as if this movement had nothing to do with the churches. The power remains the same, although it may seem at times a bit more flexible. Hence, a different strategy and different tactics for structural change seem in order. This is a new and challenging task for feminism.

This is not a question of pointing to this or that woman in a position of prestige in a diocese or a religious movement or a university. What happens is that a woman's action is always limited by the male way of understanding the world and organizing the different social institutions. In fact, it has been difficult for women in positions of power to stay faithful to their feminist practices. They end up either abdicating to the institutional power or being dismissed from their positions. If they stay, the same existing structure ends up reproducing itself indirectly, although a few small changes might be introduced. "Religious" institutions are able to absorb some reforms and some exemptions to their regular rules of conduct without any structural change. Consequently, many women speak of creating alternative structures for religious expression, but such structures or alternative locations are still not very strong on the Latin American continent. The few catholic or ecumenical nongovernmental institutions or organizations that exist are seen as parallel organizations and have little direct authority at the religious institutional level. Their existence is important, to be sure, but at present, deep down, many of them are already beginning to ask themselves whether there is any sense in seeking some sort of official connection with any ecclesial institution.[5] The preceding observations are in no way meant to emphasize our social culpability in relation to the urgent changes that need to be made. They simply reaffirm the difficulties involved in changing our cultural frameworks.

We have also observed how in Latin America as well as in other places kyriarchal control is to be found among women themselves, and with impressive force. We end up excluding ourselves among ourselves in the exercise of authority, making it impossible thereby to create alternatives to patriarchal power. We reproduce, given the lack of alternative models and adequate critical analysis, the very same behavior that we criticize. It is as if the hierarchical model formed an integral part of our conception of the sacred. The religious or sacred realm is looked upon as hierarchical in its cultural and psychological structure. The sacred introduces a hierarchical relationship among the different levels of life. It is as if, in affirming a reality or an institution or a value as sacred, we introduce ourselves into a sort of hierarchical structure that, to a certain extent, works against us. Thus, one can say that the most common model of the sacred in the Latin American religious tradition is that of patriarchy. This explains in part our difficulty as women in dealing with public power and the sacred from our reality as women. We were educated from the perspective of the sacred as patriarchal and often fell, without realizing it, into the snares of this conception of sacred power. Rarely do we reflect on the fact that what we call "sacred" is experienced in terms of socio-cultural structures that condition us. As a result of this limitation, we also never think it possible to experience the religious dimension of life according to other cultural models and from a different understanding of the sacred.

All this is compounded by the fact that the Bible called "sacred" is used as a power or "empowerment" on behalf of women. Here we find, I believe, a new point of theoretical and practical strangulation at this new moment in Latin American feminism. Indeed, the last few years have witnessed an extraordinary rescue of the Bible on the part of women, but the Bible still continues to be, in most contexts frequented by women, a "Word of God" that lives in the male church. Such is the case because most contexts from which the feminist rescue of the Bible takes place are more or less controlled by the male hierarchy and by a theology that, although it aims to be open to social questions, does not possess the right structures for bringing about relations of equality and justice in terms of gender. In one way or another, women end up suffering the consequences of their readings as a result of coercive and menacing attitudes on the part of ecclesial institutions and confessional universities.

The question before us, I believe, is to see in a different way what my and our relationship to the Bible means today. The point is not simply to use the Bible in feminist fashion by trying to do a "reading with a woman's eyes." The reason is clear: when we do so, we read from places of male control. The biblical readings promoted by the churches, parishes, and universities are framed within a religious world whose dominant power is patriarchal. A biblical framework, therefore, is not always of help in taking those steps that one would like and would need to take; in the end, such a framework turns into a sort of "ceiling" or limit beyond which one cannot proceed. In this sense, the question posed by Schüssler Fiorenza in the introduction to *But She Said*, "How can a feminist biblical hermeneutics situate its readings of the Bible in such a way that they do not reinscribe the patriarchal discourse of subordination and obedience?"[6] continues to have enormous relevance.

In this context one needs to ask as well the reason for the use of the Bible in the struggle for social and political change on the part of women. In every social and religious context, one must ascertain how the Bible has been used and is being used in the process of women's liberation. Indeed, one needs to determine whether such use of the Bible is really necessary in certain fronts of the feminine struggle, even within the Christian tradition. In my opinion, the weapons used for oppression cannot always be transformed into paths of liberation. One must have the wisdom of the moment to perceive where the small paths that lead to love are to be found.

It is clear to me that the use of the Bible has often served to reinforce authoritarian positions and has at other times prevented going beyond the Bible itself. The biblical tradition still seems to want to justify urgent actions, and one fails to understand how we fall yet again into the snares of reproducing patriarchal power. We turn to the biblical model as if it contained the most precious sources of freedom for women and men, as if it contained the most appropriate model for the practice of justice. In this turn to the Bible, we are not always successful in turning our eyes to the unjust reality in which we live and finding therein ways out of our difficulties.

For us women from the Christian tradition, the task is to reflect anew on the role of the Bible in our lives, in our struggles, in the modification of our behavior with a view toward the construction of just relations. Moreover, the question should include the need to look for noninstitutional places in which to use the wisdom of the Bible.

In the last twenty years, I believe, a particular phase of the struggle has been achieved. Through the contributions of many intellectuals and popular readings, we have succeeded in relativizing the written text and in seeing what is written as constrained by a historical, cultural, political, social, and male perspective. Many of us are no longer impressed by authoritarian images of God as identified in male figures and no longer feel like Eve, symbols of sin and fragility. However, recourse to the biblical text still seems in certain respects like a prison, because it still constitutes a strong link to the patriarchal institution that continues to dominate through the use of the book called "sacred." In a certain way, it is as if the Bible had not yet let itself loose from a dogmatic tradition that set it up as "Word of God" or "Word of Salvation." The book becomes more or less a normative example for the Christian life, so that within it are to be found the rules of conduct for our present existence. Our reading of the Bible, even a feminist reading, is more or less contaminated by the kind of dogmatic and male framework employed by the patriarchal world. The reading of the Bible is thoroughly marked by a metaphysics in which the images of God and the ways of salvation are presented as male. Even with changes in interpretation and framework, such contamination still seems strong. The heart of the problem lies, in part, in the type of relationship to the Bible produced by the patriarchal world.

I am not calling for the retirement of the Bible. I am calling for a greater feminist coherence in dealing with the Bible. I have no wish to do away with the books of the Bible as part of the history of a religious tradition, but I have no wish to affirm it any longer on the basis of a philosophy and an interpretation of the world that give no account of the complexity in which we live.

It is imperative, I believe, to turn to the fundamental values that help us to live and to see the Bible as an expression, sometimes respectful and sometimes disrespectful, of the fundamental values necessary for leading a life with dignity for all human beings. We have an urgent task before us: to capture the ambivalence and the contradiction of the Bible as one captures the ambivalence and contradiction in every human life. It is imperative somehow to lead the Bible back to the common reality of human life, that is, to "de-sacralize it" of its patriarchal sacralization and to let it become anew a human word on matters related to life and death, a word concerning the meaning of life, an ethical word, situated and dated, in dialogue with our words of today. Such a task still remains to be carried out in systematic fashion by women who work on the Bible in Latin America. Likewise, we have yet to make the philosophical rupture necessary not so much to understand the cultural productions of women and men from the point of view of other paradigms but rather to understand the "sacred" meaning that we continue to bestow on various frameworks of our religious tradition.

I propose organized action in order to take the Bible out of the control of religious universities that depend on the patriarchal power of the churches. I should like to "bring it down" to the world of Maria, the world of Isabel, the world of Maria Madalena, to the common world of women and men, so that deeds of love capable of saving life may be "exalted." I propose to let it mingle with the smell of our kitchens, of our meals, so as to rescue from it a seasoning that one could add to the "call to liberty" to which all of us, women and men, wish to respond. This would amount to turning the Bible, and more precisely the wisdom contained in it, into a reality that is mingled with our daily lives and hence capable of dialoguing with us on the basis of our own questions. The Bible can no longer be used to maintain cultural, political, and ideological fundamentalisms that mask the history of humanity and set it against a history of power legitimated by an image of God in the image of male powers.

Essentialist Metaphysical Presuppositions of Patriarchal Discourses

I begin this third phase of my reflection with a great sense of internal division. The context that, in a certain sense, gives rise to and frames this feeling of mine is my personal experience with groups that suffer as a result of the loss of loved ones. I was able to see that the Christian community that cries for and remembers its dead has no language with which to pour forth its feelings and no theology apart from that in which Christian religious culture has been passed down since the time of colonization. It is as if the poor and the less poor drew a sort of existential incision between the pain endured by the loss and the discourse of hope for eternal life, common in such painful circumstances. People speak of the sadness that surrounds the life of the loved one who has departed and then immediately conclude that this person is now watching over them. The discourse changes as if the conclusion to the discourse of suffering pointed to a different sphere of life. It is as if the tears were not endured and the pain not borne by human forces but rather by higher divinities and a discourse full of abstract and ahistorical concepts. There is a rupture of language in the midst of continuing suffering. The new language introduced attempts, it seems, to transform suffering, at least temporarily, with the hope of a life about which nothing is known.

The Christian tradition that was imparted to the poor of Latin America and was further modified by the poor themselves seems to emphasize a sort of "second history" where the dead would live. We remain in this history, and they go to this other history. This other history is a sort of "metahistory," where only perfection, kindness, and joy seem to exist. Thereby, a world opposed to the ordinary world of human coexistence is created. Here and now, we find ourselves "at war"—in the midst of suffering, hunger, pain, exile, the absurd. Expectations of assistance open up in relation to the one departed, as if we entrusted that person with the care of what they leave behind, and also of what we ask of them. Suddenly, such expectations come not from those close to the departed but rather from those who in a certain way represent the existing religious interpretation. Over and over again, they affirm, "Now the one departed is much closer. Now you have a friend in heaven."

There is a way of softening the pain by creating a type of consolation that is affirmed as coming from faith. Our culture "creates" and socializes us. It creates and socializes our feelings and emotions in almost imperceptible fashion. Along these lines, Humberto Maturana, a Chilean biologist, explains that cultural changes are possible only when there is a possibility of change in the expression of our emotions.[7] A change in the "causing of emotions" or in the forms of socializing our emotions allows for new networks of relationships among human beings and, as a result, makes possible the emergence of new cultural frameworks. Cultural values translate emotions, and emotions translate cultural values—visions of the world, expectations, hopes. All aspects of our life are interconnected.

What is clear to me is that the public religious experience of our emotions continues as if encapsulated in the old patriarchal culture. We have not yet had sufficient time or historical maturity to create new emotional relationships in line with new cognitive relationships and new forms of behavior. We fail to work on our emotional creativity and leave it more or less captive to the patriarchal cultural productions of the past. Without any doubt, our emotions are directed, shaped, channeled, and used by the culture in which we live. Our feminine and masculine emotions are related to our way of "feeling" the world, reacting to events, taking positions. In this sense, one can say, figuratively, that emotion comes before reason, that is, the way in which our emotions are expressed guides our way of acting. From this point of view, one can say that our emotions find, upon the death of a human being, a kind of cultural "habit" that allows for their expression in predetermined fashion. Similarly, our emotions with respect to national and international catastrophes are more or less shaped by the powers that control our culture.

In addition to this, one should recall that in the patriarchal tradition those who seem to have greater access to or communication with the "other world" continue to be, in the public realm, the clergy, which assumes official responsibility for religious ceremonies. Once again, the relationship between suffering and the sacred is mediated by the patriarchal religious power, as if this were the sole power authorized to immerse itself in the mysterious world of the dead. In religious celebrations the same hierarchies are reproduced. The priests occupy positions of prominence with respect to those who are suffering; those who find themselves under the burden of the loss are almost like silent spectators of the liturgical spectacle.

I myself lived through such an experience quite recently, with the loss of a great friend, Padre Humberto Plummen.[8] The people of the parish, shaken by his sudden death, reacted to suffering in different ways. This particular experience led me to reflect more vigorously on the metaphysical and essentialist presuppositions of patriarchal discourses, taking into consideration the concrete situation of thousands upon thousands of people.

The point of entry for my reflection overflows with paradoxes and contradictions as well as with the perception that, by and large, the critical discourses of patriarchal theologies have not succeeded in constructing alternative discourses and practices that bring about real changes in the existing religious culture. The texts read almost always receive the same traditional interpretations, which end up consigning death, even unjust deaths, to the mysterious designs of God. To mention this kind of collective "incompetence" in the creation of new expressions is but to affirm that the time for religious cultural change appears to be of a different sort than the time for technological change. We do not succeed in bringing about the changes that we need because patriarchal religious culture has very deep roots in the history of different human groups. We do not succeed in making our dreams a reality because our creative emotions are, in a certain sense, prisoners of the patriarchal hierarchical structure of our culture. Consequently, the task of constructing new relations and, in particular, a different kind of education of the emotions needs to begin among us. We must think about our daughters and sons and gradually opt for different steps, given what is a slow and ongoing process of change in behavior whose results cannot be foreseen; we can try, however, to lead our everyday life with *tenderness and compassion*. We are constantly challenged to avoid reproducing the forms of behavior that we criticize, to prepare ourselves and above all to prepare the new generations so that they do not fall into the snares that we have constructed for ourselves. We are called upon to reflect on life and death beyond hierarchical conceptions, but this task still needs a long historical trajectory for it to become flesh of our flesh.

It is within such a trajectory that I would place the proposed analysis of the essentialist presuppositions of our theological formation. I know from experience that a metaphysical reading of Christianity is characterized by certain fundamental points, highlighted according to the different situations and contexts in question. These can be learned through the expression of common life on the part of women and men who embrace Christianity as expression of their religious faith. For the most part, such points are not reflected upon and, as a result, appear to possess a coercive force of such intensity that people refuse to reflect upon them or to disagree with what the existing religious culture proposes for them. I should like to reflect on three such points: (1) the affirmation of an anthropology characterized by "ontological rupture"; (2) the affirmation of an epistemology characterized by cognitive leaps or ruptures; and (3) the affirmation of a history beyond the concrete history of women and men.

Anthropology of "Ontological Rupture"

What I mean by "ontological rupture" in anthropology and theology is a vision of the human being—woman and man—whereby ideals, models, ethical frames of reference seem to be projected onto suprahuman beings. This rupture entails the construction of a meaning for human life whose foundations are to be found in a vision of an idealized and divinized male human being. In this idealization certain privileged individuals can have a share, especially upon death. They become thereby models for imitation, and their historicity seems to give way to an idealization of the person.

For the purpose of my reflection here, I do not intend to call explicitly on the philosophies of Greek antiquity, where the subject was limited to noble and male citizens, nor do I intend to refer to the modernity of the Cartesian *cogito* or to European and North American postmodernity. I aim to proceed rather on the basis of a more popular, more mixed, more miscegenated philosophy, that is, a philosophy that is marked by quite different cultural origins and is prevalent within popular culture, such as that notably present in northeast Brazil. In this philosophy colonial Christianity predominates, to be sure, but in combination with black culture, indigenous culture, and other cultures that characterize our various forms of social conduct. In the cultural formation of our people, different influences of contemporary national and international cultural currents intersect one another. It is from this context of life and thought that I testify to and reflect upon the ontological rupture with which I am presently concerned. To reflect from such a place proves to be an extremely difficult task on two counts: because we leave behind the customary universality proper to male Western thinking, and because we distrust our eyes, our interpretations, since we become ever more conscious of the relativity of human beings and their quests. We feel the difficulty of finding concepts with which to express such experiences. Thus, the present reflection represents but a limited approximation to what I perceive and but one more limited interpretation of the reality in which we live.

What I do see is that in Christian anthropology as lived in these lands human beings, women and men, exist as if mirrored after a perfect being, Jesus Christ, who not only possesses every perfection one could possibly think of but also contains in his being the ability to understand all our sufferings and, to a certain extent, to bring us comfort to the extent that we accept the life experience in question. There is a human image that is reflected or mirrored in an ideal form, as if it were necessary to deny our historical, contextual face and to attempt to see ourselves in a different state of perfection. Such behavior is reflected also at other levels of our existence.

It is in this sense that our recourse to Jesus Christ preserves a philosophy that is marked by an ontological rupture. Jesus both is and is not like us. Moreover, in such is and is not, what is most emphasized is what is not. In this way we stress the ontological rupture and affirm that the ideal of women and men is different from our actual realm of possibilities. The human ideal proves absolutely inaccessible, insofar as we shall never reach the perfection asked of us. The reason is evident: ontologically, that is, in the very constitution of our being, it is impossible for us to be what we dream of being, to be human and divine at one and the same time. Jesus Christ is ontologically God and man. We are men and women. In addition, we women find ourselves at a lower degree of being: we are only and simply women.

Rarely do we ask ourselves such questions as the following: Who established these ideals? What is the origin of such proposals of perfection or such "cosmovisions," which survive in our culture through mixture with the most specialized communications technologies? Who has elevated them to the level of truths of faith or indisputable truths? Finally, how do they function today in our lives?

Some might argue that this anthropology is no longer as strong as it once was and that today, especially after the critiques of the patriarchal world on the part of feminist reason, we have gone beyond such dualistic ontology. I believe that this has yet to happen, especially in terms of Latin America in all of its immense diversity. The axiological meridian that separates men from women still endures, and with incredible strength, in our culture. Similarly, the axiological meridian that separates our history from an idealized metahistory continues as the driving force of our actions and emotions. In this particular meridian, furthermore, the recourse to the Bible plays, once again, an important role. The fundamentalist readings of the Bible, which seek justification for actions and ways of conduct that diverge from the usual, introduce the force of the Bible as an unquestionable justification for such actions and omissions. The use of the Bible as word of authority has not only caused confusion among the people but has also strengthened hierarchical and exclusive postures in all sectors of social life. The claim could be made that the Bible has also produced commitment to the cause of the poor, and this goes without question. However, the problems of clerical domination still persist, as I pointed out earlier, even in terms of projects of liberation. This weakens, of course, feminist social struggles.

The question before us has to do with how to think and live the difference of our individualities, our gender, our cultures from the perspective of affirming our interdependence. The old question, "How are we going to do that?" comes back to dwell among us and to challenge our personal and collective creativity.

Epistemology of Cognitive Leaps and Ruptures

A dualistic anthropology marked by ontological rupture is intimately accompanied by an epistemology marked by logical leaps or cognitive ruptures. I do not have in mind here a thoroughly developed philosophical epistemology, in the style of the great philosophers of the West. My intention is to capture, somewhat hesitantly, the way of knowing of the poor, especially the women, with whom I live, within the limits of my own cultural frames of reference and of the work that I have carried out. My approach to this world is, in effect, based on solidarity and on a proximity that is often ambiguous and distressing.

To begin with, I do not wish to speak of understanding on the basis of a pernicious division of knowledge according to which a number of privileged individuals have the power of knowing and make good use of it for the benefit of a few. Similarly, in keeping with this critical posture, I want to deal with the structure of understanding itself in terms of its contextualized popular patriarchal expression.

I realize that most people, in fact, have difficulty developing a historical consciousness and a historical cognitive capacity that would take in the whole of human life in all of its different artistic and religious manifestations. In point of fact, history is not historical for the majority of people. Indeed, history is historical and ahistorical in different ways for women and men to the extent that they react in different ways to the problems that life brings before them. What seems to emerge, from the point of view of a phenomenology of everyday life, is the conviction that history represents, in reality, a conjunction of beneficial and harmful forces that often function independently of individual volition on the part of human beings.

Understanding appears to be situated within this same perspective and these same limitations. To the extent that an understanding of reality escapes us, either we maintain a seemingly ingenuous attitude, or we attribute, with similarly ingenuous conviction, the benefits or malefactions of our history to supra-terrestrial forces. Such forces appear capable of intervening in negative or positive fashion in our destiny. Even if one speaks against the wealthy and the rulers, concrete action on the part of individual human beings leaves much to be desired. The hierarchical system appears to block the critique of the different historical responsibilities. It is as if the wealthy and the rulers did not believe that human beings are really capable of doing good to human beings in the same way in which it is clear that they are capable of doing evil. This cognitive culture of multiple traditions (Indigenous; African; Iberian; Asiatic; and so forth) ends up emphasizing as well a Christian life in dualistic patterns. Thus, the community of believers proves unable, for the most part, to criticize the dualistic philosophical frameworks in which Christianity has

been presented to them, not only because of the lack of critical formation but also because they belong to a "mixed" culture where different
worlds intervene in personal and social histories. There are always hidden histories and forces intervening in our history. There is always some
demon, unclean spirit, dirty soul, negative force, bad luck, intervening in
our affairs. There are also good spirits and good angels that help us. The
world of the poor is continuously split by forces extraneous to the normal course of history. Consequently, a Christology of suffering, which includes an affirmation of the magnitude of the suffering of Jesus and of
his heavenly glorification, can be received in almost uncritical fashion. In
this history, it seems, in fact, that it is pain and suffering that prove tri-
umphant in history. As a result, the expectation of something else, above
all something better, enters into the logic of the hope of the poor.

Within this cultural context, the lack of understanding with regard
to theological categories poses no problems for a large part of the Christian population of Latin America. We have no need of them in order to
continue to be religious persons. This lack of conceptual understanding
adapts itself to the world of mysteries of the poor; to their logic, inter-
mixed as it is with different logics; and to their way of dealing with those
in power or those who seem to have power. On the one hand, such theological dualism furnishes a vital means for survival; on the other hand,
it makes us easy prey for the different ideologies used in discourses that,
more or less, become part of the popular logic.

The task of education regarding the frames of reference of the poor,
and women in particular, will be possible only if the whole complex of
economic, social, and political structures comes together in the construction of a society where all, women and men, belong. In Latin America
today, a feminist critical philosophy has a chance to be fruitful only in
certain elite contexts or among certain truly exceptional groups. Thus,
yet again it is necessary, as many people have postulated, to insist not so
much on the re-education of religious frames of reference as on the empowerment of women and men in non-confessional contexts to become,
in fact, historical subjects, to understand their history within the complex of world history, and to look for ethical ways of conduct.

History beyond the Concrete History of Women and Men

Mention of essentialist metaphysical presuppositions leads us to note
that the patriarchal world speaks of history without taking into account
concrete histories, above all, the histories of women and the poor. The history pursued is a history that involves only male deeds or deeds attributed
to illustrious individuals; it is idealized history. Only the great powers
seem to have history. The greater the economic and military power, the
greater the value of such history. The greater the gross national product

of a nation or a group, the greater its historical worth. Poor countries, marginalized groups, women—all represent but auxiliary entities, secondary players, expendable in kyriarchal history.

Christianity did not remain outside this conception of history. Its most important characters have to do with the male world and the prophetic, salvific, and priestly deeds of this world. What is most important revolves around a history that is already accomplished, a past history that ends up becoming more or less normative. The present matters only in discourse, on paper, but lacks the ferment necessary to transform present history in view of the future. As a result, we women feel that the history of Christianity as narrated is still not our history. Such is the present among most women of Latin America.

Christian history is repetitive not on the basis of active memory and in dialogue with the present; rather, such repetition becomes a sort of referential criterion for all histories. All the different histories need to enter into this sort of universal history that is already finished, as if one had lived already, ahead of time, in the fullness of time. Both beginning and end appear as already on hand. Thus, for those who repeat this history, novelty is not welcome. For that reason, all variant interpretations are regarded as heterodox and even schismatic. There is not only a conflict of interpretations but also of philosophies of history.

All new events seem more or less encased within this idealized history in which the "end of times" seems to have arrived, and in this end of times men continue to play the principal role. In this patriarchal history women possess little history. The fixation of contemporary patriarchal history in Christianity may even open up some spaces for recalling the actions of some illustrious women. Once again, however, this space is made available only within the very context of patriarchal historical narration and conceptualization.

We recall that from this perspective the history of the people of God and the history of the Son of God are told in idealist terms: a history of salvation is constructed; a standardized doctrine of the resurrection is affirmed; a way of speaking about God as personal author of things and events beyond our understanding is developed. All this makes us realize how much the way in which Christianity deals with the human condition ends up disrespecting human history as it is and, within this history, disrespecting women more than men. It is imperative to break these old wineskins. They can no longer hold the new wine that is being produced. The question today, however, no longer has to do with the "it is imperative" (*é preciso*) but with the "how to" (*como fazer*). In this "how to" we women possess a particular wisdom and specific ways that need to be put into practice.

The challenge before us also involves rescuing from the biblical texts the histories of individuals who lived the same values that we wish to live. We want to reread in our own way those experiences that may echo our own experiences of today. We want to think through a different philosophy of history in which those events characterized as "foundational," those events that unleash a historical movement, are not appropriated by an elitist and sexist ideology. This is one of the challenges that we face in tearing the Christian tradition away from a metaphysical and essentialist reading of history and turning it simply into plural histories. In this regard, the contribution of Elisabeth Schüssler Fiorenza has been absolutely beyond question.

The preceding three points constitute, in a certain sense, some trails toward rethinking, from a different perspective, the essentialist presuppositions of patriarchal thought that are still present and at work among us. Such rethinking means not following the patriarchal logic, which excludes, divides, opposes, controls, and "hierarchizes." Such rethinking also means taking as our point of departure the particularity of our contexts in order to respect the individualities of our history. Such rethinking means, therefore, not forgetting the long and complex history of our lives and our plural humanity, in terms of both its culture and its individuals. Rethinking our Christian tradition from a feminist point of view does not mean a rejection of our cultural inheritance as a block, as if human history had constructed nothing of value before us. Rethinking means not to assume a patriarchal attitude with respect to our inheritance, rejecting or preserving it on the basis of the excluding logic of "either/or." Rather, as the Spanish philosopher Celia Amorós puts it, we are in need of "a comprehensive reason, a reason that is able to synthesize but that is not tormented by a compulsion to organize all of history in terms of a privileged signifying key and to see everything in terms of, under the genealogical optic of prefiguration."[9] Only then will we be able to break the totalitarianism of patriarchal culture, the essentialism of its philosophical postures, and, as Amorós again declares, only then will we "cut up the inheritance, breaking it up into its most vulnerable fissures and appropriating its valid pieces."[10] Such is the challenge of history from the point of view of feminism; to this challenge we wish to continue to respond.

By Way of Conclusion

I do not want to conclude this reflection with lessons to be kept or points to be highlighted or even with suggestions for it to be continued along this or that line. I want to express in more or less poetic fashion what remains in me at the end of this composition, in the midst of a world troubled by unjust deaths and new threats of unjust death.

There remain many mixed things, clear and obscure at the same time...

There remains the anger that hurts from our very entrails in the face of injustice, arrogance, and the misunderstandings of our world...

There remains sadness over the irrationality of the logic of violence, which grows in the name of a false freedom...

There remains fear before the imperialist patriarchal logic that arms itself and makes war, that kills in subtle and cruel fashion to try to save its wounded power...

There remains the flame that burns in our breast, feeding our passion for a more just and sisterly world...

There remain the tenderness and the love for the mysterious planet on which we live and for all those who dwell on it...

There remain the women and the men who carry lit torches and search without ceasing for their humanity...

There remain the pregnant women and the children, our future with a question mark...

There remain art, poetry, a reawakened memory, thought committed to justice, love, and tenderness...

There remain the small and fragile things of every day, capable of nourishing life in the midst of destruction and tears...

There remain flowers, gardens, birds, and stars to call to mind the ephemeral nature of our existence...

There remains gratitude to LIFE for its extraordinary work in Elisabeth Schüssler Fiorenza...

There remain my embrace and my recognition of her for having said yes to the deepest appeals of our history and her own life.

Notes

Author's Note: This study was written in honor of the biblical theologian Elisabeth Schüssler Fiorenza. Although I never set foot in her classroom, I regard her in a certain sense as a teacher of theological studies and especially of a life committed to justice. I have learned much from her by reading her articles and books as well as by listening to close friends of hers speak of her quests and her struggles. Her commitment to the cause of oppressed peoples and her clear voice in favor of feminist causes make her one of the most important thinkers of the twentieth and twenty-first centuries.

1. Elisabeth Schüssler Fiorenza, *Bread Not Stone: The Challenge of Feminist Biblical Interpretation* (Boston: Beacon Press, 1984).

2. Elisabeth Schüssler Fiorenza, *In Memory of Her: A Feminist Theological Reconstruction of Christian Origins* (New York: Crossroad, 1983).

3. Elisabeth Schüssler Fiorenza, *But She Said: Feminist Practices of Biblical Interpretation* (Boston: Beacon Press, 1992).

4. Elisabeth Schüssler Fiorenza, *Jesus: Miriam's Child, Sophia's Prophet: Critical Issues in Feminist Thought* (New York: Continuum, 1995), 17.

5. Here I have in mind especially the groups of Catholic Women for the Right to Choose present throughout Latin America.

6. Schüssler Fiorenza, *But She Said*, 5.

7. Humberto R. Maturana, *"Amor y Juego": Fundamentos olvidados del humano* (Santiago de Chile: Editorial Instituto de Terapia, 1997).

8. Fr. Plummen was a Dutch sociologist and missionary of the Redemptorist order who had lived in Brazil for almost fifty years. He worked for many years with Bishop Helder Câmara and served as director of the Institute of Theology in Recife.

9. Celia Amorós, *Hacia una crítica de la razón patriarchal* (Barcelona: Anthropos Editorial del Hombre, 1991), 103.

10. Ibid., 104.

4

DISMANTLING THE MASTER'S HOUSE WITH THE MASTER'S TOOLS

Native Feminist Liberation Theologies

Andrea Smith (Cherokee, USA)

I'm a feminist because I think anything else is unintelligent. And I just can't go with turning my brain into jello for someone else's fantasy fulfillment. I also think it's ordained by God. I really do think I have divine power on my side in that regard. To me you cannot advocate sovereignty without advocating feminism because feminism should be at its heart the same way sovereignty is. I do see feminism as ordering right relations and I think that's what Native American traditions are all about, is being in balance with one another. Being in balance with all creation, be it the environment, be it nation-to-nation, and I think feminism is that, but it does so from the particular vantage point that women are able to provide, and have always provided.[1]

Mavis Etienne, a negotiator at Oka during the Mohawk uprising, joined the struggle because she did not want her "land bulldozed to expand a golf course." Etienne says of her decision to join the struggle: "I wasn't afraid because I knew they [those opposing the Mohawks] were in the wrong, and I knew God was with me."[2]

Native women activists' utterances provide a foundation for my analysis of Native feminist theologies. Through my involvement in organizations such as Women of All Red Nations (Chicago), Incite! Women of Color against Violence (www.incite-national.org), and vari-

---

Andrea Smith, "Dismantling the Master's House with the Master's Tools: Native Feminist Liberation Theologies," *Journal of Feminist Studies in Religion* 22, no. 2 (2006): 85–97.

ous other projects, I have come to see the importance of documenting the theory produced by Native women's organizers as theory. I see this research methodology as intellectual ethnography. In my ongoing research projects on Native American feminisms, I focus on documenting and analyzing the theories produced by Native women activists that intervene both in sovereignty and feminist struggles.[3] I believe these theories can then be part of a larger collective conversation to develop Native feminist theologies. However, before I begin this task, I must first address the theological project itself within Native studies and Native communities.

Is Native Liberation Theology an Oxymoron?

After five-hundred-plus years of colonialism, patriarchy, and white supremacy, it is clear that Native communities could benefit from "liberation." However, Native religious scholars have expressed great skepticism about theology, including liberation theology, as a starting point for discussing Native religiosity. Vine Deloria, Jr., has pointed out that liberation theology is grounded in a Western European epistemological framework that is no less oppressive to Native communities than is mainstream theology. "Liberation theology," Deloria cynically argues, "was an absolute necessity if the establishment was going to continue to control the minds of minorities. If a person of a minority group had not invented it, the liberal establishment most certainly would have created it."[4] According to Deloria, Native liberation must be grounded in indigenous epistemologies—epistemologies that are inconsistent with Western epistemologies, of which liberation theology is a part. "If we are then to talk seriously about the necessity of liberation, we are talking about the destruction of the whole complex of Western theories of knowledge and the construction of a new and more comprehensive synthesis of human knowledge and experience."[5] Jace Weaver similarly argues that theology is inconsonant with indigenous worldviews, which hold that systematic study of God is both presumptuous and impossible.[6] "Traditional Native religions are integrated totally into daily activity," Weaver remarks. "They are ways of life and not sets of principles or creedal formulation ... Native 'religion' does not concern itself—does not try to know or explain—'what happens in the other world.'"[7] Even Native theologian William Baldridge states that "doing theology, thinking theologically, is a decidedly non-Indian thing to do. When I talk about Native American theology to many of my Indian friends, most of them just smile and act as if I hadn't said anything. And I am pretty sure that as far as they are concerned I truly hadn't said anything."[8]

The challenge brought forth by Native scholars/activists to other liberation theologians would be, even if we distinguish the "liberation" church from mainstream churches, can any church escape complicity in Christian imperialism? Deloria, in particular, raises the challenge that Christianity, because it is a temporally rather than a spatially based tradition (that is, it is not tied to a particular land base, but can seek converts from anywhere), is necessarily a religion tied to imperialism because it will never be content to remain within a particular place or community. Adherents of spatially based religions, however, will not try to convince other peoples of the veracity of their religious truth claims. "Once religion becomes specific to a group, its nature also appears to change, being directed to the internal mechanics of the group, not to grandiose schemes of world conquest."[9]

Hence, all Christian theology, even liberation theology, remains complicit in the missionization and genocide of Native peoples in the Americas. Robert Warrior's "Canaanites, Cowboys, and Indians," furthers Deloria's analysis. In this essay, Warrior argues that the Bible is not a liberatory text for Native peoples, especially considering the fact that the liberation motif commonly adopted by liberation theologians—the Exodus—is premised on the genocide of the indigenous people occupying the Promised Land—the Canaanites. Warrior does not argue for the historical veracity of the conquest of the Canaanites. Rather, the Exodus operates as a *narrative* of conquest—a narrative that was foundational to the European conquest of the Americas. Warrior's essay points not only to the problems with Exodus motif, but also to liberation theology's conceptualization of a God of deliverance. He contends that "as long as people believe in the Yahweh of deliverance, the world will not be safe from the Yahweh the conqueror."[10] That is, by conceptualizing ourselves as oppressed peoples who are to be delivered at all costs, we necessarily become complicit in oppressing those who stand in the way of our deliverance. Instead, Warrior argues, we need to re-conceptualize ourselves as "a society of people delivered from oppression who are not so afraid of becoming victims again that they become oppressors themselves."[11]

Comparative Study of Religion as a Colonial Project

As a result, many scholars argue that the appropriate discipline with which to study Native spiritualities is comparative religious studies.[12] Religious studies does not rely upon systematizing propositions about God, but instead explores the nature of religious experience on its own terms.[13] These arguments are compelling. However, they also fail to acknowledge religious studies as a colonizing discourse, particularly within Native communities. As one example, this colonizing discourse is evident in Emile Durkheim's *Elementary Forms of Religion*, in which Durkheim argued that the individuals best prepared to study a religious tradition are those who do not actually practice it.[14] Only the Western scientific mind has the necessary power of analysis to ascertain the nature of indigenous religion correctly; indigenous people lack the appropriate "intellectual cultivation and reflection."[15]

Durkheim's maxim continues to inform the discipline of comparative religions today. A recent exchange between Sam Gill and Christopher Jocks in the *Journal of the American Academy of Religion* shows the influence.[16] Sam Gill, a prominent non-Native scholar in the study of religion, provoked controversy when he argued that Native communities had no notions of earth as mother, that Native religions actually derived the concept from non-Native peoples.[17] Native peoples in the field of religion challenged this argument because, they argued, Gill did not know Native languages, nor did he have an in-depth understanding of Native religions, and hence was ill informed. In response, Gill wrote an essay in which he contended that because Native religious scholars subscribe to the religious beliefs they study, they are ill equipped for this type of scholarship. Like Durkheim, he implied that only those who stand outside Native religious worldviews are in a position to understand them properly.[18] "The academic study of religion has often failed to acknowledge what it is. It is academic; it is Western; it is intellectual."[19]

Romanticism about Native spirituality pervades our society. Religious studies promises the non-Indian voyeur that s/he too can understand Native religiosity. What often goes unasked, however, is, do Native communities want their religious experiences studied in academic institutions? Do Native communities want non-Natives to know about Native spiritualities? These issues are relevant not only to non-Native scholars, but to Native scholars as well, who are often accused by their communities of "telling too much."

Decolonizing Theology

In addition, rejecting theology (or any discipline for that matter) as inherently "white" presumes that Native cultures have somehow managed to remain untainted by the dominant society, or that Native communities can completely untangle themselves from the larger colonial society. Muscogee activist Roberto Mendoza has noted that this kind of separatism does "not really address the question of power. How can small communities tied in a thousand ways to the capitalist market system break out without a thorough social, economic and political revolution within the whole country?"[20] If a revolution is necessary, then it would seem wise for Native scholars and activists to use any tool that might be helpful in changing society "by any means necessary." Looking at academia, Warrior similarly argues:

> We have remained by and large caught in a death dance of de-
> pendence between, on the one hand, abandoning ourselves to
> the intellectual strategies and categories of white, European
> thought and, on the other hand, declaring that we need nothing
> outside of ourselves and our cultures in order to understand the
> world and our place in it...When we remove ourselves from this
> dichotomy, much becomes possible. We see first that the strug-
> gle for sovereignty is not a struggle to be free from the influence
> of anything outside ourselves, but a process of asserting the
> power we possess as communities and individuals to make deci-
> sions that affect our lives.[21]

Additionally, the anthropological focus of comparative religious
studies lacks an explicit concern about ethics that is integral to the discipline of theology, particularly liberation theology. It is not enough to understand or describe Native religious experience; it is also necessary to
advocate for the survival of Native spiritual practices and an end to colonialism. Liberation theology brings to Native studies an explicit concern
for the victims of colonialism. Liberation theology highlights the question, "What social movements, practices, and strategies are required 'by
any means necessary' for large-scale transformation?"[22]

As the utterances at the beginning of this essay suggest, Native
women involved in liberation struggles often participate out of a sense of
divine purpose. Whether or not they call themselves Christian, they *are*
theologizing because they are articulating what they perceive to be the relationship between spirituality, liberation, and the vision of the world they
hope to co-create. Their theologies may not be concerned with definitive
statements about faith and belief, but rather with exploring the possibilities about thinking about spirituality in light of our current political context. Furthermore, how do we release our theological imagination to develop projects of indigenous sovereignty that envision the world we
would like to live in? Such a theological reorientation is suggested by
South African theologian Itumeleng Mosala's critique of Warrior's essay.
Mosala responds that the Bible and other forms of theological discourse
are never fixed and always subject to contestation. "It is not enough to
recognize text as ideology. Interpretations of texts do alter the texts. Contrary to Warrior's argument, texts are signifying practices and therefore
they exist ideologically and permanently problematically."[23]

Mosala's approach suggests that theological discourse is never simply liberatory or oppressive, but that oppressed groups can wrest it away
from paradigms set up by dominating classes in order to further liberatory struggles.[24] Or, to quote Ghanaian theologian Emmanuel Martey,
"Unlike Audre Lorde, who might be wondering whether the master's
tools could indeed be used to dismantle the master's house, African the-

ologians are fully convinced that the gun, in efficient hands, could well kill its owner."[25]

Liberation Theology beyond the Politics of Representation

As the proliferation of black, womanist, *mujerista*, Asian, and so on, theologies indicate, liberation theologians in the United States have often relied on a politics of representation. That is, these theologies seek to represent the theological concerns of the communities from which theologians emerge. This representational strategy can in turn lend itself to totalizing and essentializing discourses about the communities theologians seek to represent. As one example, Chung Hyun Kyung's thought-provoking book on Asian women's theology raises an important challenge to Christian imperialism in the discipline of theology; however, she frequently makes broad and rather unsubstantiated claims about Asian women's religious experiences. For example: "The most prevailing image of Jesus among Asian women's theological expressions is the image of the suffering servant. Asian Christian women seem to feel most comfortable with this image of Jesus whether they are theologically conservative or progressive."[26] However, the basis of her claims seems to be limited to an analysis of the writings of Asian women theologians and eleven interviews with them.[27] It is unclear how her methodology allows her to make such broad claims about Asian women in general.[28] Many theologians, such as Chung, often assume an unproblematic relationship between their experiences in their communities and their knowledge about them. However, as Lata Mani argues: "The relationship between experience and knowledge is now seen to be one not of correspondence, but fraught with history, contingency and struggle."[29]

In addition, the theologians' positions vis-à-vis the communities they attempt to represent often allows theologians to become the self-appointed representatives of their communities regardless of whether they seek this leadership role. As a result, they may find themselves silencing the communities they wish to give voice to. Ada María Isasi-Díaz reflects upon this:

> The . . . issue to consider when dealing with the subject of presentation is that of "speaking for" others. I have insisted since the very first published writings about *mujerista* theology that this theology is but one theological elaboration of Hispanic/Latina women's liberation theology. I have in no way claimed to speak for all Latinas, nor have I claimed that my elaborations are the only reflections of the beliefs of grassroots Latinas. I have always been concerned not only about speaking "for" all Latinas but even as speaking "for" any Latina. But the fact is that because

mujerista theology is about creating a public voice for Latinas and capturing a political space for that voice, there is no other way to proceed but to speak whether "as" or "for."...The issue, then, is not whether in elaborating *mujerista* theology I speak for Latinas or not. Rather it is this: Do I speak so as to control those Latinas or to provide a platform for their voices, which are not totally separated from my own?[30]

This problem is particularly true for Native peoples; since many non-Natives have so little contact with Native people, they often have a tendency to presume that the one book that they have read by a Native author tells the truth about all Native people. It is particularly challenging for Native theologians to write theology without unwittingly encouraging their readers to make broad assumptions regarding what all Native people think about political/theological issues. By not specifically and critically analyzing their positions vis-à-vis the communities they seek to represent, liberation theologians sometimes unconsciously assume the God's eye position taken by mainstream theologians whom they oppose. As theologian David Batstone argues: "How does one talk about the marginalized without...producing a reification of the victim, which is as condescending as any fixed concept? We must take care to attend to the multiple and fluid forms that victimization takes rather than reducing the victim to a new Other, and thus finding ourselves again representing others rather than attending to how they are self-represented."[31]

On the one hand, poststructuralist analysis points to the fragmentation and discontinuities between self, experience, and identity. On the other hand, many theorists have also adopted a kind of vulgar constructionism, arguing that because axes of identities (race, class, etc.) are socially constructed, they therefore do not "really" exist. However, as Kimberle Crenshaw states: "To say that a category such as race or gender is socially constructed is not to say that category has no significance in our world."[32] She notes that social constructionism is helpful in showing how naturalized categories exclude groups and exercise power against them. Yet these categories are still performative and help shape those who are defined by them. In other words, as long as many members in society define an individual as "Indian," this category will shape her subjectivity, even if she is not comfortable with that identity. Lisa Lowe similarly contests the "racial or ethnic" subject, without dispelling the importance of identity politics. She argues that "the cultural productions of racialized women seek to articulate multiple, nonequivalent, but linked determinations without assuming their containment within the horizon of an absolute totality and its presumption of a singular subject."[33] So, as long as the categories of race, gender, and sexuality continue to shape institutional structures and our sense of selfhood, oppositional politics on the basis of these identities is critical. As Crenshaw notes, "a strong case can be made that the most critical resistance strategy for disempowered groups is to occupy and defend a politics of social location rather than to vacate it and destroy it."[34]

Elizabeth Povinelli points to a possible strategy that allows Native women to theorize as Native women while relying less on essentializing discourses about Native women. As Povinelli has so aptly demonstrated, the liberal state depends on a politics of multicultural recognition that includes "social difference without social consequence."[35] She continues: "These state, public, and capital multicultural discourses, apparatuses, and imaginaries defuse struggles for liberation waged against the modern liberal state and recuperate these struggles as moments in which the future of the nation and its core institutions and values are ensured rather than shaken."[36]

Fumitaka Matsuoka sheds further light onto this problem, noting that cultural validation is not the most important fight. The dominant culture is prepared to accommodate a little "multiculturalism"—a pow-wow here, a pipe ceremony there—as long as the structures of power are not challenged. Matsuoka states: "The central problems... have to do, ultimately, not with ethnic groupings or the distinctness of our cultural heritages as such, but with racism and its manifestations in American economic policy, social rule and class relations."[37]

Thus, this critique suggests that Native feminist theologies could focus less on a politics of representation and more on the material conditions Native women face as they are situated within the nexuses of patriarchy, colonialism, and white supremacy. That is, as Crenshaw would say, what difference does the difference Native women represent make?

Heteropatriarchy and the Nation-State

Since the theorizing of Native women's organizing and their contributions to a theological project of liberation cannot be summarized briefly, I will simply focus on the critical intervention that I think this theorizing makes. Native feminist theologies fundamentally challenge the givenness of U.S. empire and the nation-state form of governance. They further theologize possibilities of alternative forms of governance for the world. This theologizing also challenges male-dominated sovereignty and struggles for racial justice because they demonstrate that the building block of the nation-state is the heteropatriarchal family.

That is, social justice activists as well as U.S.-based liberation theologians often criticize U.S. policies, but they do not critically interrogate the contradictions between the United States articulating itself as a democratic country, on one hand, while simultaneously founding itself on the past and current genocide of Native peoples, on the other hand. That is, even progressives tend to articulate racism as a policy to be addressed *within* the constraints of the U.S. nation-state rather than understanding racism and genocide as constituitive of the United States. However, since the United States could not exist without the genocide of Native peoples, Native feminist interventions call us to question why we should presume the givenness of the United States in our long-range vision of social justice. These interventions provide a starting point for theological reflection on what exactly is a just form of governance, not only for Native peoples, but also for the rest of the world. Native women activists have begun articulating spiritually based visions of nation and sovereignty that are separate from nation-states. Whereas nation-states are governed through domination and coercion, indigenous sovereignty and nationhood are predicated on interrelatedness and responsibility. As Crystal Echohawk states: "Sovereignty is an active, living process within this knot of human, material and spiritual relationships bound together by mutual responsibilities and obligations. From that knot of relationships [are] born our histories, our identity, the traditional ways in which we govern ourselves, our beliefs, our relationship to the land, and how we feed, clothe, house and take care of our families, communities and Nations."[38] This interconnectedness exists not only among the nation's members but among all creation as well—human and nonhuman. As Sharon Venne states:

> Our spirituality and our responsibilities define our duties. We understand the concept of sovereignty as woven through a fabric that encompasses our spirituality and responsibility. This is a cyclical view of sovereignty, incorporating it into our traditional philosophy and view of our responsibilities. There it differs greatly from the concept of Western sovereignty which is based upon absolute power. For us absolute power is in the Creator and the natural order of all living things; not only in human beings ... Our sovereignty is related to our connections to the earth and is inherent.
>
> The idea of a nation did not simply apply to human beings. We call the buffalo or the wolves, the fish, the trees, and all are nations. Each is sovereign, an equal part of the creation, interdependent, interwoven, and all related.[39]

These models of sovereignty are not based on a narrow definition of nation that would entail a closely bounded community and ethnic cleansing. For example, one activist distinguishes between a chauvinistic notion of "nationalism" versus a flexible notion of "sovereignty":

> To me, nationalism is saying, our way is the only right way ... [but] I think a real true sovereignty is a real, true acceptance

of who and what's around you. Sovereignty is what you do and what you are to your own people within your own confines, but there is a realization and acceptance that there are others who are around you. And that happened even before the Europeans came, we knew about the Indians. We had alliances with some, and fights with some. Part of that sovereignty was that acceptance that they were there.

These spiritually based alternative visions of sovereignty in turn challenge the heteronormative basis of nation-building. To see the relationship between heteronormativity and the nation-state, we can turn to Charles Colson, prominent Christian Right activist and founder of Prison Fellowship, who explains why same-sex marriage leads to terrorism.

Marriage is the traditional building block of human society, intended both to unite couples and bring children into the world...There is a natural moral order for the family...The family, led by a married mother and father, is the best available structure for both child-rearing and cultural health. Marriage is not a private institution designed solely for the individual gratification of its participants. If we fail to enact a Federal Marriage Amendment, we can expect, not just more family breakdown, but also more criminals behind bars and more chaos in our streets. This is like handing moral weapons of mass destruction to those who use America's decadence to recruit more snipers and hijackers and suicide bombers.[40]

Similarly, the Christian Right *World* magazine opined that feminism contributed to the Abu Ghraib scandal by promoting women in the military.[41] When women do not know their assigned role in the gender hierarchy, they become disoriented and abuse prisoners.[42] Implicit in this analysis is that the understanding that heteropatriarchy is essential for the building of U.S. empire. That is, patriarchy is the logic that naturalizes social hierarchy. Just as men are supposed to dominate women on the basis of "natural" biology, so too should the social elites of a society naturally rule everyone else through a nation-state form of governance that is constructed through domination, violence, and control. Patriarchy, in turn, is presumed a heteronormative gender binary system. Thus, as Ann Burlein argues in *Lift High the Cross*, it may be a mistake to argue that the goal of Christian Right politics is to create a theocracy in the United States. Rather, Christian Right politics work through the private family (which is coded as white, patriarchal, and middle class) to create a "Christian America." She notes that investment in the private family makes it difficult for people to invest in more public forms of social connection. In addition, investment in the suburban private family serves to mask public disinvestment in urban areas, a disinvestment that makes the suburban lifestyle possible. The social decay in urban areas that results from this disinvestment is then construed as the result of deviance from the white, Christian family ideal rather than as the result of political and economic forces. As former head of the Christian Coalition Ralph Reed stated: "The only true solution to crime is to restore the family,"[43] and "family break-up causes poverty."[44] Concludes Burlein, "'The family' is no mere metaphor but a crucial technology by which modern power is produced and exercised."[45]

Unfortunately, as Navajo feminist scholar Jennifer Denetdale points out, the Native response to a heteronormative white, Christian America is often an equally heteronormative Native nationalism. Denetdale, in her critique of the Navajo tribal council's passage of a ban on same-sex marriage, argues that Native nations are furthering a Christian Right agenda in the name of "Indian tradition."[46] This trend is also equally apparent within racial justice struggles in other communities of color. As Cathy Cohen contends, heteronormative sovereignty or racial justice struggles will maintain rather than challenge colonialism and white supremacy because they are premised on a politics of secondary marginalization, where the most elite class of these groups will further their aspiration on the backs of those most marginalized within the community.[47] Through this process of secondary marginalization, the national or racial justice struggle takes on either implicitly or explicitly a nation-state model as its end point—a model of governance in which the elites govern the rest through violence and domination as well as exclude those who are not members of "the nation." However, as the articulations of Native women suggest, there are other models of nationhood we can envision, nations that are not based on exclusion and that are not based on secondary marginalization—nations that do not have the heteronormative, patriarchy nuclear family as their building block.

The theological imagination then becomes central to envisioning the world we would actually want to live in. At the 2005 World Liberation Theology Forum held in Porto Alegre, Brazil, indigenous peoples from Bolivia stated they know another world is possible because they see that world whenever they do their ceremonies. Native ceremonies can be a place where the present, past, and future become co-present, thereby allowing us to engage in what Native Hawaiian scholar Manu Meyer calls a racial remembering of the future. Native communities prior to colonization were not structured on the basis of hierarchy, oppression, or patriarchy. We will not recreate these communities as they existed prior to colonization because Native nations are and always have been nations that change and adapt to the surrounding circumstances. However, our understanding that it was possible to order society without structures of oppression in the past tells us that our current political and economic system is anything but natural and inevitable. If we lived differently before, we can live differently in the future. Thus, Native feminist liberation theologies can center less on representing Native women and more on calling all peoples to imagine and to help co-create a future based on the sovereignty and freedom of all peoples.

Notes

1. Andrea Smith, "Bible, Gender and Nationalism in American Indian Christian Right Activism" (PhD diss., University of California, Santa Cruz, 2002), 314, 330.

2. Mavis Etienne, "A Mohawk Peace Maker," *Indian Life* 24, no. 1 (January–February 2004): 8.

3. Quotes that are not cited come from interviews from my research. These interviews are derived primarily from women involved in Women of All Red Nations and the American Indian Movement. All are activists today.

4. Vine Deloria, Jr., *For This Land: Writings on Religion in America* (New York: Routledge, 1999), 100.

5. Ibid., 106.

6. Jace Weaver, *That the People Might Live: Native American Literatures and Native American Comunity* (Oxford: Oxford University Press, 1997), vii.

7. Ibid.

8. William Baldridge, "Toward a Native American Theology," *American Baptist Quarterly* 8 (December 1989): 228.

9. Vine Deloria, Jr., *God is Red: A Native View of Religion* (Delta: New York, 1973), 296–97.

10. Robert Warrior, "Canaanites, Cowboys, and Indians," in *Native and Christian: Indigenous Voices on Religious Identity in the United States and Canada*, ed. James Treat (New York: Routledge, 1996), 99.

11. Ibid.

12. Weaver, *That the People Might Live*, vii. Weaver argues that his work is not theology, "but a work in religious studies." He adds, however, that "the two disciplines are closer than practitioners of the latter would like to admit" (viii).

13. For a book that combines both a history of religions approach with liberation theological reflection, see Gayraud Wilmore, *Black Religion and Black Radicalism: An Interpretation of the Religious History of African Americans* (Maryknoll, NY: Orbis Books, 1996).

14. Émile Durkheim, *The Elementary Forms of Religion*, trans. Karen E. Fields (New York: Free Press, 1995), 420.

15. Ibid., 81.

16. Christopher Ronwaniènte Jocks, "American Indian Religious Traditions and the Academic Study of Religion: A Response to Sam Gill," *Journal of the American Academy of Religion* 65 (Spring 1997): 169–76.

17. Sam Gill, "The Academic Study of Religion," *Journal of the American Academy of Religion* 62 (Winter 1994): 965–75.

18. Jocks, "American Indian Religious Traditions," 169.

19. Gill, "The Academic Study of Religion," 967.

20. Roberto Mendoza, *Look! A Nation is Coming! Native Americans and the Second American Revolution* (Philadelphia: National Organization for an American Revolution, 1984), 8.

21. Warrior, "Canaanites, Cowboys, and Indians," 124.

22. David Batstone, Eduardo Mendieta, Lois Ann Lorentzen, and Dwight N. Hopkins, eds., *Liberation Theologies, Postmodernity, and the Americas* (London: Routledge, 1997), 17.

23. Itumeleng Mosala, "Why Apartheid was Right about the Unliberated Bible," *Voices from the Third World* 17, no. 1 (1994): 158.

24. Rita Nakashima Brock offers a similar analysis of the Bible. "Since I am not an essentialist in my thinking, I do not believe the Bible is inherently patriarchal. It contains a multitude of voices. To identify it uniformly as hopelessly patriarchal gives too much credit to a few elite men" ("Dusting the Bible on the Floor: A Hermeneutics of Wisdom," in *Searching the Scriptures: A Feminist Introduction*, ed. Elisabeth Schüssler Fiorenza [New York: Crossroad, 1993], 71).

25. Emmanuel Martey, *African Theology: Inculturation and Liberation* (Maryknoll, NY: Orbis Books, 1994), 46.

26. Chung Hyun Kyung, *Struggle To Be in the Sun Again: Introducing Asian Women's Theology* (Maryknoll, NY: Orbis Books, 1993), 51.

27. Ibid.,1–9.

28. Other examples of this tendency: Jon Sobrino's *Spirituality of Liberation* is filled with mass generalizations about the poor, such as "The poor accept, at least in fact...that true salvation comes only by way of their own crucifixion," but the basis of his broad-based claims about the theological convictions of "the poor" is not explicated, other than through his personal experience. See Jon Sobrino, *Spirituality of Liberation: Toward Political Holiness* (Maryknoll, NY: Orbis Books, 1988), 34.

29. Lata Mani, "Multiple Mediations: Feminist Scholarship in the Age of Multinational Reception," *Feminist Review* 35 (Summer 1990): 20.

30. Ada María Isasi-Díaz, *Mujerista Theology: A Theology for the Twenty-First Century* (Maryknoll, NY: Orbis Books, 1996), 6–7.

31. Batstone, Lorentzen, and Hopkins, *Liberation Theologies, Postmodernity, and the Americas*, 16.

32. Kimberle Crenshaw, "The Intersection of Race and Gender," in *Critical Race Theory: The Key Writings that Formed the Movement*, ed. Kimberle Crenshaw, Neil Gotanda, Gary Peller, and Kendall Thomas, (New York: New Press, 1996), 375.

33. Lisa Lowe, "Work, Immigration, Gender: New Subjects of Cultural Politics," in *The Politics of Culture in the Shadow of Culture*, ed. Lisa Lowe and David Lloyd (Durham, NC: Duke University Press, 1997), 363.

34. Crenshaw, "The Intersection of Race and Gender," 375.

35. Elizabeth Povinelli, *The Cunning of Recognition: Indigenous Alterities and the Making of Australian Multiculturalism* (Durham, NC: Duke University Press, 2002), 16.

36. Ibid., 29.

37. Fumitaka Matsuoka, *Out of Silence: Emerging Themes in Asian American Churches* (Cleveland: United Church Press, 1995), 93.

38. Crystal Echohawk, "Reflections on Sovereignty," *Indigenous Woman* 3, no. 1 (1999): 21–22.

39. Sharon Venne, "Mining and Indigenous Peoples," *Indigenous Woman* 2, no. 5 (1998): 23–25.

40. Charles Colson and Anne Morse, "The Moral Home Front," *Christianity Today* 48 (October 2004): 152.

41. Joel Belz, "No Preservatives," *World* 19 (May 22, 2004): 8; and Gene Edward Veith, "The Image War," *World* 19 (May 22, 2004): 30–35.

42. Veith, "The Image War," 30–35; Belz, "No Preservatives," 8; and Ted Olsen, "Grave Images," *Christianity Today* 48 (July 2004): 60.

43. Ralph Reed, *After the Revolution* (Dallas, TX: Word, 1990), 231.

44. Ibid., 231, 89.

45. Ann Burlein, *Lift High the Cross: Where White Supremacy and the Christian Right Converge* (Durham, NC: Duke University Press, 2002), 190.

46. Jennifer Denetdale, "Chairmen, Presidents, and Princesses: The Navajo Nation, Gender, and the Politics of Tradition," *Wicazo Sa Review* 21, no. 1 (2006): 9–28.

47. Cathy Cohen, *The Boundaries of Blackness: AIDS and the Breakdown of Black Politics* (Chicago: University of Chicago Press, 1999).

PART 2

Scripture

Words

Words that jump, that skip and that play
Words with body, everyday words
Words that sparkle with experiences, biographies, realities
Contextualities, movements, rhythms
Women, life, wisdom

Words that lament and that shout
Words weighty with suffering and complaint
Word: protest
Empire, poverty, Babylon
Women, life, wisdom

Words that flow, that evoke and that name
Indian, black, white, *mestiza*
Foremothers...
Words that cross borders
De-northing: *Nepantla, Chacana*
Women, life, wisdom

Words that disrupt and disturb
Ambiguity, deconstruction, obscurity, clarity
Word: feminism
Women, life, wisdom
Words that embrace, that convoke, that defy
Word: silence

"Words" by Maricel Mena-López and the "Feminist Intercultural Theology" symposium participants, in *Feminist Intercultural Theology: Latina Exploration for a Just World*, ed. María Pilar Aquino and Maria José Rosado-Nunes (Maryknoll, NY: Orbis Books, 2007), 23.

Liberty, empowerment, community
Women, life, wisdom

Words that jump, that skip and that play
Creativity, poetry, imagination
Dream, demand
Celebration, feast
Women, life, wisdom

5

TOWARD A POST-COLONIAL FEMINIST INTERPRETATION OF THE BIBLE

Musa W. Dube (Botswana)

Introduction

To read the Bible as a Motswana African woman is to read a Western book. For many years, I have known that "biblical Christian believers" refers to white Western believers while "pagans" refers to all non-Christian Africans.[1] I have related well to Matthew 23 and the "foolish Galatians" in Galatians 3:1, not reading Galatians and Pharisees as static historical persons but as a reference to all those who are not Christians. The rebuttal of the Pharisees in Matthew 23 has carried a painful fascination for me, for what I heard from this passage was not an old first-century story, but a familiar drama of nineteenth-twentieth century imperialist history affecting all non-Christian Africans.

What may seem to be a gross misreading and mistaken identities of biblical characters can be contested. Some may link these things to the orality of my background. Yet oral societies can read paintings. The image of Jesus was and still is that of a blue-eyed, blonde, white male, whose benevolent face, along with the similar white faces of his disciples, still grace our churches today. The image of Mary the mother of Jesus was and is that of a white woman.[2] The devil was, of course, a black, horned man (I do not know what color he is these days). Heaven was cast in Western terrain, with a riotous fusion of all Western seasons in one painting. With all these images, my misreading and mistaken identities go beyond the orality of my African background. Undoubtedly, this reading grid has a historical base, which, to my surprise, has resisted erosion from my many years of biblical studies.

This exposition highlights the fact that different readers act out the biblical story in different ways at different times in history. The Western

Musa W. Dube, "Toward a Post-Colonial Feminist Interpretation of the Bible," *Semeia* 78 (1997): 11–26.

imperial readers of the nineteenth and twentieth centuries wrote themselves into the text and characterized non-Christians as their pagan counterparts in order to validate the latter's subjugation. Recently, a wide range of readers, from textual ones to flesh and blood ones, has featured in biblical interpretation. However, biblical interpretation has yet to integrate various historical biblical readers from different points in the Christian history of the last nineteen hundred and ninety-six years. In short, the question of how different flesh and blood readers have acted out the biblical story in history, and how their act illumines some meaning of the text needs to be integrated into academic biblical studies.

The biblical story itself invites its readers to identify with it and to act it out in history. In John 20:21, for example, the resurrected Christ says, "As my Father sent me so I send you." Encapsulated in this sending is transference of power from Jesus to his disciples. The transference is a call to his hearers, readers, and believers to act out his story with almost the same authority that has characterized the Johannine Jesus. Furthermore, this transference of power, at least as it stands in the gospels (Matt 28:18–20; Luke 24:46–47) suggests that the biblical story is an unfinished story: it invites its own continuation in history; it resists the covers of our Bibles and writes itself on the pages of the earth. On these grounds, it is legitimate to hold that various biblical reader-actors, from different moments in history, should illumine the meaning and implications of the text for us.

Biblical scholars have in fact noted that the text, as we have it, already represents a drama of believers. What the narrative presents as Jesus speaking with his disciples represents the act of the first- and second-century believers. Analyzing John's text, Louis Martyn has termed this phenomenon a "two-level drama." Martyn points out that this drama did not end with Jesus' departure or the composition of the texts; rather, it continues in the person of the paraclete, operating through believers. Martyn holds that "in order for the paraclete to create the two-level drama, he must look not only like Jesus, but also like the Christian witness who is Jesus' double in that drama."[3] Consequently, it seems to me that to insist on dwelling on one historical time in this biblical drama, ignoring the continuing character of the story, is to do injustice to that very text.

Given that I come from a historical experience of the Bible functioning as an imperialist text, I know that the biblical story is a story that is acted out in history. I have, therefore, journeyed with some sense of injustice and emptiness in my academic biblical studies, where the Bible became an antiqued text, firmly contextualized in ancient times. As a biblical student, I wrestled with issues behind or in front of the text, and, sometimes, I dealt with the first three centuries. In short, I found academic biblical interpretation divorced from its historical reader-actors of the nineteenth and twentieth centuries. The approach bracketed my questions and my experience.

To be sure, this approach of situating biblical studies in ancient times has facilitated many liberating and helpful discoveries for me. For a start, it was liberating to know that biblical texts are not Anglo-Saxon books, but Jewish texts. It was also helpful to know that far from being pure (as the modern colonial Christian agents claimed), early Christianity borrowed from the non-Christian cultures of its origin. Nevertheless, I have discovered that the privileging of the ancient historical setting in the academic interpretation of the Bible is a powerful tool that divorces my experience and my questions from the field. By privileging the ancient history in biblical interpretation, the biblical texts are perfectly shielded from its various historical reader-actors. The question of confronting the imperialist manifestation of the text is neatly bracketed. However, as Ulrich Luz points out, biblical "texts have power and cannot be separated from their consequences," and, as he further notes, "Christianity, as we all know it, is far from a history of loving your enemies."[4] For me to read the Bible as an African woman and from my experience, therefore, is to be inevitably involved with the historical events of imperialism. Indeed, to read the Bible as an African is to take a perilous journey, a sinister journey that spins one back to connect with dangerous memories of slavery,[5] colonialism, apartheid, and neo-colonialism. To read the Bible as an African is to relive the painful equation of Christianity with civilization, paganism with savagery.

Luckily, early feminist readers insisted on women's experience as a valid interpretive framework.[6] My African experience has taught me that the biblical characters shift and change with time so that what were "foolish Galatians" (Gal. 3:1) may be "savage Africans," in one context and time, and something else in another; moreover, that such labels have an adverse impact upon those tagged with them. My experience has taught me that a written book does not only belong to its authors—it also belongs to its readers and users;[7] and that the history of the biblical story is not limited to the first three centuries; hence, the selection of one particular historical period as the prime reference for determining textual meaning in biblical studies is not innocent.[8] I am historically situated within this framework of facts and experiences. I, therefore, read the Bible as a black Motswana woman from the region of southern Africa, a student of religion, a survivor of colonialism, who lives in a *luta continua* (a continuous struggle) against neo-colonialism. The latter refers to "the creation of a single international (global) financial or capital market," which is impoverishing most Two-Thirds World countries with huge debts.[9] My analysis is both feminist and post-colonial.

Post-colonial, as used here, is a literary, technical term defining the setting, the use, and the classification of texts.[10] In terms of setting, it covers the period beginning with the arrival and occupation of an imperial power, the struggle against it, independence, and post-independence—a continuity that remains valid with the persistence of imperial domination.[11]

Further, as Homi Bhabha points out, post-colonial does not only define sequentiality or polarity between colonialism and independence; rather, it is a "gesture to the beyond" that seeks to "transform the present into an expanded and ex-centric site of experience and empowerment."[12] Put differently, post-colonial is not a discourse of historical accusations, but a committed search and struggle for decolonization and liberation of the oppressed. In terms of classification, it refers to a complex collection of texts that are brought, born, and used in imperial settings, to legitimate, resist, or collaborate with imperialism. While this definition is an umbrella term that includes the texts of the colonizer and the colonized, the phrase "colonial discourse" is also used to distinguish the former from the latter.[13] As an umbrella term, a post-colonial approach is best understood as a complex myriad of methods and theories that study a wide range of texts and their participation in the making or subversion of imperialism.

Although colonizing texts are mainly written by the colonizer, they also arise from the colonized. Depending on different interest groups and stages of imperial domination, the colonized can condone their oppressors, cooperate with them, or totally reject them. Since imperialism actively adopts structural strategies of assimilation or colonizing the mind, collaboration among some circles of the colonized is unavoidable. The imperialist strategy of "control-at-a-distance,"[14] for instance, engages some local groups (usually the upper class) to become its ruling representatives, and this conceals the face of the imperial oppressor among the colonized. Local groups that choose to revolt, in turn, come to fight the collaborating group but, sometimes they also come to compete for the attention of the oppressor among themselves. The enemy and its opponents are thus fully embodied within the colonized nation, a fact that is usually reflected in the wide range of texts produced in such settings.

Post-colonial theoretical frameworks were mainly developed from the analysis of nineteenth and twentieth century literature, upon the realization that texts were powerful tools for either buttressing or counteracting imperial powers. Given that imperialism has been a recurring phenomenon in the history of the world, post-colonial applicability to various other classical texts in the human history is legitimate. Its application should, indeed, open new ways to understand most of the canonized classical texts, as to how they may reflect the imperial values of their origins and how these texts have functioned in various empires that have risen and fallen in history.

Imperialism, as used here, describes the tendencies of metropolitan centers to impose their images, ideas, religions, economic structures, and political control in foreign lands.[15] Colonialism is a political manifestation of imperialism when it includes geographical control. Imperialism, however, does not always include colonialism, nor does it end with independence. The current situation of neo-colonialism/globalization indicates that imperialism does not have to include geographical possession.

In view of the fact that Christian biblical religion has been "unique in its imperial sponsorship,"[16] in ancient and current times and over different people and different places, the Bible is also a colonizing text: it has repeatedly authorized the subjugation of foreign nations and lands. Further, in view of the fact that the New Testament and many other Hebrew Bible books were born in imperialist settings, they are post-colonial books. On these grounds, I shall briefly expound on reading the Bible from a post-colonial literary perspective. In particular, I read it from my historical background as an imperial/colonial text. Then, I shall explore the intersection and implications of post-colonial and feminist reading in biblical studies. In my conclusion, I shall propose that in the post-colonial era feminist biblical readers must also become decolonizing readers.

What Is a Post-Colonial Reading of Texts?

Among its many methods, a post-colonial reading may analyze the literary constructions of colonizing texts and how they function to justify imperialism. The analysis may focus on the construction of characters, geography, travelers, gender, and unspoken intentions to highlight how these work in justifying the domination of one by another. Usually, the narrative texts construct both the colonizer and the colonized to accept the legitimacy of their respective positions. Post-colonial literary analysis, however, includes the works of decolonizing reader-writers who adopt various strategies to counteract the violence of imperialism.[17] The following exposition, however, illustrates only some of the literary constructions in colonizing texts, that is, texts designed to take possession of the minds and lands of those who are different.

To begin with characterization, the colonized and colonizer are sharply contrasted in colonizing literature. The subjugated are depicted as helpless, evil, inarticulate, backward, disorganized, lazy, exotic, and babies in need of instruction.[18] Such characters are put side by side with those in control: civilized, Christian, articulate, literate, and cultivated teachers. The contrast serves to validate the domination of the former by the latter.

Geographically, the setting of imperial narratives communicates the same ideology.[19] Some lands are depicted as empty, unoccupied, and waiting to be discovered. Some lands assume the symbol of light and holiness, while the others represent darkness, disease, and evil. The narratives also construct their readers to accept as normal the fact that someone (usually a white man) owns plantations, mines, or farms on other continents, populated and run by native servants. The geography of these narratives generally exhibits a universal and global outlook that invites expansion and relationships of domination and subjugation between nations.

Traveling is also central to colonial narratives. A few travelers,[20] mainly from the metropolitan centers, enter foreign lands. These travelers are notably authoritative strangers, who are not ignorant or dependent upon their hosts. The travelers' authority is grounded in race, religion, technology, and knowledge. They are marked by their power to see deficiency everywhere and to right this deficiency by teaching or structurally developing the colonized people to depend on them. The subjugated may travel to the lands of their masters, but as powerless strangers, such as exiles, slaves, servants, students, or refugees who depend on the benevolence of their masters.[21]

It is characteristic of colonizing texts to present an extremely gendered perspective of their subject.[22] The colonized lands are to be "entered," "penetrated," and subjugated. The colonized are symbolized by their indigenous women, who epitomize all backwardness, evil, and helplessness. The colonizers' civilization is symbolized by their women as well, who become the measure of their civilization.[23] The general picture is that imperialism is a male game with women characters articulating men's power positions in it.

It is also characteristic of colonizing texts to conceal their material interests. Nineteenth- and twentieth-century imperialism, for instance, was a power struggle of Western empires prompted by the need to create markets overseas and to import raw materials for their growing industries, but this factor was neatly wrapped in rhetorical terms such as "the duty to the natives." Imperialism was thus presented as a moral vocation to those in need of help; it hardly acknowledged its economic motivation. The hidden motives enabled the subjugated to accept their positions to some extent and the colonizers to remain firmly convinced of their good intentions even in the face of overt violence.

In sum, post-colonial texts are born in settings of intense power struggle and they articulate that struggle. In particular, colonizing texts present relationships of profound inequality, they are driven by expansionist aims, they exhibit fear of difference, they promote the authority of certain traveling strangers, and they have the tendency to disguise their economic interests under moral claims. In the words of Jerry Phillips:

> Imperialism—a system of economic, political, and cultural force that disavows borders in order to extract desirable resources and exploit an alien people—has never strayed far from a field of pedagogical imperatives, or what might be called an ideology of instruction. Christianity, Progress, Democracy, or whatever is the prevailing imperialist version of history demands of certain cultures, nations, or "chosen" races that they subject those who fall radically short of the ideal state. Subject people are "savage,"

"infantile," "untutored," "backward" or simply "underdeveloped"; as the imperialist encounters them, a model of their "uplift" is always thus entailed.[24]

Given the global impact of imperialism and its persistence, post-colonial theorists argue that its models of relationships are among the many bedrocks of oppression in most canonized texts of literature. They point out that the bracketing of imperialism as a category in Western academic schools serves to maintain the potency of these oppressive images in our thinking as well as to justify the subjugation of some nations and lands by the imperialistic metropolitan centers.[25] For this reason, I turn to arguing for the integration of post-colonial analysis into the liberationist vision of feminist biblical readers.

Intersecting Feminism and Post-Colonialism in Our Practice

With regard to white Western feminism and post-colonialism, it has been noted that the former often brackets imperialism in its analysis of male texts, or operates within imperialist frameworks of power.[26] In her book *Decolonizing Feminisms*, Laura Donaldson highlights that feminist readers use "anti-sexist rhetoric to displace questions of colonialism, racism, and their concomitant violence."[27] Donaldson points out that some feminists have theorized that man=colonizer and woman's body=colonized, a metaphorical articulation that, she notes, can be theoretically defended, but one that often fails to address colonialism as a form of oppression.[28] The latter position often obscures the fact that Western women were and are equally involved in and benefit from the imperialist oppression of Two-Thirds World women, a position that is still economically and politically in place.

The question for feminist biblical practitioners, therefore, is how to integrate post-colonial insights into their liberation discourse. Given the imperialist setting of New Testament literature, I would propose that it is imperative for feminist inclusive readings to be more suspicious of imperialism legitimation. If, for example, Matthew characterizes Pilate's wife as a prophetic woman in the trial of Jesus, an inclusive reading must be wary that this positive construction may not necessarily articulate a liberative inclusion of an outsider woman; rather, it may serve to legitimate the imperialist presence by presenting it as holy and acceptable. Elaine Wainwright's feminist inclusive reading of Matthew, for example, demonstrates insufficient suspicion toward the implied author's motivations in constructing Pilate's wife as a divine agent.[29]

Paying attention to the imperialist setting of the New Testament will also necessitate a more careful assessment of inclusive versus exclusive traditions. In this setting of a struggle for power and survival against imperial forces, an "inclusive" impulse may signal an imperialist collaboration, while an "exclusive" approach may signal a strategic resistance to imperialist powers. For instance, interpretations of Matthew 10:5–6, 15:24, and 28:18–20 must weigh out these alternatives within a Roman setting of imperialist occupation and resistance. When post-colonial analysis is integrated, the celebration of "Christian inclusiveness" versus "Jewish exclusiveness" in an imperial setting may have to be re-evaluated.[30] A post-colonial analysis necessitates identifying the Roman Empire as the enemy and the Jewish emphasis on cultural boundaries as one of strategic resistance in the face of imposed political leadership, religion, images, languages, and taxes.[31] This framework immediately calls into question the vision of Matthew 28:18–20. That is, if the Jewish people of Matthew's time were struggling to maintain their cultural boundaries against the intrusion of the Roman Empire, does not Matthew's opening of boundaries, his agenda of discipling the whole world according to the commands of Christ, indicate a collaborative stance? Matthew's command to Christianize the world ironically befriends the Roman Empire's political and cultural imposition of its structures on Jewish people and all its colonized subjects. It is when we remind ourselves that first-century Palestinian Jews were struggling to survive against the Roman Empire that Matthew's universal commission becomes a suspicious agenda—one that is driven by competition with other local groups for power and one that is consistent with the imperial ideology of disavowing boundaries and claiming cultural authority over foreign people and lands then resisting imperialism. In turn, the questioning of Matthew's worldwide agenda also helps us to understand why Christian missions (read reader-believer-actor of the Christian texts) have functioned compatibly with imperialist agendas of their countries. It also calls for a post-colonial feminist reimagining of Christian mission texts.

Similarly, the gendered construction of imperialist narratives is evident in the featuring of female characters of questionable morality and status in stories representing the penetration of other lands. A good example is Rahab, the prostitute, who becomes the point of contact in the possession of Jericho. Likewise, in both John and Matthew the Samaritan and Canaanite woman are featured in stories foreshadowing the universal mission, that is, the penetration of other lands. Both these women are characterized as either helpless or immoral, symbolizing the status of their own people and thus authorizing the subjugation of their lands. Although these women are celebrated by feminists, a post-colonial analysis detects an ideology of subjugation that proceeds by negative labeling and the use of the female gender to articulate relations of subordination and domination.

A post-colonial analysis also indicates that gender experiences in imperialist settings are different, depending on one's relation to the imperialist powers. Among the subjugated groups, women are burdened by two patriarchal systems, the national and the metropolitan one. As the national patriarchal system resists the intrusion of a foreign power, the call for protection of tradition intensifies gender constructions.[32] The enemy is the outsider and resistance calls women and men to remain faithful to national traditions. In intertestamental times, both Essenes and Pharisees are representative of this type of resistance. However, the opposite response is also common. In various revolutions and in struggles against imperialism, gender roles are often relaxed for some time, until the groups are established. Thereafter women are put back to their original place. The Jesus movement and the early church represent this type of resistance.

While women on the side of the imperialist automatically belong to a higher class, race, and sometimes religion, they still remain male objects. As attested by the biblical examples of Herod's and Pilate's wives, they are subject to male constructions in the maintenance of male power. Nonetheless, the issues of class, race, and religion are still factors of difference among the colonized and the colonizer women. Thus a feminist inclusive reading cannot equate the experience of Pilate's wife with that of the mother of Andrew, the son of Zebedee, without taking into account the former's imperialist status of exploiter and oppressor.

This brings me to a crucial question: Which feminist should read from a post-colonial perspective? As the above comments indicate, imperialism has affected all of us and its narratives construct both the powerful and the powerless—all of those who pass through formal education are inducted to accept their positions. Therefore, imperialism involves both Western and Two-Thirds World women, women of color and white women, developed and the so-called underdeveloped countries, precisely because imperialism was and still is a global event and conception that has left little or no place untouched; hence, it informs our perception of the Other.

No doubt Two-Thirds World women suffer more from imperialist intrusion; hence, they are more conscious of it. Western feminist readers, on the other hand, benefit from their social location. They can, consciously or unconsciously, bracket out a post-colonial analysis. The bracketing, however, does not only speak of one's privileged position; it also plays into the maintenance of imperialist metropolitan centers' constructions, and, worse, it hinders building "political coalitions" of resistance among feminists of various cultural persuasions.[33]

Reading for Decolonization

Among biblical and theological feminist readers, the challenge to read post-colonially for decolonization, that is, the struggle to counter imperialist violence and to seek liberating ways of interdependence, is often presented by women from Two-Thirds World settings. William R. Hutchinson, for instance, writes that "Christianity as it existed in the

West had a right not only to conquer the world but to define reality for other peoples of the world."[34] Rosemary Edet and Bette Ekeya point out that among African people there is "alienation because evangelization has not been that of cultural exchange but of cultural domination and assimilation."[35] This challenge calls for a feminist reading that does not only recover or reconstruct women's participation in early church history, but also strives to re-envision the Christian mission. For instance, how do passages like Matthew 28:18–20, Luke 24:46–47, and John 20:21 construct the power relations in the encounter with the Other? Do they propose relationships of liberating interdependence[36] between races, genders, cultures, and nations or do they propose a model of unequal inclusion? Kwok Pui-lan, grappling with the biblical models of international exchange, has suggested a "dialogical model of truth," whereby two different and equal subjects meet, and their word to each other is, "What treasures do you have to share?"[37] Such an invitation does not encounter the Other as a blank slate to be filled.

Therefore, conscious awareness of the fact that biblical texts were born in an imperialist setting and have been unique in sponsoring imperialist agendas over different times and people needs to be integrated in our feminist reading for liberation. This requires recognizing that many women in biblical religions also belong to Native American religions, African religions, and Asian religions; that this position is not only intricately related to imperialism, but must also inform our practice. This recognition implies that we are here as women in biblical religion together *with* our Other canons, written and unwritten, and they demand to be heard and read in their own right. I emphasize "other canons" because imperialism proceeds by denying the validity of the narratives and values of its victims, while it imposes its own "master narratives" on them. Furthermore, most of us experienced the Christian mission not as a liberating egalitarian movement, but as a divinely authorized patriarchal and imperial program that subjugates all those who are not Christian. Consequently, unless feminist liberation readers want to stand in continuum with the imperialist "right" of the West "to define reality for other people," the challenge is with us. It is imperative for the "women-church"[38] to become a post-colonial open-space and to read for decolonization—a practice that recognizes that we are already inscribed within an established tradition of imperial domination, collaboration, and resistance. To read for decolonization, therefore, is to consciously resist the exploitative forces of imperialism, to affirm the denied differences, and to seek liberating ways of interdependence in our multicultural and post-colonial world.

In this post-colonial interpretive open-space, feminist decolonizing readings should encourage "solidarity in multiplicity." Donaldson defines solidarity in multiplicity as a "story field" that affirms "stories" and "demands that each story negotiate its position in relation to all other stories included within the field, which in turn must recalculate their own position."[39] To translate the approach to feminist academic biblical studies, it calls for a practice of reading, imagining, and retelling biblical stories in negotiation with other religious stories in the post-colonial era. Anything short of this risks maintaining the "right" of the Christian biblical stories to remain at the highest peak of the hierarchy—a hierarchy sustained through the suppression of all other religious stories and the oppression of Two-Thirds World women.

How Can We Know and Respect the Other?[40]

Evidently, the main objective of a decolonizing reading is beyond just providing a deconstructive analysis that exposes the imperialist construction embedded in narratives. A decolonizing reading's main objective is liberation. It asks the question: "How can we know and respect the Other?" It is a struggle to conceive models that are not built along the lines of relegating all differences to deficiency. It is a struggle to build bridges for liberating interdependence cross-culturally. It is the desire to begin what have been termed "difficult dialogues,"[41] that is, to encounter and to dialogue with the different Other on a level of different and equal subjects.

At this level, a post-colonial feminist who reads for decolonization will ask how the Christian texts construct and legitimate encounters with people of different faith, race, gender, and sexuality. The phrase "difficult dialogues," indeed, accepts the fact that the construction of our narratives, hence, our thinking of the Other, has primarily operated on what Jerry Phillips has shown to be a denigrate and "uplift" model. In this imperialist model we have an aggressive inclusion but not equality. Consequently, to engage in cultivating "difficult dialogues," feminist readers must indeed become decolonizing readers: they must demonstrate awareness of imperialism as a persistent and exploitative force at a global scale, they must demonstrate a conscious adoption of resistance to imperialism, and they must struggle to map liberating ways of interdependence in our multicultural world. To bracket decolonizing is only to maintain the imperial strategies of exploitation and subjugation and to hinder building the necessary "political coalitions" among feminists of different cultures, nations, colors, classes, and sexuality.

Conclusion

In sum, the Bible as a Western book is bound to its imperialist history of subjugation and oppression. This imperialist history has constructed all of us, and its reality cannot be bracketed from our critical practice without perpetuating the history of unequal inclusion. The biblical story is at times a travel narrative; it commands its readers to travel. Consequently, the privileging of one historical time, the ancient times, in determining its meaning is ideologically suspect. Moreover, women in biblical religion also stand in other religions. The challenge, therefore, is to become decolonizing readers who seek to build true conversations of equal subjects in our post-colonial and multicultural world. Without overlooking the differences of race, sexuality, religion, and class, I am proposing that our critical practice should be multicultural in a post-colonial open-space of women of the world as equal subjects.

Notes

1. I do not consent to the use of "Africa" insofar as it implies a uniform people. My reading is representative of neither Africa nor of Botswana, my country. Africa is too large and diverse to be represented by one person's view. I am using this category insofar as I find it heavily imposed on me by the First World and because it has come to be representative of our common oppression.

2. As the new African American Bible indicates, these images are still being contested.

3. J. Louis Martyn, *History and Theology in the Fourth Gospel* (Nashville: Abingdon Press, 1979), 148.

4. Ulrich Luz points to such atrocities as the Holocaust and links them with the interpretation of the biblical text; see *Matthew in History: Interpretation, Influence, and Effects* (Minneapolis, MN: Fortress Press, 1994), 33.

5. See Katie Geneva Cannon, "Slave Ideology and Biblical Interpretation," *Semeia* 47 (1987): 9–23, on the Christian justification of the enslavement of Africans.

6. Although the category of feminist "experience" is being correctly problematized, it empowered many of us to voice our perspectives where the traditional approach insisted on neutral and disinterested methods of reading.

7. In fact, current reading theories that insist on the reader as the maker of meaning support my assertion.

8. Mary Ann Tolbert contests this dwelling on "purer origins" by pointing out that it treats those who do not share this history as somehow less important. See Mary Ann Tolbert, "Protestant Feminists and the Bible: On the Horns of a Dilemma," in *The Pleasure of Her Text: Feminist Readings of Biblical and Historical Texts*, ed. Alice Bach (Philadelphia: Trinity International, 1990), 5–23.

9. Christopher Lind, *Something's Wrong Somewhere: Globalization, Community and the Moral Economy of the Farm Crisis* (Halifax: Fernwood, 1995), 31.

10. I am grateful to Fernando Segovia for introducing me to post-colonial theories.

11. Bill Ashcroft, Gareth Griffiths, and Helen Tiffin, eds., *The Post-colonial Studies Reader* (New York: Routledge, 1995), 2.

12. Homi K. Bhabha, *The Location of Culture* (London: Routledge, 1995), 4.

13. Patrick Williams and Laura Chrisman, eds., *Colonial Discourse and Post-colonial Theory: A Reader* (New York: Columbia University Press, 1994), 5.

14. James M. Blaut, *The Colonizer's Model of the World: Geographical Diffusionism and Eurocentric History* (New York: Guilford, 1993), 70.

15. Edward W. Said, *Culture and Imperialism* (New York: Alfred A. Knopf, 1993), 9–13.

16. Wayne Meeks, *The First Urban Christians: The Social World of the Apostle Paul* (New Haven: Yale University Press, 1983), 1.

17. Barbara Harlow, *Resistance Literature* (New York: Methuen, 1987), 1–75; and Said, *Culture and Imperialism*, 191–262.

18. For examples of explicit literary colonizing constructions, see Joseph Conrad, *Heart of Darkness* and *The Secret Sharer* (New York: Bantam Books, 1981; originally printed in 1902); Rudyard Kipling, "The White Man's Burden," in *The Imperialism Reader*, ed. Louis Snyder (New York: Van Nostrand, 1962), 87–88.

19. Blaut, *The Colonizer's Model*, 69–90; and Said, *Culture and Imperialism*, 3–43.

20. The number of colonizing travelers is crucial, for it can determine the type and intensity of colonialism experienced by the colonized. For example, in areas where colonizing travelers flooded a colony such as North America, South Africa, Canada, or Australia, it led to settler colonialism, which tended to override the native groups.

21. See Fernando F. Segovia, "Toward a Hermeneutics of the Diaspora: A Hermeneutics of Otherness and Engagement," in *Reading from This Place*, vol. 1, *Social Location and Biblical Interpretation in the United States*, ed. Fernando F. Segovia and Mary Ann Tolbert (Minneapolis, MN: Fortress Press, 1995), 57–73, on the position of Hispanic-Americans in metropolitan centers of North America.

22. David Quint, *Epic and Empire* (Princeton: Princeton University Press, 1993), 31–41; Rene Maunier, *The Sociology of Colonies: An Introduction to the Study of Colonies*, vol.1 (London: Routledge, 1949), 70; and Williams and Chrisman, *Colonial Discourse*, 194.

23. Margaret Strobel, *European Women and the Second British Empire* (Bloomington, IN: Indiana University Press, 1991), 1–15.

24. Jerry Phillips, "Educating the Savages: Melville, Bloom, and the Rhetoric of Imperialist Tradition," in *Recasting the World: Writing after Colonialism*, ed. Jonathan White (Baltimore: Johns Hopkins University Press, 1993), 26.

25. Chinua Achebe, *Hopes and Impediments: Selected Essays* (New York: Doubleday, 1989), 1–20; Said, *Culture and Imperialism*, 41-43, 60-61.

26. Audre Lorde, *Sister Outsider: Essays and Speeches* (Trumansburg, NJ: Crossing Press, 1984), 66–71; Chandra Mohanty, "Under Western Eyes: Feminist Scholarship and Colonial Discourses," in *Third World Women and the Politics of Feminism*, ed. Chandra Mohanty, Ann Russo, and Lourdes Torres (Bloomington: Indiana University Press, 1991), 51–80.

27. Laura E. Donaldson, *Decolonizing Feminisms: Race, Gender, and Empire-building* (Chapel Hill: University of North Carolina Press, 1992), 62.

28. Ibid., 4–6.

29. Elaine Wainwright, *Towards a Feminist Critical Reading of the Gospel according to Matthew* (Berlin: de Gruyter, 1991), 285–86.

30. I am aware that rigid nationalism is oppressive even to its own people, but more especially to women. Nonetheless, nationalistic movements of the colonized must be seen within their contexts as a strategy of resisting the bigger enemy and as a temporary phase. Indeed, many colonized nations of the modern era adopted and used this strategy effectively.

31. Richard A. Horsley, *Jesus and the Spiral of Violence: Popular Jewish Resistance in Roman Palestine* (Minneapolis, MN: Fortress Press. 1993), 1–116.

32. Harlow, *Resistance Literature*, 28–30.

33. Mary Ann Tolbert, "Politics and Poetics of Location," in *Reading From This Place*, vol. 1, 312–14.

34. William R. Hutchinson, "A Moral Equivalent for Imperialism: Americans and the Promotion of Christian Civilization, 1880–1910," in *Missionary Ideologies in the Imperialist Era: 1880–1920*, ed. Torben Christensen and William R. Hutchinson (Aarhus: Aras, 1982), 172, as cited in Kwok Pui-lan, "Discovering the Bible in the Non-biblical World," in *Voices from the Margin: Interpreting the Bible in the Third World*, ed. R. S. Sugirtharajah (Maryknoll, NY: Orbis Books, 1991), 303.

35. Rosemary Edet and Bette Ekeya, "Church Women of Africa: A Theological Community," in *With Passion and Compassion: Third World Women Doing Theology*, ed. Virginia Fabella and Mercy Amba Oduyoye (Maryknoll, NY: Orbis Books, 1988), 3.

36. Said, *Culture and Imperialism*, 3–43, 303–36.

37. Kwok, "Discovering," 313.

38. Elisabeth Schüssler Fiorenza uses the term "women-church" to describe a feminist hermeneutical center; see "The Will to Choose or to Reject: Continuing Our Critical Work," in *Feminist Interpretation of the Bible*, ed. Letty M. Russell (Philadelphia: Westminster Press, 1985), 126–27. I am extending the boundaries of this center because for survivors of imperialism the invitation to inhabit the "ekklesia," the white male, most hierarchical and exclusive of centers, dangerously befriends the ideology of imperialism that invites its subjects to yearn for their standards even as it structurally denies them access, while at the same time denying the colonized their difference. The colonized, in other words, can enter the "ekklesia" if they forego their cultures, pursue those of their masters, or agree that their own cultural values are inferior.

39. Donaldson, *Decolonizing Feminisms*, 139.

40. See Williams and Chrisman, *Colonial Discourse*, 8. This is Edward Said's central question in his postcolonial work.

41. Jerry Phillips traces this term to Johnella Butler ("Difficult Dialogues," in *Women's Review of Books* 6, no. 5 [1989]: 16) who used it to describe "cultural negotiation between opposing ends of the earth" and Phillips uses it to point out that "for too long we have not listened to what others have to say." See Phillips, "Educating the Savages," 40–41.

6

DALIT WOMEN AND THE BIBLE

Hermeneutical and Methodological Reflections

Monica Jyotsna Melanchthon (India)

Introduction

Women in India have been reading biblical texts for several centuries but obviously with little consciousness about reading them as women or more particularly as Indian women. Because of its cultural and religious authority, the Bible has often been used to define women's place in church and society. As the basis of Christian revelation and faith, the Christian scriptures reflect women's strength as well as their subordination. But of late has come the recognition that the Bible has played a very significant role in shaping the conditions of a woman's life and that the Bible is often an instrument and a political weapon against women's liberation. Since this is true of other religious scriptures as well, it is necessary that women of all religious backgrounds start rereading their scriptures as a way of reclaiming their histories. The contents of the Bible are not accidental or the result of an alteration of the written text. That the Bible was shaped in a male-dominated and androcentric world, that councils of men shaped the canon itself, and that, over the centuries, male theologians and scholars interpreted texts that were considered to subordinate women are accepted facts. It is therefore a difficult and complex task to reconsider those texts from the perspective of women and bring to the fore an interpretation that reveals God's concern for the whole of humanity. Besides, it has been proven that the oppressed often internalize the ideals and values of the oppressor, and women are much more apt to do this because of their belief in scripture as the divine and

Monica Melanchthon, "Indian Dalit Women and the Bible: Hermeneutical and Methodological Reflections," in *Gender, Religion and Diversity: Cross-Cultural Perspectives*, ed. Ursula King and Tina Beattie (New York: Continuum, 2004), 212–24. Revised version.

revealed word of God. Hence, often, women are highly resistant to feminist interpretations.

It has been acknowledged that in the Indian context a cultural and political reform is downright impossible without a critical rereading of the scriptures. It needs to be somehow impressed upon women and men that many of the biblical statements that are considered oppressive are not necessarily factual or normative, nor do they reflect reality, but are often the wishful projections of male authors in situations where it was felt that women needed to be controlled since women were more assertive and successful. That it is only in retrospect, after women have been successfully "put in their place," that such oppressive statements appear as factual and gain the authority of norms. Thus, we have to read the scriptures from the perspective of the defeated whose defeat we do not accept as ultimate. We approach our faith from the underside of history, of God's people—we read from the perspective of woman. But which Indian woman?

Which Indian Christian Woman?

One of the most outstanding contributions of the anthropology of women has been its persistent analysis of gender symbols and sexual stereotypes. A major problem facing researchers in this area is how to explain both the enormous observable variation in cultural understandings of what the categories "man" and "woman" mean and the fact that certain notions about gender appear in a wide range of different societies. Sherry Ortner explains,

> Much of the creativity of anthropology derives from the tension between two sets of demands that we explain human universals, and that we explain cultural particulars. By this canon, woman provides us with one of the more challenging problems to be dealt with. The secondary status of woman in society is one of the true universals, a pan-cultural fact. Yet within that universal fact, the specific cultural conceptions and symbolizations of women are extraordinarily diverse and even mutually contradictory. Further the actual treatment of women and their relative power and contribution [varies] enormously from culture to culture, and over different periods in the history of particular cultural traditions. Both of these points—the universal fact and the cultural variation—constitute problems to be explained.[1]

Each society frames its concept of woman in relation to that of man; "thus woman/female/feminine are what is not man/not male/not masculine."[2] Our question in India is "what constitutes a 'woman' in the

church, given the differences in class, language, caste and culture?"
Whose list of categories does the institution adopt? What does it mean
to be female/woman in the Indian church today? Can a mixed group
comprised of varied castes, religions, languages, and cultural affiliations
answer this question? It is a question with many different answers for
women of the church in India that is located in different contexts—socially, culturally, and theologically. The need for gathering these different understandings by women has not even been felt. Where such a
process might lead us no one knows, but a church that claims to stand
in partnership with women should support such a quest. Instead the Indian church as a whole still maintains a biased view of women in general, and is therefore not able to hear what the women who do not fit
its categories have been and are saying. Lorraine Code considers the
way women are often not believed when giving witness or testifying.
She suggests that

> "truths" of the most compelling kind can simply fail to compel
> assent when the available rhetorical spaces are either closed
> against them, or so constrained in the possibilities they offer that
> what is "really" being said is slotted automatically into cate-
> gories, ready-made places, where the fit is at best crude, at worst
> distorting and damaging.[3]

She quotes society's common categories of women, categories that serve
to "tame" the "newness," the "unsettling effects," and the "danger" of
what other women are saying. The woman from whose perspective I
would like to look at the issue is that of the Indian Dalit woman.

Who Is the Indian Dalit Woman?

Dalit Women—Society's Firewood

The lives of Dalit women
Are tales of woe and agony
The darkness of unjust fate
Clothes their shame and misery

We rise up long before dawn
And run to our masters' houses
To clean and serve and hurry over
To their fields and our daily labor

We return at dusk, stumbling
Weary and anxious, to feed our

Starving families huddled in our huts
But alas, empty handed and helpless.

Exploited, hungry, weak,
Half clothed in rags
We pine away through our lives
Full of patches and doles

Our bodies are bony cages
Our lives untidy as our unkempt hair
We're earthen vessels with flickering breath
Broken bangles mock our shattered lives

Woe to the sparkling, pretty bride
The landlord lusts with his roving eye
Woe to her in in-law's household
Doomed is her married life

We go to work because we are poor
But the same silken beds mock us
While we are ravished in broad daylight
Ill-stirred our horoscopes are

Even our doddering husbands
Lying on the cots in a corner
Hiss and shout for revenge
If we cannot stand their touch.

We are not prostitutes
We are toilers with self-respect
We are Dalit women proud
We are the providers for humanity

Did God ordain our faith?
Will men decide our lives?
Are we faggots for burning in the funeral pyre?
No we will rise and free ourselves!

(Theresamma)[4]

This poem reflects to some extent the lives of poor Dalit women.
The dimension of caste, characteristic to Indian society, makes the poor
in India a group with a specific socio-cultural and historic identity. The
poor and the oppressed people in India are not a generalized category
of unfortunate people. They are the Dalits.[5] Dalit means the broken, the
oppressed, the subjugated, and the crushed. In practical terms they are

the "untouchables," who form 16 percent of the Indian population. The proportion of women to men is 927 to 1000 (1991 census), indicating that there are about 80 million Dalit women in our country. Their significance lies not in their individuality or collectiveness but in their identity as members of a socio-cultural group, ordained and fixed in a particular caste or tribe that has remained in a deprived position for centuries. Their very number demands the undivided attention of any social development, change or movement. Dalit women have been referred to as the "Dalits among the Dalits," the "thrice alienated" and the "thrice marginalized," suffering "cumulative" discrimination and subjugation for centuries, socially, culturally, and economically. The Dalit woman is thrice alienated from the resources of society owing to her gender, caste, and class. By virtue of her gender she is subordinate to the men in family and society, discriminated against for jobs, paid less, and targeted for sexual and physical abuse. By virtue of her caste, she is considered an "untouchable," her mobility is restricted, she is considered polluting and unclean, is denied jobs, legal aid, and education, and is an easy object of violence. Her economic status is low and poor; hence she is illiterate, unskilled, unorganized, dependent, and easily exploited and abused.

Reflection and experience show a direct and fundamental relationship between caste and class in the case of Dalits. The disabilities and limitations placed on Dalits in terms of education, occupation, social interaction, and social mobility have resulted in their being pushed to the lowest class—so much so that caste and class are synonymous in our society. Some prefer to call this "claste!"[6] The Dalit woman faces the same limitations and marginalizations as the men in her community but in a more severe form. With the majority in the community already landless, there is no possibility of her owning land. The restrictions on certain types of employment, the assignment of unclean work, the lack of organizing and networks, lead to further subjugation and poverty. In situations of change, women have often taken on the burden for continuing caste-based occupations and maintenance of the household. Due to the low ritual status and monetary returns that come with traditional occupations, Dalit men hesitate to continue in these professions and migrate to cities for employment, leaving the women to support and sustain the family. Women do this by engaging in occupations that are service- or craft-oriented, while also taking care of the entire household. Even where Dalit women accompany their husbands to the cities, it is the women who willingly engage in jobs as domestic helpers while the men are trying to equip themselves with new skills for new occupations. Traditional jobs are shunned by the men and hence many remain unemployed for long periods of time and the women have to support the family. The very direct and underlying supportive and reinforcing role of caste is therefore evident in our class structure. The impact of caste and class on Dalit women is more than the mere sum of these and even more than the impact of caste and class on Dalit men and non-Dalit women.[7]

The Dalit woman is thrice marginalized from all movements for social change, namely, the class movements, the caste movements, and the women's movements. Hence, amongst the vast resources developed by Indian women scholars and activists, and the contributions that Indian women have made to feminist theory and discourse internationally, one sees a very inadequate mention of Dalit women, their perspectives on things, or their contributions to the overall struggle of women for liberation. Studies on Dalit women in India are few for they have been denied a legitimate place in the academic world and are often considered to be deviations from the mainstream or irrelevant. This, I do believe, is an ahistorical and biased approach. An adequate framework for the study of the women's movement should take into account the historicity, elements of the social structure, and self-understanding and vision for society of the Dalit woman, as well as of the dialectics between Dalit women that provides a focal point for the analysis of the women's movement.

As Dalit women emerge as an identifiable category, they are playing a very significant role within the Dalit movement, addressing issues of untouchability, identity, justice, and the like. Despite this, people have tried to define the Dalit woman as a "divisive force," a tool being used to divide the Dalit movement and the women's movement, an "imaginary category" with no real identity of her own. But she is actually an "emerging category" that needs to be recognized and given space, for the caste-class-gender combination affects her in ways very different from other women within the structures of Indian society.[8] She is the victim of the most heinous forms of violence, oppression, and dehumanization. Empirical studies make it obvious that, while Dalit women share many of the same disabilities arising out of their class position with the poor in general, their caste along with Dalit men, and their gender with all other women, the extent, intensity, and depth of oppression vary. The three forces of gender, class, and caste act not only in isolation but also place specific limitations and produce forms of discrimination in combination. While it is not easy to analyze definite causal and supportive connections from one to another, their interaction and compound nature cannot be negated.

But a good source for ascertaining Dalit hopes, visions, and resolve is Dalit literature, which is marked by revolt and negativity because of its association with the hopes for liberation from the drudgery of the caste system. The language is often provocative, describing the experiences of Dalit people struggling for survival and confronting limitations, abject poverty, misery, and brutality. The literature does not reflect any established critical theory or point of view, but innate within it is a new thinking and a new point of view, a movement to bring about change. Without any established theoretical presumptions within the contemporary context, and without any impediment from status considerations within the social hierarchy, Dalit intellectualism and literature enjoy a certain freedom and result in much original thinking and intense ethical religious reflections. This is apparent in the literary characterizations of Dalit women where women are shown to take in their stride the oppression that confronts them. For example, Mina Gajbhiye in a poem entitled "The Weeping Wound of Centuries" states:

> I had sutured with difficulty
> the weeping wound of centuries.
> Those stitches are all ripped out...
> Even our old bonds of give and take are snapped.
> From now on I won't scream, "I want to live."
> From now on I'll live to die.
> Let the village become a burning ground
> along with me.
> I will not live like a pariah dog, nowhere.[9]

Another example is the story of Kashi, the heroine in the Maharastrian writer Bhimrao Shirwale's story "Livelihood."Kashi, a slum dweller, is married to Dharma, who is sent to jail for an accidental murder. To stay alive in her twenty years' wait for Dharma's release, Kashi becomes the mistress of Kesu, the one-eyed bootlegger. In her struggle for survival, the hideous looking child fathered by Kesu becomes her source of livelihood, for she allows people to hire him for a fee of twenty rupees a day to exhibit him for alms. When Kesu comes to claim his son, Kashi's life and livelihood splinter apart.[10]

Annie Namala analyzes the story and writes,

> Heroines like Kashi are a portrayal of real life Dalit women [as she tells] her story of "pathos, protest and the undefeatable will to survive," ...Kashi is the undying spirit that rises up and takes new forms every time circumstances try to crush her. She is the surge of life where the culture and value are living and life alone.[11]

Such literary characterizations filled with social content are connecting both the Dalit woman and her world anew, since they restore the mark of this exiled "other" on the many institutions—familial, psychic, and ethical—that ground her personal, and therefore as a woman also her political, life. They renew one's understanding of patriarchy and the various oppressive systems that structure and sustain it. The questions raised by these narratives and stories are frightening but full of promise.

The Christian Dalit woman, in addition to the many problems she faces in society and in her home, has to deal with discrimination by upper-caste Christians within the church as well because of her gender, her class, and her caste. While Dalit women are the most regular in terms of attendance in church and in most cases form a majority of church members, they are not always adequately represented in administrative bodies and are denied full participation. The androcentric theology and dogmas of the church and its patriarchal structures continue to subjugate the Dalit woman and to justify her weak and powerless social status by reassuring her that self-sacrifice and self-denial are a woman's best virtues. Patriarchal culture and androcentric theology have contributed to her oppression by viewing her as an inferior being who must always subordinate herself to male supremacy, as an inferior being who is always to be treated with bias and condescension. Despite all of these problems, Dalit women are strong in faith, in courage and in perseverance. They are resilient and dignified. They are hard working and are very often the primary care givers and bread earners, even in cases where the husband is present. In spite of being the most marginalized, they sustain the community and the church.[12]

Hermeneutical Considerations

Christian Dalits have had a unique and peculiar experience in relation to the biblical text. Their introduction to it, its varied influence on their existence, and the issue of its continuing relevance in their struggle for freedom and wholeness all signal the need to ask critical questions of the Bible. What should be its place in Dalit theological reflection?[13] In what sense is the Bible true? To what extent can it be trusted to accurately transmit something of the will and purpose of God? What is the relationship between the Bible and Dalit women's experience? While a full analysis of these questions and their implications would take us beyond the scope of this paper, they do point to the need to consider the significance of the Bible and Dalit experience in the doing and articulation of Dalit biblical interpretation.

But biblical interpretation in India has until very recently been too deeply formed in the Western light, or under its shadow, and where contextual attempts have been made, they have been informed mainly by the experience of the intellectual elite and brahmanical traditions—conceptual, esoteric, and far removed from the experience and reality of marginal communities namely women and Dalits. Today, when the domination of a caste and a gendered ideology in Indian society is being questioned, resisted, and confronted, it is important that biblical scholarship recognize and uplift the perspectives of women, the indigenous peoples, and the Dalit communities that have until now escaped attention or received insufficient attention in biblical interpretation. These communities have for centuries been and continue to be involved in a struggle for canonical control of the scriptures that sanctified and justi-

fied the hierarchical and discriminative system of caste and gender. De-
nial of education and therefore access to the reading of scripture has hindered them from making a contribution to the interpretation of scripture. If men and women, Dalit and non-Dalit, and indigenous peoples in
India struggle together biblically and theologically with some of the issues clamoring for attention today, it would lead to a viable and accountable Indian biblical scholarship, one that is both contextual and holistic.
It will also help us to move toward deeper self-understanding, stronger
theological persuasion, solidarity for liberation, and a clearly directed
praxis.

What is essential therefore is the employment of a liberational
hermeneutic, one that results in an interpretation of scripture that is both
liberating and provides for a liberative life for all. In other words, it is an
interpretation of scripture that ensures holistic well-being for all, for it is
God who is the Creator and author of all life and it is God who calls all
to live life and live it in its fullness. It is a perspective that pays special
attention to the socio-economic conditions, concerns, and issues of the
marginalized, namely, discrimination, suffering, language, identity,
poverty, violence, landlessness, and the like which need to be addressed
for the healing and the transformation of society and its structures as
well as the establishment of *shalom*. It is also a perspective that is open
to the diverse and varied faith, cultural, and ethnic traditions that characterize India, viewed from the vantage point of the oppressed Dalit. It
is therefore a hermeneutic that echoes the silenced voices of Dalit women
and other oppressed minorities and lifts their concerns to bring them to
the dominant academic exercise of biblical interpretation.

The Social, Political, Cultural, and Economic Context of Dalit Women

More recently, and particularly in light of the Anti-conversion Bill,
prominent leaders of the Dalit cause have been promulgating a paradigm
shift in the mission of the church. The shift emphasizes the need to work
for the economic and social empowerment of Dalits. The exegetical starting point for such a venture, if it is to become a material force capable of
gripping the Dalits, must be grounded in a materialistic epistemology that
is characterized, among other things, by its location of truth not in a world
beyond history but indeed within the crucible of historical struggles. The
social, cultural, economic, and political world of Dalit women constitutes
the valid hermeneutical starting point for reading scripture for liberation.
The theologizing and reading of scripture by Dalit women starts from the
experience of a denied humanity. Dalit women have learned hard lessons
under three gurus: poverty, caste, and gender discrimination. The first has
taught them sacrifice, patience, and forbearance. The second and third
have taught them resilience and struggle. Their theologizing, like all other
liberation theologies, starts from their experiences and their engagement.

It starts with the experience of the women at the bottom of Indian society—the experience of Dalit women. The point of departure here is women's experience in their struggle for survival and liberation.[14] The hermeneutic is therefore sensitive to both this immediate and the larger context, reflects appreciation and respect for women's experience, and acknowledges Dalit women's capacity and agency.

Dalit Feminist Consciousness

Dalit feminist/womanist consciousness is a perspective or mindset that is influenced by the context of suffering, rejection, violence, and the resolve to overcome the same. The acceptance and use of the term "Dalit" by an Indian woman or man is an expression of this awareness, an awakening to subjugation by casteist and patriarchal oppressors, and the resolve and determination to struggle and annihilate these forms of oppression and slavery.[15] "This desire to surmount repression makes their experience a legitimate and creative theological resource. It is within such experience that the affirmation of God's liberating power also takes place."[16] It includes the affirmation of one's roots; collective struggle; the experience of suffering and of liberation; and the vision of liberation and restoration.[17] These features are present in the historic struggle of the Dalits and are the ingredients that contribute to the formation of Dalit consciousness. Such consciousness is a pre-requisite for reading and interpreting the text for Dalit liberation. But this consciousness has to be infused with the ideals of feminism/womanism as well. In other words, a Dalit feminist consciousness is a frame of mind that seeks to challenge/subvert and destabilize any system or interpretation of a scriptural text that subordinates women and is critical both of the manner in which Dalit women sometimes have aided and resisted oppression and subjugation.

Discerning the "Word of God" in Community

In the context of a multi-scriptural environment, "scripture" understood as revelation that is canonized but not closed is essential for authentic and meaningful exegesis of the biblical text. Revelation is canonized, but only for the sake of making possible a multiplicity of readings in subsequent historical periods.

> Consequently, scripture as revelation canonized offers not a prescriptive meaning for all time but rather a meaning that may be characterized as "negative," ruling out a certain range of meanings, or "inductive," alluding to a certain range of meanings. According to the model, scripture becomes what one might call a guiding horizon for interpretation or, as [Clodovis] Boff puts it, a "paradigmatic message."[18]

As such, scripture enriches the ongoing hermeneutic tradition of the church through the manifold interpretations offered over time within the interpretative circle, namely the church.[19] Revelation in the present is by means of and in the light of scripture, as the church looks for the Word of God within the parameters established by scripture and its tradition of interpretation in the church.

The "Word of God" is not found in the letter of scripture but in the mutual relationship between community and scripture. Thus the meaning of scripture—the "Word of God" can be understood only within the context of the living community, namely, the church. The "Word of God" is not absolute or ahistorical. At the same time, the text is by no means wide open, subject to any interpretation by the reader. To the contrary, a hermeneutic technique should establish boundaries of meaning beyond which interpretation cannot proceed. What any hermeneutic technique cannot do is determine what might be the "right" meaning within the boundaries in question. That is a decision that calls for a creative act on the part of the reader, a response to the communication of scripture within the context of the hermeneutic circle (community). Interpretation is therefore always creative/new, more or less arbitrary, and always personal, but certainly not without limits or constraints (Boff). In other words, while the overall boundaries of interpretation can be set (by the community), the particular stance to be adopted within such boundaries—what one might call the discernment of the "Word of God" in the present situation—is not.[20] A renewed understanding of the nature and function of scripture and the notion of the "word of God" is also essential for a liberational interpretation of the text for the Dalits.

Affirmation and Transformation of Life in All Its Wholeness

The hermeneutic must have as its consequence far-reaching social changes in this society/world—changes that have political and social revolutionary significance and are hence practical, this-worldly, transforming, renewing, and transitional. The passionate and compassionate way in which women do theology is a rich contribution to theological science. The key to this theological process is the concept of life. In doing theology we find ourselves committed and faithful to all the vital elements that compose human life. Thus, without losing scientific seriousness, which includes analyzing the basic causes of women's multiple oppression, their theology and interpretations are deeply rooted in experience, in affection, in life. As Dalit women they are called to do theology passionately, a theology based on feeling as well as on knowledge, on wisdom as well as on science, a theology made not only with the mind but also with the heart, the body, the womb. Women need to work toward wholeness, and such wholeness means celebrating plurality, diversity, mutuality, and partnership, for hierarchy is inappropriate within the household of faith. The need of the hour is for open, inclusive faith communities, an inclusiveness that is open to the future of God's *shalom*. We must continue to resist everything that is alien to a process of reconnecting, to challenge those who want to cling to the old paradigm of control and exclusivism.[21]

Multi-Scriptural and Relational

Christians in India are a minority and therefore the quest for fullness of life has to be regarded as part of the larger human struggle in the community in which women of all faiths and ideological convictions are involved. This is what makes feminist hermeneutics in India different from that in the West. We cannot afford to neglect the secular, or the religious and secular efforts of women. In most countries of Asia the distinction between the secular and the religious is not as clear as is imagined by many in the West. The secular women's movement in India is called "secular" in the sense of not being obviously religious. Those in the movement are not searching for scriptural hermeneutics or a Hindu or Muslim or Buddhist theology of liberation before actually fighting for liberation, for this kind of priority does not exist in India and one should not look for it unnecessarily. There are many groups of women fighting for rights, but they do not belong to any single religious persuasion.[22] In a multi-religious society where women of different religious persuasions come together for a common human purpose in society, religious labels could become hindrances. Christians need to work together with their neighbors of other faiths and ideological convictions and should not give the impression that only Christians are actively involved in feminist hermeneutics or theology or in active struggles for women's rights.

Indian Christian women need to be liberated from a two-fold bondage, that of patriarchal hermeneutics of the Bible on the one hand and that of the scriptures of other faiths on the other. The latter have dominated and shaped the cultural ethos and social values of the Indian community for a far longer period than the Bible. Therefore, feminist hermeneutics should bring out the hidden patriarchal assumptions of all scriptures in India. A radical reassessment of the ideals of women set out in Indian scriptures is necessary. Awareness regarding this is also prevalent among women of other religious communities, and Christians need to be sensitive to them and, where necessary, cooperate with them. Thus, the quest for a specifically Dalit feminist hermeneutics in India might fulfill a larger purpose in the story of God's liberation of both women and men in the totality of a reconciled humanity.[23]

There are liberative streams within religious traditions other than the Jewish and Christian traditions as well. Christian Dalits are therefore called upon to join others (Muslim, Buddhist, Hindu Dalits) who are working to defy ancient and outmoded injunctions imposed upon them by religion and conservative men. Women's collaboration and involvement in the struggles of women of other faiths and ideologies will result in their hermeneutical antennae becoming "more sensitive to receive those gentle but by no means weak vibrations in the Bible which are now silenced by the loudspeakers controlled by men of all faiths in India."[24]

We therefore need to look at the authority and interpretation of the Bible from the perspective of women who are aware that Indian society is patriarchal and that the scriptures of Indian religions also legitimize male domination of women in hierarchical power structures in society. Women of different religious beliefs and ideological convictions in India have been struggling against this for many years. Christian women have questioned the Bible and sought to determine if it is an ally or an adversary in the struggles of women in India for freedom, self-respect, and human dignity in the community.

This calls for what Tissa Balasuriya calls a "new hermeneutic," which connects feminism and the liberation of theology. According to him, this involves recognition of the fact that there is a distinction between God's revelation at a given time as expressed by the author and how the meaning of a text is interpreted in the cultural context of another time. He writes,

> The scriptures themselves are to be subject to a transforming influence. They are not [the] total revelation of God to humanity; they are only one such revelation. We cannot limit God and God's message to the whole of humanity to only a few men from a male dominated society. We cannot limit God to one generation or impose silence on God after the death of the last apostle.[25]

As Mary Ann Tolbert says, "To understand the same God as enemy and friend, as tormentor and savior, to read the same Bible as enslaver and liberator, that is the paradoxical challenge of feminist hermeneutics."[26]

If it is good and life-giving for marginalized and excluded women, it is good for all. This rereading of the Bible in a scientific way, informed by a commitment to women's liberation and human liberation in general, has to involve a historical critical rereading of biblical and extra-biblical traditions in order to retrace the struggle of our fore-sisters for full humanhood, and to reappropriate their victories and their defeats as our own submerged history. This is of course complemented by a feminist hermeneutics of suspicion and a religious and cultural critique from the perspective of women's daily realities.

Methodological Considerations

Dalit women have traditionally been concerned not just for their own welfare but also for the welfare of their entire communities, their men, their sons, and their daughters. This inherent concern for community might lead us toward the articulation of a theology and an interpretation of the Bible that results in wholeness. Dalit women are open to dialogue and to join hands with people of other faiths and men who work for the cause of the community. This multi-dimensional and holistic approach enables them to confront the causes of oppression as they affect the community.

1. To this end Dalit women need to work toward a critical reclamation of Dalit tradition, which has been for centuries overwritten or co-opted by the dominant Hindu tradition or interpretations. It is important that Dalit women acquaint themselves with the prevailing interpretations of mainstream traditions in order to strike at their most vulnerable points. They must also seek certain provisional goals and future possibilities by which to replace prevailing norms and ideals derived from traditional interpretations, demonstrating that they are not the only possibilities and drawing upon Dalit tradition to support their stance.

2. Dalit women need to address methodological questions about how patriarchal and casteist theories and current biblical interpretations, even those by Dalit men and the dominant group, function and how they may be utilized against them. Our ideas, values, terminology, and repertoire of concepts are all products of patriarchy so that it seems impossible to maintain or develop a theoretical or methodological purity untainted by patriarchy and caste. Dalit feminism will not flourish by insisting on theoretical separatism that attempts to eliminate patriarchal and caste ingredients by isolation and distance. In fact, a familiarity with male or patriarchal methods, commitments, and values and contradictory elements and silences is beneficial to both men and women. A viable Dalit feminist methodology must therefore be the consequence of an active yet critical engagement with traditional and patriarchal methods.

3. Dalit women must use whatever remains useful in traditional discourses to create new theories, new methods, and new values that take traditional discourses as points of departure, allowing Dalit women's experiences rather than men's to select the objects and methods of investigation. By its very existence, such an approach would demonstrate that patriarchal paradigms are not universal, valid for all, but at best represent one point of view.

4. For all these, a certain amount of knowledge and skill is necessary. This would mean the creation of experts in the field with knowledge of ancient languages, which may result in some sort of elitism within the discipline. But this can be counteracted with opportunities for dialogue with women at the grassroots, for their contributions are significant and reading in community is essential. The subjectivity of both the leader and the group are taken into consideration and the active participation of both is ensured.

5. Bible study should not only end with new interpretations, it should also motivate and provoke women into action. The move from their particular experience to the Bible, from the Bible to action, and then back again to the Bible, requires a process of mutual validation between experience and text. Only then can we envision the liberation of women, renewal of the church, and transformation of society.

The methodological considerations listed above point to the need for the development of women skilled and fitted with the tools of biblical criticism and interpretation who will be able to undertake this effort. What should not be ignored and is also needed is constant engagement with the large mass of illiterate Dalit women whose experience and resultant intuitive skills could contribute to an interpretation of the text that is original and authentically Dalit.

Storytelling as Method

In the absence of a large literate mass among Dalit women, sophisticated and complex methods of biblical interpretation could prove to be a challenge. Recognition of the reality that the majority of women are non-literate highlights the need for using imaginative, informal learning strategies. Since there is an obvious bias in favor of academic learning, many women from poor rural and urban areas of India continue to feel incapable of doing biblical interpretation since they do not have access to the written text. But an emphasis on non-formal methods of Bible study in order to enable illiterate women to participate in the articulation of theology and biblical interpretation would prove beneficial. These non-formal methods, called "vernacular readings" by R. S. Sugirtharajah, are characteristic of local culture and communication processes and are distinguished from "metropolitan readings" that assume a "working universality."[27]

Ranjini Rebera points out the importance and the success of one such vernacular reading—"storytelling" as a method of interpreting the biblical text in South Asia. She claims that the use of traditional storytelling techniques, together with the hermeneutic of suspicion, enables women to release themselves from androcentric interpretative processes. It is in the last stage of being able creatively to identify with the women in the biblical story by placing them side by side with their own experiences and identities that participants in such study have achieved the greatest degree of inspiration and learning.[28]

In the act of sharing stories told personally, consciously, and politically, women begin to understand themselves and their reality better. From the depths of women's stories of joys and sorrows, triumphs and defeat, we can draw a tapestry of theological exploration and biblical interpretation that is contextual and is based on a community in struggle for humanhood. The same approach has been endorsed by Kwok Pui-lan, another Asian, who asserts that

> Bible study among Asian women is a communal event; they gather to talk about their own stories and the stories of the Bible, constructing new meanings and searching for wisdom for survival and empowerment. They treat the Bible as a living resource rather than an ancient text closed in itself.[29]

Subjective storytelling has been an important element of communication methods in Asia. The same is true of the Dalit community and such instances become a form of symbolic language that brings families and communities together, especially communities of non-literate persons. The narrating of the story becomes a vehicle for understanding attitudes, cultural taboos, relationships in families and kinship networks, and many forms of social behavior.[30] The narration also conveys the inner feelings, meanings and aspirations of the narrator.[31]

For women, the sharing of our stories has become a regular feature every time we gather for Bible study. It is an important part of our coming together, for it establishes trust and security for identifying and exploring issues. Who we are and what we are are conveyed through this mode. The stories, being personal and our very own, gain authenticity and power. Such methods of storytelling are now emerging in India and in Asia as a vehicle for gaining new insights into the biblical text and for doing theology, especially among women.[32]

Role Play as Method

The day-to-day realities of Dalit life are experienced in the body, and more in the bodies of Dalit women. The joys, the sorrows, the physical performances in the actual, ritual, and the symbolic world and the essential needs for a dignified life are part and parcel of the body's experience, and hence I see Dalit feminist/womanist methodology as basically being of a performative nature. I see Dalit women as interlocutors between their experience of dehumanization and the world of the biblical text. Their perception of their own reality and the text is marked with an intuitive component, with an emphasis on an empirical mode of experiencing reality. Precisely because of this, the Dalit reading "does not take place from the 'idealist site of inferiority' but rather from the 'bodily site of exteriority.'"[33]

In my own limited experience I have witnessed the effect that enactment of the biblical story has on women who have no access to the written text or formal tools of interpretation. Even in the secular realm, street theater or performance of short plays have been a very effective means of educating illiterate and rural people about issues, both social and political. The visual and the aural depiction of the text draws the community into the very essence and core of the story, enabling the hearer to feel, think, and relive the experience of the biblical character being enacted.[34] This approach enables the listener to enter into critical solidarity with the character and isolate interpretations derived from the experience of self-actualization or subjective experience, insights that are missed when the story is only heard.

A Dalit woman's body stooped with the load of her living would perhaps straighten into normality when stories of liberation and of women in the biblical text are heard, enacted, and therefore re-experienced. I say this knowing the very important role the Bible plays in the lives of these women. Since women are assumed to be intuitive, such a method would be effective. The problem is that society has trained women not to act. Women know things, they are intuitive, but are not encouraged to act from this knowledge, particularly if it would conflict with the environment or the status quo. Women are taught not to act aggressively even when they are being victimized. Women have to be taught to move, to act, to do what their inner voices and their bodies are saying even if it seems socially inappropriate.[35] Learning to act from our inner beings, our instinctual centers, would elicit a response that is powerful and in congruence with knowledge derived from faith and experience.

Power returns to her, to herself, and she finds the inspiration and the strength to act. The scriptural text has the power to inspire the woman when it is recounted and enacted. As a methodology and a tool for intervention, such a participatory process challenges the notion of "spectator knowledge" and enables women to discover and acknowledge the *raison d'être* of the entire interpretative process. Such a methodology also reduces imposition by an external agent when the emphasis is on the individual and her enactment of the text grounded in experience. Knowledge and insights gained through such a method are always accompanied with the fear of not fitting into any accepted theory. But if interpretations by Dalit women, particularly those of illiterate Dalit women are an integral part of biblical interpretation or women's reading of the text, then there should be little distinction between committed and skilled or formal readings of the text and informal readings of the text.

Conclusion

Every Dalit reading of the Bible forcefully claims an approach that is vested in the pain and prejudices of being discriminated against. While the need for closer cooperation and joint reading of the text by the so-called "conscientized" Dalits and intellectuals is emphasized, the critical solidarity between the two will enable the creation of new tools that would facilitate a deeper exploration of the text and the realities of Dalit women.

The oral culture of the Dalits, their creativity, their holistic approach to life, and the rich symbolism inherent in their culture needs to be explored for the purposes of identifying new and effective methods of reading the biblical text that would aid them in their struggle for liberation and provide for an engaged and meaningful conversation between biblical scholars and unlettered Dalit women.

Notes

1. Sherry Ortner, "Is Female to Male as Nature Is to Culture?" in *Woman, Culture and Society*, ed. Michelle Zimbalist Rosaldo and Louise Lampjere (Stanford: Stanford University Press, 1994), 67.

2. Lorraine Code, *Rhetorical Spaces: Essays on Gendered Locations* (New York: Routledge, 1995), 75.

3. Ibid., 61-62.

4. Theresamma, "Dalit Women—Society's Firewood," in *Towards a Dalit Theology*, ed. M. E. Prabhakar (Dehli: ISPCK, 1988), 166–67.

5. See M. E. Prabhakar, *Towards a Dalit Theology* (Delhi, ISPCK, 1988).

6. Annie Namala, "Dalit Women: The Conflict and the Dilemma," paper presented at a workshop on Dalit Women at Anveshi Research Centre for Women's Studies, 1995, 4.

7. See Leela Dube, "Caste and Women," in *Caste: Its Twentieth Century Avatar*, ed. S. R. Srinivas (New Delhi: Viking, 1996), 1–27.

8. Namala, "Dalit Women," 5.

9. Quoted by Eleanor Zelliot in *Stri Dalit Sahitya: The New Voice of Women Poets in Images of Women in Maharashtrian Literature and Religion*, ed. Anne Feldhaus (Albany: State University of New York Press, 1996), 70.

10. Bhimrao Shirwale, "Livelihood," in *Homeless in my Land: Translations from Modern Marathi Dalit Short Stories*, ed. Atjun Dangle (Mumbai: Orient Longman, 1992), 27–36.

11. Namala, "Dalit Women," 2. See also Susie Tharu's analysis of "Mother" by Baburao Bagul in *Homeless in My Land*. She writes, "For the widow-mother protagonist—and for the Dalit feminist—nothing comes so easily, yet there is in

the story the stirring of a new kind of movement: from the never ceasing shuttle between the extraditions and death that comprise her impossible life, to a struggle to leave, and in that single act to renovate the world... The beginnings of a movement, possibly, from untouchable-harijan to Dalit." Susie Tharu, "The Impossible Subject: Caste in the Scene of Desire," in *Embodiment*, ed. M. Thapan (New Delhi: Oxford University Press, 1997), 268.

12. See Monica J. Melanchthon, "Gospel and Culture: A Dalit Woman's Perspective," *Voices* 19, no. 3–4 (1995): 22.

13. Cf. Sathianathan Clarke, "Viewing the Bible through the Eyes and Ears of Subalterns in India," *Biblical Interpretation* 10, no. 3 (2002): 245–66; V. Devasahayam, *Doing Dalit Theology in Biblical Key* (Chennai: ISPCK/Gurukul, 1997); and A. Maria Arul Raja, S.J., "Towards a Dalit Reading of the Bible: Some Hermeneutical Reflections," *Jeevadhara* 26, no. 151 (1996): 29–34.

14. Virginia Fabella and Mercy Amba Oduyoye, eds., *With Passion and Compassion: Third World Women Doing Theology* (Maryknoll, NY: Orbis Books, 1988), 184–90.

15. Deenabandhu Manchala, "Reading together with the Dalits: An Exploration for Common Hermeneutical Directions amidst Plurality of Interpretations," unpublished paper, 4.

16. Ibid.

17. A. P. Nirmal, "Towards a Christian Dalit Theology," in *A Reader in Dalit Theology*, ed. A. P. Nirmal (Chennai: Gurukul, n.d.), 65–69.

18. Clodovis Boff, *Theology and Praxis: Epistemological Foundations*, trans. Robert Barr (Maryknoll, NY: Orbis Books, 1987), 140, as quoted in Fernando F. Segovia, "Liberation Hermeneutics: Revisiting the Foundations in Latin America," in *Toward a New Heaven and a New Earth: Essays in Honor of Elisabeth Schüssler Fiorenza* (Maryknoll, NY: Orbis Books, 2003), 112.

19. Ibid., 112.

20. Ibid.

21. Cf. Fabella and Oduyoye, *With Passion and Compassion*, 184–90.

22. A. S. Seetharamu, *Women in Organized Movements* (New Delhi: Ambika, 1981).

23. Stanley J. Samartha "But if It Is a Daughter She Shall Live" in *Towards a Theology of Humanhood: Women's Perspectives*, ed. Aruna Gnanadason (New Delhi: ISPCK, 1986), 106–8.

24. Ibid., 107.

25. Tissa Balasuriya, "Feminism and the Liberation of Theology," in *God, Woman and the Bible*, Logos 22 (1983): 131.

26. Mary Ann Tolbert, "Defining the Problem: The Bible and Feminist Hermeneutics," *Semeia* 28 (1983): 126.

27. R. S. Sugirtharajah, "Introduction and Some Thoughts on Asian Biblical Hermeneutics," *Biblical Interpretation* 2, no. 3 (1994): 251–63.

28. Ranjini Rebera, "Polarity or Partnership? Retelling the Story of Martha and Mary from Asian Women's Perspective (Luke 10:38-42)," *Semeia* 78 (1997): 94.

29. Kwok Pui-lan, "Discovering the Bible in a Non-Biblical World," in *Voices from the Margin: Interpreting the Bible in the Third World*, ed. R. S. Sugirtharajah (Maryknoll, NY: Orbis Books, 1991), 311.

30. Rebera, "Polarity or Partnership?" 95.

31. A. K. Ramanujan, *Folktales from India: a Selection of Oral Tales from Twenty-two Languages* (New York: Pantheon, 1991), 22, as cited in Rebera, "Polarity or Partnership?" 95.

32. Recent publications by Christian women in India have all used the method of storytelling. The real-life experience of a woman or community is narrated and then related to a biblical text to enhance the meaning of the biblical text. See Lalrinawmi Ralte et al., eds., *Envisioning a New Heaven and a New Earth* (New Delhi: NCCI/ISPCK, 1998), and Elizabeth Joy, *Lived Realities: Faith Reflections on Gender Justice* (Bangalore: JWP/CISRS, 1999).

33. A. Maria Arul Raja S.J., "Some Reflections on a Dalit Reading of the Bible" in *Frontiers of Dalit Theology*, ed. V. Devasahayam (Delhi/Chennai: ISPCK/Gurukul: 1997), 338.

34. Felix Wilfred, "Towards a Subaltern Hermeneutics: Beyond the Contemporary Polarities in the Interpretation of Religious Traditions," *Vaiharai* 1, no. 1 (1996): 77–80.

35. Vicki Noble, *Shakti Woman: Feeling our Fire, Healing our World: The New Female Shamanism* (San Francisco: Harper Collins, 1991), 8.

7

BIBLICAL TEACHINGS
AND THE HARD REALITIES OF LIFE

Jean Zaru (Palestine)

I have struggled most of my adult life with issues of theology and liberation. It has been life experience, rather than a library, that has served as my source of inspiration. My life experience has taken me to all five continents, where, over the years, I have been enormously enriched by contact with activists and theologians engaged in various struggles of liberation. My life experience is equally rooted in my identity as a Palestinian Christian woman; therefore, before I offer my contribution toward a theology of liberation, it is instructive to share some information about my context.

One of the best things that ever happened in my life was attending the Nairobi Assembly of the World Council of Churches in 1975. It led to great involvement in the ecumenical movement and travel to lands far and near, where I have met Christians from many backgrounds and cultures and encountered people of other faiths. These experiences have taught me a lot.

My first problem was always introducing myself. If I called myself a Palestinian, people might equate me with terrorism. If I said I was an Arab, I was assumed to be a Muslim, in which case people would want to know why I was even present. If I said I came from Jerusalem, thinking that this would make things clearer for my fellow Christians, someone would surely say, "Oh, you are Jewish! Shalom!" When, finally, I insisted on pointing out that I was a Christian, the inevitable final query came: "When were you converted?" I would give the only reply I could, "Sorry, I cannot give you the satisfaction of saving my soul. I am a Christian, I must tell you, because my ancestors were disciples of Christ. They

Jean Zaru, "Biblical Teachings and the Hard Realities of Life," in *Toward a New Heaven and a New Earth: Essays in Honor of Elisabeth Schüssler Fiorenza*, ed. Fernando F. Segovia (Maryknoll, NY: Orbis Books, 2003), 368-82.

were members of the first Christian church that was in Jerusalem." This, I found, was a shocking revelation for many, but I would continue, willing now to be confrontational, "My maiden name is Mikhail. My father's name is Ibrahim. My grandfather is Musa, the Arabic form of Moses. My brother's name is John. My uncles are Isaac, Jacob, Jad, David, and so on, and my grandmother's name is Sarah."

As I struggled on my journeys to affirm the presence of twelve million Arab Christians in the Middle East and of a Palestinian people struggling for justice and freedom in at least a part of their homeland, new obstacles and pressures revealed themselves. For liberal Christians, influenced by Holocaust theology and European history and guilt, I am not, as a Palestinian Christian, a part of their agenda. My very existence disturbs the balance, as if there were a balance in a situation of conflict and oppression. For fundamentalists, I am not among the chosen. Rather, I am one of the cursed. As a Palestinian, I stand in the way of the fulfillment of the prophecy of God. I cannot win, for it seems that I am not part of the theology of many of my brothers and sisters.

Yet my entire life has been affected and encompassed by biblical teachings and interpretations. As a Christian, a Palestinian, a woman, an Arab, and a Quaker, the teachings of Western churches have affected me personally and my people collectively in very specific ways. The use, and abuse, of the Bible in reflecting on the legitimacy, policies, and conduct of the state of Israel is common, especially but by no means exclusively among conservative North American Christians. They see a firm link between biblical and modern Israel. The history of condoning evil in the name of alleged biblical justification is, of course, a long one. Discrimination, oppression, and war have all been justified by references to biblical texts. In recent times, and close to home, David Ben-Gurion referred to the Bible as the "Jews' sacrosanct title-deed to Palestine . . . with a genealogy of 3,500 years."[1] In Jerusalem today, the so-called International Christian Embassy is a most overtly political supporter of Israel. Its publications proclaim that God gave the land to the Jewish people and that, therefore, God will bless or curse nations in accordance with the treatment of the chosen people of Israel.

It is appropriate, then, to begin this study with how one reads and interprets the Bible. Biblical hermeneutics deals with trying to understand what the Bible is saying to us. It is important, therefore, to be clear from the beginning what our principles of interpretation are. For me, the life and teachings of Jesus constitute the center for my readings and interpretations. Thus, I interpret both the Old and the New Testaments in that light. Justice and compassion are the central themes as I read the scriptures. God is a God of justice and compassion, not a God of war, vengeance, and exclusivity. In what follows I should like to examine a number of scriptural themes that particularly affect both my people and myself.

The Exodus

Most liberation theologians begin with the exodus. As one reads the story, one sees great miracles. A people in slavery and bondage to another were freed. However, even within the biblical narrative, there was much suffering by both the oppressed and the oppressor in the struggle for freedom. This is hinted at early on in the account. In undertaking to rescue the Israelites from their bondage, Yahweh assures them that they will be led into a "land flowing with milk and honey." Besides having milk and honey, however, the land also had an abundance of people: the Canaanites, the Hittites, and others (Exod 3:8). Most certainly, the land was not empty. Moreover, one soon learns that, according to the biblical narrative, the Israelites were required to commit genocide as an act of fidelity to God's commandments. If several texts in the Book of Exodus ascribe the future genocide to the activity of Yahweh, a number of texts in the Book of Deuteronomy attribute it to the Israelites. For example:

> But as for the towns of these peoples that Yahweh your God is giving you as an inheritance, you must not let anything that breathes remain alive. You shall annihilate them—the Hittites and the Amorites, the Canaanites and the Perizzites, the Hivites and the Jebusites—just as the Yahweh your God has commanded, so that they may not teach you to do all the abhorrent things that they do for their gods, and you thus sin against Yahweh your God. (Deut 20:16–18, NRSV)

How, one wonders, could a God of justice and compassion command the slaughter of one people to accomplish the liberation of another? When I look to Jesus' life and teachings as the way to know God, I conclude that a God of justice, love, and mercy would never have commanded that these people be killed. I am inclined to conclude that the God of that portion of the biblical account is the God of people's consciousness and perception rather than the God who really is. The biblical portrayal of the particular destiny of the Israelites, of course, is related to its concept of the "chosen people."

The Election

One of the most arresting realizations in my life comes from a tension that has persisted down through the years, related to the challenge that my personal experience poses to my religious culture. At several fundamental points my sense of what it is to be myself has not fit easily with the assertions of my faith. This is particularly true of the problem that the biblical concept of "chosen people" poses for me.

The Old Testament concept of election involves God's choice of one particular people in order to make the Godhood known to the world. Rather than suggesting a favored or special status, however, such choosing confers responsibility on the elect to know God and to make God known. Nevertheless, the notion of chosenness easily moves into a presumption of special favor, which can require separateness and which invariably introduces inequality. The biblical notion of election is problematic in itself, but, when I reflect on how it has been deployed in favor of patterns of exploitation, the moral problem is no longer merely rhetorical. Biblical chosenness has been at the heart of the ideological justification for the maltreatment of native peoples throughout the world. My own context as a Palestinian woman makes me particularly sensitive to the role this biblical notion plays in the exploitation of my people.[2]

It is equality that confers the humanizing element that brings people together. Equality abolishes all notions of inferiority and superiority and, of course, contradicts any question of the oppression of one people by another. One is very conscious of Jesus' apparent redefinition of what it is to be chosen of God: all who choose to know God and to live in relation to God become the chosen, God's children, whether male or female, Christian or Jew, Hindu or Muslim.

The Land

The question of land is central to our lives and to our self-determination as Palestinians. However, the land traditions in the Bible have been used against us. The Bible, then, became for us a tool of oppression rather than of liberation. The Zionist dream became our nightmare. My experience as a dispossessed Palestinian forces upon me an examination of such biblical land traditions. Does God promise land to one people at the expense of others and then give that people a divine mandate to cleanse the land of its inhabitants? A literalist reading of some of the earlier books of the Hebrew Bible frightens me simply as a human being. Yet the problem takes on a more immediate relevance when Jewish settlers come to the West Bank and other territories, confiscate the land, and take it for the exclusive use of Jews, claiming all the while that the land was given by God exclusively to Jews.

The Bible, for many Jews, has become a legal document that declares that "the Land" was promised to the children of Abraham and that it is still their right to lay exclusive claim to it. The "children of Abraham" are understood to include only the descendants of Isaac, when, even within the biblical narrative itself, the descendants of Abraham include those of both Isaac and Ishmael. Yet the Old Testament itself provides a different perspective on this matter:

The land shall not be sold in perpetuity, for the land is mine; for you are strangers and sojourners with me. (Lev 25:23, RSV)

The earth is the Lord's and the fullness thereof, the world and those that dwell therein. (Ps 24:1, RSV)

Moreover, there are many other biblical passages concerning the land and doing justice with it. Nevertheless, since 1948 the Palestinians have been uprooted, and, as we know only too well, they are still being displaced from their land. Israeli occupation has affected, and continues to affect, all Palestinians, regardless of where they reside throughout the world.

Women

As a Palestinian woman, I find myself struggling in yet another way. Palestinian women must work for liberation on the national front while at the same time working for liberation as women on the societal level. Like women in all societies, we Palestinian women have been cast into particular roles that have kept us subservient and have barred us from decision-making circles. Women's work has not been considered equal to men's work. The ministries of women have been considered less important than those of men. We have, then, to struggle to free ourselves from hierarchy and from the male-dominated structures of our society.

Throughout this endeavor, the liberating words and actions of Jesus become an inspiration and guide for us. Let us look at a number of women in the New Testament and see how they ministered. What was their self-image? How did Jesus respond to each of them?

John 4. My own life experience leads me to begin with a recollection of the Samaritan woman who met Jesus at the well, a well just an hour north of the place where I grew up and still live. She came in the heat of the day, the narrative tells us, because her social position did not allow her to join the other women who drew water in the cool of the morning. She was taken aback by Jesus' request for a drink. Clearly, her self-image was not a positive one. Yet Jesus, knowing all this, looked beyond it and accepted her ministry. Moreover, in forgiving her, he opened to her new possibilities for living. Sometimes, as Palestinian women, we feel the burden imposed upon the Samaritan women by their husbands. We have so many things with which to deal in our society, while, at the same time, the hierarchical structure of our church and of our whole culture hinders our growth and limits our involvement. The expectations imposed upon us by family and friends, moreover, become an overwhelming burden as we seek to be faithful to God's calling.

Luke 10:38–42. As a Palestinian woman, I find much to which I can relate in the story of Mary and Martha. First, the story deals with the relationship between two sisters, and, of course, family relationships are particularly important to us Arabs. They form the very basis of our society. In addition, the story reminds us of the gifts that are given to all of us and of the roles we all play. Jesus reminds us that, nevertheless, each one of us is unique and that, no matter who we are or what we do, each of us must be concerned with God's work and the household of life. This is not easy in a society where women are expected to do all the housework and family tasks and where, if we wish to be involved in other work, in the church or in society, we must do it in addition to the work expected of us at home. Finally, the story of Martha and Mary points to the ongoing tension, to which we can all relate, between contemplation and activity. Yet activity without contemplation is empty, and contemplation without activity is dead. The story of Martha and Mary is, of course, the *locus classicus* for reflection on the relative merits of the contemplative and the active life. Conventionally, Mary is understood to be a pious and prayerful contemplative, while Martha is seen as active but less prayerful.

Origen read Jesus' "rebuke" of Martha as justifying his own view of the subordination of the active life to the contemplative. Augustine showed a balance between the two drives, one to contemplation and the other to active service. The Cistercians too commended a combination of Martha and Mary. Among the mendicant friars, Francis had both types live together and encouraged them to exchange roles, while Aquinas insisted that Mary could not have the best portion unless she shared the fruits of her contemplation. Meister Eckhart, the famous Dominican preacher, went even further. For him it was Martha who was the more mature. The religious life of his period had quite enough "Marys" who were so caught up in their own mortifications that they did not have the freedom to follow God spontaneously or to respond to the needs of the neighbor. Martha, in Eckhart's view, was more mature than Mary, in that she had learned from experience to be both active and in essential communion with Christ. She was not so much complaining of Mary to Jesus as trying to ensure that Mary would not remain stuck in the pleasant feeling of intimacy with Jesus. Jesus, for his part, was not putting Martha in her place but was assuring her that Mary would eventually reach her full potential, by being like Martha. It was only later, when she had heard of the Ascension and had received the Holy Spirit, that Mary learned to serve—crossing the sea, preaching, teaching, and serving the disciples.

I am rather taken by Eckhart's reading of Luke's account. Yet a quick glance at some of the most recent commentaries on Luke reveals nothing of Eckhart's insight on this point. Perhaps the fear of having to become active exponents of the Word rather than mere passive ones prevents some practitioners of hermeneutics from such a reading of the text.

Mark 14:3–9 / Matthew 26:6–13. The story of the woman who wipes Jesus' feet with her ointment and her tears is one that is all too often misinterpreted. Instead of focusing on the ministry and the intentions of the woman, interpreters tend to focus on her "impurity." Jesus does not do this. Rather, he accepts her ministry, forgives her sins, and focuses on her intention. It was a radical position for a man to take in those days! For Palestinian women working and living in a traditional society, even now the dos and don'ts are very clear. Often our very ministry depends on how well we follow the expectations of our own people. If we fail to meet those expectations, our ministry is not validated; indeed, it is not even taken seriously. So, if there is any truth that I want to communicate, I must be careful to conform so as not to lose the respect of my community. Thus, I live my life in accordance with my traditional society on the one hand and in the ongoing, ever-changing larger world on the other.

A simple personal example. When people learn that I have been involved in the ecumenical movement and in theology, they react in different ways. Some are amused, some are simply scornful, and some are embarrassingly deferential. I try to explain that I am as concerned with the human condition in general as I am with specific conflicts that often represent only the tip of a pyramid of anguish and violence. I say that I am concerned with all the pain and confusion that impede our unfolding and fulfillment. My understanding of the ecumenical movement is as a movement of the Spirit, a movement that unites and reconciles us. The Spirit transforms us into a caring and sharing people, breaking down the walls that separate us. The Spirit empowers us in our struggle for justice and peace. Many argue that one's faith, or one's spirituality, is one's own private affair. I disagree, for spirituality includes all the dimensions of human, personal, and societal living that combine to make human life human—the measure of the fullness of God's gift. The human family is in crisis whenever communities and persons, including women, experience despair, hopelessness, alienation, violation, or exploitation. Many systems are interconnected, including our religious, economic, social, political, military, transportation, communication, educational, and value systems. Some of these values must be altered when we sensitize individuals and institutions to the limits and possibilities within their own cultural and ecclesiastical contexts for movement toward genuine global perspectives, engagement, and change.

Ephesians 5. I have grown up in a culture that often imposes certain traditional cultural values through which women are allotted a second-class place. This secondary place for women is frequently given biblical approval by the use of Ephesians 5 in the context of marriage services. As it is used in the liturgy, the text appears to foster in wives an attitude of submission to their husbands that is offensive to the egalitarianism one looks for between the sexes. For that reason the text is offensive. Yet, for this one should blame not Paul but his careless translators. Both the act of removing the text from its context and its common translation distort what is in the mind of the writer of Ephesians. The truth of this assertion will be conceded readily if one examines 5:15, which reads as follows:

> Therefore [in sum, or, in other words], watch carefully how you behave—not as unwise people but as wise ones—redeeming the time, for the days are evil. For that very reason do not be senseless, but understand what is the will of the Lord. And do not get drunk with wine—that is profligacy—but be filled in spirit talking to one another in psalms and hymns and spiritual songs, singing and making music to the Lord in your hearts giving thanks to God the Father always on behalf of all in the name of our Lord Jesus Christ, being subordinate to one another out of reverence for Christ, wives to your own husbands as to the Lord, for the husband is the head of the wife, as Christ is head of the church... (Eph 5:15–23)

It should be noted that the verb "be subject to" does not occur between "wives" and "your husbands" in the Greek, although translators insist on supplying it in their translations. The Revised Standard Version reads, "Wives, be subject to your husbands, as to the Lord," and the New Jerusalem Bible has, "Wives should be subject to their husbands as to the Lord." It is altogether improper to supply the words "be subject to" in this place, since such an inclusion appears to reduce the previous statement of mutual submission of all the members of the community to the one example of wives in relation to their husbands.[3] The effect of this mistranslation of the Ephesians passage is highlighted when the text of the letter is broken at verse 22 for whatever reason, liturgical or otherwise. It then appears that "being subordinate to" is an injunction only to wives with respect to their husbands, when in fact the text makes it clear that being "subordinate to" is a disposition that the writer expects of each member of the community with respect to all others. Nevertheless, this biblical passage, as it is used in the liturgy, and in the marriage rite in particular, confirms hierarchical domination in the marriage relationship. The problem is not only with the interpretation of the text but also with the way in which many understand the Bible as holding all the authority of the word of God. Yet the Word of God is much more than that. The Bible is a history of people's experiences of God and of how these people perceived God, but it is not the whole reality of God.

Maybe the letter to the Ephesians could be regarded as an achievement or an improvement in a certain historical and cultural context, where relationships were not regulated and men had many wives. This cannot be valid today. Repeating this text at all marriage ceremonies in my country confirms the subordination of women. One wonders what the effect might be if the author of the text were not so seriously misrepresented. Yet, for me, hope to overcome the powers of darkness to establish peace may be found elsewhere in Ephesians. Indeed, according to Ephesians 4:4, we are liberated from sin and division and united in the Spirit. I perceive Christ as the inward teacher, cleansing men and women of sin and bringing them back to their original state, where they were created equal in the image of God as partners and helpmates. For me the equality of women in ministry, in the business of the church, and in marriage is essential if we are to have harmonious relationships. In a community without dominance, there is no need for war, for as Paul says, "There is neither Jew nor Greek, there is neither slave nor free, there is neither male nor female, for you are all one in Christ Jesus" (Gal 3:28, RSV). Marriage within the holy community should therefore take on a meaning wholly different from that in our cultures. It must be a marriage of equals, of mutual support, so that each partner is free to follow the leadings of the Holy Spirit.

While generations of religious people have derived profit and pleasure from the retelling of biblical stories, victims of oppression—including women and Palestinians—pose fundamental moral questions with regard to the understanding of the nature of God, of God's dealings with humankind, and of human behavior. Many of these biblical traditions have been deployed in support of violent oppressive actions in a wide variety of contexts. In the spirit of contemporary moral discourse, it is a matter of grave concern that the Bible has been used and is still being used by many as a tool of colonialism, oppression, and the domination of women. Yet things are changing. As women in Palestine, we are full participants in our national struggle, but we are not fully recognized as such and are just becoming part of the decision-making structure. The Intifada of 1987–93 changed some attitudes, but there is still a long way to go. Nevertheless, women are organizing at the grassroots level and are beginning to connect the national struggle with their own need for liberation.

Peace and Nonviolence

The Bible begins and ends with promises of peace. In the beginning God created a garden. God gave the best to the man and the woman God had created. An abode of peace, order, and beauty was all they needed for a good life. At the end, another peaceable community appears. There God dwells with people on earth in a city of peace, security, and healing (Rev 21:11–14). In between, Isaiah and Micah speak of the peaceable era when swords will have been hammered into plows and spears into pruning hooks (Mic 4:3; Isa 2:4). Thus, the promise of peace is central to the biblical and Christian tradition. Peace on earth, goodwill to humankind, was the angels' song at Jesus' birth. The presence of Christ in our midst is said to bring the peace that passes all understanding (Phil 4:7). Nevertheless, the Christian tradition holds a wide range of views about peace. One could spend much time debating such views, including the division introduced by some between spiritual peace and historical peace. For me, however, much of this has a personal dimension.

All my life I have been confronted with structures of injustice that have violated my dignity and my self-esteem. The church as well as my mother taught me not to resist, that to do so would not be Christian nor in the way of peace, as both my mother and the church understood it. Until this day I vividly remember the only time my mother ever hit me and was really angry with me, when, as a child of eight, I did not listen to her but climbed the fig tree in our backyard and picked figs. My mother claimed that this made my grandmother angry and that, for that reason, I should not do it. I thought I had as much right to the tree, to my father and grandfather's property, as my grandmother. I could not understand why I could not have some of the figs. Peace, then, for my mother, meant submission and relinquishing our rights, which resulted in doing violence to others and ourselves.

The rebel in me started searching, agonizing, and inquiring. I kept asking myself, "If we say there is that of God in every person, why is it so difficult to see that of God in others? Why is there so much evil and suffering in the world?" For years I struggled with this Christian truth—that we are made in the image and likeness of God, but I was happy to learn that the indwelling divinity seemed to be a part of all religions. "The kingdom of God is within you," says Jesus. "You are the temple of God," wrote Paul. The prophet Muhammad tells his followers, "He who knows himself knows God," and many Sufis echo this. This recognition of our shared brotherhood and sisterhood convinced me that it must lead to the disappearance of exploitation, oppression, and everything that comes from false beliefs that justify themselves by degrading others. Acknowledgment of our true selves becomes revolutionary. It must, therefore, lead to great changes and to peace. Thus, the search for peace and the recognition of reality are identical.

In the war of 1948, I was only eight years old. Yet I can remember very clearly the fear. I remember hiding in the basement. I remember the refugees from the coastal plain of Palestine. My father and my older brother, hearing of their plight, took a truck with water and bread and rescued many of the women and children who were running away from the dangers of war but could not go on walking because of heat, thirst, and pain. Fifty of these people shared our house for a period of six weeks. Another one hundred camped under our pine trees. Our Friends Meeting House sheltered many families until they found a way of settling somewhere else. I have lived most of my life next to a refugee camp. The war is over, but the plight of those unfortunate people continues. A fourth generation has now been born in that camp. Can we call this peace?

In 1967, when another war broke out in the Middle East, my oldest son was eight years old. His sister was five. We were hiding in a shelter that was partially damaged, and our very lives were threatened at every moment. Then, we moved to another shelter, which we shared with thirty other children and adults. That day, two little girls died from an Israeli air raid, and overnight we found ourselves under the dominance of an alien power. To many, the evil of war is now considered less than the evil of military occupation and foreign domination. I remember, and now understand, why my aunt from Nazareth wept when we rejoiced that the war had ended. She told us, "I have lived in Nazareth since 1948 and the war has not ended. What is coming will be worse."

Four of my seven grandchildren were born during the first Intifada. One of them was six years old during the Gulf War. How much longer do we have to live with war experiences, which seem to go on from one generation to the next? I could share hundreds of such recollections—of my own fears, my children's, my grandchildren's. However, I will not; I have no wish to overwhelm either my readers or myself with this exercise.

I have lived under military occupation for almost half of my life, and it has caused me to search deep within myself. I have found that I have three loyalties. The first is to Christ, who calls us to love our enemy; the second, to aid any man or woman in need or in trouble; the third, to love our country, its people, and its way of life. This loyalty prevents us from assisting the invader. In our situation no one can set precisely the rules for us to follow, but we can testify that, in our experience, the Spirit of God leads us into the truth and provides us with proper guidance in every situation.

We have gone through circumstances of great privation and anxiety over these years. At times, this has seemed to awaken my dependence on God. What joy and hope I gain when I know that, wherever I am, whether in affluent circumstances or in poverty, whether with personal liberty or without it, I am ever under the guiding hand of God and that, wherever God has placed me, God has a service for me to render.

I call myself a Quaker or a Friend. Friends, throughout history, have maintained a testimony to peace. War, we say, is contrary to the mind of Christ. Therefore, it is laid upon us to live in the virtue of that life and that power that win through love rather than through war. This is no easy testimony. It has three aspects: refusing to take part in acts of war ourselves; striving to remove the causes of war; and using the way of love open to us to promote peace and to heal wounds.

How can I interpret this pacifism to my children and to my students when we have all been the victims of violence? How do we deal with the violence that is implicit in the structures that surround us? How do I interpret my pacifism to my children, when they see that violence seems to bring about change that benefits the violent while nonviolence appears to permit our homeland to be taken over by others? How do I show them that our faith, our pacifism, can be a practical faith, an effective pacifism?

It was at this point in my spiritual journey that I found myself at a crossroads. I could not go on because I did not know which road to take. Neither could I travel backward to the place whence I had come. New experiences prohibited that course. At times, the whole journey seemed simply too difficult. My life seemed to have turned into a jigsaw puzzle for which I could not find all the pieces. I had been taught to love my enemy, but sometimes those words simply increased the war raging within myself. How could I find peace within when I was constantly worried for the lives of my family members, for life in general? How can one find peace when life itself seems to have become a burden?

Yet I have found that peace without having to embrace with approval the violence around me. When I have the strength to endure suffering, to try again to love all men and women, I am liberated to work for peace and freedom. Love of one's enemies forces one to recognize that the enemy too is a child of God—a very necessary condition, if our enemies are ever to make the changes we are requiring of them. Still, for me this continues to be one of the hardest paths that I must walk on my spiritual journey. Thankfully, there have been milestones to show me that it is possible. There have been moments of pure joy when my soul has been washed with peace, when I have been filled with strength, when my pacifist approach to life has worked. I know that even in the midst of persecution we can find ourselves possessed by the power of divine forgiveness. God's forgiving love can burst like a flare, even in the midst of our grief and hatred, and free us to love. But one must acknowledge that there is a subtle pride in clinging to our hatreds, reminding ourselves that they are justified, perceiving ourselves as if no one else in human history has suffered as we have.

And, all the while, as Palestinians and as women, we are being told to be peaceful—but peaceful in a very different way. This peacefulness seemingly required of us means to be nice, to be passive, to permit oneself to be trampled upon. This peace is achieved by pounding our opposition to oppression into submission. It is maintained by crushing every protest against injustice. It is, simply, peace for the rulers at the expense of the ruled. We spend our daily lives as persons and as communities in the midst of violence. We find ourselves, willingly or unwillingly, participating in social organizations that practice violence and embody its principles. To promote justice we may deliberately act in violent as well as in nonviolent ways. For those who opt for violence against injustice, can we say that we would rather see them die than defend themselves? Who will throw the first stone of condemnation? Who is morally superior? When we condemn those who opt for violence, are we demonizing others in order that we may relish our own sense of greater worthiness?

Are we thus relieving ourselves of our responsibility for the sin of dealing with our brothers and sisters as if they were less than human?

As we opt for violence or nonviolence in our revolution, we understand that the liberty to choose is not always available. Pacifists and nonpacifists committed to the struggle for a just future should, I believe, regard each other as allies on most issues. The problem between these two groups does not approach in magnitude that which exists between those on the side of liberation and those who support the oppressive structures of the status quo. The gospel compels us as Christians to withhold support from such structures, and, in any case, such support is an impossible alternative for us today. Therefore, as a Quaker and as a woman, I must look to the teachings of my religious heritage, those teachings I can apply to the struggles in which I am engaged, both as a nationalist and as a feminist.

There are, of course, many contemporary ideas on revolution. These ideas have involved surface change: the transfer of power from one personality to another; the replacement of one tyranny by another. A revolution of vitality must concern itself with the triumph of human values and of human rights. Christian teachings are relevant to such a revolution. Although these teachings are essentially nonviolent, they can never be characterized as encouraging passivity or disengagement in the face of injustice. Rather, Christ's teachings are activist, highly political, and often controversial; sometimes they involve dangerous forms of engagement in social and political conflict.

In this struggle, it is my belief that means and ends should be consistent. I cannot endorse acts of violence in my day-to-day confrontations and at the same time be taken seriously when I speak of an ideal for the future that exalts wisdom, sensitivity, fairness, and compassion as basic requirements for running the world. The peculiar strength of nonviolence comes from the dual nature of its approach: the offering of respect and concern, on the one hand, while meeting injustice with noncooperation and defiance, on the other. These seemingly contradictory impulses—to rage against, while simultaneously refusing to destroy—combine to create a force worthy of nothing less than a revolution. By this I mean not just a reshuffling of death-dealing powers but a genuine restructuring of the society in which we live.

In the past few years—first in Madrid, afterwards in Oslo, and then in Washington—we all watched anxiously the unfolding of the Middle East peace process. We should not forget that the real issue of these talks is Palestine. The Palestinian people accepted an extraordinary set of compromises, compromises required of no other participant. Our experience has confirmed our worst fears: Israel is not committing itself to withdrawal, to end the military occupation, to dismantle settlements, or to Palestinian self-determination and the right of return. Such a vision of "peace," of course, is a formula for unending conflict. Cosmetic peace is not enough. The road to peace is not paved with exclusivity or with unending hostility. Rather, it grows out of reconciliation, sharing, and community. Ultimately, there can be no military option for either Palestinians or Israelis. We must, finally, live together and discover how to share the land together.

We have agreed to work for peace. Much stands in the way. The issues are clear and the dangers are very obvious. Peace is for everyone, not just for the powerful, but we cannot have peace if we continue to recite our litanies of past wrongs and past fears. We must deal with the present. We must look to the future of our children and of all humanity. We must build with new materials, with noncombustibles that will not produce yet more wars. It is up to us to remove the causes of war, but we do not seem to realize this. All too often we are indifferent. We have three meals a day. We have our jobs, our positions, and our titles. We do not want to be disturbed. We talk about peace. We have conferences. Yet, if we are not inwardly transformed, if we still seek power and position, if we are motivated by greed, if we are nationalistic, if we are bound by dogmas and beliefs for which we are willing to die and to destroy others, we cannot have peace in the world.

And what is peace? Do we perceive it as simply the absence of conflict? Conflict—internal, interpersonal, intergroup, and international conflict— is an inevitable fact of daily life. Peace consists in dealing creatively with this inevitable conflict. Peace is a process of working to resolve conflict in such a way that both sides win. Increased harmony as the outcome of conflict and conflict resolution produces real peace. We greet one another with peace. We pray for peace. We are called to be peacemakers. We are told the mission of the Savior is to be a deliverer of peace. I often quote from Ezekiel 13:10, "because they have misled my people, saying, 'Peace,' when there is no peace." Or the words of Isaiah 59:14-15, "Justice is turned back, and righteousness stands at a distance; for truth stumbles in the public square, and uprightness cannot enter. Truth is lacking, and whoever turns from evil is despoiled" (NRSV). To have peace, we must tell the truth; without truth telling there is no peacemaking.

Can we have peace without self-determination and sovereignty? Without land and water that are essential for survival? Can our society experience economic development while Israeli-imposed restrictions remain in place: roadblocks; closures; isolation; unemployment; economic marginalization and exclusion; exploitation of water, land, and people's work; and, in addition, no protection whatsoever? How can we have peace when Palestinian refugees still live in refugee camps in the Gaza Strip and the West Bank, in Jordan and Syria and Lebanon, without the right of return and compensation? When Palestinians living in the occupied territories are forced to live in *bantustans* without the right to resist (because this will be interpreted as terrorism)—and this is not called racism?

Palestinians and Israelis have no military option. We should learn how to live together as equals, as real neighbors. As our shrinking world makes us all near neighbors, we should be increasingly aware of two facts about our nature as people of this world. One is that we are very different from one another in color, lifestyles, cultures, and beliefs. The other is that we are exceedingly alike. There is a fantastic range of common needs and desires, fears and hopes, that bind us together in our humanness and in the concern for the well being of others. Maybe the time has come when we should unite in certain common affirmations of life:

- A pledge to honor and respect every race, culture, religion, and individual (no exclusiveness)

- Recognition of the claim of every individual to the resources of the earth for the necessities of human survival and the moral obligation of the more fortunate to share with the less fortunate

- The right of every individual to the use of talents, energies, and resources for the benefit of the community

- Commitment to the search for universal values, however differently expressed, that may enable the individual and the community to overcome greed, power, and self-seeking

- Affirmation of the presence of the spirit of hope and compassion, available to all, by which our lives may be made more whole, more creative, more harmonious, as we draw directly upon that power around us, and within us, and within all life.

Notes

1. David Ben-Gurion, *The Rebirth and Destiny of Israel* (New York: Philosophical Library, 1954), 100.

2. See Michael Prior's study of the role of the Bible in the exploitation of people from three different regions and periods: Latin America, South Africa, and Palestine (*The Bible and Colonialism: A Moral Critique* [Sheffield: Sheffield Academic Press, 1997]).

3. It is true that in the passage in Colossians, which has somewhat similar material, the injunction to be "subordinate" is used of wives to husbands. In that place the sentence reads, "Wives, be subordinate to your husbands as is fitting in the Lord" (Col 3:18). Here we are dealing with a different text and a different mode of expression.

8

THE SIGN OF ORPAH

Reading Ruth through Native Eyes

Laura E. Donaldson (Cherokee, USA)

Prologue: Reading in the Contact Zone

This was no party
how the house was shaking.
They were trying
to nibble my bones, gnaw
my tribal tongue.
They took turns
pretending they had the power
to disembowel my soul
and force me to give them
my face to wear
for Halloween.
They like to play
that I want to change,
that I don't mind ending myself
in their holy book.
They think they can just twist till the blood has drained
and I am as white
and delightsome
as can be.
      (Wendy Rose, "Going To War With All My Relations")[1]

The act of reading the Bible has been fraught with difficulty and contradiction for indigenous peoples. On the one hand, the translation of God's

Laura E. Donaldson, "The Sign of Orpah: Reading Ruth through Native Eyes," in *Vernac-ular Hermeneutics*, ed. R. S. Sugirtharajah (Sheffield: Sheffield Academic Press, 1999), 20–36.

Book into Native vernacular comes at a high price: the forcing of oral tongues into static alphabets and its context of a colonizing Christianity. All too often, biblical reading has produced traumatic disruptions within Native societies and facilitated what we now call culturecide. On the other hand, this depressingly long history of victimization should not obscure the ways in which Native peoples have actively resisted deracinating processes by reading the Bible on their own terms.[2] As Rigoberta Menchú (Quiché Mayan) notes in her moving *testimonio, I, Rigoberta Menchú*:

> We accept these Biblical forefathers as if they were our own an-
> cestors, while still keeping within our own culture and our own
> customs... For instance the Bible tells us that there were kings
> who beat Christ. We drew a parallel with our king, Tecún
> Umán, who was defeated and persecuted by the Spaniards, and
> we take that as our own reality.[3]

Whether Menchú and the Quiché Mayan people scan a printed page or learn the stories by heart, they claim the Bible's "reality" as their own and thus exceed the bounds of imperial exegesis. A vivid example of this dynamic emerges from the way Menchú and other women of her community learned to negotiate the biblical narratives of liberation.

As Menchú remarks, the Quiché began their reading process by searching the scripture for stories representing "each one of us." While the men of Chimel village adopted Moses and the Exodus as their paradigm text of liberation, the women preferred the tale of Judith, who "fought very hard for her people and made many attacks against the king they had then, until she finally had his head."[4] Here, the distinct hermeneutic tradition of Mayan women begins to emerge—one that does not indoctrinate the reader with the colonizer's values but rather helps them understand and respond to their own historical situation (in this case, the brutal war being waged against them by the Guatemalan regime of García Lucas). Menchú rejects the belief that the Bible, or the tale of Judith and Holofernes, themselves effect change: "It's more that each one of us learns to understand his reality and wants to devote himself to oth-ers. More than anything else, it was a form of learning for us."[5] Through this statement, she articulates a process of reading practised by many of the world's Native peoples—a process that actively selects and invents, rather than passively accepts, from the literate materials exported to them by the dominant Euro-Spanish culture. For Menchú, this transculturation of meaning emerges from the act of biblical reading in the contact zone.

In her book *Imperial Eyes: Travel Writing and Transculturation*, Mary Louise Pratt defines a contact zone as the space of colonial encounters where people who are divided both geographically and historically come into contact with each other and establish ongoing relations usually in-volving conditions of severe inequality and intractable conflict.[6] She coins this term instead of borrowing the more Eurocentric "colonial frontier" because she wants "to foreground the interactive, improvisational dimensions of colonial encounters so easily ignored or suppressed by diffusionist accounts of conquest and domination."[7] For Pratt, a "contact" perspective treats the bonds among colonizers and colonized (for example, Quiché and *Ladinos*) as implying copresence, mutual influence, and interlocking understandings, which emerge from deep asymmetries of power. In this essay, I will read the biblical book of Ruth through just such a contact perspective forged by the interaction of biblical narrative, the realities of Anglo-European imperialism, and the traditions of Cherokee women. This rereading is marked not only by the colonial history of Indian-white relations but also by the persistence of American Indian traditions; not only by Anglo-European genocide but also by Native "survivance";[8] not only by subjugation but also by resistance.

Scholars have traditionally regarded the book of Ruth as one of the Hebrew Bible's literary jewels: "a brief moment of serenity in the stormy world."[9] According to Hermann Gunkel, for example, Ruth represents one of those "glorious *poetical narratives*" which exhibits "a widow's love lasting beyond death and the grave."[10] Feminist biblical critics have persuasively challenged this view by exposing its masculinist and heterosexist bias. For these interpreters, Ruth's love embodies the love of a woman-identified woman who is forced into the patriarchal institution of levirate marriage in order to survive. It is here—with this struggle over the meaning of women in the text—that I wish to begin my own articulation of the difficult and often dangerous terrain charted by the contact zone. Like Menchú, I hope that my reading of Ruth will function as a form of learning that will enable Native people both to understand more thoroughly how biblical interpretation has impacted us and to assert our own perspectives more strongly. It seems fitting, then, that this journey begin with a crisis: the journey of Naomi and her husband, Elimelech, into Moab, the scandalous country of Lot's daughters.

The Daughters of Lot

Thus both daughters of Lot became pregnant by their father. The firstborn bore a son, and named him Moab; he is the ancestor of the Moabites to this day. (Gen 19:36–37, NRSV)

While Israel was staying at Shittim, the people began to have sexual relations with the women of Moab. These invited the people to the sacrifices of their gods, and the people ate and bowed down to their gods. Thus Israel yoked itself to the Baal of Peor, and the Lord's anger was kindled against Israel. (Num 25:1–3 NRSV)

There was a famine in the house of bread—the literal meaning of the name "Bethlehem"—and only the threat of starvation motivated Elimelech, a god-fearing Israelite, to forsake his home for the country harboring the sexually promiscuous and scandalous Moabites. Even worse, once he and his family had arrived there, their two sons defied the Hebrew proscription against foreign marriage by taking the Moabite women, Orpah and Ruth, as wives. Indeed, for centuries the Israelites had reviled this people as degenerate and, in particular, regarded Moabite women as the agents of impurity and evil. Even the name "Moab" exhibits this contempt, since it allegedly originates in the incestuous liaison between Lot and his daughters. According to the biblical narrative in Genesis 19, Lot's daughters devise a plan to get him drunk on succeeding nights so that they can seduce him. Both women become pregnant as a result, and both have sons. Lot's eldest daughter openly declares her son's origins when she calls him Moab, or "from my father." We glimpse the result of their actions in Deuteronomy, which declares that, even to the tenth generation, "no Ammonite or Moabite shall be admitted to the assembly of the Lord" (Deut 23:3).

As Randall Bailey notes in his fascinating essay on sex and sexuality in Hebrew canon narratives,

> the effect of both the narrative in Genesis 19 and the laws in Deuteronomy 23...is to label within the consciousness of the reader the view of these nations as nothing more than "incestuous bastards." Through the use of repetition in the narrative in Genesis 19...the narrator grinds home the notion of *mamzērîm* [bastards].[11]

Further, according to Bailey, this dehumanization through graphic sexual innuendo enables one to read other parts of the Deuteronomic history—David's mass slaughter of the Moabites in 2 Samuel 8:2 or the ritual humiliation of the Ammonites in 2 Samuel 12:26-31—as warranted and even meritorious.[12]

The belief in Moabite women as a hypersexualized threat to Israelite men prophetically augurs the Christian attitude toward the indigenous women of the Americas. Indeed, as early as 1511, an anonymous Dutch pamphleteer vouched that "these folke lyven lyke bestes without any reasonablenes...And the wymen be very hoote and dysposed to lecherdnes."[13] Significantly (and, I would add, symptomatically), no less a personage than Thomas Jefferson, the second president of the United States and a framer of its Constitution, forges an important link between the Israelite attitude toward the Moabites and the Christian attitude toward American Indians in his own discourse on the book of Ruth. After finishing his *Notes On the State of Virginia* (1787)[14]—one of the most

important influences upon Euramerican attitudes toward Native people
—Jefferson submitted the manuscript for comments to Charles Thomson, then Secretary of Congress. Thomson's remarks were included in the
published version because, as Jefferson enthused, "the following observations...have too much merit not to be communicated." In his response to the section that describes the nation's "Aborigines," Thomson
observes that an alleged lack of "ardor" in Indian men most probably
originated in the forwardness of their women:

> Instances similar to that of Ruth and Boaz are not uncommon
> among them. For though the women are modest and diffident,
> and so bashful that they seldom lift up their eyes, and scarce ever
> look a man full in the face, yet being brought up on great sub-
> jection, custom and manners reconcile them to modes of acting,
> which, judged of by Europeans, would be deemed inconsistent
> with the rules of female decorum and propriety.[15]

Jefferson endorses Thomson's remarks by locating the relevant biblical passage: "When Boaz had eaten and drank, and his heart was merry,
he went to lie down at the end of the heap of corn: and Ruth came softly,
and uncovered his feet, and laid her down. Ruth iii.7."[16] Although
cloaked in the rhetoric of Enlightenment gentility, the statements by
Thomson and Jefferson nevertheless disseminate a cautionary tale that is
quite similar to the one concerning the Moabites: both American Indian
and Moabite women exist as agents not only of evil and impurity but
also of men's sexual frigidity. Given such negative representations, we
need to investigate why the biblical author of Ruth chooses to foreground precisely this ideological nexus by consistently identifying the
protagonist as "Ruth of Moab."

Ruth 2:6 provides an insightful glimpse into this process. After Elimelech and his two sons die, Naomi and Ruth return to Bethlehem. Naomi
subsequently, and recklessly according to some critics, sends her daughter-in-law into the threshing fields of Boaz, a relative of her late husband,
who notices the young widow and asks his servant to whom she belongs.
"The servant who was in charge of the reapers answered, 'She is the
Moabite who came back with Naomi from the country of Moab.'" The
redundant doubling of ethnic markers in this passage—the Moabite from
the country of Moab—emphasizes the text's construction of Ruth not
only as a *gērāh*, or resident alien, but also as an alien who comes from a
despised and barbaric country. However, the significance of this particular repetition has been construed in widely variant ways.

For example, the rabbis who wrote the *Ruth Rabbah* believed that it
reinforces Ruth's role as a paradigmatic convert to Judaism who "turned
her back upon wicked Moab and its worthless idols to become a God-
fearing Jewess—loyal daughter-in-law, modest bride, renowned ancestress

of Israel's great King David."[17] The *Iggeres Shmuel* expands this view and suggests that the quality of Ruth's faith even surpasses that of Abraham since, unlike Ruth, he left home only after God commanded him to do so.[18] For more contemporary critics, the message of Ruth's identity is not one of conversion, but rather, of "interethnic bonding" that parallels the gender bond established when Naomi's daughter-in-law "clings" to her husband's mother instead of returning home.[19] William Phipps articulates this position when he argues that the repetition of "Ruth the Moabite" connotes "vital religion and ethics in a time of bigotry and mayhem,"[20] and acts as an antidote to the xenophobia of the post-exilic Jewish community. Rather than rejection of the Moabites and acceptance of the Israelites, then, Ruth's story conjures a vision of ethnic and cultural harmony through the house of David, which claims her as a direct ancestress.

While the presentation of Ruth as a character manifesting the virtues of tolerance and multiculturalism is appealing, Robert Maldonado's attempt to develop a *malinchista* hermeneutics complicates this view by exposing its political and historical ambiguities.[21] For Maldonado, a theologian of Mexican and Hungarian descent, the biblical figure of Ruth foreshadows the existence of *La Malinche*, or Doña Marina, the Aztec woman who became a consort of, and collaborator with, the conquistador, Hernán Cortés. *La Malinche*'s legacy endures not only in historical Mexican consciousness but also in its linguistic vernacular: "*Malinchista* is a common term for a person who adopts foreign values, assimilates to foreign cultures, or serves foreign interests... The usage ties the meaning of betrayal in Mexican Spanish to the history of colonialism and Indian-White relations..."[22] Yet *La Malinche* harbors deeper and even more personal levels of betrayal, since she was sold as a young girl to some Mayan trader—an experience that generated the bilingualism so crucial to her equivocal status. After she was acquired by Cortés, she was "given" to one of his officers and subsequently married to another conquistador. We begin to glimpse at least some of the complex and disturbing elements underpinning *La Malinche*'s collaboration with her colonizers. The similarities between the story of Doña Marina and the actions of Ruth lead Maldonado provocatively to ask: "Could Ruth be a Moabite Malinche?"[23] Maldonado answers his own question with a strong "maybe"—precisely because of the redundant identification of Ruth described above as well as his own investment in *mestizaje*, or the resistant discourse of racial and cultural mixing.

American Indians have a much more suspicious attitude toward the privileging of mixedness, whether it be mestizaje, métissage, or life in the borderlands. After all, "mixing" is precisely what Thomas Jefferson proposed as the final solution to the seemingly irresolvable "Indian problem." To a visiting delegation of Wyandots, Chippewas, and Shawnees he confidently predicted that "in time, you will be as we are; you will become one people with us. Your blood will mix with ours; and will spread, with ours, over this great island."[24] And what better way to accomplish this commingling than with the paradigm of intermarriage that we glimpse in the book of Ruth? Indeed, one could argue that this "moment of serenity in the stormy world" of the Hebrew Bible exists as the prototype for both the vision of Thomas Jefferson and all those who facilitated conquest of indigenous peoples through the promotion of assimilation.

This social absorption prophetically evokes the fate of many American Indian women and children. In the historically matrilineal Cherokee culture, for example, Jefferson's vision of "mingling" and the realities of intermarriage wreaked havoc upon tribal organization and development. Wives now went to live with their white husbands—a practice that was contrary to the ancient custom of husbands residing in their wives' domiciles. Further, according to Wilma Mankiller (the former Principal Chief of the Cherokee Nation), the children of these relationships assumed their father's surnames and became heirs to their father's, rather than their mother's, houses and possessions.[25] Intermarriage between whites and Indians severely disrupted the traditions of Cherokee women, since a genealogy that had for time immemorial passed from mother to son or daughter now shifted to the father and drastically curtailed women's power. In contrast to Maldonado, I would argue that the book of Ruth similarly foregrounds the use of intermarriage as an assimilationist strategy.

Soon after Ruth marries Boaz, the text states that she conceives and bears a son.

> Then Naomi took the child and laid him in her bosom, and became his nurse. The women of the neighborhood gave him a name saying, "A son has been born to Naomi." They named him Obed; he became the father of Jesse, the father of David. (Ruth 4:13–17)

As Danna Nolan Fewell and David Gunn note, through this announcement Ruth effectively disappears into the household of Boaz, and the legacy of the future king David closes the door upon her story.[26] In other words—although Fewell and Gunn do not use these terms—Ruth's assimilation becomes complete through Obed's transfer to Naomi, the proper Jewish woman, and to Boaz, the Israelite husband. The issue then becomes: What motivates this effacement and what ideological ends does it fulfill?

Even to begin answering this question, however, we must first understand how Ruth is linked to two seemingly disparate female icons—one from the Hebrew bible and the other from the annals of American Indian history: Rahab and Pocahontas. Both of these women have played important roles in the construction of national narratives and both, like *La Malinche*, have been mythologized as facilitating conquest through their relationships with colonizing men.

The Anti-Pocahontas Perplex

You made a decision. My place is with you. I go where you go.
(Stands With A Fist to John Dunbar in *Dances with Wolves*)

Rahab, of course, is Ruth's other mother-in-law and the Canaanite prostitute who gave birth to Boaz (see Matt 1:5). The events leading to this remarkable transformation of status are memorialized in the book of Joshua, chapter 2, and can be briefly summarized as follows. Joshua, who was leading the Israelite invasion of Canaan, sent two spies to reconnoiter the city of Jericho. These two men "entered the house of a prostitute whose name was Rahab and spent the night there" (2:1). When the king of Jericho heard of the spies' presence, he ordered Rahab to surrender them. She refused and hid them under stalks of flax that she had laid out on the roof. After nightfall, she visited the men and requested that, since she had dealt kindly with them, they might in turn spare her and her family "and deliver our lives from death." Jericho does indeed fall: "But Rahab the prostitute, with her family and all who belonged to her, Joshua spared. Her family has lived in Israel ever since" (Josh 6:25). For this reason, she is extolled in the Greek Bible as a paragon of faith and granted a high status as the ancestress of David and Jesus. Like her daughter-in-law Ruth, Rahab embodies a foreign woman, a Canaanite Other, who crosses over from paganism to monotheism and is rewarded for this act by absorption into the genealogy of her husband and son—in this case, into the house of Salmon and ultimately, of David. And, like Ruth, she represents the position of the indigene in the text, or of those people who occupied the Promised Land before the invasion of the Israelites.

However, the narrative figures of Rahab and Ruth conjure not only the position of the indigene in the biblical text but also the specific cultural and historical predicament of American Indian women. Cherokee scholar Rayna Green has identified this predicament as "the Pocahontas Perplex"—one of Euramerica's most important master narratives about Native women. It is named for the daughter of Powhatan and the mythology that has arisen around one of the most culturally significant encounters between Indians and whites. In this version of the story, Powhatan Indians capture Captain John Smith and his men while they are exploring the territory around what is now called Jamestown, Virginia. After marching Smith to their town, the Indians lay his head on a large stone and prepare to kill him with their clubs. Precisely at that moment, Pocahontas—the favorite daughter of Powhatan—uses her body as a human shield and prevents Smith from being executed. She then further intercedes on behalf of the English colonists, who were starving after a long winter, and consequently saves not only the colonists but also the future of English colonization.[27]

As a master narrative with an ideological function, the Pocahontas perplex construes the nobility of Pocahontas and any other Indian woman as a "princess" who "must save or give aid to white men."[28] As Green notes,

> the only good Indian—male or female, Squanto, Pocahontas, Sacagawea, Cochise, the Little Mohee or the Indian Doctor—rescues and helps white men. But the Indian woman is even more burdened by this narrow definition of a "good Indian," for it is she, not the males, whom white men desire sexually."[29]

A consequence of this desire is that the "good" feminine image also implies the "bad" one. She is the Squaw, whose degraded sexuality is vividly summarized in the frontier song, "Little Red Wing"—She "lays on her back in a cowboy shack, and lets cowboys poke her in the crack."[30] The specter of the Squaw—also known as a daughter of Lot—retroactively taints Rahab and Ruth; after all, the former earns her living as a prostitute and, according to Thomas Jefferson and company, the latter's behavior in the biblical counterpart of the cowboy shack was shockingly immoral. Such a debased starting point enables the scriptural stories to proclaim even more stridently the metamorphosis of Rahab and Ruth into the Israelite version of the Pocahontas perplex. In this scenario, Salmon and Boaz stand in for John Smith, although the result remains the same: an indigenous woman who forsakes her people and aligns herself with the men to whom Yahweh had referred when he directed the Israelites to "break down their altars, smash their pillars, burn their Asherah poles with fires, and hew down the idols of their gods, and thus blot out their name from their places" (Deut 12:3).

From an American Indian perspective, then, the midrashic interpretation of Ruth as the paradigmatic convert who "turned her back upon wicked Moab and its worthless idols to become a God-fearing Jewess"[31] seems a much more accurate description of the text's actual function than Robert Maldonado's appeal to some undecidable state of *mestizaje*. Indeed, even Ruth's name affirms the hermeneutic acumen of the rabbis, since it derives from the Hebrew root *rwh*, meaning "watering to saturation."[32] However, whereas the success of this ideological irrigation inspires rejoicing on behalf of the Israelites, it is an instance of mourning for American Indian women. Yet another relative has succumbed to—been filled up by and "saturated" by—a hegemonic culture.

Is there no hope in book of Ruth? Is it nothing but a tale of conversion/assimilation and the inevitable vanishing of the indigene in the literary and social text? In fact, there does exist a counter-narrative—a kind of anti-Pocahontas—whose presence offers some small hope to the Native reader: the sign of Orpah, sister-in-law of Ruth and the woman who returned to her mother's house.

"They broke once more into loud weeping. But while Orpah kissed her mother-in-law goodbye, Ruth clung to her" (Ruth 1:14, translation by Sasson). The figure of Orpah is mentioned only two times in the book of Ruth—1:4, which names her as one of the "Moabite wives," and 1:14, which describes her decision to part ways with Naomi and Ruth. Unfortunately, however, most contemporary scholars mimic the biblical text by leaving her to return home unattended, both literally and critically. Traditionally, Orpah generated much more scrutiny, although much of it was negative. According to midrashic literature, for example, her name allegorically connotes the opposite of Ruth's since it originates in the root 'orep, i.e., the nape of the neck, and describes how she turns the back of her neck to Naomi when she decides to return to Moab. That the sages name Orpah for this moment in her history indicates that they also consider it most important part of her story"[33] and it explicitly charges her with the narrative role of abandoner.[34] Some writers even suggest that she later becomes the mother of Goliath, the famous enemy of Israel, and that Goliath himself was "the son of a hundred fathers."[35] But what else could one expect from a "daughter of Lot?"

William Phipps expresses a more current and enlightened view of Ruth's sister-in-law:

Orpah displays wrenching ambivalence, deciding first one way and then another. She finally takes Naomi's common-sense advice and, after an affectionate goodbye, returns "to her people and to her gods." Her life is difficult enough without taking responsibility for an older widow in a land presumed to be governed by a deity different from the ones she worships (the Moabite Stone refers to Chemosh and to goddess Ashtar, or Ishtar)... She does the prudent thing and heads for her family home to await an arranged remarriage.[36]

While I do not disagree with Phipps's summary, I also believe that he fails to recognize perhaps the most important element of Orpah's decision. She does not just take the path of least resistance—the path of prudence, freedom from responsibility and passivity. Rather, Orpah returns to bēt 'immāh, "her mother's house."[37] Carol Meyers observes that the use of bēt 'immāh is quite rare in the Hebrew scriptures and indicates a family setting identified with the mother rather than the father.[38] In fact, she notes, each biblical passage using this phrase shares a similarity with all the others: a woman's story is being told; women act as agents in their own destiny; the agency of women affects other characters in the narrative; the setting is domestic; and finally, a marriage is involved.[39] Meyers further concludes that all biblical references to "the mother's house" offer female perspectives on issues that elsewhere in the Bible are viewed through a predominately androcentric lens. I would argue that the female perspective offered by "the mother's house" in Ruth is a profoundly important one for Native women, since it signifies that Orpah—the one whose sign is the back of her neck—exists as the story's most central character.

To Cherokee women, for example, Orpah connotes hope rather than perversity because she is the one who does not reject her traditions or her sacred ancestors. Like Cherokee women have done for hundreds if not thousands of years, Orpah chooses the house of her clan and spiritual mother over the desire for another culture. In fact, Cherokee women not only chose the mother's house, they also owned it (along with the property upon which it stood as well as the gardens surrounding it). Husbands customarily went to live with their wives, and the woman's family, rather than the husband's, became the primary caretakers of any children. Read through these eyes, the book of Ruth tells a very different story indeed.

Ojibway poet Kimberly Blaeser illuminates this transformative process of reading through a concept she describes as "response-ability." In her essay, "Pagans Rewriting the Bible," Blaeser defines response-ability as the need of American Indian people to "reconsider, reevaluate, reimagine what [religious] terms might mean or have meant to Indian people as well as what they might come to mean to all people."[40] This is precisely what Rigoberta Menchú accomplishes in her choosing of Judith over Moses and in her insistence that the meaning of any biblical text reflect her people's reality. It is also what I have tried to effect in my own re-reading of Ruth through a Native perspective, and more particularly, through the perspective of Cherokee women. I have reconsidered the dominant exegesis of Ruth as either a paradigm of conversion or a woman-identified woman. I have reimagined this literary jewel of the Hebrew bible as the narrative equivalent of a last arrow pageant.

During the implementation of the Dawes Act,[41] the "last-arrow pageant" was a public ritual that marked the translation of American Indian identity into its more "civilized" white counterpart. Etymologically, the word "translation" means "carried from one place to another," or transported across the borders between one language and another, one country and another, one culture and another.[42] In the context of last-arrow pageants, participants performed and acknowledged their own translation into the idiom of Euramerican culture:

> This conversion of Indians into individual landowners was ceremonialized at "last-arrow" pageants. On these occasions, the Indians were ordered by the government to attend a large assembly on the reservation. Dressed in traditional costume and carrying a bow and arrow, each Indian was individually summoned from a tepee and told to shoot an arrow. He then retreated to the tepee and reemerged wearing "civilized" clothing, symbolizing a crossing from the primitive to the modern world. Standing before a plow, the Indian was told: "Take the handle of this plow, this act means that you have chosen to live the life of the

white man—and the white man lives by work." At the close of the ceremony, each allottee was given an American flag and a purse with the instructions: "This purse will always say to you that the money you gain from your labor must be wisely kept."[43]

For "Ruth the Moabite," the translation from savagism to civilization (or from Asherah to Yahweh) similarly involves the relinquishing of her ethnic and cultural identity. For Orpah, it necessitates a courageous act of self and communal affirmation: the choosing of the indigenous mother's house over that of the alien Israelite Father.

In this interpretation, my response-ability as a person of Cherokee descent and as an informed biblical reader transforms Ruth's positive value into a negative and Orpah's negative value into a positive. Such is the epistemological vertigo inspired by reading in the contact zone. Indeed, paraphrasing Blaeser, response-ability recognizes that life—or meaning in the book of Ruth—cannot be for easy consumption. Chinese feminist theologian Kwok Pui-lan echoes a similar sentiment in her statement that "these attempts at indigenization [of the Bible] show clearly that biblical truth cannot be pre-packaged, that it must be found in the actual interaction between text and context in the concrete historical situation."[44] I can only hope that my indigenization of Ruth has located new meaning in the interaction between biblical text and American Indian context—a meaning that resists imperial exegesis and contributes to the empowerment of aboriginal peoples everywhere.

Notes

1. In Wendy Rose, *Going to War with All My Relations: New and Selected Poems* (Flagstaff, AZ: Entrada Books, 1993).

2. "Deracination" comes from the Latin word meaning "to uproot or to alienate."

3. Rigoberta Menchú, *I, Rigoberta Menchú: An Indian Woman in Guatemala*, ed. Elisabeth Burgos-Debray, trans. Ann Wright (London: Verso, 1984), 80.

4. Ibid., 131.

5. Ibid., 135.

6. Mary Louise Pratt, *Imperial Eyes: Travel Writing and Transculturation* (London: Routledge, 1992), 6.

7. Ibid., 7.

8. The term "survivance" is used by Gerald Vizenor (Chippewa) to describe the complicated gestures of Native survival in the contact zone of contemporary American culture.

9. Danna Nolan Fewell and David M. Gunn, *Compromising Redemption: Relating Characters in the Book of Ruth* (Louisville, KY: Westminster John Knox Press, 1990), 11.

10. Hermann Gunkel, *What Remains of the Old Testament and Other Essays*, trans. A. K. Dallas (New York: Macmillan, 1928), 21.

11. Randall Bailey, "They're Nothing But Incestuous Bastards: The Polemical Use of Sex and Sexuality in Hebrew Canon Narratives," in *Reading from This Place: Social Location and Biblical Interpretation in the United States*, ed. Fernando F. Segovia and Mary Ann Tolbert (Minneapolis, MN: Fortress Press, 1995), 131.

12. Ibid., 132.

13. As cited in Robert F. Berkhofer, Jr., *The White Man's Indian: Images of the American Indian from Columbus to the Present* (New York: Random House, 1978), 10.

14. Thomas Jefferson, *Notes on the State of Virginia*, ed. William Peden (New York: W. W. Norton, 1982).

15. Ibid., 201.

16. Ibid., 297. Since in Hebrew "feet" is often used as a euphemism for a man's genitals, Ruth is clearly initiating some sort of sexual encounter with Boaz.

17. Kathryn Pfisterer Darr, *Far More Precious Than Jewels: Perspectives on Biblical Women* (Louisville, KY: Westminster John Knox Press), 72.

18. Ibid., 72.

19. The verb "to cling" is particularly revealing here since its customary usage involves the relationships of husbands to wives and of humans to Yahweh. Both womanist and feminist critics have used this linguistic turn to argue for Ruth's status as a woman-identified woman, or a woman who embodied the capacity "to care passionately about the quality of another woman's life, to respect each other's choices, and to allow for each other's differences" (Renita J. Weems, *Just a Sister Away: A Womanist Vision of Women's Relationships in the Bible* [San Diego: Lura Media, 1988], 34).

20. William E. Phipps, *Assertive Biblical Women*, Contributions in Women's Studies, vol. 128 (Westport, CT: Greenwood Press), 67.

21. Robert D. Maldonado, "Reading Malinche Reading Ruth: Toward A Hermeneutics of Betrayal," *Semeia* 72 (1995): 91–109.

22. Mary Louise Pratt, "'Yo soy la malinche': Chicana Writers and the Poetics of Ethnonationalism," *Callaloo* 16 (1993): 860, as cited in Maldonado, "Reading Malinche," 99.

23. Maldonado, "Reading Malinche," 101.

24. Thomas Jefferson, *The Writings of Thomas Jefferson*, ed. Albert Ellery Bergh (Washington, DC: The Thomas Jefferson Memorial Association of the United State, 1907), 464.

25. Wilma Mankiller with Michael Wallis, *Mankiller: A Chief and Her People* (New York: St. Martin's Press, 1984), 26.

26. Fewell and Gunn, *Compromising Redemption*, 105.

27. While most Americans still believe in the myth that Pocahontas loved John Smith, a growing body of scholarship has significantly revised this tale of their encounter. Rayna Green and Kathleen Brown are among those who have persuasively argued that Smith's own account of his captivity, near-execution, and rescue by Pocahontas eloquently testifies to yet another example of misrecognized and misinterpreted cultural difference. Brown, for example, contends that Smith's recording of Pocahontas covering his body with her own was most probably part of an adoption ritual in which Powhatan defined his relationship to him as one of patriarchal dominance ("The Anglo-Alongonquian Gender Frontier," in Nancy Shoemaker, ed., *Negotiators of Change: Historical Perspec-*

tives on American Indian Women [London: Routledge, 1995), 39). Unfortunately, "Smith understood neither the ritual adoption taking place nor the significance of Powhatan's promise to make him a werowance and to 'for ever esteeme him as [he did] his son Nantaquoud'" (40). Green (in "The Pocahontas Perplex: The Image of Indian Women in American Culture," *Massachusetts Review* [Autumn 1975], 698–714) provides a further gloss when she notes that as the daughter of the tribe's leader and a woman of considerable status, Pocahontas served as Smith's "mother," for he had to be reborn, after a symbolic death, as one of the tribe. Thus, Pocahontas was not delaying Smith's execution and thwarting her own people when she threw her body over his. She was in fact acting on behalf of her people (35).

28. Green, "The Pocahontas Perplex," 703.

29. Ibid.

30. Ibid., 711.

31. Darr, *Far More Precious*, 72.

32. In *The Feminine Unconventional: Four Subversive Figures in Israel's Tradition* (Minneapolis, MN: Fortress Press, 1990), Andre LaCocque observes that most biblical exegetes "stubbornly propose" the Syriac translation of "Ruth" as an abbreviation of Re'uth, or female companion. Like other scholars who have carefully studied the book of Ruth, LaCocque persuasively argues that, philologically, the name "Ruth" has nothing to do with *r'h* (to be a companion), but rather, is a cognate of *rwh* (to water to saturation). See his discussion, 115–16.

33. Leila Leah Bronner, "A Thematic Approach to Ruth in Rabbinic Literature," in *A Feminist Companion To Ruth*, Feminist Companion to the Bible, 3, ed. Athalya Brenner (Sheffield: Sheffield Academic Press, 1993), 155.

34. Mieke Bal, *Lethal Love: Feminist Literary Readings of Biblical Love Stories* (Bloomington, IN: Indiana University Press, 1987), 74.

35. Bronner, "A Thematic Approach," 155.

36. Phipps, *Assertive Biblical Women*, 53.

37. "But Naomi said to her two daughters-in-law, 'Go back each of you to your mother's house'" (Ruth 1:8).

38. Carol L. Meyers, "Returning Home: Ruth 1.8 and the Gendering of the Book of Ruth," in *A Feminist Companion to Ruth*, 91.

39. Ibid., 109–110.

40. Kimberly M. Blaeser, "Pagans Rewriting the Bible: Heterodoxy and the Representation of Spirituality in Native American Literature," *ARIEL: A Review of International English Literature*, 25, no. 1 (1994): 13.

41. Passed in 1887 and named for its sponsor, Massachusetts senator Henry L. Dawes, the Dawes Act attempted to detribalize American Indians by privatizing communally held Indian lands and partitioning reservations into 160- and 80-acre lots subject to sale or lease by the government. Between 1887 and its end in 1934, the Dawes Act reduced the total land base of American Indian peoples by two-thirds.

42. J. Hillis Miller, *Topographies: Crossing Aesthetics* (Stanford: Stanford University Press, 1995), 316.

43. Ronald T. Takaki, *A Different Mirror: A History of Multicultural America* (Boston: Little, Brown and Company, 1993), 235–36.

44. Kwok Pui-lan, *Discovering the Bible in the Non-Biblical World* (Maryknoll, NY: Orbis Books, 1995), 11.

9

THE PATRIARCHAL HOUSEHOLD AND POWER RELATIONS BETWEEN GENDERS

Elsa Tamez (Mexico)

The Family in the Empire

For the Greeks and Romans, the family was an essential element of the society. It involved the patriarchal family, in which the father, head of the household and owner of the house, was called *paterfamilias*. He was considered the landowner and was at the same time responsible for his wife, for his children, and frequently for his grandchildren and great-grandchildren who still lived under the same roof. Those who had to submit to him were not only his own blood family but all who lived in his house: slaves, if he had any; freedmen, who legally were still tied to the head of the household; and other persons, for example, those who because of favors received from the owner of the household remained tied to him for the return of the favors. As can be seen, the term *familia* in antiquity covers not only family relationships but also all those who were dependent on and subordinate to the head of the household.

Marriage and procreation were fundamental to the patriarchal society. Carolyn Osiek and David Balch show that marriage was a social contract between two families for legitimate reproduction and the legal transmission of property.[1]

At the beginning of the first century, the emperor Augustus promulgated a law that obliged women to follow the patterns of the patriarchal household, to marry and have children. He also imposed strong sanctions against adultery committed by women.[2] The emperor was concerned that the aristocracy might not reproduce. Besides that, the gov-

---

Elsa Tamez, "The Patriarchal Household and Power Relations between Genders," in *Struggles for Power in Early Christianity* (Maryknoll, NY: Orbis Books, 2007), 27–40.

erning class and the males of the aristocracy, with their imperial ideology, were afraid that gender roles—as well as the roles of others who were subordinate to the owner of the household, such as children and slaves—might be inverted. For the aristocracy, a change in the patriarchal household would mean chaos. Greek and Roman thinkers such as Cicero, Seneca, Tacitus, Dionysius, and others repeated the vertical concepts of Aristotle with respect to the family, and, what is even more interesting, they compared the city government with the family. For them, both governments were the same. The king was like the *paterfamilias*: he should watch over and protect his subordinates and make them obey, as the father did in his household with his subordinates. The subordinates had to obey and submit to the king and the city (or imperial) authorities as the dependents of the patriarchal family submitted to the father. The patriarchal household values were intrinsically united to the values of society. For this reason it is called a patriarchal society. Elisabeth Schüssler Fiorenza rightly prefers to refer to this social setting as "kyriarchal," adding the Greek term *kyrios*, meaning "Lord."[3]

This does not mean that there were not rich women, owners of households, who demanded submission of their children, slaves, and persons who had received favors from them. This was common in the case of rich widows or rich divorced women who, because of their wealth, power, and status, received honors from their dependents and clients.[4] The patriarchal household was the ideal of the masculine and imperial or governmental ideology. In reality, wealthy women who did not submit opposed these values, as did poor women, who had to work with their husbands or alone in order to survive.

According to ancient extrabiblical documents, the participation of women in public activities in the city was ambiguous and depended not only on their gender but also on their wealth and status. Rich women could attend the theater, but they sat apart; they could also attend banquets with their husbands, but had to leave when the *symposion* began. That was a time to drink, have philosophical discussions or simple conversations, and engage in erotic activities.[5] These well-to-do women could also participate in worship activities, whether directed to the emperor or to another god or goddess, in the city or in the house, but always with marginal roles and under the orders of the men in charge. It was understood that poor women, as well as their husbands, were excluded from these social activities.

The Domestic Codes

Various texts in 1 Timothy mention the behavior of the household members: the father, the wife, the children, and the slaves. These four groups have a place and a social role to fulfill according to the ideal of the patriarchal household. In 2:11–12, the author orders women to learn in silence and not to dominate the men. Even though these texts do not necessarily refer to husband and wife, the position each one should have in society, especially the role of submission of the woman in the household, is implicit. In 3:4 one of the qualities of the supervisor (*episkopos*) of the Christian community is that "he must manage his own household well, keeping his children submissive and respectful (*semnotētos*) in every way." In 6:1–2 slaves are told to respect their masters (believers or not). The mention of these three groups of distinct members of the household, with one being superior to the other, reflects what are commonly known as "domestic codes," because they refer to the administration of the household.[6] In this way, the man, owner of the household, is the husband, father, and master to whom all must pay respect and submit.

According to some scholars, these codes go back to Aristotle (384–322 BCE), who in his work *Politics* speaks of the administration of the household, because the state is made up of family units. The parts of the family are expressed in pairs, beginning with master and slave, followed by husband and wife, concluding with father and children. Afterward, Aristotle continues his discourse basing the authority and superiority in the master, husband, and father over the slave and the rest of the household members. He also adds a fourth element to the domestic economy, namely "the art of amassing a fortune."[7]

After Aristotle, many philosophers and thinkers of antiquity continued transmitting the same idea, using similar schemes, sometimes with fixed and stereotypical forms and other times with some variants. But deep down the superiority and authority of the male as *paterfamilias* was always affirmed. For the ancient writers the authority and the subordination of the household and the city were the same. To administer the household well was a patriotic duty.[8] Any kind of inversion in the order of the household authority meant subversion, even a catastrophe, for the order of the city.

In the minds of these thinkers was the image of rich aristocratic families, since those who constituted legally formed families were free citizens and those who had houses and slaves were usually the wealthy. But the ideal was not limited to the wealthy households. Patriarchal ideology penetrated the whole of society and all social sectors. Even when the lower sectors were unable to reach the ideal because of their condition, it was assumed to be natural and logical. We see in inscriptions with epitaphs of people who were not from the elite but for some reason (commercial or another reason) had sufficient money to be able to dedicate an epitaph to a loved woman, that the praises of a mother or a wife are imbued with patriarchal ideology.

In Roman imperial times the comportment of women of the Roman elite and also those of the governing classes of the provinces changed considerably with respect to the ideal woman according to tradition. The *paterfamilias* lost power, and the women of high society achieved much liberty of movement outside the household and within marriage. They controlled properties, and they could divorce, attend banquets and public events, and be public figures, at least as city benefactors with titles of honor. Patriarchal ideals clashed with reality.[9] The Julian law of the emperor Augustus with respect to marriage and children, the satires of Juvenal and Martial about Roman matrons and their dominion, plus the continuous traditional affirmations of the majority of thinkers (including Neoplatonists, Peripatetics, Stoics, Epicureans, Hellenist Jews, and Pythagoreans) with respect to the submissive behavior of women reflect their response of rejecting women's behavior that did not conform to the domestic codes and to women's position in the patriarchal society.

The Houses Where Families Lived

Archaeological excavations have allowed us to know about the houses of the wealthy as well as the apartment buildings called *insulae*, commonly constructed for persons of modest resources. Generally books on the ancient urban environment dedicate many pages to the houses (*domus* in Latin; *oikoi* in Greek) of the rich, which have been better preserved. Nevertheless, centering so much on these houses runs the risk of losing the perspective of the contours of the whole city. The majority of the population (between 90 and 95 percent) were not members of the elite. Many of them lived in very crowded conditions in the miserable rooms of the *insulae*, which often did not have open spaces in their interior. Osiek and Balch comment, "The majority of the dwellers lived crowded in small, dark and poorly ventilated buildings, where there was neither privacy nor adequate hygiene and as a consequence the propagation of sickness was inevitable."[10] The high rate of infant mortality and reduced life expectancy at the time in which the first letter to Timothy was written were not unusual. We also have to realize that part of the population did not have sufficient money even to pay rent and they had to sleep mainly around public buildings.[11]

As the demarcation of poor neighborhoods and the city center reflected social stratification,[12] the homes also reflected the ideology of the dominant patriarchal class. This ideology was imposed with greater force in the households of the wealthy and by governments or male thinkers in their discourses and writings. In fact, as Osiek and Balch say, "One of the key functions of the wealthy households was to reinforce social status...The architecture separated slaves from property owners and dining rooms from kitchens."[13] Household property owners had enormous power over all who lived under their roof.[14]

In Ephesus, the city where Timothy's community was located, archaeologists have found various houses of the wealthy built on the hill.

The mosaics on the floors, as well as the ampleness of the perimeter, reflect the status of rich persons. It is possible that they had two or three floors. Since in the first floor there were signs of an interior garden (*peristylium*), a room where business was attended (*tablinum*), and another that could have been a multi-use room (*oecus*), it is possible that the bedrooms were on a second floor. Some of the houses in that city had a hot water system for the different rooms of the house besides having running water for baths, latrines, and the kitchen. The majority of the city's inhabitants used the city's baths and latrines and bought their food from shops on the street.

In front of these houses, before coming to the hill, were two blocks of two-story apartments (*insulae*) in which were a series of shops on the first floor and rooms for living on the second. The shops faced the street. These apartments were for persons with fewer resources, possibly the owners of the small stores that faced the street. The apartments could also have been rooms rented to poor families who lived crowded together. In other cities similar buildings of apartments (*insulae*) have been found in which the rooms, one or two small and dark spaces, were on the back side or on the second floor of the small stores.[15] Not all the *insulae* were for poor families, however. In highly populated cities such as Ostia and Rome there were *insulae* with more rooms, with even four to seven rooms in an apartment, with windows facing the street or the interior patio.[16] Except in a few cases, the *insulae* generally did not have kitchens, latrines, or baths.

The Cultural Values of Honor and Shame

Honor and shame, two values intimately related to the family and the household, were "foundational concepts of the first century."[17] Moral instructions or advice always specified what was honorable or what was not. Everyone's comportment was measured by these two concepts, which showed what people considered to be acceptable or reproachable. Whoever acted contrary to the customs valued by society suffered shame, so that the behavior of persons, families, and even communities was marked by the attention paid by others to them, according to the code of honor and shame.

Although it seems strange, these concepts were differentiated by gender in the patriarchal culture. The honor of women was not the same as that of men, and almost always women's honor was related to their sexual behavior. If a woman refused an indecent invitation, such as to have an adulterous relationship, she conserved her honor; however, if she accepted, it became a shame for her and her household. The honor of a man consisted in defending his social status and the sexual virtue of the women in his family. Honor for a woman was to maintain her virginity before marrying and to be faithful after marriage[18]—so much so that to remain a widow and never to marry again so as to remain faithful to her husband was one of the highest virtues for a woman.

The men of the household paid great attention to the sexual conduct of their women, because for them "women had a dangerous ability to bring shame to their families (especially to their male family members), through their sexual conduct."[19] That is the reason the ancient writings insist that a woman should stay in the house—this was her space and dominion—and participate as little as possible in public activities. Honor could be attained by status, power, and wealth, and by having a lifestyle designated as honorable according to the values of society.

The Patriarchal Household as an Ideal for the Concept of Family

It is important to underline that when we speak of household (*oikos*) in antiquity, we are not only referring to the place or building but also to the family and the conduct of the family in the household. The ideal of family—and here we have to underline *ideal*—was that the wife, the children, and the slaves if there were slaves—that is, all of the dependents of the head (man)— submitted in obedience to him, because he was the husband, the father, and the master. The space reserved for women was in the house. This was the ideal that may have existed in the ancient Greek and Roman households in the times of the Republic. By the middle of the Hellenistic period, however, there had already been generated a change in that the *paterfamilias* had lost certain power in his household and women had reached a certain level of independence.[20] Thus, in the Roman Empire the patriarchal household remained as only an ideal of the male and governing elite, filled with nostalgia and discontent in the face of contrary conduct of women, especially wealthy women. On the other hand, as has already been said, the ideal conduct within the household was associated more with the elite than with those who did not belong to it. The construction of houses for the rich could have favored this ideal conduct for the patriarchal family in the wealthy citizen class. Women could stay in the spaces assigned to them,[21] but they did not do so. Moreover, in the *insulae*, without latrines or kitchens, women were obligated to use public space—not because they rebelled but because of need. In the small rooms of the apartments of the poor *insulae* there was barely room for a father, mother, and two or three children. Nevertheless, we would have to realize that, if the family had a small shop on the first floor, the owner could have one or two slaves who would live in the workshop or store itself.

Besides, neither non-citizens nor slaves could legally marry. The so-called domestic codes that required obedience and submission to the *paterfamilias* by the wife, children, and slaves, were an ideal almost impossible to strictly follow, whether because of social and legal changes in the society with respect to women or conditions of the lower classes, who were the majority of the inhabitants of the city. The patriarchal ideal was one thing, the social reality was another.

Nevertheless, it is important to take into account that those domestic codes or norms did not go out of existence; on the contrary, they were internalized also by the non-elite,[22] even by the poor. The codes always appeared as profound cultural values and as a model to follow, according to the moral or apologetical discourse. The codes continued to be a force that, even without a corresponding practice, served to restrict and crush aspirations to equality between family members. We will see later how in the first letter to Timothy these values were affirmed and applied to all the families of different social strata.

For our study it is important to ask ourselves, when speaking of the household and domestic codes, if these codes really pertained only to the rich who had houses or mansions (*oikos/domus*) or if they could also have referred to people who lived in *insulae* for well-off persons,[23] as well as those who lived in *insulae* that had one or two rooms. The majority of the commentaries and books that deal with the theme of domestic administration refer only to the houses of the rich. This is because the literature that deals with this question refers only to the wealthy. Nevertheless, taking into account the interiorization of patriarchal values and the existence of families that had small businesses and workshops in which the father, mother, children, and maybe one or two slaves worked, it is logical to think of an administration and patriarchal relationships between those members in which the domestic codes were also applied. This point is important because, as we will see in 1 Timothy 3:1–7, certain qualities required of the supervisor will be those that have to do with the administration of the household. If we affirm that only the rich administer a household, the requirements of the supervisors could be filled only by the wealthy members of the community, which would be a contradiction with respect to the author's confrontation with the rich, according to our interpretation.

Let us now analyze the texts against the background of a patriarchal culture as we have described it in reference to the family, the household, and the values of honor and shame in antiquity. We will begin by studying again 1 Timothy 2:8–15, but now from the perspective of gender.

Against Women Who Teach and Have Authority over Men

The Text: 1 Timothy 2:8–12

> 8 I desire, then, that in every place the men should pray, lifting up holy hands without anger or argument; 9 also that the women should dress themselves modestly and decently in suit-

able clothing, not with their hair braided, or with gold, pearls, or expensive clothes, [10] but with good works, as is proper for women who profess reverence for God. [11] Let women learn in silence with full submission. [12] I permit no woman to teach or have authority over a man; she is to keep silent.

The context of the instruction is the liturgical assembly or the Christian community, in which the men should pray with hands raised and the women should not dress in an ostentatious manner. That is what most of the commentaries on the letter say. If that is so, then it deals with an assembly where men and women actively participated in prayer,[24] but because of the struggles for power the author wanted to eliminate the participation of women in the teaching. To teach (*didaskalein*) could here be a technical term meaning to teach that which is official or the tradition.[25] Chapter 3 of the letter, where the qualities of supervisor are indicated, where men are assigned, also seems to reinforce the context of the community. However, it could be that verses 11 and 12 of chapter 2 also applied to women outside the context of the Christian community. The text gives the impression that the author wants submissive and resigned conduct, rather than the exercise of teaching and authority over men, to be applied also in the daily life of women.[26]

The author deemed the presence of rich women to be threatening because they probably tried to use their wealth, status, and power to dominate the rest of the members, including the official leadership. The text, because it is situated within the first instructions and written in a negative tone, indicates that there was a problem with this kind of woman. The different instruction for men and women is notable (v. 8). However, the main point of the letter is not in this conflictive situation, which probably involved only a small number of women benefactors or patrons. What is an issue, however, is the author's instruction on how to resolve the problem. Instead of resolving it in a non-authoritarian manner, he turns to the patriarchal ideology of those times—not only to call attention to the rich women causing the problem, but to subjugate all the women, because patriarchal ideology is directed to all women, regardless of their social class.

To tell women how they should dress, even though here it is to avoid the contrast of the clothing worn by the rich and the poor of the assembly, is part of patriarchal ideology. The terms "decently," "modestly," "restraint," and "discretion," for example, in spite of the fact that the author contrasts them with ostentatious hairdos, jewels, and costly clothing, still reflect the values that patriarchal society assigns to the feminine gender. By applying to women the terms *aidous* ("discretion, modesty") and *sōphrōsynēs* ("self-control, restraint"), the author causes the reader to think of "chastity," sexual purity. It is because patriarchal ideology has associated women throughout history with sex and temptation.

Shame is for women who dress with insolence and liberty. That is why, as we have seen, the men of the household—fathers, brothers, uncles, grand-fathers—had the task of controlling the women so they would not be sexually provocative and damage the family's honor.

Thus the author of the letter gives instructions that the rich women not use jewels and expensive clothing in order to reduce the social inequality within the Christian community,[27] but at the same time the patriarchal ideology tells women how they should dress, using terms with connotations associated with chastity. For our reading of the Bible, what is important is to contrast the ostentatious with what is modest and simple, not with chastity. The problem is not the women's sexual provocation, but the ostentation of some of the wealthy women of the community.

If we do not show the real contrast, which is simplicity versus ostentation, the ambiguity of verse 9a leads some interpreters to assume uncritically certain values assigned to women in keeping with their feminine gender. That is why some commentators read here an instruction directed to ornamentation in the women's finery, in the sense that they should not dress in a flirtatious manner, but chastely:

> Knowing that the dress and ornamentation was an area of preoccupation for women, and that there is danger in falling into insolence and indiscretion, Paul focuses on this point in his advice and instruction to the women when referring to their manner of dressing.[28]

In this comment George W. Knight III forgets that men in antiquity as well as today like to preoccupy themselves with how they dress and flirt with women. Jerome D. Quinn and William C. Wacker translate *kosmein* as "to make oneself attractive,"[29] adding that it is oriented to the feminine role assigned by culture, and that if *kosmein* ("to adorn oneself") referred to men, it certainly would not have been translated "to make oneself attractive."

We note, then, two problems in 2:9: the text itself and the interpretations of the text. In both, the ideology of patriarchal society is present in assigning virtues in accord with gender. The concepts of family, household, honor, and shame have not varied much in the essentials. Our patriarchal culture today has deep roots in the Greco-Roman culture, the mother of Western culture.

Verse 10 continues the exhortation on clothing, now in a metaphoric sense. If v. 9 contrasted simplicity with ostentation, now the ostentation is contrasted with good works. The author underlines that in the end what is basic is that appearances are not important. In fact, to dress with simplicity is not a virtue in itself; it is the way humble persons in the community normally dress. Most important are good works. To profess reverence for God (*eusebeia*) means that women give testimony of their spirituality, their manner of being, as followers of Jesus. Godliness, *eusebeia*, is not a transaction, as some of the community thought (6:5), even if it is true that costly clothing gives status and power. *Eusebeia* is a spirituality oriented toward the words of Jesus (6:3), and it is reflected in the practice of good works.[30]

In 2:11–12 the mandates that women should learn in silence with full submission and should not teach or have authority over men come out of the context of struggles for power. That probably means that some rich women took on positions of leadership simply because of their donations to the Christian community. Now, analyzing the texts from the perspective of gender, we see that the author tries to resolve the problem by going back to the domestic codes of patriarchal ideology. Instead of asking his delegate Timothy to discuss the model of leadership in terms of the "democratic" principles inherited from Jesus, in which the criterion of social condition would favor the poor, independent of gender, the author adopts the values of Greco-Roman patriarchal society, excluding women from teaching and obligating them to keep quiet and to learn.

Verses 11 and 12 bring us to the problem of other teachings and theologies considered heresies by the author, and, as it is probably these same women who hold those teachings, the text also tries to resolve that problem by going back to the traditional ideas about women's comportment in the household and society. The terms "to learn" (*manthaneto*) and "to teach" (*didaskein*) in the polemical context of other teachings and on the assumption that the women adopted the "other teachings" imply that the women teach without knowledge and therefore should learn in submission and silence—that is, without debating, questioning, or giving their opinion. In sum, the traditional ideas present in the domestic codes of patriarchal ideology, which exclude all women from teaching and leadership, are used by the author to resolve a circumstantial problem: a number of rich women dominated the community and probably taught something that the author did not like.

Some of the later writings of the New Testament, such as Ephesians, Colossians, and 1 Peter, repeat, although with certain variations of reciprocity, the traditional domestic codes reflecting the dominant ideal of a patriarchal society in tension with the women's conduct. In 1 Timothy and Titus the ideal of the submissive woman appears but in a context that mixes the domestic with the community; that is, the author links the conduct of the household with the conduct in the household church and society.[31] This is why the domestic codes here are not so clear as in Ephesians and Colossians. The author of 1 Timothy and Titus has as his point of departure the conduct of the household according to the codes and is interested that this conduct be extended to the household church. It is not an accident that the author uses "household" (*oikos*) to refer to the church (*ekklēsia*):

> I am writing these instructions to you so that, if I am delayed,
> you may know how one ought to behave in the household of
> God, which is the church of the living God, the pillar and bul-
> wark of the truth. (1 Tim. 3:14–15)

We find, then, not only an a-critical reproduction of the domestic codes
but a conscious assimilation of these with the intention of putting the
rich women in their place, according to the patriarchal ideal—but as
women, not as wealthy. As to rich women, it seems as if the author is
ambiguous about the values of society, defining the rich, among them
the women, as generous givers, but as people who should not boast and
claim honors (6:17–19); besides that, he reminds them that the love of
money is the root of all evil. So we find a contradiction in the author:
in a certain sense he follows the tradition of Jesus (6:3) with respect to
the wealthy, but not with respect to women or slaves. The dominant patriarchal ideology is present here, as among the male thinkers and leaders of the time. Thus, when confronted with struggles for power, the author totally delegitimizes the rich women—as women according to the
patriarchal ideal; as rich according to the tradition of Jesus. From the
perspective of gender and class the author wants to annul the participation of these dominant women. Since they are women, he wants them
to be silent, not to teach, but to be submissive. Since they are rich, he
wants their donations to be generous, but he does not want them to impose themselves because of their wealth and power.

If it is true that this situation occurs because of the power struggles
in the household church, it should not seem strange that the author includes instructions directed to the slaves. That men and women slaves
must be respectful of their masters and mistresses and serve them well is
not in contradiction with the author's negative posture toward the rich
and the love of money. The slaves can serve their masters and mistresses
well because this does not affect the polemic of leadership with respect
to gender. The concern of the author is not the same in relation to slaves:
it was the surrounding society that disapproved of the mixing of distinct
social strata within the same community.

Notes

1. Carolyn Osiek and David L. Balch, *Families in the New Testament World:
Households and House Churches* (Louisville, KY: Westminster John Knox Press,
1997), 216.

2. The imperial policy on the obligations of marriage appears in the Julian
laws on marriage. See Mary R. Lefkowitz and Maureen B. Fant, *Women's Life
in Greece and Rome* (Baltimore: Johns Hopkins University Press, 1991), 104ff.

3. Elisabeth Schüssler Fiorenza, *Jesus: Miriam's Child, Sophia's Prophet:
Critical Issues in Feminist Christology* (New York: Continuum, 1995), 14.

4. James M. Arlandson, *Women, Class and Society in Early Christianity: Models from Luke-Acts* (Peabody, MA: Hendrickson, 1997), 503.

5. Ekkehard W. Stegemann and Wolfgang Stegemann, *Historia social del cristianismo primitivo: Los inicios en el judaísmo y las communidades cristianos en el mundo mediterraneo* (Estella: Verbo Divino, 2001), 503.

6. Two excellent studies on this theme are David L. Balch, *Let Wives Be Submissive: The Domestic Code in 1 Peter* (Atlanta: Scholars Press, 1981); and David C. Verner, *The Household of God: The Social World of the Pastoral Letters* (Chico, CA: Scholars Press, 1983). Balch analyzes the domestic codes that have to do with the administration of the household. Verner also analyzes those codes that go beyond the behavior in the household and have to do with the social placement of the members and names them "social station codes."

7. Aristotle, *Politics*, trans. Benjamin Jowett (Mineola, NY: Dover Publications, 2000).

8. Verner, *The Household of God*, 85.

9. See ibid., 64–70.

10. Osiek and Balch, *Families in the New Testament World*, 32. The various data here presented come from Osiek and Balch; Verner, *The Household of God*; Arlandson, *Women, Class and Society*; and Stegemann and Stegemann, *Historia social del cristianismo primitivo*.

11. Verner, *The Household of God*, 58.

12. For a sketch of a typical Greco-Roman city, see Richard L. Rohrbaugh, "The Pre-industrial City in Luke-Acts," in the *Social World of Luke-Acts: Models for Interpretation*, ed. Jerome H. Neyrey (Peabody, MA: Hendrickson, 1991), 135.

13. Osiek and Balch, *Families in the New Testament World*, 215.

14. According to Osiek and Balch, in the houses of the rich can be observed "the status and its difference" between family members and between wealthy families. With certain variations, in a typical house of a rich person immediately after the entrance was a public reception area for any matter or business (*atrium*); there was a container to collect rain water. Behind this place (*atrium*), in some houses there was a large room where the owner of the house attended to his private matters and business and received the more private visitors, and, given the ample space there, the scribes and helpers could also be there. Alongside this room was a corridor (*andron*) that led to an interior garden (*peristylium*) surrounded with columns, where the luxury and sumptuousness of the house were exhibited. There were mosaics, busts of heroes or great teachers or gods or other extravagant objects, depending on whether the owner was a philosopher, a devotee, or a merchant who became sufficiently rich so as to have a house of this type. In a more interior place of the house could be found one or more dining rooms (*triclinium*), according to the number of members and status of the family. The Romans ate reclining on cushions, looking toward the center where there was a low table. It seems as if only men ate in this posture; the children and women sat to eat. In the triclinium about three cushions would fit where two to five diners reclined. Some houses had one room, called the *oecus*, which was used by everyone. Servant or slave quarters such as the kitchen or storage rooms were neglected, dark, and dirty; at the same time bedrooms were small and dark. Frequently the houses had a store that faced the streets.

15. See Étienne Morin, *El Puerto de Roma en el siglo II de nuestra era Ostia*, trans. Seve Calleja (Bilbao: Mensajero, 1995), 34–38.

16. See the house of Diana in Ostia.

17. See Bruce J. Malina, *The New Testament World: Insights from Cultural Anthropology*, 3rd ed. (Louisville, KY: Westminster John Knox Press, 2001); David A. deSilva, *Honor, Patronage, Kinship and Purity: Unlocking New Testament Culture* (Downers Grove, IL: Intervarsity Press, 2000), 23.

18. Osiek and Balch, *Families in the New Testament World*, 216.

19. Ibid.

20. See Verner, *The Household of God*, 55ff.

21. Even in the Roman Empire there was in the house a corridor called *andron* (for males), which marked a public space for males. It was understood that women would stay in the back part of the house, which was private.

22. There are inscriptions by people in modest social positions in which the family praised the deceased using the same patriarchal ideal used by the wealthy families.

23. We have evidence of apartments (*insulae*) that had four or even seven rooms such as those discovered in Ostia. See Osiek and Balch, *Families in the New Testament World*, 18.

24. Some commentators separate v. 8 from v. 9 as independent contexts; however, the Greek term *hōsautōs* ("likewise, in the same way") unites them, as do the verb "I desire" and the infinitives "to pray" and "to adorn."

25. Phillip Towner, *The Goal of Our Instruction: The Structure of Theology and Ethics in the Pastoral Epistles* (Sheffield: Sheffield Academic Press, 1989), 123.

26. J. M. Holmes, *Text in a Whirlwind: A Critique of Four Exegetical Devices in 1 Timothy 2:9-15* (Sheffield: Sheffield Academic Press, 2000), 59.

27. Philip Towner recognizes that, if in fact there is a sexual connotation in "discretion" and "self control," behind the instruction there could have been something more that would affect the social and economic divisions; see *The Goal of Our Instruction*, 208.

28. George W. Knight III, *The Pastoral Epistles: A Commentary on the Greek Text*, New International Greek Testament Commentary (Grand Rapids, MI: Eerdmans, 1992), 133.

29. Jerome D. Quinn and William C. Wacker, *The First and Second Letters to Timothy* (Grand Rapids, MI: Eerdmans, 1995), 216.

30. On the concept of "godliness," see chapter 1 in Elsa Tamez, *Struggles for Power in Early Christianity: A Study of the First Letter to Timothy* (Maryknoll, NY: Orbis Books, 2007).

31. The author of 1 Timothy adapts with great liberty both the domestic codes and the codes of social placement. See Verner, *The Household of God*, 106ff.

PART 3
Christology

The Star of Christ

In the dark of the night
A Star, hope and light
Not to the kings, ranks and rich
But to the humble seekers of truth
And to the poor wandering shepherds

In the manger where the animals
Serving the needs of people are tied and herded
Christ, the savior of the world is born
Not to the kings, ranks and rich
But in the manger, the place of the lowly creatures
To the humble seekers of true life
And to the poor and heavy laden

Within the thick and high walls
    of the palaces and mansions
Where the bright chandeliers
    are the reality immediate and imperative
On the streets where mounting neon signs
    of all colors imaginable
    intoxicate and dominate all the eye sight inhabitable
Those who have locked themselves up all
    determined in the darkness of today's harshness
The star cannot be perceived
Purity of a star light is the curse of blindness

The star, the symbol of hope and light
Hope for the higher meaning of life

Lee Sun Ai Park, "The Star of Christ," *In God's Image* (December 1988): 3; used with permission of the Asian Women's Resource Centre for Culture and Theology.

Hope for the betterment of human situation
Caught deep in sin
Glory for self, egoism of individuals and groups alike
Dividing, hurting, making the helpless wail and moan
While the wicked enjoy the riches and power only for themselves
Far from love that is saving
Far from grace that is transcending
Self, culture, traditions, laws and orders
The guarantors of evil structures

It is not the law that saves but grace
For St. Paul, the Christ was Grace
Who was born in a manger
Lived a full love of humanity
In faith to God of love and justice

Jesus who fed the hungry, healed the sick
Cleansed the demons and raised the dead
Was crucified and resurrected
The true child of God, nature of God in flesh
Is the Christ, hope and light for me and the world

—Lee Sun Ai Park (Korea)

10

JESUS CHRIST

Mercy Amba Oduyoye (Ghana)

The Context

African Christian theology is decidedly contextual, and this contribution on Jesus by an African woman will stay in that mode and reflect the
faith of African Christian women in the African context. Jesus Christ yes-
terday, today, and tomorrow requires that each generation declare its
faith in relation to its today. It is, therefore, natural that the Christologies
African women were fed should reflect the faith of those who brought
Christianity to Africa and the African men who did most of the interpretation and transmission. Having heard all this, African women today can
announce in their own words the one in whom they have believed.

The intention of this chapter is to survey the language of African
Christian women about Jesus and, through that, to build up a profile of
the Jesus in their Christianity. We begin with a note on sources, as the
expected "library study" of this subject will yield very little that is of the
provenance of women. We then sample the oral Christology which is our
key source, as most of what is written by African women began as oral
contributions to study groups and conferences. The third section is this
writer's assessment of what is being said about Jesus and why.

In the past thirty years or so, several Christological models have appeared in books written by men theologians of Africa.[1] They share the
emphases of the Western churches but several go beyond these. They are
grounded in the classical Christian approach that identifies "Savior
myths" with biblical narratives and attempt to answer the question:
"Who is the Savior?" The classical divine-human motif is stated as a matter of faith and not debated, as was common in the early church. African
theologians transmit as an article of faith the divine human person whose

Mercy Amba Oduyoye, "Jesus Christ," in *The Cambridge Companion to Feminist Theology*, ed. Susan Frank Parsons (Cambridge: Cambridge University Press, 2002), 151–70.
Reprinted with the permission of Cambridge University Press.

sacrifice on the cross is salvific. As a human being, the Savior is a pastor and an example for human life. As a human being, his role is like that of royalty in traditional African communities, a representative and leader, but it is as divine that the Savior is victorious over death.

The divinity of the Christ experienced through the Bible is that of one in control of the universe and history. The Christ controls evil and is a wonder-worker. In times of crisis, the Christ is expected to intervene directly on the side of the good, for God is the giver of good. In the gospels, the Christ is seen as a healer, an exorcist, and a companion. All these notions feature in African Christologies and influence what women, too, say about Jesus.

In dealing with Christologies in Africa, one finds two major trends, the inculturationalist and the liberationist. The first type is that of those who consciously appropriate Africa's traditional experience of God. We note that the Greek Bible imagery that forms the foundations of traditional Christologies has appropriated beliefs and language from Jewish religion, as well as Greco-Roman paradigms. To talk intelligently about new experience, one cannot but build upon what is known. African religion and culture furnish the language of Christologies that describe Jesus as an ancestor, a king, or elder brother. These carry notions of mediatorship and authority. It is as an ancestor that Jesus stands between humanity and God as the spokesperson, as the *Okyeame*; Jesus is interpreter and advocate. We name ourselves Christians after his being the Christ, just as we name our children after our worthy forebears.

We say Christ is king and we see the lives of royal leaders who were compassionate and brave community builders. We see the royal leaders of the Akan, who bear the title *Osagyefo*, the one who saves the battle, the victorious warrior, and we see Jesus as *Nana*, both ancestor and royalty. In several African traditional cultures, the rulers are regarded as hedged by divinity, and so one is able to talk about the Christ being both divine and human without raising the philosophical debates of early Christianity. So, praying to and through Jesus follows naturally and is practiced as the spirituality of the religion that enables Christians to face the daily realities of life.

Women have employed cultural paradigms to describe their belief in Jesus, but those that are most favored are the cultural ones that are also liberative. They employ myths of wonder-workers who save their communities from hunger and from the onslaught of their enemies, both physical and spiritual. The women's Christology in large measure therefore falls within the category of the liberationist types. Jesus is the brother or kin who frees women from the domination of inhuman husbands. Women relate more easily to the Christ who knew hunger, thirst, and homelessness, and see Jesus as oppressed by the culture of his own people. Jesus the liberator is a paradigm for the critique of culture that most African women theologians do.

The faith in and the language about Jesus that is reviewed here has become written theology within the last two decades or so; nonetheless, they are of African hue and have their roots in African Christianity in particular. The language about Jesus is heard in songs with lyrics created by both women and men and sung lustily in churches and in TV drama. There are several women's singing groups that have recorded cassettes sold on our streets, and songs are sung by people at work, at play, or while traveling. The name of Jesus is therefore on the lips, in the ears, and before the eyes of all, including those of other faiths.

Ghana, the country of my birth, today wears many placards bearing slogans that contain the name of Jesus. When you greet anyone in the streets and ask, "How do you do?" they will profess their faith by telling you, "*Yesu adom*"—"by the grace of Jesus." This version replaces the traditional "by the grace of God," which has become insufficient, as God was in Ghana before Christianity came and our Muslim sisters and brothers punctuate all hopes and plans and inquiries after their state of being with "*Insha Allah*"—by the will of Allah (God). Specifying the name of Jesus, therefore, properly claims Christian particularity. Who Jesus is to Ghanaian Christians is written largely in their songs, prayers, and sayings. The first full text of individual spirituality anchored in Jesus and coming from an African woman with no formal schooling is a publication with the English title *Jesus of the Deep Forest*.[2]

The Texts

Jesus of the Deep Forest signifies the place of Jesus in the life of people both rural and urban. It is the prayers they pray to Jesus and the praises they give to him. One could almost say that, of the women "writing theologians" of Africa, Afua Kuma is the first, and she paved the way by pointing to the central theme of Christology. She will be our first source, and she represents the women who weave lyrics about Jesus and pour their hearts out in prayer and praise at all times and in all places, the women whose theology gets "reduced" into writing by those who can write.

Our second source is the writings of the women who belong to the Ecumenical Association of Third World Theologians (EATWOT) or to the Circle of Concerned African Women Theologians (the Circle). In the 1980s, EATWOT called attention to the Christologies of the Third World and generated many studies on the subject of Jesus. It is in this context that African women members of the association contributed to the publication, *With Passion and Compassion: Third World Women Doing Theology*.[3] The Circle, with its initial focus on religion and culture, had ecclesiology as its main theological schema, but naturally the subject of Jesus looms large in its members' reflection. The first publication of the Circle, *Talitha Qumi!*, features two Bible studies (on Luke

8:40–46, and 1:42) and one article on that subject that can aid us in our study. The series of *Circle Books* and reflections published in the newsletter *Amka* also provide relevant references.[4]

Our third source will be the writings of individual African women in other anthologies. An example of this is Anne Nasimiyu's "Christology and an African Woman's Experience" in Robert Schreiter's *Faces of Jesus In Africa*.[5] Individually authored books on the subject by women are rare, but there is a chapter on Jesus in this writer's *Hearing and Knowing*. Teresa Okure's opus on mission can, of course, be read from the perspective of Christology and so can Christina Landman's, *The Piety of South African Women*.[6]

Oral Christology

In *Jesus of the Deep Forest* by Afua Kuma, our example of oral Christology, one encounters numerous astonishing reversals of so-called natural laws and unexpected outcomes of simple actions. Jesus is the one who catches birds from the depths of the ocean and fish from the heights of the trees. These reversals are then reflected in magnificent types of deeds in the lives of people. Jesus, the Great Provider under all circumstances, brings wealth to widows and orphans and is the friend of the aged. Jesus frees children from the fear of *kakae* (the monster) and breaks the will of the murderer. It is Jesus who has accepted the poor and given them glory. Jesus clears the forest of all evil spirits, making it safe for hunters. Imagery that is in keeping with the stilling of the storm abounds in oral Christology.

The motif of Savior and liberator is very strong in this and other reflections on Jesus by women. For Afua Kuma, the Exodus becomes another motif. Jesus is Yahweh of the Exodus, who defeated Pharaoh and his troops and becomes the sun ahead of Israel and lightning behind them. He is given the Akan title "*Osagyefo*, the one who saves the battle" and so we can depend on him to win life's battles. Other biblical images, like good shepherd, healer, and the compassionate one, are seen together with cultural ones such as "the mighty edifice that accommodates all corners," while provision of hospitality common to both serves as the very antidote to death. Whatever the situation, Jesus has the last word. There are no life challenges for which the power of Jesus is found unequal to the task of achieving victory. The following excerpt from *Jesus of the Deep Forest* illustrates the ethos of this publication:

> All-powerful Jesus who engages in marvelous deeds, he is the one called Hero *Okatakyi*! Of all earthly dominions he is master; the Python not overcome with mere sticks, the Big Boat which cannot be sunk.

Jesus, Saviour of the poor, who brightens up our faces! *Damjo-Adu*: the clever one. We rely on you as the tongue relies on the mouth.

The great Rock we hide behind: the great forest canopy that gives cool shade: the Big Tree that lifts its vines to peep at the heavens, the magnificent Tree whose dripping leaves encourage the luxuriant growth.[7]

Several images in Afua Kuma come from gospel-events involving Jesus and women. "Women recognize his uniqueness and put their cloths on the ground for him. A woman anoints him as Messiah, friend and Saviour."[8]

Reflecting on Jesus is not simply an intellectual task or one of personal spirituality. Afua Kuma, like many African women theologians, speaks as an evangelist. "Follow Jesus," she says, and not only will you witness miracles, but for you will come grace, blessings, eternal life, and peace. The cross of Jesus, she says, is like a net with which Jesus gathers in people; it is the bridge from this life to eternal life. The word of Jesus is the highway along which we should walk. She therefore prays to Jesus: "Use us to do your will for you have cleansed us with your blood."[9] This saving blood motif is featuring more and more frequently in song and in prayers in this period of deliverance-seeking. The royal blood of Jesus, precious and potent, has given us health and happiness, for it has overcome and kept at bay the power of demons. This living faith is proclaimed daily in the churches, in store fronts, on vehicles, and even in the designs of clothes people wear.

Written Christology

"There is a concrete history that is lived which is prior to the history that is recounted. That lived history in all its concreteness is the ultimate ground of all the history that is written."[10] Christologies, therefore, are the results of questions asked by succeeding generations of theologians, the interpreters of the history of Jesus. The vocabulary of African women's theology is focused on Jesus, rarely on Christ or Christ Jesus. Few questions are asked beyond that of the human response to that history. The oral affirmations ask hardly any questions, but Rosemary Edet insists that some women do ask questions of this Jesus-story. As a Nigerian woman she could ask: "Who is the Christ to the Nigerian Woman? What type of Christ does she know? How does she relate to this Christ?"[11] The spirituality of the majority of African women moves us to conclude that it is the personality of the one about whom the gospel speaks that draws prayer and praise from them. The songs about Jesus proclaim royalty, king of kings. Jesus is the first and the best of all that is counted good in humanity, and best and first of all good professionals who keep human beings and human communities in a state of health and general well-being. Predominant is Jesus the wonder-worker. Essentially, what we get from African women is an affirmation of faith such as is stated by Rosemary Edet: "Jesus is the Son of God, son of Mary, sent by the Father to our planet to redeem mankind from sin and death and to restore them to grace."[12]

Snippets from the contributors to this volume follow the same train of reflections as in "Christ and the Nigerian Womanhood" in Edet and Umeagudosu's book.[13] In the same publication, A. E. Kwazu writes, "Jesus was born on earth to reform man who has completely deviated from God's call to being good."[14] Akon E. Udo affirms, "God has sent Jesus Christ to the world to break the barriers of culture and sexism, that is why the names of women appear in the genealogy of Jesus Christ."[15] This inclusiveness of the mission of God is then illustrated by Jesus' example of giving women the mandate to "Go and tell" of the resurrection (Mark 16:7).

In response to this inclusive mission, African women are heard loud and clear singing the redemptive love of Jesus the liberator. Jesus accomplishes God's mission by setting women free from sexism, oppression, and marginalization through his death and resurrection, and both women and men are made members of God's household and of the same royal priesthood as men.[16] In *Talitha Qumi!*, we read: "The ultimate mission of Jesus was to bring healing, life and dignity to the suffering. Jesus came to give voice to the voiceless."[17]

Teresa M. Hinga's contribution in *The Will to Arise: Jesus Christ and the Liberation of Women* offers a section on "Christology and African Women: The Ambivalence of the Encounter." She discusses two faces of Christ that are prevalent in African Christologies—the Colonial Christ who is a warrior-king, whose followers sang "Soldiers of Christ Arise" as they battled against other religions and cultures and indeed races, and the Imperial Christ, the conquering Christ of the missionaries who did battle for Africa, on behalf of the missionaries. Africans embraced this version of Christianity as a "means of social and economic mobility"—hence the reports we have of mass conversions in some parts of Africa. Hinga states that African women were among those who perceived the emancipating impulses of Christianity and turned to it. Women were among those who took refuge at the mission stations. The early missionary period in Africa presented a Christ who had two faces, the conqueror who inspires the subjugation of people and their cultures while promoting the liberation of individuals from the oppression generated by their environment. The Jesus of missionary praxis in Africa was an ambiguous Christ. Thus it is that he has acquired many faces on the continent.

The Christ of missionary teaching, based mostly on the Bible, adds complexity to this scenario. Hinga discusses three of its dimensions. The first is that of personal Savior and personal friend—accepting people as they are and meeting their needs at a very personal level—Jesus "friend of the lonely" and "healer of those who are sick, whether spiritually or physically."[18] The title "friend" is "one of the most popular among women, precisely because they need such a personal friend the most." Thus the heightened image of Jesus as the Christ who helps them to bear their griefs, loneliness, and suffering is a welcome one indeed.[19] Women's oral Christologies reflect this history and have been translated into the written ones.

Hinga observes that, in African women's theology, the "Image of Christ is a blend of Christology with pneumatology. Jesus is seen as the embodiment of the spirit, the power of God, and the dispenser of the same to all who follow him."[20] This "pneumatic Christology" is very popular among women, for here Christ is the voice of the voiceless and the power of the powerless on the models sculptured by Afua Kuma. African women do need such a Christ, for they are often expected to be mute and to accept oppression. The Spirit empowers them to enjoy a lively spiritual life that cannot be controlled by the official powers of the church. In this way they are able to defy unjust authority and repressive structures and to stand against cultural demands that go against the spirit of Jesus.

The Christ, the iconoclastic prophet-critic of the status quo that "engenders social injustices and marginalisation of some in society" illustrates "some of the defining characteristics of the Christ whom women confess":

> For Christ to become meaningful in the context of women's search for emancipation, he would need to be a concrete and personal figure who engenders hope in the oppressed by taking their [women's] side, to give them confidence and courage to persevere.[21]

Jesus has to be the Christ on the side of the powerless to empower them, the one who is concerned with the lot of victims of social injustice and with the dismantling of unjust social structures. However, the concern most heard these days is deliverance from "Satanic Bondage," and from demons who seem to have become very active in the Africa of the last decades of the twentieth century. The need for deliverance has revived traditional religious methods. Most especially, the importance of blood in African religions is reflected in the central place given to the blood of Jesus in women's theological imagery and, indeed, in much of "deliverance spirituality" of contemporary African Christianity. Just one example should suffice.

Grace Duah, a "deliverance Minister," in her book, *Deliverance: Fact or Fantasy?* includes puberty rites for girls that open the doors for demon possession, to demonstrate how easily people can come under the influence of demons and so need deliverance. She writes in her introduction:

> Jesus came not only to give us the highest form of deliverance, i.e., Salvation—Deliverance from a Kingdom of sin and darkness into a Kingdom of Righteousness and light—but also to give us deliverance from demonic obsession, demonic oppression, and demonic possession, as well as all forms of fleshly enslavement.[22]

Rosemary Edet, a foundation member of the Circle, reflects this in her contribution to the Circle's inaugural conference. Looking at the life of Jesus, she points out that "Christ has triumphed over illness, blood taboos, women's rituals and the conventions of society."[23] She is, of course, referring to rituals and conventions that are inimical to women's well-being. These are the ones that Grace Duah is referring to as providing opportunities for demons to possess women.

Jesus has become for us a liberator by countering misogynist culture. After all, says Edet, Jesus' humanity is the humanity of a woman; no human father contributed. The touch of the "bleeding woman" has become a very important image not only for healing, but also for total liberation from all that oppresses women culturally and makes Jesus Savior *par excellence*, as we saw in the oral Christology. Therefore Margaret Obaga, commenting on the salvific role of the Christ, puts her emphasis on the breaking down of walls of hostilities created by religion and culture. She writes: "The breaking of the wall therefore meant the abolishing of all external customs and taboos of Judaism which created and perpetuated a state of enmity between Jews and Gentiles."[24] In her discussion of Ephesians 2:15, she calls attention to contemporary gender issues that are a source of subjugation for women in Africa.

In Afua Kuma, as in most of the writings under review, salvation comes to women and men alike. Even so, Afua Kuma does have feminist consciousness. In Edet, this consciousness is explicit in the very title of her paper, but even here the starting point is the universal appeal. She notes that Jesus is "sensitive to the oppression of the weak and the helpless, took them on in his incarnation," as a carpenter's son from a nondescript town.[25] This is heightened by his interpretation of Messiahship, which he portrayed "not as king but as a servant by contradicting in his life and person, the messianic expectation of Israel." Jessica Nakawombe is even more explicit with regard to this. She states bluntly that:

> Jesus was born of Mary, a good and godly woman. She was the obedient vessel through which Christ was conceived of the Holy

Spirit. She was given a unique part to play in the outworking of God's plan for the salvation of humankind, for the Incarnation and the virgin birth have had a tremendous significance for Christology.[26]

The women cling to the full humanity of the Christ in order to honor their own humanity and to insist on the link between the human and the divine in all persons as it was in Jesus. The church's imagery of Jesus, which marginalizes women, is therefore non-biblical, and contemporary women theologians of other continents have traced the history of this state of affairs. For Edet, this process was most evident in the Constantinian era, with its return to the royal ideology of the Davidic Messiah that made the Christ the "pantokrator," reinforcing the distance between Christ and the feminine.[27] The Jesus of African women's Christology is the Jesus of the Bible and of whatever scholarship aids the identification of this Jesus and the context in which he lived his earthly life.

Another historical development highlighted by Edet is the Aristotelian desecration of womanhood. This desacralization of the feminine has succeeded in making the totality of the *imago dei* male, says Edet. Consequently, women have had to lead the Christian community toward a "return to the Christ of the gospels, his Person and his words and deeds."[28] It is in this tradition that African women's Christology stands:

> Africans in general have a holistic view of life which demands a Christ who affects the whole of life for there is nothing that is not the realm of God if it is true that God made everything and keeps them in being. God as father is beneficent but there are good and evil forces operating in the world. These affect humanity. In short, a Nigerian woman is a victim of evil forces like witches, hunger, infant mortality as well as the triple oppression of culture, religion and socio-economy. How does Christ function within this situation? If Jesus did take on himself our weakness and injustice at his incarnation, then he is a suffering Christ, a liberating Christ and a friend.[29]

Continuing with the Christological texts of African women, we call attention now to *With Passion and Compassion*. In this publication, Térèsa Souga from Cameroon, writing on "The Christ Event," introduces her reflections with what she titles, "My Act of Faith." She has as her opening sentence, "Jesus Christ means everything to me... Christ is the true Human, the one who makes it possible for all persons to reach fulfillment and to overcome the historic alienation weighing them down."[30] Similarly, Afua Kuma would recite the traditional praise of enablers saying: Jesus is the big tree that makes it possible for the climbing plant to reach the sun. Souga's theology is deeply informed by Philippians 2:9–11, an affirmation of faith that enables her to link the suffering and resurrection of Jesus with women.[31] This, she says, is the source and motivation of African women's spirituality. She writes: "The realism of the cross every day tells me, as a woman of the Third World, that the laws of history can be overcome by means of crucified love."[32] Jesus bears a message of liberation for every human being and especially for those in social categories that are most disadvantaged.

Jesus "delivers women from every infirmity and suffering."[33] Souga has in view Africa's threefold captivity—cultural, spiritual, socio-economic—when she writes, "there can be no understanding of Jesus Christ outside of the situation in which we seek to understand ourselves."[34] "It is by way of these situations that Jesus bears on his person the condition of the weak, and hence that of women" (Luke 2:6-7, 22-24; John 2:46).[35] In the light of Christ, if Jesus is the God who has become weakness in our context, in his identity as God-Man, Jesus takes on the condition of the African woman. Souga surmises that the correlation between women's experience and liberation in Jesus Christ "leads us to discover that Jesus reveals God in the various kinds of bonds connecting him to women throughout the Gospels." Paul emphasizes the realism of the incarnation with a legacy of faith saying, "When the times were fulfilled, the son of God was born of a woman."[36] Afua Kuma would have said Jesus is the royal one who chooses to live as the common poor so that the common poor might appropriate the dignity of being human:

> Looking at Africa, I wondered how I could write on a subject that suggests or points towards hope and renewed life in a continent that for decades has witnessed unending violence, suffering and death. A critical reflection on the resurrected Christ, the one Paul knew and wrote about in the epistles, however, reminded me of the crucified and suffering Christ who faced violence and death. The awareness gave me the courage to write about the labour pains experienced by all creation in Africa as a Christian woman.[37]

The image of Jesus as the suffering servant is very prominent in the writings of African women theologians. Most, like Rosemary Edet and Nyambura Njoroge, describe Jesus as identifying with the suffering of humanity, especially that of women. In this vein, Edet describes Jesus as "the revelation of God's self-giving suffering and enduring love to humanity."[38]

This suffering love moves into healing the hurts of humanity and so Christ the healer is very popular with church women. Ada Nyaga brings out the results of this love among human beings when she writes:

Similarly, Jesus calls us to revise our ways of thinking and asks us to reconsider what it means to be a woman in our new understanding. Just as Jesus forced the ruler of a synagogue to reconsider what it means to work on the Sabbath, when he showed his compassion for a crippled woman by healing her (Luke 13:10–17), there is an obvious need today to awaken women and free them from socio-cultural and theological restrictions based on a false understanding of the Bible.[39]

Suffering love operating in the incarnation wipes off the dirt that hides the glory of our true humanity, that which we believe is of the *imago dei*. Healing here includes liberating women from all evil and life-denying forces, enabling the fullness of all we know of perfect womanhood to be revealed. Jesus is the friend who enables women to overcome the difficulties of life and restores to them the dignity of being in the image of God, having annulled the stigma of blood taboos used as a separation of women's humanity. Akon E. Udo affirms that Jesus Christ has broken the barriers of distinction between men and women and used his precious blood to seal the broken relationships and to make men and women one in himself.[40] Mercy Amba Oduyoye and Elizabeth Amoah state in *With Passion and Compassion* that:

> the Christ for us is the Jesus of Nazareth who agreed to be God's "Sacrificial Lamb," thus teaching that true and living sacrifice is that which is freely and consciously made; and who pointed to the example of the widow who gave all she had in response to God's love. Christ is the Jesus of Nazareth who approved of the costly sacrifice of the woman with the expensive oil, who anointed him (king, prophet, priest) in preparation for his burial, thereby also approving all that is noble, lovely, loving and motivated by love and gratitude.[41]

Louise Tappa of Cameroon in *With Passion and Compassion*, states that "the task of Christology is to work out the full meaning of the reality of the Christ-event for humankind." Doctrinal Christology, which reduces the Christ to a positive but sublime abstraction, can be and is ignored "when the time comes to translate it into the life of our communities." Tappa continues: "that is why even to the present it has been possible to interpret the doctrines of the incarnation (liberation) and of expiation (reconciliation) in terms that leave intact the social structures and models of our communities, including the church."[42] Like Afua Kuma, Tappa proposes another procedure, which she says is much simpler but no less Christological. It is to put more emphasis on the praxis of Jesus himself, even though she occasionally refers also to Jesus' teaching.

Summary and Reflections

These works and words of Jesus, culled from the reflections of African women on Jesus, constitute the Christologies that they are developing and which embolden them to work and to speak for Jesus toward the liberation of the world in fulfillment of the *missio dei*. "The Christ of history is the one who defined his mission as a mission of liberation" (Luke 4:18–19). The Christ of dogma therefore plays only a marginal role in the women's affirmations about Jesus, who defined liberation by his quotation from Isaiah 61, and whose actions revealed that "the truly spiritual is that which embraces all the material and physical life of the human being and our communities" (Mark 5:21–34).[43]

Elizabeth Amoah and Mercy Amba Oduyoye, writing on "The Christ for African Women," point out that Jesus, the Messiah, is God-sent and the anointed of God. The messianic imagery is very powerful in Ghana and is reflected in Afua Kuma's praises that make references to what priests are teaching when they speak of deliverance. The influence of male theologians is evident in how large the cross looms in the theology of women like Afua Kuma. As noted earlier, she points out that the cross "has become the fishing net of Jesus. It is also the bridge from which Christians can jump into the pool of saving blood that leads to everlasting life."[44] The emphasis of women, however, is not that we emulate the suffering, but that it become the source of our liberation. We do not only admire Jesus, but we are caught in the net of liberation which we believe will bring us into fullness of life:

> The Christ whom African women worship, honor and depend on is the victorious Christ, knowing that evil is a reality. Death and life-denying forces are the experience of women, and so Christ, who countered these forces and who gave back her child to the widow of Nain, is the African woman's Christ.[45]

Ghana must have great hunger in its history, as is evidenced in folktales and legend. The more recent 1983 drought revives this reality, and so a Savior is certainly the one who can keep us whole, integrating body and soul and enabling us to enhance the quality of our lives. Jesus of Nazareth was all of this; his earthly life and today his name and spirit keep the liberative ministry alive. With Jesus we do not need guns and bullets to make the enemy disappear, since, as Afua Kuma points out, we only need to "tell Jesus." "I'm going to tell Jesus about it, today my husband is a lawyer. How eloquent he is!"[46]

Deliverance from death into life is often discussed by African women in the context of aspects of cultural practice that they experience as negative in their quest for fullness of life:

This Christ is the liberator from the burden of disease and the ostracism of a society riddled with blood-taboos and theories of inauspiciousness arising out of women's blood. Christ liberated women by being born of Mary, demanding that the woman bent double with gynecological disorders should stand up straight. The practice of making women become silent "beasts" of societies' burdens, bent double under racism, poverty, and lack of appreciation of what fullness of womanhood should be, has been annulled and countered by Christ. Christ transcends and transforms culture and has liberated us to do the same.[47]

African women's experiences lead them into Christological language that does not come to African men. Hence Tappa can say: "I am convinced that Jesus died so that the patriarchal God might die and that Jesus rose so that the true God revealed in Jesus might rise in our lives, and in our communities."[48]

Souga and others have reiterated that it is by self-emptying that we become filled with the spirit of Jesus. What African women reject is the combination of cross and sacrifice laid on them by people who have no intention of walking those paths themselves. They would argue that the calls to take up the cross and to self-emptying are directed to all who would be called Christians; those calls are not sensitive to gender, race, or class. Amoah and Oduyoye, commenting on Kuma, highlight the same point.[49]

The vividness of this drama of jumping from bridges into pools of blood, even when blood has been the main source of women's marginalization, signifies the intensity of their spirituality of relating their lives to what the life of Jesus means to them. For them, Christology is not words or reasoning about Jesus, but an actuality in their lives. This is a life of faith, not of theological debates. It is a spirituality to overcome evil and oppression and to lift up constant thanks to God.

It is difficult to say whether the language of intimate relationships with Jesus, as used by African women, is to be read as eroticism or mysticism. What is clear, however, is that their spirituality is the result of this type of Christology. They find an affirmation of their personhood and worth in the person of Jesus, born of a woman without the participation of a man. The significance for them is that "womanness" contains the fullness of "humanness." By this they counter earlier assertions that a woman by herself is not fully human. This eroticism-mysticism enables them to understand suffering as related to crucified love with an anticipation of transformation and shalom.

Hinga has suggested that it is the lack of male companionship that drives women into the near-erotic language of Jesus as husband. Afua Kuma relies on Jesus, her husband, who is a lawyer who liberates her from the hands of oppressive legal procedures with his eloquence. The only time Jesus appeared in the diary of Dutch-Afrikaans woman, Alie Badenhorst (1866–1908), was when even God "The Strong One, the Powerful Father in heaven" had seemed impotent to deliver her. When she thought her last hour had come, "she left a message for her husband with her son, that she was going to Jesus and that she would wait for him there."[50] Thus for her—as for many African women, products of the same European missionary theology—Jesus is the last sure haven. While life lasts, however, African women theologians would suggest that Christology should be about reclaiming and reasserting the role of "Jesus Christ as Liberator and a saviour of women."[51]

> I am married to Jesus, Satan leave me alone.
> My husband is coming
> To take me away
> Into everlasting love.[52]

Afua Kuma is not afraid of court cases, for her "husband" Jesus is a most eloquent lawyer. Christina Landman, who has documented *The Piety of South African Women* from diaries, has several examples of this type of language from both African and Afrikaner women of South Africa under the influence of European Calvinism. In the context of "racial persecution (black women) and suburban boredom" for white women, pious women escaped "into the arms of Jesus," who suffered for them and continues to suffer with them. Landman comments: "Where there is suffering, a woman is in control,"[53] and oh, how Africa suffers. It is African women's experience that, where there is suffering, the powers that be, usually men, would allow women to take control. Women derive power from caring and being caregivers, a role that puts them on the side of the Christ. The hallowing of suffering, however, is rejected in the theology of several African women theologians who see this as a source of patriarchal domestication. The cross and suffering of Jesus are not to be perpetuated but rather decried and prevented.

The victorious Christ of Afua Kuma is clearly the Jesus of the writing theologians. Jesus turns death into life and overcomes the life-denying forces that dog our way. He conquers death and restores life to all who believe in him. Having triumphed over death, he has become our liberator by countering women-denying culture. After all—is his own humanity not that of a woman?[54]

My reading of African women's theology is that they have had no problem particularizing the "Christ of God" in the man of Nazareth. They know of saviors in their own histories; some are men, others are women. Their stance is that the maleness of Jesus is unjustly capitalized on by those who want to exclude women, but that does not detract from the fact that in Jesus' own practice, inclusion is the norm. What Rosemary Edet says about the humanity of Jesus is that it is the humanity of woman, and African women should and do claim Jesus as their liberator. They claim the soundly constructed so-called feminine traits they find in Jesus—his care and compassion for the weak and excluded. The anti-hunger ministry, healing, and the place of children in his words and works—all go together to create a bonding around women's lives that African women feel with Jesus. He is one of us, knows our world, and can therefore accompany us in our daily joys and struggles.

What alienates some African women is the interpretation of revelation that suggests that before Jesus Africans had not encountered God and that without Jesus all are doomed. Christian exclusiveness is in large measure not biblical and must therefore not be allowed to become an obstacle in the multi-religious communities of Africa. African women theologians have often reinterpreted the exclusiveness of John as a directive to walk in the path of Jesus. Elizabeth Amoah would say, "Jesus is the only way" is a call to the recognition that to make salvation a reality for all, we all should walk in the way of Jesus and live the truth of the implication of a kenotic life.[55]

There has been no need to insist on the Christ as the wisdom of God. The biblical references to *Sophia* as eternally with God have not played a significant role in this theology. What is clear is that wisdom language would be associated with fairness in dealings among humans and fidelity to the will of God that Jesus exemplified. Thus Christology is reflected in spirituality.

African Christian women attribute the positive outcome of their endeavors to God or Jesus and to the guidance and protection of the Holy Spirit. They learn from biblical narrators and from stories of liberation that others have attributed to their faith in Jesus. They cling to their own faith in the liberating powers of Jesus and expect them to work in their own lives. Living under conditions of such hardship, African women and men have learned to identify the good, attribute it to God in Christ, and live a life of prayer in the anticipation that the liberative potential of the person of Jesus will become a reality in their lives.

The victory of Jesus is not over other nations and cultures. It is over death and life-denying forces. The Jesus "who countered these forces and gave back her child to the widow of Nain, is the African woman's Christ." Jesus of Nazareth, by the counter-cultural relations he established with women, has become for us the Christ, the anointed one who liberates, the companion, friend, teacher, and true "Child of Woman"— "Child of Woman" truly, because in Christ the fullness of all that we know of perfect womanhood is revealed. The Christ for us is the Jesus of Nazareth who agreed to be God's sacrificial lamb, thus teaching that true and living sacrifice is that which is freely and consciously made. Jesus of Nazareth, designated "the Christ," is the one who has broken down the barriers we have erected between God and us as well as among us. The Christ is the Reconciler calling us back to our true selves, to one another, and to God, thereby saving us from isolation and alienation which is the lack of community that is the real experience of death.[56]

"The Christ of the women of Africa upholds not only motherhood, but all who like Jesus of Nazareth perform 'mothering roles' of bringing out the best in all around them." The present profit-centered economies of our world deny responsibilities to bring life to the dying and to empower those challenged by the multitude of impairments that many have to live with. Justine Kahungu Mbwiti, in a study of Jesus and a Samaritan woman (John 4:1-42), draws out several of the images of Jesus that empower African women. As rural women, they see the scandal of the incarnation, the appearance of God in the hinterlands of the Roman Empire, as God coming to their rural and slum situations. They relate to Jesus who deliberately shakes what was customary as a sign of renewal that opens for them the space to put critical questions to what is traditional. They refer to the scandalous action in the temple (John 2:13–16), and the many violations of the Sabbath (John 5:1–18) as affirmations that life is to be lived consciously and conscientiously. Jesus becomes therefore not just the one by whom God saves; He is Himself the Savior.[57]

We may conclude with another survey treatment of Christology in African women's theology, in Mabel Morny's contribution to *Talitha Qumi!* "Christ Restores to Life." She states: "When I think of liberation, a vision comes into my mind. A vision of a fuller and less injured life in a world where people can say 'I' with happiness; a vision is a means of restoring life."[58] Morny tries to develop an understanding of Christ as the liberator of all people; she writes as an African woman within the context of situations in Africa—cultural, social, religious, economic, and political. She writes in a context in which women resort to Jesus as the liberator from bondage, all that makes them less than what God intended them to be. Christology becomes a study of the Jesus who responds to African women's experiences of fear, uncertainty, sickness, illiteracy, hunger, spousal aggression, and distortion of the image of their humanity.

African women theologians think in inclusive terms, hence the emphasis on Jesus for all people, in every particular context and in all situations. At the same time, these theologians wish to maintain the relations the individual can establish with the Christ, as each is unique, and each is a child of God. My reading of African women's Christology, as it appears in the writings of the Circle of Concerned African Women Theologians, may therefore be summed up in the words of the workshop on "Jesus Christ and the Liberation of Women":

> Jesus Christ is liberator and a saviour of women from all the oppressive contexts discussed and empowerer of women in their contexts of powerlessness, and their friend and ally in the context of alienation and pain that women may be confronted with.[59]

Notes

1. In this series one finds J. N. K. Mugambi and Laurenti Magesa, eds., *Jesus in African Christianity: Experimentation and Diversity in African Christology* (Nairobi: Initiatives Ltd., 1989); John S. Pobee, ed., *Exploring Afro-Christology* (New York: Peter Lang, 1992); Enyi Ben Udoh, *Guest Christology: An Interpretative View of the Christological Problem in Africa* (New York: Peter Lang, 1988).

2. Afua Kuma, *Jesus of the Deep Forest*, ed. and trans. Peter Kwasi Ameyaw, Fr. Jon Kirby SVD, et al. (Accra: Asempa Press, 1980). The rendering here is by Mercy Amba Oduyoye.

3. Virginia Fabella and Mercy Amba Oduyoye, eds., *With Passion and Compassion: Third World Women Doing Theology* (Maryknoll, NY: Orbis Books, 1988).

4. Since the initiation of the Circle of Concerned African Women Theologians in 1989, the following anthologies and four issues of *Amka* have been published: Mercy Amba Oduyoye and Musimbi R. A. Kanyoro, eds., *Talitha Qumi!: Proceedings of the Convocation of African Women Theologians* (Ibadan: Daystar Press, 1989 and 1990); idem., eds., *The Will to Arise: Women, Tradition and the Church in Africa* (Maryknoll, NY: Orbis Books, 1992); Rosemary N. Edet and Meg A. Umeagudosu, eds., *Life, Women and Culture: Theological Reflection; Proceedings of the National Conference of the Circle of African Women Theologians 1990* (Lagos: African Heritage Research and Publications, 1991); Justine Kahungi Mbwiti and Couthon M. Fassinou, et al., *Le canari d'eau Fraiche au L'hospitalité Africaine* (Lubumbashi: Éditions de Chemins de Vie, 1996); Musimbi R. A. Kanyoro and Nyambura J. Njoroge, eds., *Groaning in Faith: African Women in the Household of God* (Nairobi: Acton Publishers, 1996); Elizabeth Amoah, ed., *Where God Reigns: Reflections On Women in God's World* (Accra: Sam Woode Ltd., 1997); Grace Wamui and Mary Getui, eds., *Violence Against Women: Reflections by Kenyan Women Theologians* (Nairobi: Acton Publishers, 1996); Mercy A. Oduyoye, ed., *Transforming Power: Women in the Household of God. Proceedings of the Pan-African Conference of the Circle of Concerned African Women Theologians* (Accra: Sam Woode Ltd., 1997).

5. Robert J. Schreiter, ed., *Faces of Jesus in Africa* (Maryknoll, NY: Orbis Books, 1988); Denise Ackermann, et al., eds., *Women Hold up Half the Sky: Women in the Church in South Africa* (Pietermaritzburg: Cluster Publications, 1991).

6. Mercy Amba Oduyoye, *Hearing and Knowing: Theological Reflections on Christianity in Africa* (Maryknoll, NY: Orbis Books, 1986); Teresa Okure, *Johannine Approach to Mission: A Contextual Study of John 4:1–42* (Tübingen: J. C. B. Mohr/Paul Siebeck Verlag, 1988); and Christina Landman, *The Piety of South African Women* (Pretoria: C. B. Powell Bible Centre, UNISA, 1999).

7. Kuma, *Jesus of the Deep Forest*, 5.

8. Ibid.

9. Ibid.

10. Rosemary Edet, "Christ and the Nigerian Womanhood," in Edet and Umeagudosu, *Life, Women and Culture*, 177.

11. Ibid.

12. Ibid. Note that inclusive language, even on the horizontal level, is not common with African women, most of whose mother tongues have non-gendered pronouns and words for humanity.

13. Edet, "Christ and the Nigerian Womanhood," 177–93.

14. A. E. Kwazu, "Church Leadership and the Nigerian Woman," in Edet and Umeagudosu, *Life, Women and Culture*, 94.

15. Akon E. Udo, "The Emerging Spiritualities of Women in Nigeria," in Edet and Umeagudosu, *Life, Women and Culture*, 102.

16. Akon E. Udo, "Women in God's World: Some Biblical Affirmations," in Amoah, *Where God Reigns*, 20–25.

17. Musimbi R. A. Kanyoro, "Daughter, Arise: Luke 8:40-56," in Oduyoye and Kanyoro, *Talitha Qumi!* 59.

18. Teresa M. Hinga, "Jesus Christ and the Liberation of Women in Africa," in Oduyoye and Kanyoro, *The Will to Arise*, 190.

19. Hinga, "Jesus Christ," 191; See also Christine Landman, *The Piety of South African Women*, 19, 51.

20. Hinga, "Jesus Christ," 191.

21. Ibid., 191–92.

22. Grace Duah, *Deliverance: Fact or Fantasy?* (no publication details available).

23. Rosemary N. Edet, "Christianity and African Women's Rituals," in Oduyoye and Kanyoro, *The Will to Arise*, 26–29.

24. Margaret K. Obaga, "Women are Members of God's Commonwealth," in Kanyoro and Njoroge, *Groaning in Faith*, 69.

25. Edet, "Christ and the Nigerian Womanhood," 178.

26. Jessica Keturah Nakawombe, "Women in the Kingdom of God," in Kanyoro and Njoroge, *Groaning in Faith*, 47. See also Betty Govinden on the link between Christology and Mariology in Kanyoro and Njoroge, *Groaning in Faith*, 122–23.

27. Edet, "Christ and the Nigerian Womanhood," 183. Note, however, that it seems that, for women like Afua Kuma, this "pantokrator" is not a distant emperor, but the African ruler into whose courts all can run for refuge, for food, for fairness, and for fair-play.

28. Edet, "Christ and the Nigerian Womanhood," 184.

29. Ibid., 184–85.

30. Térèsa Souga, "The Christ Event from the Viewpoint of African Women: A Catholic Perspective," in Fabella and Oduyoye, *With Passion and Compassion*, 22.

31. Ibid., 28–29.

32. Ibid., 22.

33. Ibid., 24.

34. Ibid., 26.

35. Ibid., 28.

36. Ibid.

37. Nyambura Njoroge, "Groaning and Languishing in Labour Pains," in Kanyoro and Njoroge, eds., *Groaning in Faith*, 4.

38. Edet, "Christ and the Nigerian Womanhood," 185.

39. Ada Nyaga, "Women's Dignity and Worth in God's Kingdom," in Kanyoro and Njoroge, *Groaning in Faith*, 81.

40. Akon E. Udo, "Emerging Spiritualities of Women in Nigeria," in Edet and Umeagudosu, *Life, Women and Culture*, 105.

41. Mercy Amba Oduyoye and Elizabeth Amoah, "The Christ for African Women," in Fabella and Oduyoye, *With Passion and Compassion*, 44. The sacrifice involved in the widow's mite, however, does raise a question. Is Jesus only approving her action or also illustrating how religious obligations can rob the poor of even the little they have for sustaining their lives?

42. Louise Tappa, "The Christ-Event: A Protestant Perspective," in Fabella and Oduyoye, *With Passion and Compassion*, 31.

43. Ibid., 31–32.

44. As quoted by Oduyoye and Amoah in "The Christ for African Women," 43.

45. Ibid.

46. Kuma, *Jesus of the Deep Forest*, 42.

47. Oduyoye and Amoah, "The Christ for African Women," 43.

48. Tappa, "The Christ-Event," 34.

49. Oduyoye and Amoah, "The Christ for African Women," 44.

50. Landman, *The Piety of South African Women*, 63.

51. Oduyoye and Kanyoro, *Talitha Qumi!* 206.

52. Conversations on Christology with Pastor Pamela Martin, Baptist from Cameroon, November 1999.

53. Landman, *The Piety of South African Women*, 29.

54. Edet, "Christ and the Nigerian Womanhood," 187.

55. Conversations on Christology with Dr. Elizabeth Amoah, June 1999.

56. Landman, *The Piety of South African Women*, 34.

57. Justine Kahungu Mbwiti, "Jesus and the Samaritan Woman," in Oduyoye and Kanyoro, *Talitha Qumi!* 63–76. At the time of this writing, the name of the country was Zaire; it is now the Democratic Republic of the Congo, a nation still crying for shalom.

58. Mabel S. Morny, "Christ Restores to Life," in Oduyoye and Kanyoro, *Talitha Qumi!* 145–49.

59. Workshop on "Jesus Christ and the Liberation of the African Woman," in Oduyoye and Kanyoro, *Talitha Qumi!* 206.

11

THE SUFFERING CHRIST AND THE ASIAN BODY

Sharon A. Bong (Malaysia)

A theology that matters is one that is embodied. That Asian Christian theology is "body language, heart semantics or soul-syntax" reclaims the body and its corporeality in theologizing from the lived experiences of the grassroots and, in particular, women.[1] It is premised on the historical and material conditions of specific Asian communities and articulated from their positions of marginality *and* agency. And it effects the following doctrinal transgressions. It is first an antithesis to the denigration of the body fed by the church's tacit valorization of asceticism and residual misogyny of the (male) spirit/(female) body duality. Second, it embodies the humanization of God in the body of Christ that suffers, resists, and heals and in so doing, eschews a Godhead that is disembodied. And third, it rejects the exegetic "violence of abstraction"[2] by foregrounding faith and praxis toward the realization of a local/global community that is more equitable, just, and sustainable from within the church and beyond.

In contrast, from my personal standpoint as an Asian-Malaysian Catholic feminist, the platter of doctrinal interpretation of the "economy of 'signs'" served on women's bodies, sexuality, and roles has become not only unsavory but also distasteful.[3] Women are equal but different within the equation of the complementarity of the sexes. Second, women are divested of the capacity to act *"in persona Christi"* (imaging Christ) notwithstanding their "feminine genius." This essential lack inherent in the ontology of woman, her very being, affords the irrefutable and therefore irreversible rationale to women's exclusion from priestly ordination.[4] And third, extolling the virtue of "heroic love" of women who refuse to abort a fetus resulting from "the injustice of rape"[5] evinces the "violence of abstraction" of a theology disconnected from the signs of

---

Sharon A. Bong, "Suffering, Resisting, Healing: An Asian View of the Body," in *Body and Religion*, ed. Regina Ammicht Quinn and Elsa Tamez, *Concilium* 2002, no. 2 (London: SCM Press, 2002), 122–29.

the times. Its maturity date for those who inhabit and negotiate their bodies and sexualities within the intersection of gender, race, caste, class, cultures, and religions has long expired.

Bodies that suffer, bodies that resist, and bodies that heal constitute the life-blood, sinew, and fiber of Christian theologies from Asia. In this article, with "an economy" of words, I reflect on the centrality and limits of theologizing on the materiality of bodies that are pathologized (bodies that suffer), politicized (bodies that resist), and spiritualized (bodies that heal).

Bodies That Suffer

Imaging a suffering Christ is literalized in women (and men) who are dehumanized. An embodied theology in faithful allegiance to Christ's preferential option and actualization of scarred bodies confers hermeneutical privilege on the biblical poor. It does so in recognition of the lived realities of Asian women (and men) who are pinioned by structural and systemic violence in the form of gender, racial, caste, class, cultural, and religious oppressions.

The bodies that suffer are thus those who know (suffering) as opposed to the primacy of historically laudable mediators of knowledge, translators of experience, and codifiers of faith. And they are mothers, wives, daughters, sisters who are victims and survivors of familial violence in the form of female infanticide, incest, dowry deaths, honor killings, domestic violence (which includes marital rape); communal and military violence in the mass rape of women from ethnic minorities, outcast (i.e., Dalit of India) or indigenous communities; state violence manifest in rape, torture, summary executions and forced relocation, labor and deportation of women in situations of armed conflict; and global violence through the trafficking of women and girls and inhumane treatment of migrant and sex workers and disenfranchised sexual minorities. They are the 12,612 dowry deaths recorded across India in 1998–99 where new brides were starved, beaten, tortured, imprisoned at home and/or doused with paraffin and set alight by their husbands or mothers-in-law because their families failed to make "adequate" dowry payments to the husband's family.[6]

It is women's bodies constructed as repositories and markers of ethnic, cultural, and religious boundaries that result in women's greater vulnerability to racism, racial and ethnic discrimination, xenophobia and related intolerance which not only affect women in different ways and degrees from men but also exacerbate gender-based violence.[7] It is the 168 Indonesian women and girls of mostly Chinese descent who were gang raped in the streets and raped in front of their families during the mid-May 1998 Jakarta riots.[8]

It is the appropriation of women's bodies as a site of contestation between fundamentalism and feminism: where women's bodies in the former ideology serve as retainers of pristine and immutable identity and in the latter as breeding ground for polluting and subversive change. The scene is the 1994 Cairo International Conference on Population and Development (ICPD); the script, "replete with death threats from militant Egyptian Muslim groups, eschatological rhetoric from the Vatican" amid the dissonant chorus of women's health, rights, and empowerment; and the "prop," women's bodies, their sexuality, and their roles in family and society.[9]

It is the inscription of women's bodies as lesser that is the foundational premise of son-preference endemic in Asian cultures and, contentiously, in the church. This predisposes a girl-child to a life of gender-based violence, in particular early marriage (including child marriage) and sexual exploitation, and of deprivation in terms of adequate access to food, health, education, and love. Nearly one-seventh of Chinese baby girls are missing—for every 100 girls registered at birth, there are 118 little boys—as a result of female infanticide (or baby dumping) and prenatal sex selection (illegal, selective abortion) as extensions of son-preference.[10]

The democratization of Asian theology reinstates the primacy of bodies that suffer into the body of the canon. Hermeneutical privilege is thus accorded to them and the "community becomes the theologian."[11] They thereby serve as the pulse of Asian theologies of liberation for they liberate theology from its doctrinal abstractions, hegemony, and disconnectedness. To illustrate the centrality of the oppressed as the foundational basis of theologies from Asia, "Dalit theology" or "No people's theology" embraces the "no-humanness" of Dalits (pariahs of Indian society) as symptomatic of the negation of their humanity, yet strives to realize their "full divinity" as created in God's image (*imago Dei*).[12] In doing so, theologies premised on bodies that suffer call for the "primacy of the anthropological element over the ecclesiastical," "utopian over the factual," "critical over the dogmatic," "social over the personal" and "orthopraxis over orthodoxy."[13]

Theologizing from the vantage point of the marginalized does not detract from but essentially concretizes Christ's preferential option for the poor: where one's compassion and interconnectedness with those who are more dispirited is the hallmark of Two-Thirds world women and men *doing* theology. It stretches the limits of Christianity as an eschatological faith premised on the potential and obligation of human agency to evince a better tomorrow today: to approximate a heaven on earth. This conviction then materializes into a catalytic spirit that embraces solidarity with the marginalized and culminates in an "eruption from below."[14] In profoundly identifying with the poor, in being a servant to the poor, in conferring upon the poor the dignity of self-determination, theologians reinstate the plural and radical voice of the marginalized of Asia as the cornerstone of theologies of, for and by Asians.

However, eschewing an exegetic "violence of abstraction" runs the risk of pathologizing bodies that suffer: of inscribing Asian bodies, particularly Asian women's bodies, as weak, infirm, and violated. On one level, the inferiorization, subjugation, and victimization of women and the girl-child from birth to grave substantiate bodies that suffer as knowing subjects of theological discourse as argued above. But hermeneutical and political privileging of bodies that suffer is also problematized. For instance, the "theology of 'the poor woman' in Asia" has its discursive limits as Wong Wai Ching deconstructs the monolithic categorization of "the poor woman" as a metonym for human suffering. Within the economy of a nationalist rhetoric and strategy that dichotomizes the colonized Asian against the Western imperialist, women's individuated historical and political agency is often subsumed. Women's bodies are on the one hand homogenously constructed as victimized to justify colonial intervention in the form of civilizing missions; on the other hand, they are propped up as barometers of national essence to preserve tradition and to fortify resistance. Within a postcolonial identity politics, woman is thus doubly colonized: denigrated as "poor woman" and idealized as "superwoman."[15]

Bodies That Resist

Theologizing therefore begins with an awareness of the pitfalls of pathologizing and its attendant risks of romanticizing and appropriating the narratives of subjugated positions. It follows through with a conviction that foregrounding bodies that suffer as the foundational premise of theology would potentially illuminate the underlying causes of structural and systemic sin toward the realization of a transformative vision of the world. Solidarity with the oppressed and substantiation of our collective and reciprocal self-worth and determination thus serve as prerequisites to the authentication of embodied theologies from Asia.

As such, hermeneutical subjects or bodies that know are also bodies that resist. In breaking the silence on sexuality, they generate new ways of seeing that are grounded, specific, and critical. This type of theologizing is thus those who challenge homophobia and heterosexism in negotiating sexuality from a human rights perspective[16]: whereby women—as affirmed in the Beijing Platform for Action, the international blueprint of women's human rights—are "to have control over and decide freely and responsibly on matters related to their sexuality, including sexual and reproductive health, free of coercion, discrimination and violence."[17] It is those who recognize that empowering women does not disempower men in stemming the HIV/AIDS pandemic in Asia: that more gender-equitable relationships significantly reduce the risk of vulnerability of both women and men to HIV infection.[18] It is those who redefine virginity on their own terms in embracing chastity of mind, body, and spirit and those who reject the construct of virginity as proof of a woman's marriageable worth.[19] It is those who demystify the regulation of women's sexuality and representation as "ornamented surface" for the gratification of male pleasure and gaze.[20] It is the 80 comfort women who broke the silence of their victimization in a mock tribunal on Japan's World War II enslavement of at least 200,000 women in military brothels in occupied territories in South East Asia and East Asia.[21]

It is the bodies that resist seamless categorizations within the plurality and proliferation of identities embroiled in multi-ethnic, multi-cultural, and multi-religious contexts in Asia compounded by the disparity between the haves and have-nots therein. It is the implausibility and indecency of ranking hierarchically suffering and resistant bodies. It is Vietnamese women opting for cosmetic surgery in pursuit of the idealization of Western standards of beauty to embellish their Asian features and Bangladeshi women who as survivors of acid attacks get reconstructive surgery to refigure physical but not emotional scars.[22] It is not de-sexualizing the grassroots as bodies that suffer and bodies that resist in agitating for structural change within the church and society. It is avoiding the violent othering of the Other in embracing gay, lesbian, bisexual, trans-sexual, trans-gendered and other disinherited bodies as well as the single, widowed, and childless as deviations from normative heterosexual and (re)productive relations. It is recognizing that the bodies that do not have enough to eat, bodies that overeat, and bodies that refuse to eat rest on the same continuum of need. It is coming to terms with the inequitable distribution of the world's resources that accounts for hunger and obesity as corollary eating disorders. And it is being aware that voluntary starvation is paradoxically a protest against the construction of women's bodies and regulation of women's sexualities as well as an eroticization of thinness as a beauty myth that is internally inflicted.

Bodies That Heal

In "an epistemology of the broken body," the restoration of bodies that suffer and bodies that resist becomes the dialectical site of redemption, for, as Chung Hyun Kyung contends, "to be human is to suffer and resist" and "to be human is to be created in God's image."[23] For Asians, where the spirit is corporeal and the body (and sexuality) sacred, by inference, the body is the spirit. The configuration of the human person as both body *and* spirit reinstates not only human agency but also human worth and, in repositioning the spirit as corporeal and the body as sacred, Asian theologians depart from doctrinal eschatology that maintains the inferiorization of material and sexualized bodies.

The benchmark of Christianity in Asia is its insistence on praxis—faith translated as compassionate identification and solidarity with the marginalized. The Asian sense of ecclesiastical mission as premised on the "epistemology of the broken body"—alluding simultaneously to the crucifixion of Christ as/and bodies that suffer, resist, and heal—attests to the concretization of a transformative faith that witnesses the transition from *"anthropocentrism to life-centrism"* and the adoption of "voluntary [spiritual] poverty" in dialectical opposition to "forced [material] poverty."[24] Embodied theologies thus problematize dualisms such as mind/body, spirit/matter, abstract/concrete, objective/subjective, theory/praxis, universal/particular, observer/observed, and male/female.

For Asian theologies, the representation of God in the anthropomorphic Christ is both transcendent *and* immanent. God therefore is not immutable and dispassionate but is embodied in and through the oppressed. The phenomenon of a *"christological transformation"* is exacted through the use of "religio-political symbols" to encapsulate unique images of Christ concordant with the experiences of Asian peoples.[25] The postcolonial portrayal of Jesus as "liberator, revolutionary, and political martyr" mirrors the political martyrdom of Filipino women in their relentless crusade for social transformation: that they "do not merely accompany Christ to Calvary as spectators [but also] carry the cross with him and undergo his passion in an act of identification with his suffering" and in so doing, resurrect "the *Bagong Kristo* (the New Christ)" that resides within them.[26] Through a "christology from below"[27] God is thus transmuted and humanized. Knowledge of God as omniscient, omnipresent, and omnipotent is arbitrated through the agency of the suffering and resistant, and God the Signifier thus becomes known, present, and empowering.

An emerging Asian spirituality of, for and by Asian people is fundamentally a theology that necessitates the politics of difference and the politics of identity premised on the socially determinate lives of its knowing subjects—the bodies that suffer, resist, and are healed. A theology that matters is a theology that is embodied. And a theology that is embodied is sound theology. The spirituality of Asian people affords a site of theological inquiry to the question of praxis or committed action. The politicization of spirituality and the spiritualization of politics endemic in Asian theologizing prophetically herald the eschatological promise of begetting a heaven on earth. It is the realization of an equitable, just, and sustainable global/local community from within the church and beyond. It is in the context of Asia, ceasing to wonder at the extent to which favoring sons and neglecting daughters is sanctioned by the "economy of 'signs'" of the body of the church.

Notes

1. C. S. Song, quoted in Charles Elliott, *Sword and Spirit* (London: BBC Books, 1989), 42.

2. Chung Hyun Kyung, *Struggle to Be the Sun Again: Introducing Asian Women's Theology* (Maryknoll, NY: Orbis Books, 1990), 101.

3. "Pope John Paul II's Letter to Women," issued July 10, 1995 to address the Fourth United Nations World Conference on Women, Beijing (paragraph 11), http://www.womenpriests.org/church/Beijing.htm.

4. Sally M. Vance-Trembath, "John Paul II's *Ut Unum Sint* and Conversation with Women," *Theological Studies* 60 (1999): 103.

5. "Pope John Paul II's Letter to Women," paragraph 5.

6. BBC News, "Jail Crisis for Dowry Crimes," June 1, 2000, <http://news.bbc.co.uk/hi/english/south_asia/n ewsid _772000/772896.stm>.

7. The Asia-Pacific NGO (non-governmental organization) Position Paper prepared for the 45th Session of the UN Commission on Status of Women (CSW), New York, March 6–16, 2001, as well as the recent World Conference against Racism, Racial Discrimination, Xenophobia and Related Intolerance (WCAR), Durban, South Africa, August 31–September 7, 2001. The paper was originally drafted by the Asia Pacific Forum on Women, Law and Development (APWLD), based in Chiangmai, Thailand, in consultation with women's NGOs and other grass-roots organizations in the Asia-Pacific region, <http://194.78.216.158/whrnet3/wcar/key_docs/intersection.htm>.

8. *New Straits Times Press* (Kuala Lumpur, Malaysia), August 18, 1998, 20.

9. Lynn P. Freedman, "The Challenge of Fundamentalisms," *Reproductive Health Matters* 8 (November 1996): 56.

10. BBC News, "China's Unwanted Girls," August 23, 2001, <http://news.bbc.co.uk/hi/english/world/asia-pacific/newsid_1506000/1506469.stm>.

11. Chung, *Struggle to Be the Sun Again*, 103.

12. Arvind P. Nirmal, "Toward a Christian Dalit Theology," in *Frontiers in Asian Christian Theology: Emerging Trends*, ed. R. S. Sugirtharajah (Maryknoll, NY: Orbis Books, 1994), 34, 40.

13. Alfred T. Hennelly, *Liberation Theology: A Documentary History* (Maryknoll, NY: Orbis Books, 1990), 160–61.

14. Jojo M. Fung, SJ, *Shoes-Off Barefoot We Walk: A Theology of Shoes-Off* (Kuala Lumpur: Longman Malaysia, 1992), 79.

15. Wong Wai Ching, "Negotiating for a Postcolonial Identity: Theology of 'the Poor Woman' in Asia," *Journal of Feminist Studies in Religion* 16, no. 2 (2000): 9.

16. beng hui, "Time's Up! Moving Sexuality Rights in Malaysia into the New Millennium," *Women in Action*, 1999, http://www.isiswomen.org/wia/wia199/sex00006.html.

17. United Nations, *The Beijing Declaration and the Platform for Action, Fourth World Conference on Women, Beijing, China, 4–15 September 1995*, paragraph 96.

18. Geeta Rao Gupta, "Gender, Sexuality and HIV/AIDS: The What, the Why, and the How," Plenary Address, 12th International AIDS Conference, Durban, South Africa, July 12, 2000.

19. Celeste Cinco, "Virginity in the 90s: Young Filipinas Face up to Contending Pressures [of] Virginity," *Women in Action*, 1999, <http://www.isiswomen.org/wia/wia199/sex00008.html>.

20. Young-Hee Shim, "Gender and Body Politics in Korea: Focusing on the Making of the Feminine Body," *Asian Women* 6 (June 1998): 23.

21. *AP International*, "Mock Tribunal for Sex Slaves Opens," December 8, 2000, <http://freegroups.net/groups/end-times_news/0::4744read.html>.

22. BBC News, "Vietnam: West is Best for Beauty," January 11, 1999, <http://news.bbc.co.uk/hi/english/world/asia-pacific/newsid_ 250000/250630.stm>, and "Joyous Homecoming for Acid Attack Victims," July 22, 1999, <http://news.bbcco.uk/hi/english/world/south_asia/newsid_401000/ 401993.stm>.

23. Chung, *Struggle to Be the Sun Again*, 39, 47.

24. Ibid., 42–43.

25. Ibid., 62.

26. Ibid., 63–64. Wong Wai Ching cautions that such postcolonial discourse, which polarizes Western imperialist/Asian colonized in politicizing Christ's salvific mission, runs the risk of "normalization and routinization of one kind of women's experience—that is, as victims of foreign and home exploitation—and one form of women's agency—that is, as national-liberation combatants." See Wong, "Negotiating for a Postcolonial Identity," 21.

27. Chung, *Struggle to Be the Sun Again*, 60.

12

AUSTRALIAN ABORIGINAL WOMEN'S CHRISTOLOGIES

Lee Miena Skye (Palawa, Australia)

Australian Aboriginal women were pursued by a paradoxical Christology through the missiology of colonialism. The paradox intended to save, but instead brought about spiritual, cultural and physical, actual genocide. The Aboriginal people of Australia were considered to be less than human and, therefore, were not treated as if they were human. Hence, there was a meager attempt to understand the meaning of their culture and ways by a common *Weltanschauung* (worldview) shared by a colonialist church and state. A new paradox has occurred in the present day, however, when there is an intense interest in understanding the Aboriginal tribal ways and culture in order to save this world. The Aboriginal scientific system, which allows people to fit into rather than outside of the ecology, has been and is being investigated because, unlike the Western world and in M. J. Christie's words, it does not place "humanity apart from and above the natural world."[1] Consequently, the Indigenous people of Australia will be the messengers of a new ecological vision and ecotheology/creation theology for the new millennium.

Aboriginal people's *Weltanschauungen* are being investigated by the Western world for all possible answers for survival in a world in crisis: the environment; the threat of nuclear war; poverty; disease; the lack of mental, spiritual, and physical wholeness of humanity. Westerners look to a race of people who have "survived" since time began, with very few of these aspects of crisis in their history. The study of racial ontology and epistemology reveals a race with a deeper "spiritualness" than Western ontology and epistemology. A study of the genetics of memory helps to

Lee Miena Skye, "*Kerygmatics* of the New Millennium: The Message This Study of Australian Aboriginal Women's Christologies Gives to Future Generations," in *Kerygmatics of the New Millennium: A Study of Australian Aboriginal Women's Christology* (Delhi: ISPCK, 2007), 99–109.

support this theory. Hence, this ontological quality is what, significantly, separates Australian Aboriginal and Western ontology; therefore, it seems an intense study of this major aspect of Australian Aboriginal ontology is where the core of knowledge for human survival will be found.

Such an ontology with a central characteristic of deeper spiritualness reveals a culture that does not have a work-ethic ideology, as is the case with Western culture, but works only to survive, and "balances" the rest of existence with rest and recreation. The gender structure within the traditional cultures is balanced and egalitarian; men and women see their role as one of partnership. Aboriginals were constantly referred to as "savages" by the colonialists, but that has not been my experience of my Tasmanian Aboriginal culture. Aboriginal children were never physically hit as a part of chastisement; if any chastisement was necessary, it occurred only after initiation. The children were treated as extremely precious, as gifts from God, to be celebrated and cherished. This is my memory of the treatment I received from my Aboriginal grandfather; it is impossible for me to perceive my ancestors in white terms. The Aboriginal culture places little value on the material things of life, only on what contributes to human "happiness"—being: wholeness, harmony, physical survival, and love. Hence, these cultural ways that arise out of a deep spiritualness give a strong message to the generations of the future regarding what is essential for survival and quality existence.

The phenomenon is that, in spite of a paradoxical, phantom, intrinsically violent and unhealthy Christology inherited from colonialism, some Aboriginal people became Christian, as did many generations that followed. None were more exploited, from then until now, than Australian Indigenous women; they are on the lowest rung of the Australian social order and experience a "quadric-dimensional" oppression of racism, classism, sexism (including heterosexism), and naturism. The answer to the phenomenon seems to be that, in spite of the legacy of a violent Christology and the multilayered oppression these women experience, they have found a gentle Christ who tenderly and solidly comforts, identifies with, supports, and empowers them in their *Sitze im Leben* (settings in life). This I see as one of the most important messages Australian Aboriginal women give to future generations, white, black, and of color—the "real and true" insight they have into the being of Christ, born out of the incredible depths of their suffering; in this, they are significantly the *kerygmatics* of the new millennium in their Christologies.

While interviewing the women in order to document their Christologies, I became aware of their remarkable "benevolence," even in a state of suffering virtually incomprehensible to white people. This benevolence toward their oppressors, I believe, contains a message to future generations. Thus, combined with their real and true insight into Christ came an expression of benevolence. This charitable attitude was displayed in the interest in "education," as a means of helping Aboriginal people be able to communicate with white people and thus assist in bringing about reconciliation. White people, however, do not seem to have seen a need to initiate the learning of Aboriginal peoples' languages for mutual benefit. A positive activity in the area of education has been the training of Indigenous teachers for Indigenous students; this can be effective if the teachers are allowed to employ their own methodologies for teaching and are not hindered by the hegemonic bureaucracy. Indigenous support for and interest in education is something that I think is of value for future generations to contemplate and consider.

One of the interviewees of my research, who is a teacher, remarked on how she preferred a teaching methodology that was designed to educate her students about the "spiritual" things of life, and she liked to put this into practice by being guided spiritually. This teaching methodology would be very alien to a white culture that possessed an ontology strongly anchored in the intellect. The emphasis on the *spirit* in all areas of their lives would have to be the strongest characteristic of Australian Aboriginal ontological and epistemological expression. Even their perception of Christ is centered on his spiritual reality. There are healing methods that are centered on a combination of Aboriginal and Christian spirituality; these methods display a common, accepted practice among Australian Aboriginal Christian women to inculturate the spirituality of Christ into Aboriginal spirituality. In the area of Western psychology and practice in Australia, physicians have begun to recognize the power Aboriginal elders have in healing Indigenous people with diagnosed mental health problems. The elders bring these people into the life of the spirit and help to establish their Aboriginal identity. The fundamental message the Aboriginal Christian women are offering here to others is that wholeness requires mental, physical, and spiritual balance. Fortunately, the Western world is beginning to look at Aboriginal *Weltanschauung* to aid in mental health, as it knows its Western philosophies and medicines are limited in establishing mental wholeness.

Aboriginal spirituality is diverse in its healing concepts and practices from tribe to tribe, but there are major common healing concepts such as stillness, a natural closeness to God, and an intimate relationship with nature. The Aboriginal elders will bring those of their people who are ill in contact with these concepts. In the stillness, you come in touch with the spirit within you. This is how you come in touch with the Spirit of God within you. It is only in that stillness that you become aware of the Spirit of God within you also existing without. You then become aware that the Spirit of God existing without is "one" with all that is living. This is the first important step in healing, coming to know what the Spirit is; this method can be followed by anyone, of any culture, who wants to get in touch with their spiritual-self and spiritual reality, and to begin the process of balancing the mental, physical, and spiritual, which is very important for human wholeness. The next important step in healing is the establishing of Aboriginal identity, coming to know one's roots and uniqueness, as an individual and as part of a community; this creates a sense of "belonging," which is extremely important, and the building up of self-esteem.

The majority of Australian Aboriginal women interviewed suggested that the activities that would be of the greatest value to Indigenous people of the future were to establish Aboriginal "identity" and to walk close to God. The importance of establishing Aboriginal identity cannot be over-emphasized. These people are dispossessed, mentally, physically, and spiritually in their *Sitz im Leben* due to the effects of white hegemonic culture; this has to be reversed. The message of establishing identity is an important one for other Indigenous cultures throughout the world who have suffered at the hands of other hegemonic cultures.

When Aboriginal women are encouraging other people to walk close to God, it is God as seen through their eyes; that perception is one that is unique, intimate, and powerful, reflected in their Christologies. To them, God and Christ are one and the same. This characteristic of their Christologies they share with the Christologies of other black women and women of color from throughout the world. There are other attributes of their Christologies that are shared with the Christologies of these women from other cultures. They share a view of Christ who identifies with and supports them in their liberation from a quadri-dimensional oppression of racism, classism, sexism (including heterosexism), and naturism. Australian Aboriginal Christian women are not interested in issues centered around the gender of Christ, as is the case with white Christian feminists; their interest is centred more on his "humanity" and "saving power." This aspect of their Christologies they also share with the Christologies of their black sisters and sisters of color. Hence, there are "universal" attributes that Australian Indigenous Christian women share with other black women and women of color from throughout the world in their Christologies. In this, Australian Aboriginal Christian women are contributing to the universal academic area of womanist theology, strengthening its foundation for the generations to come and, thus, building a more solid foundation for universal healing of Christian Indigenous women struggling in hegemonic cultures.

There are other attributes of their Christologies that they do not necessarily share with their black sisters and sisters of color in the area of Christology. The understanding of the "sacredness" of life and land, and especially land, is very strong in their Christologies in comparison to the Christologies of their sisters from other black cultures and cultures of color. The strong connection Australian Aboriginal women have to land/nature/creation and to the source of creation is a unique aspect of their Christologies and calls for a methodology for doing Christology within this context. The majority of Australian Aboriginal Christian women interviewed inculturate the Spirit of Christ into their Indigenous spirituality. A Creation/Identity methodology[2] for doing Christology helps to articulate this inculturation. The methodology affirms the sacredness of creation and allows for the flourishing of identity with the Creator/Source and the natural environment. Thus, Christ becomes "one" with creation. I see this methodology as the most valuable contribution Australian Aboriginal Christian women make to the generations of the new millennium. This contribution will have benefits not only for Aboriginal women, but also for all people of black cultures and cultures of color, and for white people as well, doing Christology. A Creation/Identity methodology anchors Christ in creation, uniting spirit and nature, which is a major negative dualism that has existed for too long in Western culture. The end of this dualism in Western consciousness will help in shaping human attitudes toward the environment; the importance of this cannot be overstated in our state of universal environmental crisis. A Creation/ Identity methodology for doing Christology allows Christ to be inculturated into whatever conception one has of God in one's culture; if the conception of God is female, then Christ becomes One-with-the-feminine-principle, hence, helping to end the male/female dualism, another major negative dualism in Western consciousness.

There is a relationship that exists between church and state in the Western world in the areas of morality and ethics; the changes in Christology in the church, therefore, will in turn affect the moral and ethical conscience of society. Thus, a Creation/Identity methodology for doing Christology can have resounding positive effects on church, and then state, in the Western world of the future.

Australian Aboriginal women doing Christology by using a Creation/Identity methodology will produce "new" Christologies that reflect their individual tribal spirituality/culture. The Christologies, therefore, will reflect differing images of Christ after being inculturated into their creation and religious stories, beliefs, and ways. The common characteristics that these Christologies will share, however, is that they will be ecowomanist, contextual, ecumenical, and inclusive. In their ecowomanist aspect, they are fighting for liberation from the oppression of naturism, an oppression exercised by white hegemonic culture; in this characteristic of their Christologies they contribute to the academic area of creation theology, which is and must be a domain of social ethics. Their Christologies will be contextual because the uniqueness of their *Sitz im Leben* demands such a perspective; this demand was the influence behind the development of Creation/Identity methodology for doing Christology, and in this they are liberated from Christologies written for women of a different *Sitz im Leben* and *Weltanschauung*. They will expound Christologies that reflect their Indigenous theologies with strong links to the Source of Creation and land/nature/creation. In this, they contribute to creation spirituality because their Christology is done through the study of creation and its interrelating spiritual relationships.

The ecumenical aspect of the Christologies comes about by the willingness of the women to inculturate Christ, a God brought to them by a hegemonic culture and spirituality, into their Aboriginal spirituality. This ecumenical aspect is significant in that it displays a great closeness to the Spirit of Christ, even if the vehicle for this savior is their oppressors. Their depth of closeness to Christ and their benevolent attitude toward their oppressors are strong messages indeed, now and in the future, for generations dealing with the plight of imposed Christianity. The inclusive aspect of their Christologies expounds their interest in keeping harmony in human relationships; to these women, Christ is inculturated into all of humanity; there is no hierarchical manifestation, no male/female dualism, only humankind being united in Christ. This aspect of their Christologies reflects Aboriginal culture's egalitarian and community outlook.

This inclusive aspect as well as all the other aspects of Australian Aboriginal women's Christologies just discussed, utilized in an Creation/Identity methodology, make critical contributions to liberation theology and spirituality while witnessing to the depth of the reality of Christ and the attitude to hold while experiencing oppression and encouraging the seeking of peace and harmony in all one's relationships with humankind and creation. This is a collective message of justice/wholeness/truth/peace being found for the Australian Indigenous Christian woman, and an encouragement for others to seek and find the same within the uniqueness of their *Sitz im Leben* and *Weltanschauung*.

Australian Aboriginal women using a Creation/Identity methodology for doing Christology will be aware of the common conception in Aboriginal spirituality of the sacredness of life, an attitude that encompasses all of creation. By the inculturation of the sacredness of the Spirit of Christ into the sacredness of all life, there is a unification of both Aboriginal and white spirituality; this activity witnesses in turn the inculturation of Christ, linked to the sacredness of all life, into white culture. This means a witness to the liberation of the oppressor from destructive Christologies that separate spirit from matter, people from each other, and humankind from nature. In the spiritual concept of the sacredness of all of life, a contribution is made to earth-based spiritualities, the theology of the Creator Spirit, and Christian sacramentalism. Therefore, Australian Aboriginal women doing Christology, using a Creation/Identity methodology, contribute to spiritualities and theologies that emphasize the sacredness of life: the earth, individuals, communities, the cosmos.

The aspect of Aboriginal spirituality that understands the earth as mother when it is united with the Spirit of Christ not only is the uniting of the feminine and masculine principles but also is the joining of the living Spirit of Christ with the living spirit of the earth. In this activity, Creation/Identity Christological methodology contributes to Gaia Spirituality, which sees the earth as a female, living, spiritual entity.

In this Earth Mother spirituality, along with all other aspects of Australian spirituality inculturated with the Spirit of Christ, is the witness to the end of the dualism of black and white spirituality; hence, Australian Aboriginal women using an Creation/Identity Christological methodology will help to create new Christologies that contribute to universal health and harmony, and to display the possibility that such positive things can be achieved in future generations.

Australian Aboriginal women using a Creation/Identity Christological methodology will contribute to theologies and spiritualities that are seeking the right mind-set, philosophy, or religious practice for the salvation of our world, in human and earth wholeness, in its permanent, unchangeable, symbiotic relationship. The importance of this contribution is urgent in a world at war with the earth and with itself. In light of this important contribution on a global scale, and all the other extremely valuable messages Australian Aboriginal Christian women can give to the generations of the new millennium, the value of the womanist perspective for interpreting one's *Sitz im Leben* is undeniable. I hope this thesis will encourage Australian Aboriginal Christian women to adopt this perspective in their cognitive thinking and to receive the benefits it will bring in liberation and wholeness to them, individually, and to the community.

The message Australian Aboriginal Christian women interviewed for this thesis and those Christian women who are part of the Australian Aboriginal community of women of my lived experience give to the church of the future is the need for its indigenization and for a holistic ministry that will help contribute to the mental, physical, and spiritual wholeness of Aboriginal people. Fundamentalism is responsible for Australian Aboriginal people receiving an incorrect biblical hermeneutic, and through the indigenization of the church we hope to see a rereading of scripture in the Australian Indigenous context. This reading done by Australian Aboriginal women in the contexts of their individual tribal theologies, racial and gender ontologies and epistemologies, in the view of Will Coleman, will offer theologies that will help reformulate all theological languages[3]; the women, as Matthew Fox suggests, in being an authentic source of revelation, are the primary spiritual directors for future generations.[4]

This thesis has taken us on a journey from the times of colonialism when Australian Aboriginal women received a violent Christology, through the development of their own Christologies that reveal the "real and true Christ," born out of the depths of their suffering, which is their legacy for the generations to come. I have the honor of documenting their Christologies for the first time in history. I hope that anyone who takes this journey while reading this thesis will be overwhelmed, as I have been, by the immense healing value the documentation and evaluation of these Christologies will have not only for Australian Aboriginal women but also for anyone from any culture or gender who is seeking healing for our earth and its people.

As a *Palawa*, a Tasmanian Aboriginal, I have grown up in a community of Indigenous women who have constantly questioned "why" this tremendous suffering occurred, and why it still occurs to our people. I hope this thesis has helped to answer this question in some way, and provided a path for healing. Mostly, I hope that this thesis helps first of all to ensure that the physical genocide of my people will never be forgotten and, second, to provide ways of healing for Australian Aboriginal Christian women experiencing the effects of genocide. The most powerful message Australian Aboriginal Christian women give to the generations of the new millennium is to please let there be no more genocide in the history of humanity! Please let the pain that is expressed in this poem, written by a *Palawa* woman, never occur again:

Why?

Across the Strait is Tasmania
A place that was once *Koorie* Land
A place that belonged to our people
As they wandered with love of their land

They roamed the hills and the mountains
Swam in the vast flowing sea
LIVED on this land of beauty
Land that was happy and free

They didn't need houses to live in
Their home was the land it was free
They didn't need medical treatment
Their medicine came from the Tree

No prison was there to hold them
For they were all happy and free
Our people the Tasmanian *Koories*!
Who lived on their land so free

They didn't have clocks to remind them
They knew what the weather should be
As they looked up above it would tell them
What the forecast for tomorrow would be

Then without warning it happened!!!
A tragedy no-one wanted to see

As they watched from the shore
A ship came sailing to their land
The land of the free

With fear in their eyes they stood watching not knowing
What was to be—
As the guns fired death lay all around them
The horror no one wanted to see
Killed by the guns of the white man
Killed on their own sacred Land

They didn't hurt anybody
They didn't take any land
After 200 years they have waited
And still they cannot understand

Why did they kill our people?...
Why did they take our land?...
Why?...

—Brenda Campbell (1983)

Notes

1. M. J. Christie, "Aboriginal Science for the Ecologically Sustainable Future," *Aboriginal Science Teachers Journal* 37, no. 1 (March, 1991): 26–31.

2. This concept was given to the author in an oral communication by Anne Pattel-Gray.

3. Will Coleman, "Tribal Talk: Black Theology in Postmodern Configurations," *Theology Today* 50, no. 1 (April, 1993): 68–77.

4. Matthew Fox, *Original Blessing: A Primer in Creation Spirituality Presented in Four Paths, Twenty-Six Themes, and Two Questions* (Santa Fe, NM: Bear & Company, 1983), 267–70.

13

JESUS AND MARY DANCE WITH THE ORISHAS
Theological Elements in Interreligious Dialogue

Clara Luz Ajo Lázaro (Cuba)

He was standing in one of the last benches of the old church of Pueblo Nuevo. His white clothes stood out in the tenuous, welcoming shadows. As he approached me, I could see his kindly, smiling mulatto face and his green eyes that shone as he beheld his mother, who was coming toward him, trailing the golden cape of her virginal attire. The Mass was ending, and many people were in a hurry to leave, making the classic sign of the cross after hearing the final blessing. Mary, also in a hurry, was gesturing to her son, "Come on, son, it's getting late." He got up. Despite his handsome, attractive appearance and the brightness in his expressive eyes, people hardly looked at him. Making his way forward among the crowd, greeting here and there, Jesus reached his mother, and both went out onto the street.

In the distance the drums announcing the *Wemilere*[1] could already be heard. Holding hands, Jesus and Mary quickly moved in the direction of the house-shrine where the saint's feast being announced by the drums would be celebrated. The house was close by, in the same neighborhood as the church they had just left after taking part in Sunday Mass.

The day was becoming liturgy, was becoming shared life, life in the realm of the sacred, and Jesus and Mary were totally involved in the celebrations, first in the church and afterward in the *Wemilere*. A Sunday of celebration, a meeting of the sacred and the human in a blend of all the gestures, sounds, aromas, colors, form and content, words and images through which ordinary people orient their daily lives within celebrative moments and in intimate relation with the sacred.

Clara Luz Ajo Lázaro, "Jesus and Mary Dance with the *Orishas*: Theological Elements in Interreligious Dialogue," in *Feminist Intercultural Theology: Latina Exploration for a Just World*, ed. María Pilar Aquino and Maria José Rosado-Nunes (Maryknoll, NY: Orbis Books, 2007), 109–24.

Mary and Jesus Left from Mass and Went to Dance with the *Orishas*

This story, fruit of my imagination, is simply a fanciful way of ex-
pressing what can be experienced in a transcultured[2] religiosity, which in
the Cuban context finds daily expression in constant exercises of encul-
turation. This experience is one of dialogue and interaction, not for the
purpose of imposing forms, ideas, or concepts, but for sharing and being
enriched in a mutual interchange of expressions that become blended
and fused almost imperceptibly for ordinary people, who are the prime
subjects of this experience. They have known how to draw on, and at the
same time contribute to, a rich spirituality that has dialogued with itself
since the epoch when our ancestors arrived from Africa, made into
slaves—and it still continues that dialogue.

My interest is to study some of the theological elements that express
the faith of a large part of our Cuban people, elements that are created
and re-created by the people through their religious experiences and
practices. To that end I take as points of reference two diverse Cuban religious universes, namely, the Rule of Ocha or Santería and Christian belief and practice. In both traditions Jesus and Mary constitute important
figures in people's experience of the sacred. This experience has been
transformed by a process of transculturation. Above all, through the
faith of the slaves, it has produced an enriching encounter between the
Catholic saints and the *orishas* of African origin.

The religious factor is a decisive component in the whole formation
process of the Cuban ethnic character, and it displays a great wealth of
theological elements that have been reshaped by the people's faith. In the
course of almost four centuries these elements have been engaging in a
constant process of interchange, assimilation, and fusion. Such experiences open up for us today new avenues of theological reflection.

From the Mass to the Wemilere and from the Wemilere to the Mass

For many people in today's Cuba, it is quite natural to participate both
in the Mass and other church activities and also in rituals of Santería or other
Afro-Cuban religious worship. When I speak of church, I am referring to the
Catholic Church or the Episcopal Church, which are the Christian denomi-
nations that in some way allow their members to live this religious duality.

If we examine the origins of Santería, we find that this interrelation
between Christianity and elements of the African traditions arose
through a process of transculturation that structured and shaped Cuban
society. This process began at the very start of colonization and took
place primarily among the indigenous cultures of the peoples that originally populated our lands; it then took place between these cultures and
the culture of the whites who came from Spain; later, large numbers of

Africans of different ethnic groups, brought to Cuba as slaves, became integrated into this process; and eventually others also were included: Jews, French, English, Chinese, and people from all corners of the earth.[3]

The Africans, however, were a most important element for nurturing and molding Cuban culture. Of all the different ethnic groups that were introduced into Cuban territory,[4] the Yoruba, who came from former Dahomey, Togo, and especially southeastern Nigeria, were those who had the greatest cultural influence.[5] They came from urban civilizations that were culturally quite advanced; they had a developed agriculture, traded with other regions, and possessed artistic skills that made their cultural influence dominant in Cuba, especially in the more western parts of the country, such as Matanzas and La Habana. The Yoruba, called *lucumíes* in Cuba, also brought with them their religious beliefs, for their divinities (*orishas*) traveled along with them in the slave ships. Slowly but surely, many of the religious practices of the *lucumíes* were assimilated into the Christian tradition they found here.

Certain social and cultural factors contributed to this interchange and assimilation of religious elements between the two traditions. First of all, although the Catholic Church of Cuba sought to evangelize the slaves and rid them of their native religious beliefs (at least, this was one of the arguments given for participating wholeheartedly in the slavery business), a major part of the clergy were slave-owners, so that their material interests ended up prevailing over their supposedly missionary intentions. That is to say, the priests did not concern themselves much with catechizing the slaves, since that would mean taking slaves away from their work. At the same time, the colonialist masters applied cruel and violent methods, which made the slaves reject both their unethical behavior and their Christianity as unworthy of imitation. Besides these problems there were linguistic difficulties, for the custom of performing the Catholic rituals in Latin was quite foreign to African customs and traditions. Moreover, the slave-owners sought to preserve ethnic, linguistic, and religious differences among the slaves in order to avoid uprisings and riots in the barracks. On some feast days, though, there was a certain tolerance of organization, which allowed the people to play their drums and dance according to their traditions. Such moments were taken advantage of by the slaves to celebrate their liturgical rites and invoke their divinities.

In addition, there existed among the Africans associations called *cabildos* or *cofradías*, which provided them a legal space for organizing meetings. In the *cabildos* men and women of one ethnic group met together for the sake of helping one another and maintaining their culture.[6] The *cabildos* allowed the slaves to preserve their own customs and traditions as if they were still in their places of origin, and they were also able maintain their own religious hierarchies, which were recognized and respected by all the members. The *cofradías* were somewhat similar, but they were of Spanish origin, and they brought together Africans of different ethnic groups to celebrate Christian feasts.

Although these organizations had functions that were ostensibly social, they were of fundamental importance for the religious life of the
African slaves and for freed persons as well. These spaces allowed them
to keep alive their traditions and religious customs, disguised behind
Christian norms and practices. The ceremonies with African rituals
joined together and fused with those of the Catholic tradition. In some
cases the organization was given the name of a saint, and processions
were made to the parish church so that the priest in charge could bless
the saint's image. Afterward the people celebrated the feast by playing
their drums and dancing according to their own traditions. The *cabildos*
often took the name of an African deity; they were spaces in which the
language of origin was recalled and taught, and the traditional African
religious rituals found protection there.

In the course of time the *cabildos* and the *cofradías* extended to all
parts of the country, and the colonial government placed many limitations
on them. They finally underwent a process of fusion, so that not only people of African descent but also people of other ethnic groups participated
in them. At the end of the nineteenth century many of these organizations
were transformed into house-shrines, where a saint or a deity was wor-
shiped and where African rituals with Christian elements were practiced.

The transcultural give-and-take gradually transformed many aspects
of ritual, customs, and traditions. Throughout this whole process, the
slave *lucumíes*, from the Yoruba tradition, put Christian names on their
gods and goddesses, taking cues from external similarities that they
found between the deities and the saints; they also borrowed elements of
the Catholic liturgy to celebrate their own religious rites. The result of
this process was that the *orishas*, African divinities of the Yoruba tradition, were commonly "canonized." At the start, this was a strategic act
aimed at hiding or disguising the African deities, but little by little these
strategies became new pathways, new cultic elements, and new ritual expressions. As a genuinely Cuban creation, Santería transformed the original African elements, keeping some of them and adding new elements.

The saints of the Christian tradition came down from their altars to
join with the African *orishas* and to share with them their characteristics,
virtues and defects, ritual elements, spiritual gifts, and healing energies.
The saints came out from the parish Mass to become part of the
Wemilere. They entered into the people's humble houses, communing
closely with the men and women, children and elders, and in the process
became much more human. In this way, the *orishas* have themselves been
transformed, taking on a Cuban identity and becoming Cuban gods and
goddesses of African origin. For that reason we find a major portion of
the Cuban population who, with no feeling of dogmatic sectarianism,
proceed tranquilly from Mass to the *Wemilere* or from the *Wemilere* to
Mass. The people themselves have established the interreligious dialogue; they have broken the barriers and the limits between the Mass and
the *Wemilere*, between the parish church and the house-shrine.

Elements That Dialogue

The theological elements that enter into the dialogue between these two religious universes come from all levels of the religious expression of those who are the prime participants in the dialogue: from their world-view, from their myths and symbols, from the characteristics of the divinities and the believers' relationship with them, from their rituals and other aspects of life. All this is reflected in ordinary human relations and in the way people face their day-to-day problems.

Of course, Jesus and Mary are sacred images that form a very important part of the religious symbolism of believers, but people have practiced a certain deconstruction of the traditional images. Believers have developed a new relation with these two figures as a result of their proceeding back and forth between the *Wemilere* and the parish Mass, and that new relation challenges us to find new ways of formulating our theological reflection.

The Child Jesus and the Old Jesus

In Santería, the creation of the world and of people is not done by the supreme God.[7] Rather, God creates the *orishas*, and it is they who make the earth, the universe and people—and afterward they come to live with them. The supreme God breathes life into people, but afterward he draws apart and remains distant and indifferent to human problems. The *orishas* are the ones who govern the world and remain in contact with people. These divinities have attitudes that are completely anthropomorphic; they have all the imperfections and virtues of human beings. In Yoruba tradition, good and evil are two inseparable aspects of existence, and both are mixed together in the divinities; they behave like humans and live intimately related to them. Each one of them has been endowed with one of the powers of the supreme God.[8]

In Cuba these divinities are individual and personal, and each believer has his or her own. The relation between the *orisha* and the believer is described by Verger as "pure force, immaterial *aché*[9] that becomes perceptible only to those persons who incorporate themselves into one of them, . . . who become a vehicle that allows the *orisha* to return to earth in order to greet and to receive tokens of respect from the descendants who have evoked him."[10]

The figure of Jesus appears in relation to the manifestations, avatars, or "ways"[11] of two important *orishas*, Obatalá and Elegguá.

The *child Jesus*, through the transculturation[12] process, is related to Elegguá, the *orisha* who is owner of the ways, the one who opens and closes the ways of people's destiny. One has to count on him for any major life decision. He not only opens up the ways but also cares for houses, and for that reason his image is generally positioned behind the doors. What is interesting is that since the time of our African ancestors

Eleggúa has been conceived of as a mischievous child; he is unpredictable, as is destiny, which can be either very good or very bad. He is the messenger of Olófin, who told him, "Since you, the smallest one, are my messenger, you will be the greatest on earth and in heaven, and people will not be able to do anything without counting on you."[13]

Believers and practitioners of this Cuban religious tradition consider this relationship to be perfectly valid. Eleggúa is a child, owner of the ways and the life destinies of people; he can open or close horizons; he can provide well-being and growth in the future life; he is the messenger of Olófin—after all, he is the child Jesus! This strategic relation was established by our African foreparents, but today it is fully accepted by all who practice Santería, even while they confess themselves to be Christians and attend church.

An ancient story, "The Child of Atocha," tells of a boy who went to a prison carrying a basket full of bread and a bucket full of water. He gave food and drink to countless prisoners, but the basket of bread and the bucket of water always remained as full as when he started. According to the legend, this child was the same Jesus Christ who came as a child to attend to the material and spiritual needs of the prisoners.[14] This story was told by old African slave women to illustrate the relationship between Eleggúa and the child Jesus. We see the miracle of feeding, of filling hungry stomachs, as a gesture that identifies Jesus. This story of the child recalls the words of the gospel: "But Jesus called for them [the children] and said, 'Let the little children come to me, and do not stop them; for it is to such as these that the kingdom of God belongs. Truly I tell you, whoever does not receive the kingdom of God as a little child will never enter it'" (Lk 18:16–17; cf. Mt 19:13–15; Mk 10:13–16).

It is significant that Eleggúa is first in everything: the first to eat at the time of the ritual sacrifices, the first to be offered gifts, the first to be praised in the *Wemilere*, which begins with drumming and songs to Eleggúa and also ends with hymns to this mischievous, playful little god. Eleggúa is always present in the homes; he is the guardian and the caretaker of domestic space. He is also the first to be consulted when future plans and projects are being prepared or when people have problems or difficulties in their lives.

The symbol of the child is an important part of people's faith; it is synonymous with security, future growth, creativity, and foresight. Popular mysticism makes freshly present the messianic prophecy of First Isaiah (chapters 1–39). As Nancy Cardoso Pereira points out: "The child is just this: he is and will be. Through this ambiguity of present and future we can approach the child as a prophetic category. The child is event, expectation, incarnation."[15]

Of course, the wisdom of the people's mysticism allows for Eleggúa to take on negative characteristics. Indeed, all the *orishas* can show a negative side: none of them represents extreme purity. All of them represent the contradictions of life, so that each may present certain negative aspects. Elegguá's negative side is called Echu, which is the incarnation of the bad things, the human problems, and the tragic misfortunes that come along in life. According to tradition, Echu lives in the streets and in the bush; if he manages to enter into a house, difficulties and tragedies will start for the family.

Natalia Bolívar Aróstegui states that

> the Elegguá-Echu pair is the mythical expression of the inevitable relationship between the positive and the negative. For the Yorubas, the house signifies the refuge *par excellence*, the privileged place to escape the avatars of destiny. Elegguá dwells at the very door of the house, marking with his presence the boundary between two worlds: the internal world of security and the external world of danger. Security cannot exist, however, without danger, nor can calm exist without anxiety; for that reason, the Elegguá-Echu pair is indissoluble, despite their opposition.[16]

That is the reason, in my opinion, that the saints of the church became more human in the process of transculturation. Such human qualities as fragility, error, and evil are also found in these anthropomorphic manifestations of the divine; the gods and the saints are seen as persons who have their defects and their virtues. The experience of the sacred forms an integral part of the mystery that includes the ambiguous and paradoxical character of existence.

The *old Jesus* is a figure that appears in some of the manifestations of Obbatalá, who is one of the principal *orishas*. His statue is placed in the first division of the shelf called *canastillero*, where the devotees of the saints keep their images.[17] Obbatalá is considered to be the creator of human beings, the one who sculpted them from clay so that Olófin would then place the breath of life in them. He is the deity that represents purity; he is master of all that is white; and he is lord of the head, of thoughts, and of dreams. In various of his manifestations or ways, he is associated with Jesus of Nazareth,[18] but he is generally pictured as a stooped, trembling little old man. He is the *orisha* of peace and harmony, much respected by all, capable of calming the worst manifestations of wrath in the rest of the *orishas*. White is his color, and he is a symbol of intelligence, experience, and discretion.

Apart from being identified with Jesus of Nazareth, Obbatalá assumes another interesting form in the process of transculturation, namely, a feminine image that relates Obbatalá to the saints of the Christian tradition, and especially to the Virgin Mary as Our Lady of Ransom. On the altars of the house-shrines we will find images of Jesus and Our Lady of Ransom placed quite close together beside the container for the natural elements that represent Obbatalá, this *orisha* who is master of all that is white.

In keeping with Yoruba tradition, the Cuban gods and goddesses of African origin behave like humans and show human imperfections. One of the old stories of the Yoruba tradition tells that when Olódùmaré gave Obbatalá the task of creating the earth and human beings, Obbatalá did not make the things the way he should have. Rather, he got drunk on palm wine and his rival Odduwa had to take over the job of creating earth. Obbatalá was then given the task of creating human beings, and he was forbidden to drink palm wine. According to the story, however, he sometimes gave in to his vice, so that some of his human sculptures came out badly shaped—thus does the tradition explain birth defects.

Important elements of this interreligious dialogue are the way humans are formed from the dust of the earth and the way people's lives are inevitably interwoven with good and evil. The earth is seen as a great womb, a giant pumpkin, a fertile belly in which all life comes to birth. The first ancestors were born of the clay of the earth, which was their original matter. Death returns to the earth all that belongs to it, thus allowing rebirth; when biological life ceases, the earth receives the bodies back into itself, thus regaining its generative capacity. The origin of life and of bodies is closely related to nature's vital elements: light, air, water, and earth. In these elements are found the principles or forces *iwà*, *axé*, and *àbá*, which are divine energies regulating all existence.

Each *orisha* represents the archetype of a different personality, and we find in the Yoruba pantheon almost all the most general archetypes of human psychology. At the same time, each *orisha* is related to one of the forces of nature. In this way important relationships are established among divinities, personalities, and natural forces.

Jesus and Mary also form part of these interrelationships. It is significant that in the process of transculturation Jesus assumes archetypal forms that have generally been avoided by Western civilization, such as the young and the elderly. Also, when Our Lady of Ransom is related to the *orisha* that is responsible for the creation of human beings, we become aware that many symbolic elements involved in the deconstruction of traditional images have ended up enriching the people's spirituality.

Two Faces of Mary: Goddess Mother and Goddess of Love and Sensuality

The process of transculturation has given Mary many faces that become manifest through the feminine *orishas* and the relationships between them and the saints of the Catholic tradition. Mary has come down from her high altar, donned the clothes of the common women, and remained there with them—for that reason she is much loved and venerated. We would like to examine now two faces of Mary that are of great importance in the religiosity of the Cuban people: Mary the mother, related to Yemayá, the goddess of the seas; and Mary the goddess of love and sensuality, related to Ochún, the goddess of fresh water.

Mary and Yemayá are two divinities that in Cuba have become united in the transculturation process, whereby they have come to share many elements that transform and enhance both of them. The Virgin of the Regla is the name of the black Mary, who is patroness of fishers; her sanctuary is located in the town of Regla, in La Habana province, where she is venerated both by Christians and by devotees of Santería.

The Virgin of Regla and Yemayá represent the archetype of the mother who protects and gives life. In the Santería tradition, Yemayá is the queen of all waters, mistress of the fresh water that she gives to Ochún and also of the salty sea waters from which life emerged. She is considered the mother of all the *orishas*, the mother of all life. The name Yemayá means "mother whose children are fish." Originally she was the *orisha* of a Yoruba nation called Egbá, in a part of Africa where there still exists a river that bears her name, Yemoja.

In Cuba she is called the goddess of intelligence and is the symbol of the balanced person. She is considered to be a mother who is judicious, kind, protective, understanding of her children, and rather stern; when she becomes angry she can be quite terrible. She is like the sea, which can be quite beautiful when calm but quite fearful in times of tempest.

The fusion of Yemayá with the Virgin of Regla shows a face of Mary quite different from the traditional image of the humble and chaste Virgin, since Yemayá, though she is a good mother, is also a single mother. The stories tell of her love affairs with various *orishas* and also of her strong character, expressed in her tenacity and valor. Yemayá therefore is not a model of maternity that can be used for controlling the sexuality and the bodies of women. The fusion of the two images has been enriched with the common people's spirituality, which brings them close to the real lives of women. Thus these images become creative and transformative forces that destroy the traditional stereotypes of the Virgin Mary and project rather the image of a mother who affirms her body and her sexuality in a free and responsible manner.

Mary and Ochún, the goddess of love and sensuality, show us the other face of Mary, one that is a good mirror of the Cuban woman. Ochún is a goddess of the Yoruba pantheon that has passed through a process of transformation and adaptation and thus become one of the most important deities in Santería. In Cuba, Ochún ceases to be African and becomes mulatto, Creole, or Cuban; she is the muse of many poets and painters, who re-create her cinnamon-colored skin, her long tresses, and her warm sensuality. She is the symbol of coquetry, of grace, of beauty, and of feminine sensuality. She is the goddess of love and fecundity, the patroness of pregnancies, the protectress of women with child. The devotees of Santería say that she takes care of women's wombs and recently born children.

When we study the African roots of this *orisha*, we see that her origins go back to Nigeria, where she is the goddess of the river (Ijebu/Ijexá) that bears her name and that runs the length of Nigeria. Her great ancestral mothers are the Iyàmi-Ajé or the Iyàmi Osàròngà, which in the Yoruba tongue mean "my mother sorceress"; they are also called *iyá àgbá* (old, respectable mother) or *eleye* (mistress of the birds).

As the stories go, Ochún maintains strong ties with these ancestral mothers, thanks to which she possesses the power of fertility.[19]

In the Yoruba region the Iyàmi traditionally represented the mystical powers of women, which were feared and respected. These ancestral mothers were considered sorceresses and might be called the matriarchs of Yoruba tradition. They appear in the ancient myths of creation and so reveal an epoch when women were the ones who had charge of the most important matters of the community, including the cult of the ancestors. They had control of the powers of the tradition, which later passed into the hands of the men.

In this tradition the Iyàmi represent those feminine powers in their most dangerous and fearful aspect. They were the so-called Great Angry Mothers, without whose leave life could not continue; they were considered sorceresses (*àjé*), but not in the popular meaning that that word has today. According to Pierre Verger:

> The matter of the sorceresses in relation to the so-called traditional religions was not always treated with due caution. That is to say, since sorcery was always from the start considered to be an extremely anti-social activity, people thought it could not form part of the religion of a human community. In the Yoruba religion, however, these women were considered sorceresses because their activities were directly related to the divinities, to the *orishas* and to the myths of the creation of the world.[20]

In Cuba, just as in Brazil, the powers of the Iyàmi appear in the more socialized form of the feminine *orishas*, such as Ochún, Yemayá, Oyá Yansá, Nanà Burukú, Obba, and Yewa.

In Cuba, as in Africa, Ochún is called Iyálóde, a title conferred on her to indicate that she is the person who occupies the most important place among all women. According to Verger, she is the one who controls women. In one story she is presented as the head of the sorceresses, and she distributes among them birds, the power source of the *àjé* (sorceresses). She sells in the marketplace, but she also represents women in the king's palace and in the council of the elders. She is also present in the local tribunal if a woman is involved in a trial. Outside the tribunal, she herself performs the function of arbiter of the problems that might arise among women. This is the most honorable title that a woman can receive; it places her automatically at the head of women and makes her the representative of the *àiyé* of the ancestral feminine power.

Water and earth are the conducting elements for the *axé*, the feminine generative force that is in the earth's waters: the water of rain, rivers, lakes, and springs, and even the water of the sea. In the Santería tradition Ochún is closely linked to Yemayá, and in some of her manifestations or "ways," she dwells beside Yemayá in the mouth of the rivers, where river and sea join together. The Cuban tradition contains stories that tell how Yemayá cares for Ochún, protects her as a sister, and shares her riches with her, including the river as a place to dwell.

Ochún is transformed into the Cuban mulatto woman throughout all the process of transculturation. If we ask practitioners of Santería what Ochún is like, they will always describe a Cuban woman, sensual, flirtatious, happy, amusing, a lover of dancing and feasting. She loves to entice by adorning herself and dressing up in fine clothes. She is generally described as a honey-skinned mulatto with clear eyes, long curly hair, and a beautiful, sensual body. While possessing great powers, she is compassionate and miraculous; she is affectionate and as sweet as the honey she loves, but also willful and harsh when she gets angry.

She is considered mistress of the earth's fresh waters, without which life would be impossible, but she is also mistress of the sweet waters of the sexes, also essential for life. She represents the lively, free, daring woman who is mistress of herself. She possesses femininity, but not of the submissive, complacent type. Rather, her femininity is powerful, liberated, sensual, sure of itself, and in control of its sexuality; it is a femininity that is able to obtain anything through its charms. The African slaves called her the *panchákara*, which in the Lucumi language spoken in Cuba means "prostitute" or even "whore goddess." To be sure, this title is considered one of power and is used only by the more experienced practitioners of Santería, and always with the greatest respect and admiration, not in a pejorative sense. This is one of the most popular and best-known ways or manifestations of Ochún, in which she is known by the name Yeyé Kari or Yeyé Moró.

Ochún is also associated with the Virgin of Charity of Copper (Cobre), the patroness of Cuba. What has made possible this relationship between the sensual Ochún and the pure and chaste Virgin?

Poets have called her the dark-skinned Virgin, and historians have called her the Mambisa Virgin, as have all the people who have felt her support during the long years of struggling for freedom. Much venerated by the Cuban people, she is a *mestiza* or mulatto Virgin who reflects in her face a broad blend of Hispanic, Indian, African, and Creole origins. Precisely that blend of races of our Cuban ethnicity has made Cachita or Cari, as she is affectionately called by devotees, a most important part of popular religious expression in Cuba. In her there takes place an integration of many devotions that have been the heritage of centuries of Hispanic, Native American, African, and Creole traditions. In her, all of them become fused and transculturated, producing a popular Cuban religious expression that is today practiced by the great majority of our people. From the sixteenth century down to the present, such devotion has been capable of uniting the faith and the beliefs of all the different social groups that make up our nationality.

One day in 1613 a statue appeared floating in the waters of the Bay of Nipe, on the northeastern coast of the island; it was recovered by two Indian farmworkers and a ten-year-old African slave. Attached to the statue was a small tablet with an inscription that reads, "I am the Virgin of Charity."

A number of factors led the slaves to associate the Virgin of Charity with the goddess of African origin. First, the Indians had already associated the Virgin with their own goddess Atarex, adored as the engendering mother, and this association must in some way have influenced the later relations between the Indians and the Africans. Second, the Virgin was the patroness who presided over the religious celebrations in the copper mines of El Cobre, where women worked at removing the mineral from the river. Ochún's traditional mineral was copper, and her traditional color was yellow. In Africa, Ochún was the goddess related to the river waters, the goddess of fertility who gave women their children. The Virgin, wearing a yellow cape, held a child in her arms, and she had been found floating in the water. All the legends told of her disappearing and then reappearing again, soaking wet.

This fusion of Virgin and goddess took place in a process that was accompanied by struggles and rebellions, in the midst of a long history in which *mestizos*, mulattos, blacks, and whites united and fought for their rights to land and independence. Meanwhile, the dark-skinned Virgin and the goddess of love became blended to the point of forming an integral part of people's daily life. The pure Virgin was humanized and transformed into a real woman of the people, a joyful, dancing, sensual Cuban *mulata*, thus breaking with the stereotypes that Western tradition had imposed on her by making her forbiddingly holy.

In our days Ochún and Cachita are joined together; they are one and the same divinity, although with very different historical origins. Santería has fused them, and they are found one beside the other on the altars, in the rituals, and in the feasts dedicated to Ochún. September 8, the day when people traditionally celebrate the appearance of the Virgin of Charity in the waters of the Bay of Nipe, is a feast day both for the Catholic Church and for the devotees of Santería; the one has Masses, processions, and other activities for the dark-skinned Virgin of Charity, while the others adorn her altars with flowers and hold a vigil in which candles are lit before her image. The Virgin, dressed in her golden tunic, is always brightly shining beside the *asentamiento* of Ochún, which is a porcelain or clay recipient in which are kept the elements of the river that contain the *axé* of the *orisha*. The candles are lit at midnight, and at that moment everyone prays and asks the Virgin for peace, health, and prosperity. Christian prayers such as the Our Father and the Hail Mary are said, and Christian hymns are sung, while a bell is sounded for Ochún (called *agogo*); finally, some hymns are sung in Yoruba. It is a unique blend of traditions that the people have achieved by breaking through the barriers of religious sectarianism, in the same way that Ochún and Cachita were able to break down and deconstruct the barriers of conventionality and traditionalism that have kept women imprisoned in rigorous patterns of conduct.

Inexhaustible is the wealth of symbols, ritual elements, spiritual gifts, and sacred energies that we find in the relationship that the Cuban faithful have established between these two expressions of traditional religion. By means of such simple, sincere interreligious dialogue, which seeks not to impose criteria or concepts but rather to give and receive with the believers' open, faith-filled hearts, we find ourselves challenged to open up new avenues in Cuban feminist theological reflection. The drums continue to sound, blending with the church bells. And Jesus and Mary are still dancing in the great circle, with all the *orishas*.

Notes

1. The religious expression called Rule of Ocha or Santería is one of the most extended religious traditions of African origin in Cuba. It arose at the end of the sixteenth century through a process in which elements of the African cultures and religions, introduced into the island during the epoch of slavery, became mixed and fused with elements of Christian tradition and with other social and cultural factors. Such blending gave rise to this popular religious expression, which is today practiced by a large part of the Cuban population. The *Wemilere* is one of the liturgical rituals of Santería.

2. "All transculturation is a process in which something is always given in exchange for what is received; it is a give-and-take [*toma y daca*], as the Spanish say. It is a process in which both parts of the equation end up changed and in which a new reality emerges, one that is not simply a mechanical agglomeration of features, or even a mosaic, but a new, original and independent phenomenon...Transculturation as a term describes a process in which there is no one given culture to which another has to conform, but there is rather a transition between the two cultures. Both are active and contribute with their respective features, and both cooperate in the advent of a new reality to civilization" (Fernando Ortiz, *Contrapunteo cubano del tabaco y el azúcar* [Havana: Ciencias Sociales, 1983], xxxiii).

3. Ibid., 243.

4. Fernando Ortiz mentions ninety-nine different ethnic groups. See *Los negros esclavos*, 3rd ed. (Havana: Ciencias Sociales, 1975), 100. Other authors have furthered the studies made by Ortiz; among them, Rafael López Valdez states that the number of ethnic groups introduced into Cuba reached one thousand (see "Presencia étnica de los esclavos de Tiguaboa (Guantánamo) entre los años 1789 y 1844," *Revista José Martí* 77, no. 3 [1956]: 14–21).

5. All the peoples and tribes living in this region and speaking the Yoruba language were identified by this name. Yoruba is therefore "a basically linguistic denomination, although these tribes were linked by the same culture and their belief in a common origin" (Natalia Bolívar Aróstegui, *Los orishas en Cuba* [Havana: P. M. Ediciones, 1994], 3).

6. This type of organization arose at the beginning of the slave epoch, during the sixteenth and seventeenth centuries, when slavery in Cuba had not acquired the rigor and violence that it had in later centuries.

7. The name of this supreme god is Olòfin Olóòrun Olódùmarè. Each of these names represents functions and forces that are active in the world. Olòfin

is the creative force that made the *orishas*, the world, the animals, and the people; it is the cause and the reason-for-being of all things. Olóòrun is the sun, heat, light, the basic vital energy for all that makes up life on earth. Olódùmaré represents universal law, the laws of nature and of all existence.

8. "Each *orisha* becomes an archetype of an activity, a profession or a function; they are complementary to one another and represent the whole complex of forces that govern the world" (Pierre Verger, *Orixás: Deuses iorùbás na Africa e no novo mundo* [São Paulo: Editora Corrupio, 1981], 21).

9. For the Yoruba there are three forces that make possible and regulate all that exists in the universe: *iwà*, *axé* (*aché*), and *àbá*. The *iwà* allows generic existence; the *axé* (*aché*) is the power of realization that energizes existence and allows it to arise; the *àbá* is the power that endows purpose, gives direction, and accompanies the *axé* (*aché*). Existence develops through these tissues of forces and principles in a continual search for balance among the elements.

10. Verger, *Orixás*, 19.

11. All these divinities have different ways of manifesting themselves, which in Cuba are called "ways" or "avatars."

12. I do not use the term "syncretism" because it is not the most appropriate for describing the fusion that comes about between the African divinities and the saints of the Christian tradition. Besides, it is a term that has been quite manipulated. I prefer to use the term "transculturation."

13. Verger, *Orixás*, 27.

14. This legend, inherited from Spanish Catholicism, is known as the story of "The Child of Atocha." For more details see Aróstegui, *Los orishas en Cuba*, 35.

15. Nancy Cardoso Pereira, "El Mesías siempre debe ser niño," *Revista Ribla* 24 (1996): 17–24.

16. Aróstegui, *Los orishas en Cuba*, 28.

17. The *canastillero* is a piece of furniture that has an important ritual function; all devotees of Santería have one. It is a sort of cupboard with various divisions and is kept in the room of the saints in the house-shrines. In the *canastillero* are placed the *asentamientos* of the *orishas* in accord with their hierarchy, as well as a series of objects and attributes that correspond to them according to the tradition. The *asentamientos* are containers of clay or porcelain that contain natural objects that are charged with the energies of the different *orishas*. To indicate its hierarchical importance, the *asentamiento* of Obbatalá is always in the first division of the *canastillero*. Generally, domestic cabinets and cupboards are modified to serve as *canastilleros*.

18. In these ways or avatars he is known as Obbatalá Ocha Griñán, Obbatalá Obá Lufón, or Obbatalá Obá Moró. For more information on this, see Lydia Cabrera, *El Monte* (Miami: Ediciones Universal, 1992), 306–9; and Aróstegui, *Los orishas en Cuba*, 94–120.

19. Pierre Verger, "Grandeza e decadência do culto de Iyàmi Òsòrònga (Minha Mãe Feiticeira) entre os Yorùbá," in *As senhoras so pássaro da noite: Escritos sobre a religião dos orixás* V, ed. Carlos Eugênio Marcondes de Moura (São Paulo: Universidade de São Paulo (Edusp), Axis Mundo, 1994), 16.

20. Ibid., 16–17.

PART 4

Body, Sexuality, and Spirituality

The Lord's Prayer

Eternal Spirit,
Earth-maker, Pain-bearer, Life-giver,
Source of all that is and that shall be,
Father and Mother of us all,
Loving God, in whom is heaven:

The hallowing of your name echo through the universe!
The way of your justice be followed by the peoples of the world!
Your heavenly will be done by all created beings!
Your commonwealth of peace and freedom
    sustain our hope and come on earth!

With the bread we need for today, feed us.
In the hurts we absorb from one another, forgive us.
In times of temptation and test, strengthen us.
From trial too great to endure, spare us.
From the grip of all that is evil, free us.
For you reign in the glory of the power that is love,
    now and for ever. Amen.

—From *A New Zealand Prayer Book*

"The Lord's Prayer," in *A New Zealand Prayer Book* (Auckland: Collins, 1989), 181.

14

HIV/AIDS

An African Theological Response in Mission

Isabel Apawo Phiri (Malawi)

Every first Saturday afternoon of the month a group of twenty ecumenical women from different parts of Africa meet at my house in Pietermaritzburg, South Africa, to discuss issues that affect women in the
church and society. We call ourselves "Women of Faith" who are implementing the mission of Jesus as described in Luke 4:18–19. As participants in God's mission, we equip ourselves with knowledge of what is
happening in our churches and societies so that our responses may be
contextual. On March 6, 2004, we chose to talk about HIV/AIDS and
African women. One of us passionately argued that we need not worry
about being infected with the virus, because as long as we remained
faithful to our husbands and prayed for our protection, God was going
to hear our prayers and protect us from the virus. She equated HIV with
punishment from God for the disobedient. Yet within our group there
was one woman who had shared with us that she was living with HIV,
which she got while she was already a committed Christian and faithful
wife. Her husband died in 2002 of AIDS and she lamented over why her
husband did not disclose his status soon enough to take advantage of the
availability of anti-retroviral therapy in South Africa as she has done.
She also told us how every day she wakes up at 4:00 in the morning to
go to her Pentecostal church to pray for healing.

The discussion of this day left us divided in our responses to
HIV/AIDS because it raised deep issues that required a theological reflection that is contextual to the continent of Africa: ecumenical in nature
and dealing with the problems of African women. The central theological issue that the women battled with was: "Why do human beings suf-

Isabel Apawo Phiri, "HIV/AIDS: An African Theological Response in Mission," *Ecumenical Review* 56, no. 4 (2004): 422–31.

fer and how does one conduct mission in the context of suffering?" While it was clear to the women that our role is to participate in God's mission to the oppressed and the poor of our communities so that all people can experience the presence of God's reign here on earth, which is also yet to come, questions were raised about the status before God of people who are already infected. If one believes strongly that HIV/AIDS is a punishment from God for the disobedient, then what kind of mission is directed to the infected? Is HIV/AIDS a punishment from God or is suffering necessarily a result of sin? Does God use HIV/AIDS and suffering to bring people to God-self? Why does God allow the faithful partners, who are committed to prayer, to get infected? Is there room for the justification of unjust systems that cause people to suffer unnecessarily? Why is there still stigma among the people of God toward people with HIV/AIDS? Can faithful married women protect themselves from the virus? Why do some people get infected and not others, while they are all praying to God for protection? Is there hope for the infected and affected of HIV/AIDS? This paper is too short to deal adequately with all the questions raised above. Before dealing with some of these challenging questions that take us into a discussion of theodicy, it is very important that I locate myself so that the reader may understand what is influencing my theology of mission and HIV/AIDS. I locate myself within African women's theologies as propagated by the Circle of Concerned African Women Theologians (hereafter, the Circle).

African Women's Theologies

African women's theologies belong to a wider family of feminist theology, which is further categorized under liberation theology. Both theologies are different varieties of Christian theology and they acquired their names on the basis of context and approach. On the African continent, we have a number of liberation theologies. The African Christian women have called their theological reflection of the African context "African women's theologies."

Why theologies and not just theology? The word "theologies" is used in its plural form because African women theologians want to acknowledge the fact that even within Africa, there is diversity of women's experiences due to differences in race, culture, politics, economy, and religions. Despite the differences in terminology, all women would like to see the end of sexism in their lives and the establishment of a more just society of men and women who seek the well-being of the other. African women theologians are seeking restoration of the present life from death-promoting activities. African women's theologies actively engage with the society to bring holistic healing in today's world that is polluted with HIV/AIDS.[1]

HIV/AIDS as an Urgent Issue for the Theology of Mission in Africa

The theological issues raised by the "women of faith" group represent an ongoing theological discussion on the mission of the church in Africa in the context of HIV/AIDS. Since the advent of HIV/AIDS in Africa, which was more than twenty years ago, the church in Africa has struggled in reading the signs of the times with regard to HIV/AIDS. The statement that "HIV/AIDS is a punishment from God" was the predominant initial theological stand of the church. Why? This was linked to the mode of transmission of the virus in Africa. While in Europe and America the spread of HIV is mainly through homosexual relationships, in Africa it is predominantly through multiple heterosexual relationships. It therefore became easy for the church in Africa to argue that abstinence from pre-marital sex and faithfulness in marriages is the solution to the spread of HIV. People who do not follow such church teaching are the ones who get infected with the HIV as punishment from God for their disobedience.[2] This belief was further strengthened by the African worldview that individual sins affect the whole community.[3] The result was an approach that promoted the HIV/AIDS stigma and prevented the church from reaching out in mission to the affected and infected. Discrimination went further to the extent that some Christian doctors and nurses did not see that it was their mission to treat patients with AIDS. The Christian doctors and nurses justified their actions by stating that they did not want to interfere with God's punishment of people with AIDS.

The interpretation of HIV/AIDS as a punishment for sin not only comes from the church but is also internalized by the infected, thereby increasing their suffering. Moji Ruele has rightly argued that "Spiritually, HIV/AIDS sufferers experience a crisis. They ask why they are the ones affected. Whether God loves them. Whether they have sinned or are just unlucky. Is the disease a form of punishment from God?"[4] The church people's simplistic understanding of the existence and spread of HIV in Africa is where the church missed the mark. That simplistic understanding has remained a major issue that still interferes with the church in Africa's mission to those infected and affected with HIV/AIDS. The fact that the church has preached about abstinence and faithfulness for a very long time and still is not winning with these messages has caused the ecumenical church in Africa to take a critical look at itself. This is reflected in the November 2001 action plan of the international and African ecumenical organizations that participated in a World Council of Churches global consultation on an ecumenical response to the challenge of HIV/AIDS in Africa held in Nairobi, Kenya. This consultation produced a plan of action as a guideline for African churches, para-church organizations, and ecumenical partners in responding to the plague of AIDS.

At the consultation, the church admitted that knowingly and un-
knowingly it has contributed to the spread of the HIV. Church leaders
acknowledged that the way scriptures have been interpreted and the emphasis on the theology of sin, among other issues, have helped to promote the stigmatization, exclusion, and suffering of people with HIV or
AIDS. They also came to the realization that HIV/AIDS is there in the
church among the children of God. Therefore, they said,

> Given the extreme urgency of this situation, and the conviction
> that the churches do have a distinctive role to play in the response
> to the pandemic, what is needed is a rethinking of our mission,
> and the transformation of our structures and ways of working.[5]

The consultation outlined a plan of action in the areas of theology
and ethics, prevention, care and counseling people living with
HIV/AIDS, education, training support, treatment, advocacy, gender,
culture, liturgy, and resources. It also proposed the inclusion of
HIV/AIDS in the theological curriculum. International and African
church leaders recommended the formation of the Ecumenical
HIV/AIDS Initiative in Africa (EHAIA) to coordinate the shift in the
church's theology and mission with regard to HIV/AIDS.

African women theologians chose to make HIV/AIDS the main issue
for their work in theology from 2002 to 2007. This was the Circle's contribution to the ecumenical movement's response to HIV/AIDS in Africa.

The Circle and HIV/AIDS: A Gender-based Response

The Circle has highlighted the relationship of gender to HIV/AIDS.
Philippe Denis has rightly said "HIV/AIDS is ultimately a gender
issue."[6] This statement is supported by the fact that in sub-Saharan
Africa marriage is a major risk factor for any African woman to contract HIV.[7] Teenage girls between the ages of fifteen to twenty-four in
sub-Saharan Africa are five times more likely to be infected than boys
of the same age range.[8]

African women theologians' writings have shown that in Africa
marriage is at the center of the African community.[9] Yet marriage is also
the center of patriarchy, which constructs the subordinate position of
African women. This position does not work well in the era of
HIV/AIDS, when research shows that there are more new infections of
HIV among married women than any other group.[10] It has been argued
by the World Health Organization that the major reason why this is the
case is because of "the sexual and economic subordination of
women."[11] Articles in two of the Circle's publications, *The Will to
Arise*[12] and *Violence against Women*,[13] have described very clearly the

subordinate position of women in Africa. As long as women continue to be put in a subordinate position through the literalistic interpretation of Bible teachings and African cultural practices, it will be difficult to control HIV/AIDS in Africa.

Women are also caregivers for those infected with HIV/AIDS and they take care of the orphans with minimal economic and social support. HIV/AIDS has brought us to a theology of praxis that looks at everyone as an agent of change to promote life. African women theologians have also agreed that research into religious, cultural, and social practices that make women vulnerable to HIV/AIDS is an insufficient contribution. These theologians have taken upon themselves the task of engagement with the community to save lives.[14]

A Challenge for a New Theology

First and foremost, the creation of a new theology that deals with HIV/AIDS needs to acknowledge that HIV is more than a medical condition. It calls Christians to examine also their religious and cultural beliefs and practices in their understanding of mission. Since it is generally accepted among scholars of mission that the mission of the church models itself on the mission of Jesus Christ which has its origins in the mission of the triune God,[15] reflection on a new theology is based on how the church understands itself as having been sent by God to bring wholeness to a broken world.

Second, a mission-oriented theology of HIV/AIDS acknowledges that the Bible is central in Africa and is used as authoritative within the church.[16] Whenever the church is seeking direction, the Bible is consulted in all circumstances. Musa Dube has rightly stated that it is therefore not surprising that in this era of the HIV/AIDS pandemic the church has gone back to the Bible to search for knowledge concerning the disease, healing, stigma and isolation, guilt and fear, caring, death and dying.[17] The major problem of African Christians is their uncritical reading of the Bible, which becomes dangerous in the era of HIV/AIDS as it leads to wrong interpretations. Nevertheless, African theology has shown the similarities between the Old Testament and African beliefs and practices. Therefore Africa is now exploring new ways of reading and interpreting the Bible that equip the church to move away from a theology of HIV/AIDS as a punishment from God to a theology of God who is in solidarity with the HIV/AIDS affected and infected people in the same way that liberation theologies have depicted God as being on the same side as the poor and the marginalized. God, Jesus Christ and the church in Africa are being described as present wherever one finds HIV/AIDS.[18]

Third, HIV/AIDS is also causing African women theologians to revisit the question of why human beings suffer. I agree with Musimbi

Kanyoro who has stated: "To do theology in Africa today is to do theology among a people with much suffering. There is so much death on our continent that reality makes a mockery of the bravery of Job, the biblical giant of tribulations."[19] HIV/AIDS has just added to the intensity of suffering on the continent. African women agree that suffering is part of human life and it should not necessarily be interpreted as a result of sin, for not everyone suffers as a result of sin. This is particularly true in the case of HIV/AIDS. While it is true that having multiple sexual partners increases the chances of getting infected with HIV, it is also true to argue that there are a lot of spouses (especially women) who have been faithful to their partners but still have ended up being infected with the virus. In addition, there are also children who have been infected by their mothers at birth. So why would God want to punish this large group of people whose suffering is not associated with any sin of their own?

The theology that says people suffer because of moral failure is based on Augustine's theodicy that argues that there is a link between natural disasters and moral weakness. Ronald Nicolson has stated that Augustinian theodicy "believes that somehow pain, sickness, famine and death are entirely the consequence of the disobedience of Adam and Eve and their descendants. In this view, it is not God but humans who are responsible for all the suffering in the world."[20] In the context of HIV/AIDS, this view translates to blaming the infected for sinning. It can also be extended to include structural sins that create an atmosphere that is conducive to the spread of HIV. For example, poverty has forced many women to have multiple sex partners so that they can earn money for self-sustenance. The practice of migrant labor has also created an atmosphere of multiple sex partners that has made it easy to get infected with the virus. It can be argued that what is sinful is to accept unjust systems that cause people to suffer unnecessarily. This calls for a theology that goes beyond looking at the HIV pandemic as a moral failure or God punishing the infected and affected with stigma and death, for this theology does not explain why some people in Europe and America also practice the system of having many sexual partners but do not get infected with the virus. It also does not explain why some people in Europe and America live very long lives with the virus while in Africa they die quickly. Current research has revealed that HIV/AIDS is preventable, manageable, and controllable if there is solidarity at individual, family, community, national, and international levels in taking responsibility and sharing resources.

Fourth, the issue of HIV/AIDS is also connected to conceptions of life. The theology of creation as depicted in Genesis 1–2 shows what is in God's plan for the sacredness of all life. There is interdependency and goodness of creation. The same image is depicted in African creation myths. God's image is found in both men and women. The world of HIV/AIDS is a broken world of Genesis 3, where quality of life does not exclude suffering. However, in the conception of quality of life in the time of HIV/AIDS, everyone is called upon to protect life as opposed to destroying life. This raises ethical and theological questions about denying a person with AIDS the right to a decent life through medication that reduces opportunistic infections. As mentioned already, this is done by some professional Christian service providers. It is also done at the government level where medication is not made accessible or affordable to the majority of the sufferers. Where is the message of the God of love and compassion for the oppressed and discriminated against? When Jesus was extending healing to all who needed it, he did not ask how the person got sick. His concern was to bring about the kingdom of God on earth by restoring health. So why should the body of Jesus, the church, behave differently when met with the crisis of ministering to those infected and affected by HIV/AIDS?

The theology of the sacredness of life also includes taking responsibility to protect life that has already been infected so that the infection is contained. It involves the protection of life that has not been infected yet. The methodology of protecting life has been riddled with theological debates as to how this may best be done. The majority of the churches in Africa have stuck with the message of abstinence and faithfulness and fought vigorously against the use of condoms on the understanding that condoms promote promiscuous behavior. For some African women theologians, the process of protecting life does not exclude the responsible use of condoms despite the protest of some African church leaders. This is because African women are aware that regardless of the constant message of abstinence and faithfulness, the majority of Christians are not following the church's message. Therefore, while we are sorting out our power games surrounding patriarchy and the sanctity of marriage as originally intended by God, life has to be protected by whatever means is available today.

Although some from the women of faith group suggested dependence on prayer for the protection of the life of married women from HIV/AIDS, the experience of other women from the same group has shown that this cannot be achieved by prayer alone. Praying women have been infected with HIV/AIDS by their spouses, but not because they did not have enough faith to prevent the infection. Prayer without appropriate knowledge is dangerous[21] and has led so many Christians to death. This is where one has to apply wisdom as given by God. As stated in the book of James,[22] if people lack wisdom, let them ask for it from God. God is the one who gives appropriate wisdom for each crisis because God has not stopped revealing God-self in each situation that confronts humanity.

Fifth, HIV/AIDS has also raised the issue of corporate sin that calls for all people to re-examine their private and public lives in order to protect life. It does not make sense that one part of humanity can have a

quality life even after infection with HIV while the other half dies quickly
due to poverty and curable opportunist infections. This is where the message of Jesus in Luke 4:18–19 defines the mission of the church to deal
with all forms of oppression that include social injustice, disease,
poverty, and racial and sexual discrimination and to promote liberation,
social justice, life, and healing. Globalization has not promoted equal
distribution of drugs to all the infected people of the world.

Sixth, healing was central in the mission of Jesus and it is important
in the African worldview. This explains why the churches that have
taken seriously physical healing in Africa are very popular.[23] In such
churches, Jesus is the healer, even though the medical world has not yet
found a cure for HIV/AIDS. It is common in Africa to see desperate cases
of people with AIDS being taken to churches that practice the ministry
of healing. Despite the fact that many people who are critically ill die at
the churches, people do not lose hope in a God who is a healer. They still
go to church in droves to seek Jesus the healer. Jesus becomes their last
hope. They hope for physical healing. Hope in Jesus as healer is what
gives them motivation to face another day, even up to the deathbed. They
cling to hope for healing. These cases show that, while it is important to
understand the medical side of HIV/AIDS, the spiritual side is equally
important. Nicolson has also rightly argued: "While not pretending that
there are easy solutions, a major contribution which the churches can
make to the issue is to hold fast to the hope that solutions will be found
and that in the end God is victorious (John 16:33)."[24]

Conclusion

The way forward for all the theologies of Africa is to unite and take
the current context of HIV/AIDS into theological reflection. It has been
argued in this paper that the theology that views HIV/AIDS as a punishment from God ought to be rejected, for it is life-denying and contrary to the holistic message of the mission of God. Real church involvement in the combat against HIV/AIDS needs to recognize that sexual
sins are not the sins that bring the wrath of God on humanity. Every sin
is the same before God. Bad things happen to good and bad people alike
because of the existence of evil in the world. However, that does not
mean God has lost control of the world. God is in the world, siding with
the oppressed. God is on the side of those affected and infected with
HIV/AIDS. How they got the virus is immaterial to Jesus. Therefore it
should not be an issue for the body of Christ. What is required from the
church, the body of Christ, is commitment to fight against the spread of
the virus with all available resources. Presenting a God of compassion
rather than a God of wrath is central when dealing with the infected and
affected. Jesus came to establish the reign of God on earth. It is the re-

sponsibility of the church to work in conjunction with God to realize the reign of God now as the church continues to hope for the final realization of the reign of God for the whole creation and the whole human community. While HIV/AIDS brings fear and desperate actions, the message of the church should continue to promote life in all its fullness. The reign of God on earth entails peace and justice, healed relations between individual people in the broader society, between the people of God, as well as peace between humankind and nature. HIV/AIDS is now forcing the church to develop a comprehensive theology that addresses all areas of human suffering with the aim of bringing hope in the midst of suffering.

Notes

1. Isabel Apawo Phiri, "Contextual Theologies of Southern Africa," in *An Introduction to Third World Theologies*, ed. John Parratt (Cambridge: Cambridge University Press, 2004), 151.

2. Dorothy Scarborough, "HIV/AIDS: The Response of the Church," in *Journal of Constructive Theology* 7, no. 1 (July 2001): 3–16.

3. Stuart C. Bate, "Responsible Healing in a World of HIV/AIDS," in *Responsibility in a Time of AIDS: A Pastoral Response by Catholic Theologians and AIDS Activists in Southern Africa*, ed. Stuart C. Bate (Pietermaritzburg: Cluster Publications, 2003), 158–59.

4. Moji A. Ruele, "Facing the Challenges of HIV/AIDS in Southern Africa: Towards a Theology of Life," in *HIV/AIDS and the Curriculum: Methods of Integrating HIV/AIDS in Theological Programmes*, ed. Musa W. Dube (Geneva: World Council of Churches, 2003), 79.

5. See Plan of Action: The Ecumenical Response to HIV/AIDS in Africa Report, November 25–28, 2001, 3.

6. Philippe Denis, "Sexuality and AIDS in South Africa," *Journal of Theology for Southern Africa* 115 (March 2003): 75.

7. S. Baden and H. Wach, *Gender, HIV/AIDS Transmission and Impact: A Review of Issues and Evidence*, no. 7 (Brighton: Institute of Development Studies, 1998).

8. Hunger Project, 2001, no. 1.

9. For example see Mercy Amba Oduyoye, *Daughters of Anowa: African Women and Patriarchy* (Maryknoll, NY: Orbis Books, 1995); chapter 6 (pp. 131–53) is on marriage and patriarchy.

10. Judith van Woudenberg, *Women Coping with HIV/AIDS* (Amsterdam: Royal Tropical Institute, 1998).

11. Gillian Paterson, *Women in the Time of AIDS: Women, Health and the Challenge of HIV* (Maryknoll, NY: Orbis Books, 1996).

12. Mercy Amba Oduyoye and Musimbi R. A. Kanyoro, eds., *The Will to Arise: Women, Tradition and the Church in Africa* (Maryknoll, NY: Orbis Books, 2001).

13. Grace Wamue and Mary Getui, eds., *Violence Against Women: Reflections by Kenyan Women Theologians* (Nairobi: Acton Publishers, 1996).

14. Isabel Apawo Phiri, "African Women of Faith Speak Out in an HIV/AIDS Era," in *African Women, HIV/AIDS and Faith Communities*, ed. Isabel Apawo Phiri, Beverley Haddad, and Madipoane Masenya (Pietermaritzburg: Cluster Publications, 2003), 8.

15. Gabriel L. Afagbegee, "Responsibility and Media in a Time of HIV/AIDS" in *Responsibility in the Time of AIDS*, 124.

16. Sam Oleka, "The Authority of the Bible in the African Context," in *Issues in African Christian Theology*, ed. Samuel Ngewa Mark Shaw and Tite Tieno (Nairobi: East African Educational Publications, 1998), 75–103.

17. Musa W. Dube, "HIV and AIDS Curriculum for Theological Institutions in Africa," in *African Women, HIV/AIDS and Faith Communities*, 224.

18. Ronald Nicolson, *God in AIDS* (Pietermaritzburg: Cluster Publications, 1995).

19. Musimbi R. A. Kanyoro, *Introducing Feminist Cultural Hermeneutics: An African Perspective* (Sheffield: Sheffield Academic Press, 2002), 24.

20. Nicolson, *God in AIDS*, 26.

21. In Hosea 4:6 the Lord is quoted to have said, "My people are destroyed for lack of knowledge."

22. James 1:5 and 3:17.

23. Isabel Apawo Phiri, "African Women in Mission: Two Case Studies from Malawi," *Missionalia* 28, nos. 2/3 (November 2000): 267–93, and Phiri, "Healed from AIDS: The Testimony of Pastor Fridah Mzumara-Ngulube of Barak Ministries Lusaka Zambia," *Journal of Constructive Theology* 7, no. 1 (July 2001): 63–81.

24. Nicolson, *God in AIDS*, 42.

15

WOMEN, FAITH, MARRIAGE

A Feminist Look at the Challenges for Women

Meng Yanling (China)

In the opinion of Wang Meixiu, associate professor of history at Beijing University, in the socio-cultural value system, marriage and family are the social institutions most sensitive and responsive to changes in social life. Social change and development will inevitably be reflected in ethical relations within the family and in the moral standards of marriage. We can say that changes in the concepts of marriage and family reflect changes, developments, and progress in the entire system of social and cultural mores. This point is expressed not only in society, but is particularly evident in the church, because there is a concentration of women believers in the church. As a woman pastor, I naturally connect very easily with women in the church, who frequently come to tell me privately of the conflicts and difficulties they face, and to find support and help in their faith. The greatest number of problems facing women are marriage problems, because even today, women see marriage as the most important aspect of their lives.

Once, following a sermon, a sister poured out to me the humiliations and sufferings of her twenty-year marriage. I was deeply shaken, and this gave me greater recognition of the importance of feminist theology and feminist biblical interpretation. Reading the Bible from a feminist perspective, uncovering the experience and spiritual language of women that has been ignored by men, interpreting the Bible from within the context women face, and giving women support and guidance in faith are clearly of extreme importance.

Meng Yanling, "Women, Faith, Marriage: A Feminist Look at the Challeges for Women," *Chinese Theological Review* 18 (2004): 85–100. Translated by Janice Wickeri and edited by Kwok Pui-lan.

Marriage and Compromise between Chinese Culture
and Christian Faith

Contemporary Chinese society can only be an extension of Chinese history. Contemporary Chinese culture, while containing new modern concepts and consciousness, inherits and critiques the traditional culture of the Chinese people and extends it in a reasonable way. Traditional Chinese culture undoubtedly has a profound impact on the lives of Chinese women, their values, choices of roles, and future development.

Traditional Chinese society was one in which men were honored and women despised. This was evident and undebatable. For two thousand years of Chinese civilization, women were kept at the margins of society. The nature and status of women were never valued or affirmed. A traditional Chinese saying goes: Three things are unfilial and the most serious is to be without progeny. Here progeny refers, not to daughters, but to sons who could carry on the family name, authority, and property. Another traditional saying has it that the most beautiful daughter cannot match a splayfooted son. In the extreme poverty of the old society, female infanticide was a common way of reducing the number of mouths to feed.

Throughout her life, a woman was confined by family regulations. The scope of her everyday activities was restricted to the home. The Book of Rites set down the role of women as one of inner spaces: confined to the inner quarters where men might not enter. While men went out and about, women were confined within. Men spoke of things beyond the home, women did not. In sum, traditional social rules for women were nearly all about establishing, maintaining, and strengthening the family order. The restrictions of feudal propriety placed upon women contained many unique and unequal demands.

There are a number of famous passages in the Book of Rites whose subtext is to discourage an independent character or social position for women. With regard to the female intellect, for example, it was said that "a virtuous woman is without talent." Economically, women had no right to property and the names of women were not recorded in the family's genealogy. Women were forced to observe so-called female virtues, to be Confucian paragons. A Song-dynasty Confucian saying had it that starvation is a small matter, while loss of virtue is serious. The truly virtuous women who died rather than compromise their virtue were rewarded with memorial arches constructed in their honor. Economically women were dependent on others. And the Book of Rites says that "women are subservient. As children they obey their fathers and brothers. When married, they obey their husbands. As widows, they obey their sons."

These special rules built a human wall around women, excluding them from acting as social subjects outside the home. The female gender made women into political, economic, and cultural outsiders. The traditional Chinese woman, whether in reality or in literature, had only two paths open to her, the same paths open to Hua Mulan [the fifth-century woman warrior]: taking on a male role, fighting the enemy, and acting as part of the feudal system, or going back home and waiting to become a wife. This was the context for a woman. We could say that marriage and family were, for all intents and purposes, the sum total of the space allotted to the traditional woman for her existence. The man always held authority and he placed on woman a consciousness more in line with his own tastes. Thus the image of the traditional woman was created in accord with male imagination and desires. The role of women, their nature, and their position were all controlled, defined, and interpreted by men. The signifying of women in patriarchal society became a process by which women were gradually depreciated and oppressed.

Modern women inherit the concept of marriage from tradition, but they also live in modernity. Traditional Chinese marriage has been attacked and influenced by modern thought. Threats to modern marriage come mainly from the impact of materialism, consumerism, and hedonism, such that romance and sex have become commodities. Since the twentieth century, developed countries have experienced a whole host of vast changes in the realm of sex, what has been called the sexual revolution, which has in effect been a comprehensive challenge to traditional sexual relationships and ethics, causing people to rethink, reevaluate, and readjust sexual tradition. This sexual revolution reached its height in the 1960s. Under attack in this revolution, the traditional system of morality and values (in the West) collapsed.

As it happened, in the 1970s and 1980s, China was implementing a policy of reform and liberalization; the gates of China were open to the world. As good and bad things rushed in from the developed countries, the Chinese people, with their souls too long held down, rushed to absorb these things from outside. There was no time to consider, the mind simply took it all in, including some moral and ethical ideas that were too radical and liberal and thus assailed traditional Chinese marriage and family. As one American historian has pointed out, the assault brought about by the sexual revolution is nearly global, and its greatest assault on the human soul is moral confusion. Traditional, Confucian-, Buddhist- and Daoist-influenced ethics and morality have experienced an unprecedented challenge. Trial marriage, living together before marriage, and extra-marital affairs are no longer novelties. The divorce rate has risen sharply and as a result there are currently many single-parent households.

It is especially among young people that the concept of family has diminished, as individualism and hedonism have surged. With a concept of marriage and family in which pleasure is the goal and no one takes responsibility, people seek only to satisfy their own desires and ignore the needs of the family. Many people see marital affections as a private matter unrelated to others, separate from morality, chastity, and responsibility. The traditional conception of marriage and family has been shaken. People are no longer willing to shoulder a lifetime of responsibility. Popular sayings along the lines of "Who cares whether the mountains crumble as long as I get mine" or "Live it up" reflect the current attitude. Margaret Thatcher reflected a typical critique of the situation when she said in March 1983 that we are now being paid back for what was sown in the 1960s. The families of many Christian women in China experience such attacks, and, not only their families, but they themselves experience the effects of this so-called modern thinking.

The effects of traditional Chinese culture on female Christians are profound and far-reaching; some are more affected by traditional culture, while others are more affected by modern trends.

As a Christian woman, one lives, on the one hand, within Chinese culture, while at the same time one is influenced by biblical culture. A Christian woman stresses understanding marriage and family from a biblical standpoint, and her views on this are frequently taken from those of her preachers and pastors. Though sixty to seventy percent of believers in the church are women, it is mostly men who stand in the pulpits and teach and lead. Male pastors can speak only from their own standpoint, while most ordinary women Christians do not have the capacity to interpret the Bible on their own. Thus, their understanding of the Bible must come from pastors. Because these women have a pious faith, one that upholds the authority of the Bible, they do not dare question the teaching of the preacher in any way. The message the majority of women believers get from preachers is that women in the family should be long-suffering and obedient. In fact, sometimes it is not that a male preacher is deliberately biased against women but simply because he is a man that he has no way to understand the inner struggles of women, and so it is easy for him to overlook the female situation. It is also extremely difficult for women in a congregation to pour out sufferings from their marriages and families to male pastors. And it is difficult for male pastors to identify with these sisters in the way a woman pastor can.

A high government male official once moderated a conference on women in which he heard real stories of discrimination against women and harm done to the rights of women. He lamented at the end of the conference, "Men do not deliberately discriminate against women; we have mothers, and what son would discriminate against his mother? But men do indeed fail to think about or often forget the rights of women or ignore the needs of women." And in the church, too, it is often for the same reason that male pastors, deliberately or not, ignore the situation and experience of women.

Even in the course of giving a sermon, a preacher is frequently unable to transcend culture in (his) interpretation of the Bible. The Bible was revealed by God; it transcends all culture and penetrates through all culture. The revelation of God had to be expressed in human language and, in the course of being expressed, was inevitably influenced by Hebrew culture. The Bible was born out of a culture that honored men and despised women and so it reflected this phenomenon. If we pay no attention to historical context and background in our biblical interpretation, but simply apply things mechanically, we turn the revelation of God into a fossilized word, and not the living Word.

In teaching women the church most often uses the words of Paul, such as, "Wives be subject to your husbands as you are to the Lord. For the husband is the head of the wife just as Christ is the head of the church, the body of which he is the Savior. Just as the Church is subject to Christ, so also wives ought to be, in everything, to their husbands. Husbands, love your wives, just as Christ loved the church and gave himself up for her" (Eph 5:22–25). "But I want you to understand that Christ is the head of every man, and the husband is the head of his wife, and God is the head of Christ" (1 Cor 11:13). "Wives be subject to your husbands as is fitting in the Lord" (1 Cor 3:18).

There are many such passages. Women were told to be obedient, enduring, and humble. Because we have not transcended the influence of culture in our biblical interpretation, women are caught in conflicting interpretations. Wong Wai Ching of the Chinese University of Hong Kong says, "On the one hand, the church teaches brothers and sisters to love one another, that we are all made in the precious image of God; but on the other hand, it teaches that men are the main and women the subordinate gender and that sisters ought to obey their husbands and moreover, ought to make the home their ultimate base of service if they wish to be in accord with biblical truth."[1]

Of course, a woman has an irreplaceable function in the construction of the family. She plays an important role in building harmonious family relations, in the education of children, and in care for the elderly. Research has shown that care for pre-school age children is borne by the wife in over 60 percent of households and that women themselves feel this is their responsibility. Today we have, on the one hand, a rising body of public opinion that would like to see women return to the home as housewives, and on the other, a society that still judges women according to male values, ignoring the efforts of women in marriage and the home. This being the case, if women want to gain recognition and respect, they must expend greater effort and gain success in the workplace and professions.

In their view of marriage, Chinese Christian women are influenced by society and culture on the one hand and church teachings on the other. Within the church there are times when culture is equated with truth, to the extent that men and women are seen as unequal. The church must first deal with such phenomena; otherwise it will be powerless to take up its mission of responding to the times. Women within the church will more and more sense their isolation from their surrounding environment and feel unsure in facing real issues; they will experience a clash between faith and real life.

Biblical Teachings on Marriage from a Feminist Perspective

Let us consider first of all the position God gave to women at their creation. In the first creation story in Genesis, "the peak of creation came when humanity was created, because the result of the creation of other things and beings was 'good' and that of the creation of humanity was 'very good.'"[2] This creation story says, "in the image of God he created them; male and female he created them" (Gen 1:27). In this P account of creation, male and female are united, not separated; from this union, we can infer that neither is higher or lower than the other. Male chauvinists usually take the second creation story as evidence for male superiority, especially Genesis 2:18: "Then the Lord God said, 'It is not good that man should be alone; I will make him a helper as his partner.'" The word helper here has no sense of higher or lower either. Help (*ezer*) occurs a dozen times in the Old Testament and in many instances it refers to the work of Yahweh and has no meaning of grade or level attached to it.[3] Chapter 2, verse 10 is best translated as "but for the man there was not found an equal helper." In general when the Bible mentions "helper," it refers to the role and not the status. Helper here is used to express the idea of complementarity, and not a conferral of status, so most scholars take this helper not as simply helping in the work of everyday life or child bearing, but as a mutual partner. Thus, we best understand helper as a role, a kind of post: a helper is one who has the role of knowing when to extend a hand in aid, like God who gives human beings aid in time of need but does not spoil the people he loves. When the man, on seeing the woman, calls her "bone of my bone, flesh of my flesh," this is a fuller expression of their mutual complementarity, of their union. Only when male and female are united, mutually helping, can perfection be achieved. Thus, the most important message Genesis 2 has for us is not the order of creation but the mystery of human connection, that "they become one flesh." Between male and female there is not opposition, but mutual help.[4]

It is Paul who mentions the male-female relationship within marriage most frequently in the Bible and there are several instances in his discussion of marriage that are frequently quoted by Christians, especially that in Ephesians 5:22–25 quoted above. However, "be subject to" here is not a command, but a sincere exhortation; the best translation of the Greek verb is "voluntary obedience."[5] A wife is obedient to a husband just as the church is obedient to Christ. Christians do not obey Christ because of a command from God; their obedience stems from willing and joyful hearts. At the same time, Paul is at pains to point out that Christ is the head of the church, something quite different from the husband being the head of the wife. Therefore, he particularly emphasizes "the body of which he (Christ) is the Savior." By saying this, Paul shows that he knows his comparison is not exact. Christ is the Savior of the church, but the husband is far from being the savior of the wife.[6] At the same time we must not forget that Paul has a teaching for the husband: to love his wife as Christ loves the church. Paul tells us that the love of a husband for his wife is a high form of love and its mark is self-sacrifice, not self-satisfaction. The goal of such love is the well being of the loved one. And Paul says: "Husbands should love their wives as they do their own bodies" (Eph 5:28). This is not to demonstrate the limits of husbandly love, to say that as much as he loves himself he should love his wife; rather it refers to the nature of the relationship between husband and wife, which is the foundation of his love. The husband should love the wife because she is part of his body.[7]

In the Bible we find that some passages in Paul's letter express the idea of equality: "As many of you as were baptized into Christ have clothed yourselves with Christ. There is no longer Jew or Greek, there is no longer slave or free, there is no longer male and female; for all of you are one in Christ Jesus" (Gal. 3:27-28). But there is also what looks like a belittling of women: "Let a woman learn in silence with full submission. I permit no woman to teach or to have authority over a man; she is to keep silent. For Adam was formed first, then Eve; and Adam was not deceived, but the woman was deceived and became a transgressor" (1 Tim 2:11–14), and so on. In these passages, we see a Paul who is contradictory, conflicted. But we must not forget that Paul was situated in a male-dominated social environment. Paul was attempting to bring the fellowship of the Christian ideal of male-female equality and the culture of the time into harmony. Cultural comparison must be synchronic and not diachronic. In those times, discrimination against women was a global phenomenon. When Paul said the husband was head, it was to say that, like Christ, he should love his wife with a self-sacrificing love. And in those times, this was quite a breakthrough.

When we study the Bible, Wong Wai Ching says, "we unconsciously hold particular cultural values as sacred, with the result that, in order to uphold gender values that were in force in some culture, we maintain that the Bible has these unchangeable teachings or principles. Such a method only serves to continually diminish the richness of the Bible and forcefully homogenize the varied voices of the Bible. This limits Christians' interest in and intellectual exploration of the world of the Bible."[8]

The Predicament of Modern Christian Women and the Way Out

Along with reform and liberalization and economic development in China, people are moving from being closed-in toward liberty, from poverty to affluence, and at the same time, people's values and ethics are also undergoing continual transformation. The family is the most fundamental social unit and is most sensitive to these changes. Societal changes have led to a higher rate of family breakup. The divorce rate remains at a high level and continues to rise even higher, and a substantial number of extra-marital affairs leads to the breakup of families. When marriage is breaking up, it is women who are in the weaker position. The instability of modern marriage means that women cannot rely on their husbands forever. Women must be strong and independent and seek their own worth and status.

There are many women in the Bible who can serve as models. Hebrew society was a male-oriented society and for the most part women were not entered in genealogies. But four women appear in Jesus' genealogy, which means they are unusual, set apart from the norm. I think the reason these women won recognition was precisely because of their courage and self-reliance, their strong characters and unyielding aspirations.

Tamar, for example, was much to be pitied. She was married to Er, the firstborn son of Judah, but because "he was wicked in the sight of the Lord, the Lord put him to death." According to Hebrew custom (Deut 25:5–10) she was then married to another of the sons of Judah, Onan, but her fate was the same, for the Lord was displeased at the sin of Onan and put him to death also. Tamar was again plunged into widowhood. What is more, Judah believed she has caused his sons' deaths, and was unwilling to let his youngest son marry her. We could say that her fate was at its nadir, because in Hebrew society if a woman wanted to change her status, she usually did it by giving birth. Though women were not valued, mothers were both valued and highly respected. We see in the Bible that every woman paid great attention to the matter of bearing children, and often prayed to have many offspring. Moreover, they frequently felt pride or humiliation over how many children they bore or did not bear. And they could be ridiculed if they were barren. Biblical scholars believe that the reason Hebrew society placed such a high value on childbearing and gave high status to mothers was based on people's misunderstanding of the promise of God: "I will put enmity between you and the woman, between your offspring and hers, he will strike your head" (Gen 3:15). They believed that only after a woman had produced offspring did she have a part in the promise of God and have value. In her hopeless situation, Tamar tried to have a son with Judah to continue her dead husband's name. Though we may look askance at Tamar's method, as the weaker sex, Tamar had no other way out. This was her only way of struggling for her rights and status. Thus, Judah said, "She is more righteous than I." For her own future and her own worth and dignity, she was willing to risk her life to get a son from Judah. I very much admire her courage and spirit of self-reliance. It was because of her perseverance and determination that she saw light in her hopeless situation.

In the same way, every Christian reverences Mary, Jesus' mother. When we mention Mary, we think of her gentleness, virtues, and endurance, for these are men's ideal image of the Holy Mother. Our definition of Mary has always been based on a male aesthetic. But when I do a close reading of the passages about Mary, I find that actually her most important virtues, courage and strength, are often overlooked. The angel appeared to Mary, telling her that she was to bear a child. To a young virgin, this must have been a tremendous challenge, especially in the Jewish society of the time. In those days it was not permitted for a young woman betrothed but not yet married to become pregnant, and Joseph thought of dismissing her quietly (Mt 1:19). In the face of great pressures, Mary courageously accepted the divine plan: "Here am I, the servant of the Lord; let it be with me according to your word" (Lk 1:38). In the days to come, Mary, with the strength and endurance of a mother, accompanied her son through every sort of situation and faced every kind of challenge. At the foot of the cross on Golgotha, we see a great mother, who with incomparable strength stood by her son to the end. Actually, what we notice first about Mary is her courage and strength, and not the way she is seen according to a male perspective.

These women are excellent models for us. The courage, strength, and self-reliance we see in them are qualities needed by women in every age. And it is because of these wonderful qualities that they are recognized and honored.

Wong Wai Ching says,

> In its missionary efforts, early Christianity gave women a double-edged sword: faith both restricted them and gave them new stimulation and imagination. Thus, three "backhanded" phenomena quietly crept in: when missionaries intended to "save" oppressed Chinese women through Christianity, women missionaries were seeking their own independent roles outside their own country. As women missionaries blessed wholeheartedly good wives and mothers, Christian women in China were inspired by the way these foreign women lived their lives, and found that women might have choices outside the home. Christian women worked through the church and its western network to struggle for gender equality. It can be said that once the missionaries, with their western colonial consciousness, met up with women who were seeking self-liberation and space for development, the result could not have been imagined at the outset.[9]

Today, Christian women also gain strength and help from faith, cast off their dependence on their husbands or others, and thus raise the status of women in the home. Of course, self-reliance is much more difficult for women than for men, whether in the past or today. We hear often about women's crisis, women's tragedy, and women's predicament.

The establishment of the market economy and economic development do not automatically bring freedom and independence to women.

One important aspect for women in ridding themselves of reliance on men is to go into society and find gainful employment. This will enable women to have an independent voice in the home and control over income and finances. In such an environment, women will naturally have greater choice and opportunities. At the same time, however, there will be greater challenges and even potential for harm.

Because of the rapid development of the market economy and the weakening of traditional moral standards, it is more difficult for women to rely on men and find protection and escape. If women do not improve themselves, there will inevitably be more of the past repeating itself in modern dress. In such circumstances, women must strengthen their quest for freedom and independence and raise their educational level in order to strengthen their ability to meet challenges. But one characteristic of the economic revolution embodied in the market economy has been the marginalization of Chinese women in the labor force. The rate of female unemployment is high, their choice of work is limited, and in some professions the gender gap is fairly serious. The force of public opinion compels them to be marginalized. Therefore, women must expend a great deal more effort in making themselves independent than men.

As China makes the transition from traditional to modern, modern women undergo a profound and difficult transformation. In their everyday lives, women frequently find themselves in a double bind. Their progress and development are always accompanied by the contradiction that they cannot fulfill all that is expected of them. When social conditions are not yet perfect, women must give up one thing in order to get another. Faced with a changed aesthetics of the times, women have made the painful discovery that success in a profession does not mean success as a woman, but just the opposite. For a woman, success engenders in other people a sense that she has gotten off track; when people term her a strong woman, it may not be a compliment. There needs to be a comprehensive integration of the modern women's liberation movement and the movement toward development. There needs to be a kind of negotiation between traditional culture and modern culture, social reality and Christian faith, to enable modern women to develop their character in a healthy manner.

Theological Theory Integrated with Christian Reality

The rise of the feminist movement was a response and a resistance to a culture that had made men the center of humankind. As Christianity grew and developed in human society, it was naturally influenced by patriarchal thinking in a profound way. Feminist theology was born in response to this androcentric traditional theology. Western feminist theology was born out of the modern human rights movement, though it has far exceeded this movement. From the 1960s till today, it has been like a brilliant rising star, not easily ignored. Whether in terms of theological theory or in practice, it has made important contributions. Many seminaries have courses in feminist theology and many theologians and clergy have set up church organizations to protect and promote the rights of women. The focal point of feminist theology is to rediscover the experience of women that has been ignored, and, through new interpretations of the Bible, to reveal patriarchal influences on traditional theology, to develop more inclusive theological language and contents, and to emphasize male-female partnership, interdependence, complementarity, and equality in friendship and love.

At the same time, theological reflection can be enriched by taking the context seriously for reflection, exploring the signs of the times, questioning unequal phenomena, and affirming the importance and inspiration of the feminist movement. Feminist theology also needs to understand gender inequality in social structures and women's predicament, so that it can oppose female subordination, gender stereotypes, and language and actions that oppress women. Women should understand the significance, dignity, and value of being women and put ideas into concrete action, promoting the struggle for the dignity and power of women and abolishing roles and images men have forced on women. Their question should be not "What do others want me to be?" but rather "Who am I?"

Feminist scholar Zhou Bi-e says, "on the surface, women/gender studies and feminism seem to be popular, but in fact, whether in academia or in the cultural system, they are marginalized. They are not the mainstream, but are almost without recognition. In such an unfriendly environment, to announce that one is a feminist or to identify with women's studies, takes quite a bit of courage."[10]

It is difficult for people to accept Chinese feminist theology because of the influence of traditional culture on the one hand, and because of misunderstanding of many biblical passages on the other. So from the very beginning the term "feminist theology" often raises a lot of doubts, even a lot of hackles. But I believe it is a very suitable term to express an important theological trend in the church today. Perhaps in the course of its development, there has been this or that type of deviation, but no development leads smoothly from beginning to maturity and perfection. There must be a process of searching and exploration before moving onto a healthy path.

Feminist theology is just beginning in the Chinese Church, and in theory and practice, it is a bit scattered and superficial. Theoretical research has so far made little impact on the concrete reality. Christians with a consciousness of gender equality are mostly intellectuals; many ordinary female believers have no such consciousness, and this may be due to the fact that all the promoters of feminism come from among intellectuals.

Women from middle and lower classes, because of their circumstances and limitations, have no resources for resisting men, so the idea of gender equality is, for them, nothing more than empty talk. Women who lack resources need help in all areas. There are women who have long lived in violent marriages and women whose husbands have had many affairs. Because these women have no defined work themselves, they have no income and no ability or opportunity to struggle for themselves. They must accept their situations, endure abuse, or live in what are marriages in name only. Their most urgent need is the concrete help of the church and other institutions to enable them to have the ability to live independently and give them practical guidance from a faith point of view.

I am greatly concerned about women, not only because I am a woman, but also because God gives to men and women the same grace. It is also because when growing up and now I have encountered so many great, strong, fighting women. In their homes, workplace, and society, they have used their weak shoulders to uphold a home, the sky, a whole era.

Notes

1. Wong Wai Ching, *Xingbie yishi yu shengjing quanxi* (Gender consciousness and biblical interpretation) (Hong Kong: Chinese Christian Literature Council, Ltd., 2000), 24.

2. Dai Haohui, "Funü yu gudai quanxi" (Women and ancient interpretation), in *Dujing, yanjing, xijing* (Bible reading, study and interpretation), ed. Lu Longuang (Hong Kong: Chung Chi College, Chinese University of Hong Kong, 2000), 94.

3. See Yang Keqin, *Nünan zhijian* (Between male and female) (Hong Kong: Alliance Bible Seminary, 1995), 59.

4. Wang Peng, "On Paul's Prohibitions on Women in 1 Corinthians," *Chinese Theological Review* 15 (2001): 88.

5. Fung Guotai, *Yifusuoshu* (Ephesians) (Hong Kong: Tiandao Publisher, 1998), 136.

6. Ibid.

7. Charles Hodge, *A Commentary on the Epistle to the Ephesians* (Grand Rapids, MI: Eerdmans, 1950), 332.

8. Wong, *Xingbie yishi*, 24.

9. Wong Wai Ching, "Zongjiao wenhua yu funü" (Religion and women), (paper presented at Chinese Culture and Women Conference, Beijing, 2002).

10. Zhou Bi-e, address at the Gender and Society Conference, Qinghua University, 2002.

16

CATHOLICISM AND WOMEN'S RIGHTS AS HUMAN RIGHTS

Maria José Rosado-Nunes (Brazil)

Catholicism and Women's Human Rights

The concept of "rights of man" should be understood in the context of modernity's ambition to forge, for the first time in the world's history, a universal consensus.[1] This ideology of rights, charged with paradoxes and limitations, is founded on an Enlightenment concept of "mankind" and was formed by breaking away from Catholic principles. In a book about the social teaching of the church Charles Curran points to the strong opposition of the Catholic Church to the concept of human rights in the nineteenth century. Human rights, he says,

> were identified with the Enlightenment in the philosophical realm. Pius IX's Syllabus of Errors and Leo XIII's condemnation of modern freedoms illustrate this perspective. The Enlighten-ment grounded human rights in the freedom and autonomy of the individual person, which Catholicism strongly opposed. The person is not autonomous precisely because human beings are related to God as well as to the world itself... Catholic moral theology insisted on duties and not on rights.[2]

From Human Nature to Individual Freedom

Under a liberal conception of society, humankind, and the world, "the rights of man" are based on three suppositions: an extensive, abstract

---

Maria José Rosado-Nunes, "Catholicism and Women's Rights as Human Rights," in *Rights of Women*, ed. The Concilium Foundation, *Concilium* 2002, no. 5 (London: SCM Press, 2002), 50–63. English language translation © SCM Press. Used by permission of SCM Press.

concept of "humanity"; a concept of rights for which "humanity" is the only necessary condition; and the realization of the individual as a social unit resulting from these rights. According to Emile Poulat, these suppositions underlying the liberal theory of rights explain the unending and perhaps insurmountable conflict between Catholicism and liberalism, which never ceases to repeat itself. It is possible to consider this conflict in the light of the new problems brought about by bioethics: contraception, abortion, euthanasia and, in broader terms, sexuality.[3]

The conflict between Catholicism and liberalism can be seen in the way law has developed and how the concept of nature has changed. Natural law, the common denominator of Christianity and modernity, has transformed itself in a radical way. "With modern science, like science itself, modern law repudiates the Christian conception of nature created by scholastic thought, according to Aristotle."[4] If the basis for Christian ideas is to be found in the affirmation of God as the primary cause and ultimate foundation, scientific thought and modern law are supported by the social contract and by a certain conception of reasoning—which discards appeals to divinity. "In this effort of scientific and legal construction emerges a new man: the *individual* and his *conscience*, master of himself; his judgments and his decisions."[5] The "man" born out of the Protestant Reformation is obliged to obey his conscience alone. "Without doubt," says Curran,

> natural law fitted very well with nineteenth-century papal opposition to liberalism. Philosophical liberalism so exalted human reason that it denied the divine and cut off human reality from any relationship to God and God's law. Aquinas insisted on the role of human reason but regarded human reason as related to the divine reason through mediation.[6]

According to Christianity, all liberty is a gift from God; it is not inherent in the individual and is not a source of rights. "To the contrary, all efforts of the modern spirit will tend to abolish this arbitrariness and set it free, offering human nature something which until then [has] depended on a higher order."[7] Such a transformation, in the legal realm, meant the invention of the individual as a "social unit and its corollary: one man equals one man." This principle of individuality not only opposed the Catholic social order, but also the religious order. As such, a conflict of rights developed:

> The right of the individual to freedom of conscience, opinion, and religion; the right of Catholicism, held as a state religion, to represent the absolute truth and extract the social consequences which seemed to result...Liberal individualism secreted social atheism: a lay society no longer needed God to govern its steps

and kept him in the sphere of private life, and in the intimacy of conscience and family."[8]

Even recognizing a dramatic change in Catholic thought across the 1920s, Curran points to the maintenance of such opposition to the liberal affirmation of individual freedom.

> There is no doubt that a very significant change occurred in the twentieth century as Catholic social teaching came to a greater appreciation of the freedom, dignity, and rights of the individual person. Yet although Catholic social teaching did learn from philosophical liberalism and human experience, it cannot and will not accept liberalism's individualistic understanding of the human person.[9]

The Role of Maternity

These discussions may help to shed light on the ways in which the Catholic Church manifests itself by violating the fundamental rights of women. An analysis of the "unending and insurmountable" conflict between liberal ideas and Christian conceptions may help in understanding the reasons why Catholicism rises up against women's struggles for autonomy.

Feminism sets out to affirm rights and individual liberties by proclaiming that women, as social subjects, are citizens, with the right to interfere in the political sphere of society; and that they, as individuals, have the right to control their own sexuality and reproductive capability. In the field of reproductive rights, "the issue of individual autonomy—so deeply valued by contemporary feminism—as a fundamental point of the exercise of liberty is the basic inspiration for the growth and adaptation of this field of law."[10] On the opposite side, Catholicism propagates a traditional conception of women and identifies their essence in maternity. The roles reserved by traditional Catholic doctrine for women are as wives and mothers. Thus, the affirmation of individual rights for women becomes incompatible with the staunch affirmations of the Catholic religion. Patrick Snyder, while analyzing the position of Pope John Paul II, says that "as an absolute, for Pope John Paul II maternity defines in one fell swoop the nature, dignity, vocation, and the temporal and spiritual essence of women." This pope considered one of the errors of feminism to be exactly the fact that it aims to "'liberate' women...from that which is their specific vocation of mother and wife."[11] Curran affirms that

> the male perspective comes through in almost every document of Catholic social teaching. Women tend to be invisible in the earlier

documents, except in discussions of the family. Within the family, however, the earlier documents clearly portray and extol the subordinate position of women. Even today the role of women is primarily as mothers and educators of their children in the home."[12]

The Catholic Church is allergic to liberalism which upholds modern conceptions of autonomy and the claims of women to their self-determination. These claims are also found within Catholicism itself. The enormous development of feminist theology has laid the foundation for a consistent claim of Catholic women for autonomy and for respect of their dignity as human beings, including in the controversial field of sexuality and reproduction. A Catholic theologian, Monique Dumais, critically states: "One of the main claims of women is to control their own bodies. How can one feel like a person when that which is closest to one, one's own body, escapes one and is made dependent on others and under the authority of others?"[13]

Human Rights, Feminism, and Women's Rights

Within the liberal field of supporting individual rights, the notion of human rights has been, and continues to be, critically incorporated and restated by women. As Susan Moller Okin points out:

> The recognition of women's rights as human rights has been taking place on the global stage—from the grassroots to the international conference levels—in the last two decades. This has required considerable rethinking of human rights. Many specific human rights that are crucial to women's well-being need to be identified and acted on to stop clearly gender-related wrongs ... such rights cannot be recognized as human rights without some significant challenges both to that concept itself and to some institutions basic to the various human cultures, certainly families and religions.[14]

Against the Male Bias

One of the feminist critiques to the human rights thinking and priorities is their "male bias." As stated, the problem is that the "male model" under existing theories and priorities of human rights prevents the incorporation of women's life experience into the core of the discourse. Problems considered to be private, such as rape, domestic violence, claims for sexual freedom, as well as unequal opportunities for education, employment, and health care, were virtually ignored until women asked for their inclusion at the Vienna and Beijing Conferences (World Conference on Human Rights, held in 1993; Fourth World Conference on Women, held in 1995). Though of great importance for women, these rights were considered to be in the private realm and were off the human rights agenda. As Charlotte Bunch, one of the prime movers to get them on this agenda, has said: "They have been largely invisible and/or are dismissed as private family, cultural or religious rather than political matters."[15]

According to Okin, some other

> recognized human rights abuses have specifically gender-related forms that were not typically recognized as human rights abuses . . . Also, there was little acknowledgment until recently of women's particular vulnerability to poverty and need for basic social services, such as health care, because of both their biological reproductive capacity and their assumption, in virtually all societies, of greater responsibility for children.[16]

Reproductive and Social Rights

Southern feminists laid special claim to the incorporation of reproductive and social rights under the notion of women's human rights. "Reproductive rights are a recent concept arising out of women's own reflection and include individual, collective and social rights, in addition to other rights related to maternity, conception and contraception, family planning, among others which integrate fundamental rights."[17] Such a widening of rights allows for the possibility that a woman can control her sexuality and reproductive capability as part of the realization of women's citizenship. In the words of Sia Nowrojec,

> Women's reproductive health must be understood within a wide approach of human development, in order to promote the well-being of people and women's full citizenship . . . The perspective of reproductive rights and health formulated by the network Dawn-Mudar is grounded on the principles of human rights to rescue the question of reproduction from isolation.[18]

According to Irene León, the reformulation of human rights proposed by Latin American women includes economic, social, cultural, civil, and political rights, covering the area of individual rights as collective rights.[19] Calling for the inclusion of social rights and reproductive rights into the scope of human rights, women contribute to the development of the concept of citizenship and democracy by projecting a new model of society, which demands social reform and a change in mental attitudes.[20]

On the other hand, the critical vision of liberalism "as a political and economic doctrine in which the market is perceived as the driving force of the possibilities of choice, and accumulation and competition are the basic values sustaining it"[21] leads to the suggestion of a Latin American critique perspective on human rights. The document prepared by the Ad Hoc Coordinating Committee of Non-Profit Organizations at the Regional Human Rights Conference held in Costa Rica in 1992 states:

> The application of neo-liberal policies and structural adjustment programs deny economic, social, cultural, civil, and political rights to our peoples since these measures have increased poverty and discrimination by polarizing our societies and leading discriminated groups to subsistence levels; women, Latin Americans of African and Native (South) American heritage, those living with HIV/AIDS, the disabled, those forced to relocate, and migrant workers, have all experienced a decline in their already anguishing situations.[22]

Interdependence

The understanding that connects individual and collective rights instead of setting them in opposition to each other leads to a more comprehensive approach to human rights. While liberal-individualism treats group and individualized interests as being in competition with each other, feminists offer an understanding of the interdependence of these interests. The abstract and atomistic liberal model of the individual leads to an under-valuation or an ignoring of significant aspects of human experience, thus making it difficult to address social needs. Brazilian feminists affirm:

> The action of feminist movements turns to the transformation of gender relations as its historical direction. In this sense, the struggle for women's rights is part of a social transformation process searching for equality, social justice, freedom, etc. The institution of women as political subjects is the core of political action; it is its greatest achievement and at the same time its historical contribution to women's movements in general.[23]

As many analyses of women's participation at the international meetings of the 1980s and 1990s indicate, this critical feminist assumption of human rights as women's rights has led to changes in final documents. Activists present in Vienna, Cairo, and Beijing have been exercising significant influence on issues relating to such topics as the conception of family, the adoption of inclusive language, and a historical turn in the understanding of matters of population. Okin shows how areas like religion and family have begun to be affected by the recognition of women as holders of full human rights. The Beijing Platform for Action added to the right to freedom of thought, conscience, and religion: "However, it is acknowledged that any form of extremism may have a negative impact on women and can lead to violence and discrimination." Even when it is not clear what "extremism" means, notes Okin,[24] it is significant that religion and family are recognized as not always "unmitigated goods, at least from the point of view of women seeking equal rights." Feminists have shown that families considered in a more concrete and less idealized approach are not always a safe place for women. As Okin points out,

> Many violations of women's basic human rights both occur *within* [families] and are justified by reference to culture, religion or tradition. So recognizing women's rights as human rights means looking at the institutions of family, religion and culture or tradition in a new light.[25]

Thus women's reformulation of the liberal concept of human rights so that women's individual rights are integrated into collective rights and include sexual and reproductive rights as well as the ideal of social justice challenges the religious concept of human rights. In the case of Catholicism, this vision of rights that affirm the importance of individual autonomy, present in a liberal vision but connected to social rights, is particularly antagonistic, as we will see.

The Fundamentalist Face of Catholicism in Brazil and Women's Rights

Can we appropriately talk of fundamentalism when Catholicism is at stake? Commenting on the books of Martin Marty and others on fundamentalism, Rosemary Radford Ruether points out the fact that they include Catholic and Protestant right-wing groups in the wave of contemporary fundamentalisms. All fundamentalist movements seem to have in common "a rejection of modernity and efforts to re-establish the public role of religion, if not religious states, to counter what was seen as evil secularity, with its lack of established public values." However from Ruether's point of view, the authors have overlooked

> perhaps the most striking similarity of all... their efforts to re-establish rigid patriarchal control over women and their hostility to women's equality, autonomous agency and the right to

control their own sexuality and fertility... The Vatican is hardly less obsessed [than other right-wing groups] with women's equality and reproductive rights as the epitome of evil modern secularity and the cause of civilization's demise.[26]

Courtney Howland points to two main characteristics of religious fundamentalism. The first has to do with how "fundamentalists are particularly concerned with women's sexuality—as a danger and a threat to society—and thus are keen to regulate and control women's sexuality and reproduction through a variety of measures... and thus a number of norms are aimed at making sure that women's sexuality is controlled—not by women—but by men." The second characteristic is the tendency of religious fundamentalism "to take political action aimed at conforming a state's [a country's] law to religious doctrine, particularly in areas affecting women's rights."[27] The Brazilian Catholic Church is a clear example of this kind of religious fundamentalism.[28]

Problems after a Good Beginning

Unlike the situation in other countries, the relationship of Brazilian feminists with the Catholic Church has not always been one of mutual opposition. In the 1970s, the Catholic Church in Brazil offered an important space for protest against the military dictatorship that had existed from the 1960s through the 1980s. During this period, there were feminist and left wing party alliances with the Catholic Church.[29] The firm opposition to the military regime by key members of the Catholic hierarchy and the church's privileged position in negotiations with the state greatly boosted the institution's credibility in the eyes of the left wing groups with which feminists were allied or to which they belonged. The women's movement was therefore able to find allies in the Catholic Church who supported campaigns for day care centers, lowering the cost of living, freeing political prisoners, and the like.

Because of the church's social penetration and its power to influence society, feminist struggles were amplified by this alliance. Through the action of the Base Ecclesial Communities (CEBs) in the 1970s, many poor Catholic women from outer urban communities and rural areas took on social and political struggles. According to their testimony in various surveys, it was the Catholic Church that took to the streets. In the process, many of these women met with feminists and assimilated their ideas, sharpening their critical awareness in relation to their own situations "as women" not only in society; but also in the church itself.[30]

However, the alliance between the Catholic Church and the women's movement at times placed constraints on women's demands and limited the issues debated by the movement. As the military began liberalizing the regime in the 1980s and feminists explicitly extended their demands to include the right of women to decide sexual matters freely, including the right to interrupt unwanted pregnancies, the Catholic Church reacted adversely, and conflict entered into the relationship. The ambiguity in the Brazilian Catholic Church toward social issues is maintained by engaging in social discourse over some issues while at the same time siding with the conservative or fundamentalist positions of the Vatican on matters of sexual mores.

Three Examples

A few recent examples may help to illustrate the matter. The first example demonstrates the commitment of certain sectors of the church to issues of social justice. In 1998, the worst drought in over fifteen years afflicted the north of Brazil. Neither the government nor the media, and not even the president himself, addressed the problem, much less were prepared to do anything about it. Men, women, and children were dying. Finally, the Catholic bishops of Brazil broke the silence and dramatically announced to the starving that they had the right to loot the supermarkets for the food that they needed to live. In fact, the people had already begun this type of action, but the bishops gave their blessing in support. Television, radio, and newspapers then began reporting on the drought and the looting of food. Finally, the president spoke publicly for the first time about the problem. After having announced measures to help the needy population, he called on the courts legally to prosecute "those" who were encouraging the looting, in a clear reference to the bishops' action. But it was in fact the bishops' outspoken stance that finally provoked a response by the government to the crucial problem of the drought. Many judges and lawyers publicly supported the bishops by stating that stealing food in order to avoid starvation was not a crime and could be justified.

A second example concerns individual rights and social responsibility with respect to human reproduction in cases of rape and pregnancy. In a rural part of the state of Rio de Janeiro, an eleven-year-old girl was raped and became pregnant. She, with the support of her parents, decided to undergo an abortion, which in this case is permitted by Brazilian law. Meanwhile, Catholic religious groups, supported by the local priest, pressured the girl and her family into changing their minds. Thus, the resource of religious argumentation was used to compel a child who had become pregnant by the violence of rape to continue her pregnancy.

Another recent episode is also revealing. Under Brazilian law, women may legally have an abortion for one of two reasons: rape and whenever a woman's life is endangered.[31] But public hospitals do not provide abortions, so poor women are not protected by this law, and many die. Provoked by continuous political action by the women's movement, legislators proposed a law forcing public hospitals to perform legal abortions. Congress held a special session to discuss the issue. Catholic feminists, including myself, attended. A Catholic priest and his supporters also attended. He brought a voting girl with him, making a ridiculous spectacle by presenting her to the entire session and saying, "This child would not be alive if abortion were legal."

These cases illustrate the two-sided nature of Brazilian Catholicism, and allow us to better understand the difficulty faced by Catholic women in continuing to subscribe to this religious creed and, at the same time, to defend their feminist ideas. Their support of the church's action in the struggle for social justice does not prevent them from criticizing Catholic positions with respect to sexual and reproductive rights.

Courtney Howland, in discussing a possible definition of religious fundamentalism, argues that "the experience of many religious women who have suffered under fundamentalism and fought to resist it" must be considered. She states that

> fundamentalism is real and has meaning for numbers of religious women from different religions and countries who experience it as a very real threat to their freedom and often their lives. These women perceive themselves to be religious despite their resistance to fundamentalist trends within their religion, and may perceive themselves to be feminists despite the intensity of their religious belief.[32]

Following the Sexual Morals of Rome?

In reality, this is the experience of many Catholic women and feminists in Brazil. They swing between affirming their religious faith and the need to defend the more elementary rights of women in search of their autonomy. This is the context in which the fundamentalist face of Brazilian Catholicism should be analyzed. Returning to Howland's text, we find a conceptualization of religious fundamentalism that includes, on the one hand, principles of doctrine and, on the other, political action aimed at bringing national legislation in line with religious norms.[33] The teachings of the Brazilian Catholic Church have always faithfully followed the sexual morals of Rome. The Roman Catholic position on sexuality and reproduction is well known, and has the effect of limiting the value of women to the biological capabilities that allow them to generate new human beings. Women's demands for recognition of their moral capability to make decisions that are acceptable from ethical and religious standpoints, of their right to decide matters affecting their own lives and bodies, of their experiences as appropriate for Christian reflection in the sphere of sexual morals, all produce situations of conflict within the Catholic Church. As Howland and many others have noted, any change in the patriarchal organization of the family or attempt to enhance women's autonomy in the sphere of sexuality and reproduction threatens the basis of Catholic belief and tradition.[34]

Catholic doctrine pervades Brazilian culture. As has been noted,

> The Catholic patriarchal order is so deeply rooted in our culture that it does not require justification; it imposes itself as self-evident and is considered "natural": [Pierre] Bourdieu points out the great difficulty in analyzing this cultural logic due to the fact that the institution for more than a millennium has been woven into social structures and mental thought processes and attitudes, such that analysts run the risk of using certain categories of perception and thought as instruments of knowledge which should rather be dealt with as objects of study.[35]

In the area of political action, the Catholic Church has a history of constant interference in issues relating to sexuality and reproduction. By making use of the considerable social power that it still enjoys in Brazil, this religious institution acts as a major pressure group by lobbying the government and Congress and by influencing the mass media. In maintaining its traditional principle of the inseparability of sexuality and procreation, its aim is to

> influence or even define the content of social policy and legislation. The result of this is that dialogue with the representatives of the executive and legislative branches is, in general, continually under the censuring influence of a transcendental and theological order. This situation has resulted in the obstruction of, and delays in, the implementation of social programs, as in the case of the PAISM (Program of Total Assistance for Women's Health), which had its inauguration as an official program delayed because of the Church attempting to remove the IUD (intra-uterine contraceptive device) from the list of contraceptive methods to be offered by the state social services. The controversy finally ended with the inclusion of this method, but meanwhile this has given the religious wing an opportunity to promulgate so-called "natural" methods. In addition, the Church has succeeded in delaying, or even in some cases entirely preventing, the distribution of informative materials produced by feminist groups at the request of the Ministry of Health.[36]

There are many other examples. The situation with regard to abortion in Brazil is the clearest example of Catholic intervention in the most basic of women's rights: the right to control our own bodies; the right to live our sexuality in a free and responsible way; and the right to decide our own reproductive capacity. In the past few years, the Catholic Church, allied with other religious groups and retrogressive forces of society, has been active in the Brazilian Congress in preventing public access to the voluntary interruption of pregnancy. It has tried both to eliminate the laws that allow for abortion in some circumstances and to prevent further liberalization of the abortion laws. As demonstrated above, the church also seeks to place obstacles in the way of allowing public health services to provide abortions in situations where the abortion should be legal, thereby effectively preventing poor women from exercising their rights under the law.

The Roman Catholic Church in Brazil, both because of its doctrine in dealing with sexual morality and reproduction and because of its political action in these areas, is one of the most powerful adversaries of the development and affirmation of women's reproductive health and rights. Its opposition to the expansion of the scope of autonomy of thought and action for women is what we characterize as the fundamentalist face of Brazilian Catholicism.

Since the initial publication of this article, the Catholic Church's institutional politics have consolidated changes that had begun some years before. The papacies of John Paul II and Benedict XVI have moved the church toward a more conservative vision and practice. These popes have chosen new bishops for the Brazilian Catholic Church from priests who did not share the same line of thinking on liberation theology as their predecessors. The result has been a totally different composition of the Brazilian National Conference of Bishops. At the same time, new Pentecostal religions have emerged and rapidly developed, attracting followers from the Catholic Church. To confront the loss of followers and to respond to the new Roman directions, the Brazilian Catholic Church has shifted its pastoral politics from the Base Ecclesial Communities to parish organizations and to charismatic forms of the faith.

Notes

Texts not originally in English have been translated by the author. An earlier version of this article was published in Courtney W. Howland, *Religious Fundamentalism and the Human Rights of Women* (New York: St. Martin's Press, 1999), 293–302.

1. Emile Poulat, *Les Discours sur Les Droits de L'Homme. Ses Paradoxes et Ses Contraintes, Extrait: Actes de la IIIème Rencontre (Discourse on the Rights of Man: Its Paradoxes and Limits}* (Tunis: Centre D'Études et Recherches Economiques et Sociales, 1986), 27.

2. Charles E. Curran, *Catholic Social Teaching: A Historical, Theological and Ethical Analysis*, (Washington, DC: Georgetown University Press, 2002), 215.

3. Poulat, *Les Discours sur Les Droits de L'Homme*, 28.

4. Ibid, 29.

5. Ibid.

6. Curran, *Catholic Social Teaching*, 25.

7. Poulat, *Les Discours sur Les Droits de L'Homme*, 32.

8. Ibid, 33–34.

9. Curran, *Catholic Social Teaching*, 221.

10. Maria Betânia Ávila, "Modernidade e Cidadania Reprodutiva," *Revista Estudos Feministas* 1 (1993): 382–90.

11. Patrick Snyder, *Le Féminisme Selon Jean-Paul II: Une Négation du Déterminisme Corporel de la Femme* (mimeo), 5, 3.

12. Curran, *Catholic Social Teaching*, 94.

13. Cited in Snyder, *Le Féminisme Selon Jean-Paul II*, 5.

14. Susan Moller Okin, "Feminism, Women's Humans Rights, and Cultural Differences," *Hypatia* 13, no. 2 (1998): 32.

15. Quoted in Okin, "Feminism, Women's Humans Rights, and Cultural Differences," 39.

16. Ibid, 35.

17. Ibid, 14.

18. Sia Nowrojec, *População e Direitos Reprodutivos. Perspectivas Feministas do Sul*, trans. Renato Aguiar (Rio de Janeiro: Rede Dawn-Mudar, 1994), 13.

19. Irene Léon, *La Perspetiva Latinoamericana*, Serviço Informativo, Separata, 1 (February 1993): 166.

20. Ávila, "Modernidade e Cidadania Reprodutiva," 390.

21. Ibid., 387.

22. Léon, *La Perspetiva Latinoamericana*, iii.

23. Betânia Ávila and Sonia Corrêa, "Movimento de Mulheres: Questões para Pensar-se seus Rumos," 1, in: http://www.ibase.org.br/paginas/movimento.htm

24. Okin, "Feminism," 41.

25. Ibid, 39.

26. Rosemary Radford Ruether, "The War on Women," *Conscience: A New Journal of Prochoice Catholic Opinion* 22, no. 4 (2001-2002): 26.

27. Courtney Howland, ed., *Religious Fundamentalisms and the Human Rights of Women* (New York: St. Martin's Press, 1999), xii, xx.

28. On May 19, 2002, one of the most important Brazilian newspapers reported a confrontation between Catholic bishops and feminists on the ratification of the Convention on the Elimination of All Forms of Discrimination against Women (CEDAW). While feminists acted in favor of the ratification, Catholic bishops tried to convince the Brazilian parliament to reject the Convention (*O Estado de Sao Paulo*, May 19, 2002).

29. Leila de Andrade Linhares Barsted, "Legalização e Descriminalização do Aborto no Brasil; 10 Anos de Luta Feminista," *Revista Estudos Feministas* 1 (1992): 104–8.

30. Maria José Fontelas Rosado-Nunes, "De Mulheres, Sexo e Igreja: Uma Pesquisa e Muitas Interrogações," in *Alternativas Escassas: Saúde, Sexualidade e Reprodução na América Latina*, Séries Editora 34, ed. Albertina O. Costa and Tina Amado (Rio de Janeiro: PRODIR/F.C.C., 1994), 175, 177–78, 186–94.

31. Decreta-Lei no. 2848, December 7, 1940, art. 128, Penal Code.

32. Courtney W. Howland, "The Challenge of Religious Fundamentalism to the Liberty and Equality Rights of Women: An Analysis Under the United Nations Charter," *Columbia Journal of International Law* 35, no. 2 (1997): 271–80.

33. Ibid., 277–79, 289–96.

34. Howland, "The Challenge of Religious Fundamentalism," 273–76; Geraldine Sharp, "The Control of Reproduction and Patriarchy in the Church: Catholicism and Women's Rights as Human Rights of Pope John Paul II," Document for International Society for the Sociology of Religion, Laval University, Quebec, Canada, June 1995; and idem., "The Changing Nature of the Marriage Contract," *Theology and Sexuality* 6 (1996): 49–60.

35. Consuelo Maria Mejóa, "Normas y Valores de la Iglesia Catolica en la Sexualidad y la Reproducción: Nuevas Perspectivas," paper given at Seminário Nacional sobre Políticas Sociales, Sexualidad y Salud Reproductiva, Sala Afonso Reyes, el Colégio de México, 20/21 (November 1996): 3.

36. Ávila, "Modernidade e Cidadania Reprodutiva," 389-90.

17

WOMEN'S SPIRITUALITY FOR JUSTICE

Carmelita Usog (Philippines)

Our Context

Over the centuries, Philippine society has been subjected to different waves of colonization and thus developed people who are submissive yet also critical. This experience of domination has also shaped the
economic and political landscape of the present society. The subjugation
and exploitation of the Filipino people by foreign powers and the native
elite form one strand of the Philippine reality. The other strand is the
people's resistance and struggle against foreign rulers and their native
collaborators.

Since both economic and political power is controlled by a few, the
situation among the masses is both oppressive and dehumanizing. The Fil-
ipinos are left with nothing but the need to defend themselves. *"Kapit sa
patalim"* ["clinging to a sharp knife"] is a local saying that is often heard
when the people seek to redress their grievances through violent means.

Women have also been very much affected by the different waves of
colonization, which confined their participation in society to domestic affairs in contrast with their active involvement in the community prior to
the coming of the colonizers. The birth of resistance movements
prompted women to look into their situation and reclaim the legacy of the
past. The liberation of women cannot be achieved by men making con-
cessions to women. It can be realized only through organized struggle by
women in the economic, social and political spheres. The call is for
women to participate actively in people's struggle whether it is in the parliament or in the street or in armed struggle. This is no ordinary struggle.
It is a struggle that will lead to societal liberation and therefore it demands
total commitment. It is our task to challenge oppressive structures that

Carmelita Usog, "Women's Spirituality for Justice," in *Ecclesia of Women in Asia: Gathering the Voices of the Silenced*, ed. Evelyn Monterio and Antoinette Gutzler (Delhi:
ISPCK, 2005), 227–41.

curtail women's full personhood and deny their full membership in society. Women, whether as individuals or as a group, are denied their rightful share of the land and its produce. The arena of women's political struggle encompasses the entire social structure: from workers and peasants resisting the grip of transnational corporations to nuns and lay people becoming integrated with slum dwellers and the urban poor.[1]

It was economic deterioration and political oppression that prompted the Philippine Church, especially the clergy and nuns, to undergo a transformation. The priests, nuns, and lay workers journeyed with the masses in social action, basic ecclesial communities working side-by-side with the workers, students, and urban slum dwellers caught up in the resurgence of nationalist mobilization. These church workers took to heart the challenge of the Synod of Bishops' document, *Justice in the World*, which states that:

> Action on behalf of justice and participation in the transformation of the world fully appear to us as a constitutive dimension of the proclamation of the Gospel or, in other words, of the church's mission for the redemption of the human race and its liberation from every oppressive situation.[2]

In the Philippines, many church workers opted to do organizing work with the peasants, workers, and urban poor communities. With the growing feminist awareness, ministry to and for women was given importance. Some religious congregations encouraged sisters to launch into direct apostolate with the masses. The Association of Major Religious Superiors of the Philippines (AMRSP) has been supportive of the different task forces that serve the masses, groups such as the Rural Missionaries of the Philippines and the Women and Gender Commission. Religious congregations continued to review their aims and mission to find a more meaningful way of living their option for the poor. These involvements are at once healing and rewarding to women. They restore one's openness to wholeness and the holy. The work also responds to a crisis situation on a spiritual level. The solitude-solidarity connection is a recurrent theme in feminine spirituality or "womanspirit."[3]

Grounding and Reflection

When Mary's *Magnificat* in the Gospel of Luke is read from a feminist perspective, it gives another picture of Mary—a woman who is deeply in touch with the life situation of the people and who takes upon herself the pain and hardships that the people feel under the patriarchal and exploitative Roman Empire. The song of Mary is a classic example *par excellence* of a woman's spirituality that is based on justice. It is a favorite of many church workers who strive to be relevant and consistent to the faith they profess and proclaim.

One of those who opted to sing Mary's song during the First Quarter Storm[4] was Sr. Asuncion Martinez, ICM, a valiant woman who, till the very end of her life, was unceasingly committed to social transformation. In her memoirs she wrote:

> The revolution of LIFE among the toiling masses has still to happen. They still have no rice to eat, no decent home to live in, no land of their own to till. Millions are jobless, and millions more are buried in exploitative factories, chained hopelessly inside the "Haciendas" or marginalized in the wilderness of isolated forests and mountains. Thousands of babies are still dying of sickness and hunger.[5]

Another woman who has had several brushes with death but never ceased to witness to life is Mary Rosario Battung, RGS. She expressed her involvement first with the urban poor and then with rural grassroots women. In her attempt to live a life of struggle and resistance to unjust structures, she declared:

> The urban poor's just and organized struggle for land inspired and challenged us—lay and religious interdisciplinary groups—to organize ourselves as Friends of Zone One Tondo Organization (ZOTO). Their living example impelled us to work together ecumenically, to break the barriers of our tightly held dogmas and to live simply in inter-congregational communities. Thus in the early 1970s, we who were being formed as religious or who were studying Theology got ourselves enrolled in the people's community "school life" ...*upang pandayin sa patuloy nating pakikibaka*...to be forged in the crucible of continuing struggle.[6]

Yet another prominent figure in both the academy and the people's movement (especially the women's movement) is Sr. Mary John Mananzan, OSB. The La Tondena strike in 1975 brought her face-to-face with the harsh realities of the Philippine situation and was the genesis of her involvement with church-related groups working for social transformation. In the early 1980s she and other activist women facilitated the formation of a Women's Organization—Pilipina then GABRIELA. In her book *Challenges to the Inner Room* Mananzan recalls:

> A telephone brigade gathered a group of priests, sisters and seminarians to the La Tondena strike. I was among them. And that was my first encounter with military brutality. The military beat up the workers, pushed them into buses and hauled them all to

prison. At that moment I felt that Christ himself would not ask them to offer the other cheek.[7]

These are only a few among the many women who live out their faith in dialogue with their *Sitz im Leben* (setting in life).

After Vatican II, the phrase "preferential option for the poor" was the catalyst for many church workers to take the poor seriously. A certain kind of spirituality is needed to be at the service of the poor and accompany them in their struggles. To be a transforming leaven in society requires a spirituality with a social face, social commitment, and political option.[8] The definition of spirituality needs to be redefined.

As one who strives to live out the faith I profess within the context of the struggle toward total liberation, I have moved in my spirituality from a vertical and possessive "Me and my God" to an experience of God that is more liberating. I would like to start with these lines that I wrote as a hallmark of my transformation.

Resurgence ... Upsurge for New Hope

To lament of the past
To hold on to a thousand "if onlys"
    Would only add another coating
    To realities embedded out of bitterness.

        Pain is a driving force
        Anger can be converted to compassion
        COMPASSION ... the birth of renewed commitment
        COMMITMENT ... to the long fought struggle
            Of the millions who are imprisoned
            In unjust and inhuman structures.

The passion to seek freedom mounts up
    Explosion followed, accompanied by action
    Fears tend to block the momentum
    Establishing an equilibrium was horrendous task YET done.

        Passion ...
            Tension increased ...
        Compassion ...
            Commitment deepened.

I dare to stand,
    To struggle,
    To fight,
For the long sought FREEDOM.[9]

This poem, written in 1991, speaks of the crisis and difficulty that I went through as a church worker immersed in the situation of the struggling masses. It is also reflective of the journey of many church workers, especially women who have opted to tread the paths less traveled towards the realization of new and relevant ministries. The verses too, are an overture and salute to the journey of the entire Filipino people.

And yet the history of the Filipino people is not only a history of oppression and suffering. It is also a history of resistance and struggle for total liberation. The extreme poverty of the masses (about 77 percent of the population live below the poverty level), and the injustice and dehumanizing situations experienced by more than half of the Filipino people are not merely statistical data but living testimonies to a nation very much in need of development, liberation, and transformation. This reality is both a challenge and a task.

There are those who simply reach out to the poor and give them some of what they have. Others try to dig deeper and understand why there is a growing disparity between the wealthy and the poor. Still others are moved from asking questions and analyzing the answers to engaging in concrete actions with and for the struggling masses. Together with the people they chart a better future toward a society that is more just and humane. This is where the liberation movement is heading. This is also where the so-called progressive church is aligning its response to the situation.

In a nation where 90 percent of the population is Christian, one grapples with the haunting questions: "What makes me different from other believers? How should I live out the faith today *vis-à-vis* the stark realities of poverty, injustice and dehumanizing situations?" The task laid before each one is to respond to these realities and to heal the wounds of the masses, wounds that are the effects of capitalism, ongoing militarization in the rural areas, destruction of the environment, and massive land conversion. All of these are hallmarks of a sick society, a condition worsened by the growing number of unemployed and underemployed. This in turn results in gender inequality where women are on the underside of society—abused and marginalized. The "Philippines 2000" espoused by the present administration aggravated the situation. What was at stake was life itself, which is sacred, and should be preserved and protected.

Those persons who have combined the challenges of ideology and religion to forge their way in challenging ministries have inspired committed Christians to find more meaningful involvements. In the process they have faced threats and the risk of being misunderstood, labeled, and even persecuted.

Living Christian ideals has its twists and turns, growth and crises, fulfillment and disillusionment as one adapts to one's *Sitz im Leben*. One's way of life is greatly affected by the signs of the times. A crises-laden society is home to persons with varying degrees of skills for listening and action. The progressive church in the Philippines has been actively supporting struggles for liberation through its programs and alternative institutions. At the forefront are women—both religious and lay—who have dedicated their lives to work for justice and social transformation. This requires openness to the Spirit that moves a person beyond fears, doubts, and hesitation.

Spirituality Redefined: Women's Spirituality as Spirituality for Justice

Spirituality is life lived to the full. Traditional views of spirituality that were shaped by a dichotomy between body and spirit resulted in persons who spent most of their time cleansing their souls in order to be saved. However, recent developments in theology as well as attention to socio-political contexts have changed many perceptions of and practices in spirituality. There was also the need to break the myth that spirituality is an exclusive domain of those affiliated with religious congregations.

Women are now drawn into a struggle for social justice and that demands time, energy, and commitment. Convinced that all forms of injustice should be eradicated through whatever means, one is tempted to do everything to correct the situation. One is often confronted with having to conform to a functional and performance-oriented society or risk paying the price of being different.[10]

Women's ministry is a personal service of one human being to another in the name of Christ. Women ministers have led the way in identifying with the oppressed and in a real commitment of personal and communal resources for the promotion of social justice both on a national and global level.[11]

Through the ages there have always been women who expressed their faith experience of the Divine in various ways. Some of them were influenced by male dominant figures, such as religious leaders. Hildegard of Bingen and Julian of Norwich, who despite rejection and criticism lived out their faith in a manner they felt comfortable with, are worthy of special mention. Even though Hildegard was a cloistered abbess and an enclosed nun, she was by no means cut off from the turbulent world of the twelfth century.[12] She counseled many individuals and involved herself in the political struggles of both the church and the empire with a boldness that was rooted in her prophetic task.[13] Julian of Norwich, on the other hand, made a radical decision to be an anchoress (akin to the life of a hermit but her dwelling place was attached to a church). She was one of those who spoke of God as father and mother. In her *Showings*, Julian declared:

As truly as God is our Father, so truly is God our Mother, and he revealed that in everything, and especially in these sweet words he says: I am he; that is to say: I am he, the power of goodness of fatherhood; I am he, the wisdom and the lovingness of motherhood; I am he the light and the grace which is blessed love;...I am he who makes you love; I am he who makes you to long; I am he the endless fulfilling of all true desires.[14]

These two women were ahead of their time as they expressed their spirituality in a way that differed from the standard norm.

An individual's faith expressions (e.g., prayer, image of God, etc.) are shaped by his or her community, class, race, sex, and so forth. In the process, these elements evolve into ways of living and responding to the divine presence in every creature. This is spirituality. It includes and expresses one's critical appraisal of history and culture. There is no such thing as a "fixed" spirituality, especially when one is always in dialogue with life and open to new ways of being, that is, open to the creative spirit moving in all of creation. Spirituality has to do with the age-old quest for fulfillment and liberation; it points toward transcendence amidst the confusion of human experience. It can be described as a process of transformation and growth. It is an organic and dynamic part of the human development of individual and society. Samuel Ryan, a Jesuit theologian from India, defines spirituality as:

> the openness and response-ability that goes beyond mere accountability to the willingness and readiness to respond to situations of importance for life. This spirituality constructs and nurtures what makes for fuller life, for finer humanity and for a new earth. The Spirit's action in people's lives is thus experienced as an energizing force not only for attitudinal and structural change, but also for "combat" in defense of shared freedom and life in community.[15]

In the early 1990s, the members of the Ecumenical Association of Third World Theologians (EATWOT) began to articulate a spirituality relevant to the realities in their countries of origin. The Philippine delegates to the Third Asian Theological Conference (ATC III), a sub-regional conference of EATWOT, had in-depth discussions among themselves as well as a series of consultations with the masses and resource persons in the fields of anthropology and social sciences. Their report expressed that:

> A Philippine spirituality that springs from the involvement in liberation struggles—whether against economic exploitation, political repression, gender oppression, ethnic discrimination, or ecological destruction—is necessarily an integrated one. It is a holistic spirituality in touch with the movement of the Holy

Spirit, not only in people's lives but also in the whole of creation. It is a spirituality rooted in our Christian faith tradition and at the same time aware of our animist roots that consider sacred our soil, forests, rivers. It is concerned with concrete bodily needs and yet also caught up with the spiritual world that has produced a richness of popular symbols and rituals. In our search for a genuinely liberating spirituality, we find a need for both analytical and intuitive minds regarding reality, for both structural and cultural analysis to situate the role of popular beliefs in people's struggles, for both concrete action for justice and silent contemplation.[16]

This paper affirms the importance of the dialectic between theory and the actual life situation of the people. Spirituality does not grow in a vacuum but develops through one's integration and immersion in people's lives and struggles. Armed with compassion and commitment to work for a better and transformed society, one hopes for the coming of God's "*basileia*" (kin-dom of God). As people are systematically devalued and degraded, it is women who suffer the most, as they are the first to be sold or exchanged for food or even the first to die (as in the case of female infanticide in rural areas of India).

A spirituality that grows out of the struggle to dismantle unjust structures draws strength from both the Hebrew and Christian traditions. Two biblical texts that clearly demonstrate this point are Leviticus 25 and Luke 4:18–19. Leviticus 25:8–13 declares:

> You shall count off seven weeks of years, seven times seven years, so that the period of the seven weeks of years gives forty-nine years. Then you shall have the trumpet sounded loud; on the tenth day of the seventh month; on the day of the atonement—you shall have the trumpet sounded throughout all your land. And you shall hallow the fiftieth year and you shall proclaim liberty throughout the land to all its inhabitants. It shall be a jubilee year for you; you shall return, every one of you to your family. The fiftieth year shall be a jubilee year for you: you shall sow, or reap the aftergrowth, or harvest the unpruned vines. For it is jubilee; it shall be holy to you; you shall eat only what the field itself produces. In this year of jubilee you shall return, every one of you, to your property. (NRSV)

The second text, Luke 4:18–19, is considered the Magna Carta for those involved in justice making.

> The Spirit of God is upon me.
> God has anointed me to preach the Good News to the poor,

God has sent me to proclaim liberty to the captives,
And recovery of sight to the blind,
To set free the oppressed,
To announce the year when God will save all people.

These two texts speak of re-orientation of resources, social justice, and liberty. Bernadette Mbuy-Beya, an African theologian, writes:

It is useless to groan over the oppression and misery of the people while those who govern do so with impunity. Faith in Jesus Christ and love of neighbor must lead the Christian to concrete commitment in the struggle for the liberation of the oppressed and the transformation of the world.[17]

What Does a Spirituality of Justice Entail?

Justice has to do with the way in which society is organized and how wealth is distributed. Building a society with just structures requires committed action. A spirituality of justice means confronting the everyday pain and humiliation that people experience in a given society.[18] It is a commitment *to* and a stance *for* those who suffer. This spirituality is a cry for justice; it is a power that resists the limiting and death-dealing structures in society. It resists dehumanization and fulfills the quest for self-discovery, self-affirmation, and self-inclusion, for all of us in the human community have the urge to live and to live fully as human beings.[19] The core of a spirituality of justice touches the deepest part of ourselves and allows God, who resides in each one of us, to move us to wholeness while we also work for wholeness in our community and society.

A spirituality for justice means being mutually accountable to and for each other regardless of religious denomination; it has a profound respect for ecumenism. Elisabeth Schüssler Fiorenza suggests the model of *ekklesia*.

It is an invitation to gather together those who in the angry power of the spirit are sent forth to feed, heal and liberate the women. It unmasks and sets us free from the structural sins and alienation of sexism, racism and exploitation and propels us to become children and spokeswomen of God.[20]

Liturgy and Symbols

As one embraces new ways of living out our faith, one is also faced with the question of relevant symbols and ways of celebration. In many women's rituals, telling stories of women are preferred to the reading of some texts from scripture. There is also a movement away from the leader (priest) as center of the ritual to community participation. Symbols that are part of women's lives, such as woven fabrics, potted plants, soil, flowers, salt, candles, and so forth are used as part of the celebration.

Using an embodied ritual and liturgy allows participants free expression for prayer. Women's issues such as violence against women (rape, incest, prostitution), exploitation in the labor force, and discrimination, among others, are always integrated within the liturgy. This embodied ritual is also an actualization of the call to reconstruct the meaning of woman's body, which is the seat or locus of exploitation, and reclaim it as hallowed ground and a temple of the spirit. Women's spirituality for justice enhances connectedness and solidarity with all victims and at the same time develops in each one a movement from being victim to being survivor. Maria Harris maintains that this is a call to fidelity in relationship, a continuing struggle to share the gifts of God's good earth, finding out what belongs to whom and giving it back.[21]

The call of women today is to integrate prayer and justice as suggested by the prophet Micah:

What does the Lord require of you
But to do justice and to love kindness
And to walk humbly with your God. (Mic 6:8)

A spirituality for justice invites each one to join protest marches to demonstrate our resistance to unjust structures and laws and at the same time listen to women's stories and accounts of exploitation. This calls for dynamism; passivity is a way of the past.

The Challenge

Women's spirituality for justice can blossom only if the liberating Spirit is allowed to move us beyond our fears, doubts, hesitations, and insecurities. Everything and everyone is related. No one can be herself without doing work for justice.[22] Maria Harris provides some basic steps:

You shall hold the resources of God's earth tenderly, and with
a light touch,
You shall remember you are a steward of the gifts of the earth;
you did not make them.
You will give thanks minute by minute for your food, your
shelter, your clothes.
You will not turn your eyes from the suffering of others.

You will believe and teach children to believe we are never
    diminished by giving.[23]

A complete reworking of values and outlook are needed so that we
can really actualize what Harris has prescribed. Relationships of mutuality are needed instead of relationships of domination and exploitation.
It is only when the structures that support *kyriarchy*[24] (a more complex
social pyramid of graduated domination and subordination) are broken
that women will be really free.

Women's spirituality for justice is not a path of disintegration but of
wholeness. Following the example of Jesus of Nazareth one needs to
have an integrated rhythm of prayer and action—always mindful of the
presence of the liberating spirit blowing in us and through us.

Finally, a spirituality for justice is not the end but a vehicle for the
"birthing of new persons and society and renewed creation." Schüssler
Fiorenza reminds us of the hallmarks of this spirituality: commitment,
accountability, and solidarity.[25] For this spirituality to grow one should
not lose sight of the poor and the struggling women, one should feel with
them, listen to them, and celebrate life and healing with them. Only then
can we truly feel SHE WHO IS incarnate.

We pray:

Creative darkness, you have sent us the Sun of Justice,
Who reveals your truth to all people.
Liberating Strength, you have made known through your mes-
    sengers and prophets
Through the ages that you are the God of Life and not Death.
The God of freedom and not bondage
The God of love and not of domination
The God of creativity and not division

Strengthen your people Holy Sustainer
Against Exploitation and for Happiness
That we might struggle for justice and liberation
Against every deprivation of body and soul.

And always may we know: Your Strength and your Love
Nurture us, Gentle Wisdom, now and the times of our despair.
    AMEN.[26]

Notes

1. E. San Juan, *Crisis in the Philippines: The Making of a Revolution* (Philippines: National Bookstore, 1988), 29.

2. Synod of Bishops, *Justice in the World*, 1971.

3. Susan Muto, *Womanspirit: Reclaiming the Deep Feminine in our Human Spirituality* (New York: Crossroad, 1991), 60–65.

4. A period in our history (1970s) that galvanized the protest against the heightened economic crisis, government militarism, and martial law. This also gave birth to several grassroots organizations.

5. Asuncion Martinez, *I Climb Mountains: Selected Writings of Sr. Asuncion Martinez, ICM* (Quezon City: Mga Kaisa, 1988), 8.

6. Mary Rosario Battung, "Urban Poor," in *Witness and Hope amid Struggle: Towards a Theology and Spirituality of Struggle, Book II*, ed. Victoria Narciso-Apuan et al. (Quezon City: Milcar Printing, 1991), 29.

7. Sr. Mary John Mananzan, OSB, *Challenges to the Inner Room: Selected Essays and Speeches on Women* (Manila: Institute of Women Studies, St. Scholastica's College, 1998), 5, 16.

8. Samuel Amirham and Liberato Bautista, eds., *Those Who Would Give Light Must Endure Burning* (Philippines: National Council of Churches in the Philippines, 1987), 7.

9. Carmelita M. Usog, unpublished poem.

10. Amirham and Bautista, *Those Who Would Give Light*, 7.

11. Joann Wolski Conn, *Women's Spirituality: Resources for Christian Development* (New York: Paulist Press, 1986), 34–35.

12. Renate Craine, *Hildegard: Prophet of the Cosmic Christ* (New York: Crossroad, 1998), 21.

13. Fiona Bowie and Oliver Davies, eds., *Hildegard of Bingen: Mystical Writings* (New York: Crossroad), 7.

14. Gloria Durka, *Praying with Julian of Norwich* (Winona, MN: St. Mary's Press, 1989), 47.

15. Virginia Fabella, Peter K. H. Lee, and David Kwang-sun Suh, eds., *Asian Christian Spirituality: Reclaiming Traditions* (Maryknoll, NY: Orbis Books, 1992), 3.

16. Carlos Abesamis et al., "A Philippine Search for Liberation Spirituality" in *Asian Christian Spirituality*, 85–104.

17. K. C. Abraham and Bernadette Mbuy-Beya, eds., *Spirituality of the Third World* (Maryknoll, NY: Orbis Books, 1994), 67.

18. Ibid, 77.

19. Ibid.

20. Elisabeth Schüssler Fiorenza, "Gather in My Name: Toward a Christian Feminist Spirituality," in *Discipleship of Equals* (New York: Crossroad, 1993), 199.

21. Maria Harris, *Dance of the Spirit: The Seven Steps of Women's Spirituality* (New York: Bantam, 1993), 132.

22. Ibid., 133.

23. Ibid.

24. Elisabeth Schüssler Fiorenza, *Jesus: Miriam's child, Sophia's Prophet: Critical Issues in Feminist Christology* (New York: Continuum, 1995), 14.

25. Schüssler Fiorenza, "Gather in My Name," 200.

26. Author's collection.

Selected Bibliography

GENERAL

Fabella, Virginia, and Mercy Amba Oduyoye, eds. *With Passion and Compassion: Third World Women Doing Theology.* Maryknoll, NY: Orbis Books, 1988.

Kanyoro, Musimbi R. A., ed. *In Search of a Round Table: Gender, Theology, and Church Leadership.* Geneva: World Council of Churches, 1997.

King, Ursula, ed. *Feminist Theology from the Third World.* Maryknoll, NY: Orbis Books, 1994.

Mananzan, Mary John, et al., eds. *Women Resisting Violence: Spirituality for Life.* Maryknoll, NY: Orbis Books, 1996.

Ortega, Ofelia, ed. *Women's Visions: Theological Reflection, Celebration, Action.* Geneva: World Council of Churches, 1995.

Pobee, John S., ed. *Culture, Women and Theology.* Delhi: ISPCK, 1994.

————, and Bärbel von Wartenberg-Potter, eds. *New Eyes for Reading: Biblical and Theological Reflections by Women of the Third World.* Oak Parks: Meyer Stone Books, 1987.

Ruether, Rosemary Radford, ed. *Women Healing Earth: Third World Women on Ecology, Feminism, and Religion.* Maryknoll, NY. Orbis Books, 1996.

Russell, Letty M., et al., eds. *Inheriting Our Mothers' Gardens: Feminist Theology in Third World Perspective.* Louisville, KY: Westminster, 1988.

Schüssler Fiorenza, Elisabeth, and M. Shawn Copeland, eds. *Feminist Theology in Different Contexts. Concilium* 1996, no. 1. Maryknoll, NY: Orbis Books, 1996.

AFRICA

Ackermann, Denise. *After the Locusts: Letters from the Landscape of Faith.* Grand Rapids, MI: Eerdmans, 2003.

————, et al., eds. *Claiming Our Footprints: South African Women Reflect on Context, Identity and Spirituality.* Matieland, South Africa : EFSA Institute for Theological and Interdisciplinary Research, 2000.

————, Jonathan A. Draper, and Emma Mashinini, eds. *Women Hold Up Half of the Sky: Women in the Church in Southern Africa.* Pietermaritzburg: Cluster Publications, 1991.

Amoah, Elizabeth, ed. *Where God Reigns: Reflections on Women in God's World.* Accra: Sam-Woode Ltd., 1997.

Dube, Musa W. *The HIV/AIDS Bible: Selected Essays.* Scranton: University of Scranton Press, 2008.

————. *Postcolonial Feminist Interpretation of the Bible.* St. Louis: Chalice Press, 2000.

————, ed. *Other Ways of Reading: African Women and the Bible*. Atlanta: Society of Biblical Literature, 2001.

————, and Musimbi R. A. Kanyoro, eds. *Grant Me Justice! HIV/AIDS and Gender Reading of the Bible*. Pietermaritzburg: Cluster Publications, 2004.

Kanyoro, Musimbi R. A. *Introducing Feminist Cultural Hermeneutics: An African Perspective*. Cleveland: Pilgrim Press, 2002.

————, and Nyambura J. Njoroge, eds. *Groaning in Faith: African Women in the Household of God*. Nairobi: Acton Publishers, 1996.

Njoroge, Nyambura J. *Kiamka Kia Ngo: African Christian Feminist Ethic of Resistance and Transformation*. Legon: Assempa Publishers, 2000.

————, and Musa W. Dube, eds. *Talitha Cum! Theologies of African Women*. Pietermaritzburg: Cluster Publications, 2001.

Oduyoye, Mercy Amba. *Beads and Strands: Reflections of an African Woman on Christianity in Africa*. Maryknoll, NY: Orbis Books, 2004.

————. *Daughters of Anowa: African Women and Patriarchy*. Maryknoll, NY: Orbis Books, 1995.

————. *Hearing and Knowing: Theological Reflections on Christianity in Africa*. Maryknoll, NY: Orbis Books, 1986.

————. *Introducing African Women's Theology*. Cleveland: Pilgrim Press, 2001.

————. *Who Will Roll the Stone Away? The Ecumenical Decade of Churches in Solidarity with Women*. Geneva: World Council of Churches, 1990.

————, ed. *Transforming Power: Women in the Household of God*. Accra: Sam-Woode, 1997.

————, and Musimbi R. A. Kanyoro, eds. *Talitha Qumi! 1989 Conference Proceedings*. Ibaden: Daystar, 1990.

————, and Musimbi R. A. Kanyoro, eds. *The Will to Arise: Women, Tradition, and the Church in Africa*. Maryknoll, NY: Orbis Books, 1992.

Phiri, Isabel Apawo. *Women, Patriarchy and Presbyterianism: Chewa Women of Central Malawi*. Blantyre: CLAIM, 1997.

————, Beverley Haddad, and Madipoane Masenya, eds. *African Women, HIV/AIDS, and Faith Communities*. Pietermaritzburg: Cluster Publications, 2003.

————, Devakarsham Betty Govinden, and Sarojini Nadar, eds. *Her-Stories: Hidden Histories of Women of Faith*. Pietermaritzburg: Cluster Publications, 2002.

————, and Sarojini Nadar, eds. *African Women, Religion, and Health: Essays in Honor of Mercy Amba Ewudziwa Oduyoye*. Maryknoll, NY: Orbis Books, 2006.

————, and Sarojini Nadar, eds. *On Being Church: African Women's Voices and Visions*. Geneva: World Council of Churches, 2005.

Wamue, Grace, and Mary Getui, eds. *Violence against Women: Reflections by Kenyan Women Theologians*. Nairobi: Acton Publishers, 1996.

ASIA

Abraham, Ducie, et al., eds. *Asian Women Doing Theology: Report from the Singapore Conference, November 2–27, 1987*. Hong Kong: Asian Women's Resource Center for Culture and Theology (AWRC), 1989.

————, Sun Ai Lee Park, and Yvonne Dahlin, eds. *Faith Renewed I: A Report on the First Asian Women's Consultation on Interfaith Dialogue, November 1–8, 1989. Kuala Lumpur, Malaysia*. Hong Kong: AWRC, 1989.

Asian Women's Resource Center for Culture and Theology. *Faith Renewed II: A Report on the Second Asian Women's Consultation on Interfaith Dialogue, November1–7, 1991, Colombo, Sri Lanka.* Seoul: AWRC, 1991.

———. *Introduction to Asian Feminist Perspectives on Religions: Toward Interfaith Dialogue.* Kuala Lumpur: AWRC, 2008.

———. *Introduction to Asian Feminist Theologies.* Kuala Lumpur: AWRC, 2005.

———. *Telling HerStory: Introduction to an Asian Feminist Re-reading of History.* Kuala Lumpur: AWRC, 2006.

Barton, Mukti. *Scripture as Empowerment for Liberation and Justice: The Experience of Christian and Muslim Women in Bangladesh.* Bristol: University of Bristol, 1999.

Brazal, Agnes M., and Andrea Lizares Si, eds. *Body and Sexuality: Theological-Pastoral Perspectives of Women in Asia.* Quezon City, Philippines: Ateneo de Manila University Press, 2007.

Choi Hee An. *Korean Women and God: Experiencing God in a Multi-Religious Colonial Context.* Maryknoll, NY: Orbis Books, 2005.

Chun Kwang-Rye, Yoshiko Isshiki, Hisako Kinukawa, and Satoko Yamaguchi. *Women Moving Mountains: Feminist Theology in Japan.* Kuala Lumpur: AWRC, 2000.

Chung Hyun Kyung. *Struggle to Be the Sun Again: Introducing Asian Women's Theology.* Maryknoll, NY: Orbis Books, 1990.

Chung Meehyun, ed. *Breaking Silence: Theology from Asian Women.* Delhi: ISPCK, 2006.

Fabella, Virginia. *Beyond Bonding: A Third World Women's Theological Journey.* Manila: Eumenical Association of Third World Theologians, 1993.

———, and Sun Ai Lee Park, eds. *We Dare to Dream: Doing Theology as Asian Women.* Maryknoll, NY: Orbis Books, 1988.

Gnanadason, Aruna. *Listen to the Women! Listen to the Earth!* Geneva: World Council of Churches, 2005.

———. *No Longer a Secret: The Church and Violence against Women.* Geneva: World Council of Churches, 1993.

———, ed. *Towards a Theology of Humanhood: Women's Perspectives.* Delhi: ISPCK, 1986.

In God's Image. Quarterly journal published by Asian Women's Resource Centre for Culture and Theology, Yogyakarta, Indonesia.

Katoppo, Marianne. *Compassionate and Free: An Asian Women's Theology.* Geneva: World Council of Churches, 1979.

Kinukawa, Hisako. *Women and Jesus in Mark: A Japanese Feminist Perspective.* Maryknoll, NY: Orbis Books, 1994.

Kwok Pui-lan. *Introducing Asian Feminist Theology.* Sheffield: Sheffield Academic Press, 2000.

Lee Oo-Chung. *In Search for Our Grandmothers' Spirituality.* Seoul: AWRC. 1994.

———, et al., eds. *Women of Courage: Asian Women Reading the Bible.* Seoul: AWRC, 1992.

Mananzan, Mary John, ed. *Women, Religion, and Spirituality in Asia.* Manila: St. Scholastica's College, 2004.

———, ed. *Essays on Women.* Rev. ed. Manila: St. Scholastica's College, 1991.

Monteiro, Evelyn, and Antoinette Gutzler, eds. *Ecclesia of Women in Asia: Gathering the Voices of the Silenced*. Delhi: ISPCK, 2005.

Orevillo-Montenegro, Muriel. *The Jesus of Asian Women*. Maryknoll, NY: Orbis Books, 2006.

Ralte, Lalrinawmi, and Evangeline Anderson-Rajkumar, eds. *Feminist Hermeneutics*. Delhi: ISPCK, 2002.

———, and Stella Faria, eds. *Waging Peace: Building a World in which Life Matters: Festschrift to Honour Gabriele Dietrich*. Delhi: ISPCK, 2004.

———, et al., eds. *Envisioning a New Heaven and New Earth*. Delhi: ISPCK, 1998.

Yamaguchi, Satoko. *Mary and Martha: Women in the World of Jesus*. Maryknoll, NY: Orbis Books, 2002.

LATIN AMERICA

Althaus-Reid, Marcella. *From Feminist Theology to Indecent Theology: Readings on Poverty, Sexual Identity, and God*. London: SCM Press, 2004.

———. *Indecent Theology: Theological Perversions in Sex, Gender and Politics*. London: Routledge, 2000.

———. *The Queer God*. London: Routledge, 2003.

Aquino, María Pilar. *Our Cry for Life: Feminist Theology from Latin America*. Maryknoll, NY: Orbis Books, 1993.

———, and Maria José Rosado-Nunes, eds. *Feminist Intercultural Theology: Latina Explorations for a Just World*. Maryknoll, NY: Orbis Books, 2007.

Con-spirando: Revista latinoamericana de ecofeminismo, espiritualidad y teología. Journal published by the Con-spirando Collective in Santiago, Chile.

Gebara, Ivone. *Longing for Running Water: Ecofeminism and Liberation*. Minneapolis, MN: Fortress Press, 1999.

———. *Out of the Depths: Women's Experience of Evil and Salvation*. Minneapolis, MN: Fortress Press, 2002.

———, and María Clara Bingemer. *Mary: Mother of God, Mother of the Poor*. Maryknoll, NY: Orbis Books, 1987.

Ress, Mary Judith, ed. *Circling In, Circling Out: A Con-spirando Reader*. Santiago, Chile: The Con-spirando Collective, 2005.

Tamez, Elsa. *Against Machismo*. New York: Meyer Stone Books, 1987.

———. *The Amnesty of Grace: Justification by Faith from a Latin American Perspective*, trans. Sharon H. Ringe. Nashville: Abingdon Press, 1993.

———. *Bible of the Oppressed*, trans. Matthew J. O'Connell. Maryknoll, NY: Orbis Books, 1982.

———. *The Scandalous Message of James: Faith without Works is Dead*, trans. John Eagleson. New York: Crossroad, 1990.

———. *Struggles for Power in Early Christianity: A Study of the First Letter to Timothy*, trans. Gloria Kinsler. Maryknoll, NY: Orbis Books, 2007.

———. *When the Horizons Close: Rereading Ecclesiastes*, trans. Margaret Wilde. Maryknoll, NY: Orbis Books, 2000.

———, ed. *Through Her Eyes: Women's Theology from Latin America*. Maryknoll, NY: Orbis Books, 1989.

INDIGENOUS

Donaldson, Laura E. *Decolonizing Feminisms: Race, Gender, and Empire Building*. Chapel Hill: University of North Carolina Press, 1992.

Pattel-Gray, Anne. *The Great White Flood: Racism in Australia, Critically from an Aboriginal Historico-Theological Viewpoint*. Atlanta: Scholars Press, 1998.

———. *Through Aboriginal Eyes: The Cry from the Wilderness*. Geneva: World Council of Churches, 1991.

Skye, Lee Miena. *Kerygmatics of the New Millennium: A Study of Australian Aboriginal Women's Christology*. Delhi: ISPCK, 2007.

Smith, Andrea. *Conquest: Sexual Violence and American Indian Genocide*. Cambridge, MA: South End Press, 2005.

———. *Native Americans and the Christian Right: The Gendered Politics of Unlikely Alliances*. Durham, NC: Duke University Press, 2008.

Contributors

Clara Luz Ajo Lázaro, a Cuban, received her doctorate from Universadade Metodista in São Paulo and specializes in historical theology. She is a lay Anglican theologian and professor of systematic theology at the Seminario Evangélico de Teología (Matanzas, Cuba) and a member of the Commission of Theological Studies for Latin America and the Caribbean of the American Episcopal Church. Her publications include *Teología Género: Selección de Textos* (2002) and other articles.

Sharon A. Bong, a Catholic woman from Malaysia, received her Ph.D. from the Department of Religious Studies at Lancaster University, United Kingdom, and is senior lecturer in gender studies at Monash University in Malaysia. She was a specialist writer with the New Straits Time Press and a Programme Officer (publications) at ARROW, the Asian-Pacific Resource and Research Center for Women. The author of *The Tension between Women's Rights and Religions: The Case of Malaysia* (2006), she is doing research on sexuality and religion through narratives of persons in same-sex partnerships in a Southeast Asian context.

Laura E. Donaldson, of Cherokee and Scotch-Irish descent, is a professor of English and American Indian Studies at Cornell University in Ithaca, New York. She works at the intersection of postcolonial, feminist, religious, and Native perspectives and teaches courses in early American literatures and religion. She also directs a Telluride Association summer program at Cornell on democracy and diversity. When she is not teaching or writing, Laura raises registered Navajo Churro and Icelandic sheep, whose fleece she hand processes and spins.

Musa W. Dube, from Botswana, is an activist-scholar whose expertise is in postcolonial feminist interpretations of the Bible. She is a professor in the Department of Theology and Religious Studies at the University of Botswana. She has worked for the World Council of Churches as an HIV/AIDS and theological consultant for churches and theological institutions in Africa. She has authored and edited many volumes, including *The HIV/AIDS Bible: Selected Essays* (2008), *HIV/AIDS and the Curriculum: Methods of Integrating HIV/AIDS in Theological Programs* (2003), *Other Ways of Reading: African Women and the Bible* (2001), and *Postcolonial Feminist Interpretation of the Bible* (2000).

Ivone Gebara is Brazilian and belongs to the religious order of the Sisters of Our Lady (Canonesses of St. Augustine). She was a professor at the Theological Institute of Recife for nearly two decades, and she worked among women in poor neighborhoods. Well known for her work on ecofeminism and liberation theology, her many books include *Out of the Depths: Women's Experience of Evil and Salvation* (2002), *Longing for Running Water: Ecofeminism and Liberation* (1999), and *Mary: Mother of God, Mother of the Poor* (with María Clara Bingemer, 1987).

Musimbi R. A. Kanyoro, from Kenya, is the director of the Population Program at the Parkard Foundation and former general secretary of World YWCA in Geneva. She has deep roots in the ecumenical movement, and she served as executive secretary of the Program for Women and Society at the Lutheran World Federation. With Mercy Amba Oduyoye, she co-founded the Circle of Concerned African Women Theologians, and coordinated it from 1998 to 2006. She received her Ph.D. from the University of Texas in Austin and her D.Min from San Francisco Theological Seminary. She is the author of *Introducing Feminist Cultural Hermeneutics: An African Perspective* (2002) and coeditor of *Grant Me Justice! HIV/AIDS and Gender Reading of the Bible* (2004), *Groaning in Faith: African Women in the Household of God* (1996), and other volumes.

Kwok Pui-lan was born in Hong Kong and is the William F. Cole Professor of Christian Theology and Spirituality at the Episcopal Divinity School in Cambridge, Massachusetts. Her publications include *Postcolonial Imagination and Feminist Theology* (2005), *Introducing Asian Feminist Theology* (2000), and *Discovering the Bible in the Non-Biblical World* (1995). She is the coeditor of *Off the Menu: Asian and Asian North American Women's Religion and Theology* (2007), and, most recently, of *Women and Christianity* in 4 volumes (2010).

Monica Jyotsna Melanchthon, Indian, is a professor of Old Testament Studies at the Gurukul Lutheran Theological College and Research Institute in Chennai, South India. She has a special interest in Dalit theology and feminist theology and has lectured internationally on these subjects. Author of numerous articles, she is the author of *Rejection by God: The History and Significance of the Rejection Motif in the Hebrew Bible* (2001).

Meng Yanling, from China, received her M.Div. degree from Nanjing Union Theological Seminary. She began teaching at Nanjing Union Theological Seminary in 2000, offering courses in Old Testament, women in the Old Testament, and feminist theology. She was ordained a pastor in 2002. During 2006–2007, she was visiting scholar at Emmanuel College, University of Toronto. Currently she is studying Hebrew and Greek at Emmanuel College in preparation for her doctoral program.

Mercy Amba Oduyoye, a Ghanaian, is director of the Institute of African Women in Religion and Culture, Accra, Ghana. A pioneer in African women's theology, she was co-founder of the Circle of Concerned African Women Theologians. She was former president of the Ecumenical Association of Third World Theologians and former Deputy General Secretary of the World Council of Churches. Her many books include *Beads and Strands: Reflections of an African Woman on Christianity in Africa* (2004), *Introducing African Women's Theology* (2001), *Daughters of Anowa: African Women and Patriarchy* (1995), and *Hearing and Knowing: Theological Reflections on Christianity in Africa* (1986).

Isabel Apawo Phiri, from Malawi, was the general coordinator of the Circle of Concerned African Women Theologians from 2002 to 2007. She is a professor of African theology in the School of Theology, University of KwaZulu-Natal, Pietermaritzburg, South Africa. She is the author of *Women, Patriarchy and Presbyterianism: Chewa Women of Central Malawi* (1997) and coeditor of *African Women, Religion, and Health: Essays in Honor of Mercy Amba Ewudziwa Oduyoye* (2006), *On Being Church: African Women's Voices and Visions* (2005), *African Women, HIV/AIDS, and Faith Communities* (2003), and *Her-Stories: Hidden Histories of Women of Faith* (2002).

Maria José Rosado-Nunes, Brazilian, is a graduate professor of sociology of religion and feminism at Pontifícia Universidade Católica de São Paulo in Brazil. She received her Ph.D. in sociology from the École des Hautes Études en Sciences Sociales of Paris. She is the founder and coordinator of the organization Catholics for the Right to Decide in Brazil. She was a visiting professor at Harvard University in 2003 and was among fifty-one Brazilian women nominated for the Nobel Peace Prize in 2005. Her published works include *Vida Religiosa nos Meios Populares* (1985) and numerous articles on the Catholic Church and feminism.

Lee Miena Skye is a womanist (black feminist) theologian, a Tasmanian Aboriginal, a Palawa, descended from the last "full blood" before the genocide. She made a historic presentation at the Parliament of the World's Religions Congress at Montreal in 2006 and won the Women's Scholars in Religion and Theology scholarship to present a paper at the University of Auckland in 2008. She completed a post-doctoral fellowship at Harvard Divinity School in 2009 and is the author of *Kerygmatics of the New Millennium: A Study of Australian Aboriginal Women's Christology* (2007) and other essays.

Andrea Smith, Cherokee, is the U.S. coordinator of the Ecumenical Association of Third World Theologians. She is also a co-founder of Incite! Women of Color Against Violence and the Boarding School Healing Project. She is the author of *Native Americans and the Christian Right: The Gendered Politics of Unlikely Alliances* (2008) and *Conquest: Sexual Violence and American Indian Genocide* (2005). She currently teaches at the University of California at Riverside.

Elsa Tamez, a Methodist born in Mexico, is one of the principal initiators and developers of the feminist perspective of Latin American feminist theology. She is Professor Emerita of Biblical Studies and former principal of the Latin American Biblical University in San Jóse, Costa Rica. Currently she is a translation consultant of the United Bible Societies. Her many books include *Struggles for Power in Early Christianity: A Study of the First Letter to Timothy* (2007), *When the Horizons Close: Rereading Ecclesiastes* (2000), and *The Amnesty of Grace: Justification by Faith from a Latin American Perspective* (1993). She was editor of *Through Her Eyes: Women's Theology from Latin America* (1989).

Carmelita Usog from the Philippines is an administrator and professor at St. Scholastica's College in Manila. She teaches theology and women's studies at St. Scholastica's and also teaches part time at the Institute of Formation and

Religious Studies. Active in the ecumenical movement, she is the Asian women's coordinator of the Ecumenical Association of Third World Theologians. She received her D.Min. degree from the Catholic Theological Union in Chicago and has written essays on women's theology and theological perspectives on poverty and violence against women.

Wong Wai Ching Angela, from Hong Kong, is an associate professor in the Department of Cultural and Religious Studies and head of the Graduate Division of Gender Studies at the Chinese University of Hong Kong. She was formerly chairperson and Asia-Pacific regional secretary of the World Student Christian Federation and is a member of the presidium of the Christian Conference of Asia. She is the author of *"The Poor Woman": A Critical Analysis of Asian Theology and Contemporary Chinese Fiction by Women* (2002) and many articles and several books in Chinese.

Jean Zaru, from Ramallah, Palestine, has been a leader in the Palestinian Quaker community and a pioneer in women's equality. In addition to serving as clerk of the Ramallah Friends Meeting, Zaru was a founding member and vice-chair of Sabeel, an ecumenical Palestine liberation theology center in Jerusalem. She was vice-president of the World YWCA and served on the Central Committee of the World Council of Churches and on the Working Group in Interfaith Dialogue. She is the author of *Occupied with Nonviolence: A Palestinian Woman Speaks* (2008).

Of Related Interest

The Jesus of Asian Women
Muriel Orevillo-Montengro

978-1-57075-533-0

A critical survey of Asian Christologies that focuses on the need to recognize and end the oppressed condition of Asian women who suffer from poverty, cultural strictures, gender discrimination, and a lack of access to basic human rights.

Female Circumcision
The Interplay of Religion, Culture, and Gender in Kenya
Mary Nyangweso Wangila
Foreword by Mercy Amba Oduyoye

978-1-57075-710-5

"A careful, balanced study of an extremely troubling issue. . . . An important book for anyone concerned about cross-cultural approaches to ethics, the status of women worldwide, and the need for women's voices to be heard in all of this."
—*Margaret A. Farley, Yale University*

Korean Women and God
Experiencing God in a Multi-religious Colonial Context
Choi Hee An

978-1-57075-622-8

"Dr. Choi articulates how Korean women . . . acquire new identites through naming their own God. . . . The book advances the discourse on cross-cultural theology and ministry."
—*Kwok Pui-lan, Episcopal Divinity School, Cambridge MA.*

Please support your local bookstore, or call 1-800-258-5838.
For a free catalog, please write us at
Orbis Books, Box 302
Maryknoll, NY 10545-0302
or visit our website at www.orbisbooks.com.

Thank you for reading *Hope Abundant: Third World and Indigenous Women's Theology*. We hope you profited from it.